explorer
NEW YORK

Mick Sinclair

AA Publishing

Written by Mick Sinclair
Revision verified by Mick Sinclair
Original photography by Richard Elliott

Revised second edition 1996
First published 1994

Edited, designed and produced by AA Publishing
1994,1996. © The Automobile Association 1994, 1996.
Maps © The Automobile Association 1994, 1996.

Distributed in the United Kingdom by AA Publishing,
Norfolk House, Priestley Road, Basingstoke, Hampshire,
RG24 9NY.

The contents of this publication are believed correct at the
time of printing. Nevertheless, the publishers cannot be
held responsible for any errors or omissions or for
changes in the details given in this guide or for the conse-
quences of any reliance on the information provided by
the same. Assessments of attractions, hotels, restaurants and so forth are based upon the author's own personal experience and, therefore, descriptions given in this
guide necessarily contain an element of subjective
opinion which may not reflect the publishers' opinion or
dictate a reader's own experiences on another occasion.
We have tried to ensure accuracy in this guide, but
things do change and we would be grateful if readers
would advise us of any inaccuracies they may encounter.

A CIP catalogue record for this book is available from the
British Library.

ISBN 0 7495 1364 0

Published by AA Publishing (a trading name of
Automobile Association Developments Limited,
whose registered office is Norfolk House,
Priestley Road, Basingstoke, Hampshire, RG24
9NY. Registered number 1878835).

Colour separation: LC Repro & Sons Ltd,
Aldermaston

Printed and bound in Italy by Printer Trento srl

Cover picture: Park Avenue at night
Page 4: Yellow cabs
Page 5 (top): Relaxing outside the Metropolitan Museum
of Art
Pages 6–7 (top): Evening lights of Manhattan
Page 9: Hot dog stand

*The Empire State Building casts its shadow over
Midtown Manhattan*

Besides *Explorer New York*, Mick Sinclair is the author of
the AA's *Explorer California* and Duncan-Petersen's
Versatile California, and has written or co-written three
titles – *Florida*, *Scandinavia* and *California* – for the Rough
Guide series. His newspaper and magazine reviews and
features on travel, culture and the arts have appeared all
over the world.

How to use this book

This book is divided into five main sections:

❏ Section 1: ***New York Is***
discusses aspects of life and living today, from streetlife to art

❏ Section 2: ***New York Was***
places the city in its historical context and explores those past events whose influences are felt to this day

❏ Section 3: ***A to Z Section***
covers places to visit, including walks and excursions, and lists itineraries, tips for those on a tight budget and sightseeing ideas for children. Within this section fall the Focus-on articles, which consider a variety of subjects in greater detail

❏ Section 4: ***Travel Facts***
contains the strictly practical information vital for a successful trip

❏ Section 5:
Hotels and Restaurants
lists recommended establishments throughout New York, giving a brief résumé of their attractions

How to use the star rating
Most of the places described in this book have been given a separate rating:

▶▶▶   **Do not miss**

▶▶   **Highly recommended**

▶   **Worth seeing**

   Not essential viewing

Map references
To make the location of a particular place easier to find, every main entry in this book has a map reference to the right of its name. This comprises a number, followed by a letter, followed by another number, such as 176B3. The first number (176) refers to the page on which the map can be found; the letter (B) and the second number (3) pinpoint the square in which the main entry is located. The maps on the inside front cover and inside back cover are referred to as IFC and IBC respectively.

Contents

*Sign-cleaning on the corner of
Seventh Avenue and Broadway*

This quick-reference guide high-lights the features of the book you will use most often: the maps; the introductory features; the Focus-on articles; the walks and the excursions.

Statue of Liberty

New York fire engine

J P MacBean
A confirmed New Yorker, J P MacBean lives in the King/Charlton/Vandam historic district of the South Village next to SoHo. His books include *New York: Heart of the City* and *New York City 1989,* and he writes extensively on travel, food, theatre, restaurants and New York for newspapers and periodicals. From 1989 to 1990 he was Editorial Coordinator of *The Big Apple Guide – The Official Guide to New York City.*

Harvey Chipkin
Harvey Chipkin was born and raised in New York City and has spent all of his life in the city or within easy striking distance. For many years he has written about travel for major consumer and trade magazines.

My New York
by J P MacBean

To reach the heart of the Big Apple and to feel its pulse, two activities are absolutely necessary: walking and talking. You must walk the city's streets – exploring its neighborhoods, marveling at its architecture, soaking up its sights and sounds – and you must talk with its people in all their infinite variety. Not everyone, of course, and not in every section of the city: prudence is the international catchword these days in a troubled world.

Here are a few personal directions to the heartbeat of my metropolis. On a fine day, in any season, enter Central Park at Fifth Avenue and 59th Street and stroll to Bethesda Fountain in the middle of the park at 72nd Street. Buy a hot dog from a vendor, sit on a bench and strike up a conversation with a neighbor. On another day, stop in a store like Tiffany's and casually chat with a salesperson (believe me, visitors fascinate them). Spend an evening in Greenwich Village (the West Village): have a meal in a small restaurant and swap stories with the waiters and your fellow diners. Or drop by the estimable (and Kosher) Second Avenue Deli (in the East Village at 10th Street) and let the uninhibited waiters tease you. Go to an Off-Broadway show (get the tickets at the half-price 'TKTS' booths) and, during the intermission, discuss the performance with your seat mates and the ushers.

All of these activities are modest in price; and talk, as always, is cheap. In New York, it is also easy. In fact, I often think that everyone in my gregarious city is a music box, just waiting for its lid to be lifted.

My New York
by Harvey Chipkin

As a native New Yorker, I can only imagine the excitement of taking that first step onto a sidewalk and being swept up into the energy, the passion and the electricity that is New York.

I can't experience the thrill of a first stroll in Manhattan's Chinatown, along the very Italian Arthur Avenue in the Bronx, or through the wildly diverse Flushing district of Queens – neighborhoods as foreign as any city abroad. Lost to me is the anticipation of the first visit to 'tourist clichés' that are in fact wonders of the world, such as the Empire State Building and the Statue of Liberty.

But as a native I do get to enjoy some advantages: I've watched trendy neighborhoods superimposed over once-neglected districts (witness SoHo and TriBeCa); I know how newcomers keep the city stew of food, music and culture bitingly fresh and boiling hot; and I can remember that before brunch was invented New York on a Sunday used to be as sleepy as an Iowa farm town.

So much for the native's advantages and disadvantages. The point is that New York possesses a magical appeal that can turn all of us into tourists – whether we see it for the first time as an adult, or from our earliest days.

■ **Great museums, fantastic architecture, luxurious hotels and every imaginable kind of restaurant; New York has them all – but only by stepping out among the sights, smells and sounds that fill its streets will you begin to feel the true pulse of the mighty city ...■**

Non-stop streets A New York street can be a lonely place but seldom – morning, noon or night – will it be an empty one. Around 5am, the first batches of briefcase-carrying commuters emerge from the city's subway stations, just in time to see the nightclubbers heading for home.

A few hours later, young people make their way to school; soon after, the first lunch-seeking office workers begin filing on to the sidewalks. By early afternoon, the early-rising commuters are already making for the stations and by dusk Midtown Manhattan is buzzing with pre-theatre diners. In Greenwich Village, meanwhile, the bars and clubs prepare for another long, busy night.

New York without traffic jams is unthinkable

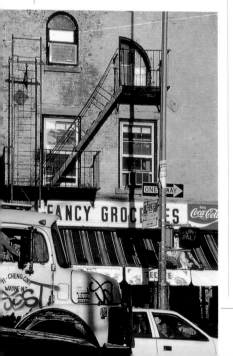

❑ The 12,000 yellow taxis that cruise New York's streets are much more than merely a quick (traffic permitting) way of travelling from A to B. Enshrined in city mythology, taxis have inspired a TV series (*Taxi*, which made a star of Danny de Vito), been represented as small yellow rectangles in a major painting – Mondrian's *Broadway Boogie-Woogie* (displayed at New York's Museum of Modern Art) – and, like taxis the world over, are infamously hard to find when it rains.

But why are they yellow? Because John Hertz, who founded the Yellow Cab Company in 1907, read a survey carried out by the University of Chicago which found that yellow was the colour most people found easiest to spot. ❑

Off the street One contributory factor to the round-the-clock hubbub on New York's streets is the size and price of the apartments that rise above them. Most Manhattan apartments are small and, except for a few rent-controlled properties, extremely expensive. Rather than stay indoors contemplating how many dollars each square foot of home space is costing them, New Yorkers rush out at every opportunity to eat, drink and socialise – and to remind each other why they live in such a pricey place.

Street deals Free enterprise rules the New York streets. A food-stand on every corner means appetites can be quelled – often surprisingly well – without ever venturing inside a restaurant. Bookworms can shop at makeshift outdoor tables which offer reading material ranging from brand-new discounted hard-backs to used paperbacks. Many New York apartments have been furnished by purchases from street markets, where the merchandise ranges from eccentric lumps of junk to three-piece suites.

Even if it rains, there is no need to dodge inside for shelter. As the first drops fall, street-corner traders appear from nowhere bearing armfuls of cheap umbrellas.

Tompkins Square Park. Street culture comes in many guises

Street traffic Listen to cyclists and truck-drivers locked in verbal combat at traffic lights, after jostling for prime position the length of the last block. Careful eavesdropping may provide you with useful ammunition should *you* ever find it necessary to exchange unpleasantries with a New Yorker.

Watch for roller-skaters who choose to dice with death by weaving through Fifth Avenue's rush-hour traffic and grabbing hold of passing vehicles for a free tug.

If you see a stretch limousine, in which the well-heeled make forays to the city's most exclusive stores, glide to a halt as you walk along the street, act like a New Yorker: stop and stare shamelessly at whoever steps out.

❑ Everyone knows New York is nicknamed the Big Apple but nobody is sure of the origins of the term. Musicians, gangsters and horse-racing devotees have all been cited as its source, but the phrase's recent popularity stems from a tourism campaign launched in 1971. ❑

Dirty streets With federal funding cut by 20 per cent in the 12 years from 1980, the US's most glamorous city is, sometimes literally, falling to pieces. Many city bridges have not seen fresh paint for 10 years and are in urgent need of maintenance; pot-holes are a common sight on city streets – some neighbourhoods are littered with them. In a bizarre twist to the city's rubbish-disposal problems, the New York Sanitation Department

loses two or three of its 18-ton refuse trucks to thieves every year. Each vehicle is worth $110,000.

Mean streets Every day in New York, 1,800 serious crimes are reported, hundreds of handbags or wallets are snatched and five murders are committed. You will be less likely to appear among these statistics if you read the Survival guide featured on pages 54–5.

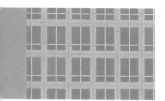

■ **For anyone, anywhere, with aspirations, New York is the place to be. Whether you want to sing and dance your way to fame, make a mint on Wall Street, or start a new life in a new land, New York is – as it has always been – a true beacon of opportunity ...■**

High finance For those who can stand the stresses and strains, the heady world of New York high finance offers rewards unimagined and a level of power few outside the realms of international politics ever experience.

Take one look at the glass-and-steel high-rise towers of the Manhattan skyline, and it should be no surprise that nearly 3,000 major international companies are based here. Among them are six of the seven largest banks which between them account for a quarter of the world's banking business.

Cab driving – a steady living

Industrial giants such as the international oil companies may have blue-collar workforces around the globe but their companies are driven by decisions made in the penthouse boardrooms of their Manhattan headquarters. These decisions not only directly affect the livelihoods of millions but indirectly influence the well-being of the US – and the world – economy.

❏ During the 1980s, a surging New York Stock Exchange helped create the yuppie and the junk-bond millionaire. Following the stock-market crashes of 1987 and 1989 – when a few of the more unscrupulous went to jail – overnight fortunes have been harder to find. The New York Stock Exchange continues to be pre-eminent in the financial field, however, despite being challenged by Nasdaq, an electronic, screen-based exchange through which shares are traded in information, life science and bio-technology companies. Nasdaq's rise was aided by the phenomenal success of small-capitalisation computer companies during the 1980s. ❏

Taxi-drivers It may not be the most glamorous occupation, but shortly after the internal combustion engine replaced the horse on the New York streets, driving a taxi became the staple first job of arriving immigrants.

Currently, less than 11 per cent of applications for cab-driving jobs are from native-born New Yorkers. Almost half the existing taxi force originate on the Indian subcontinent – reflecting the ethnic origins of new immigrants.

Many of these newly arrived taxi-drivers may have a university degree, or years of experience in accountancy, medicine or some other profession in their native land. Being a cabbie in New York, however, means steady wages and a chance to provide their children with a standard of education not available back home.

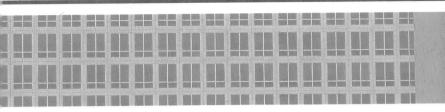

Unconventional lifestyles Many come to New York simply for the opportunity to live as they want to. Multi-coloured hair and bizarre attire seldom raise eyebrows on Manhattan's seen-it-all-before streets. Should a nocturnal lifestyle appeal, avid nightclubbers can enjoy themselves every night, sleep all day and never feel that New York life is passing them by.

coveted by ambitious news-gatherers across the country. Some New York-based magazines enjoy worldwide esteem. In recent years, the *New Yorker*, *Vanity Fair* and *Vogue* have had little trouble in luring overseas talent and have raised some eyebrows by appointing British editors to their most coveted jobs.

Most of the country's major publishers are based in New York, which attracts writers – both American and émigré – to the city and gives editors the chance to work with some of the world's most celebrated literary names.

New Yorkers have learned to take the eccentric in their stride

New York also promises a supportive infrastructure for gays and lesbians, many of whom arrive to escape discrimination in jobs and housing elsewhere.

Publishing The New York-based *Wall Street Journal* and the *New York Times* lead the country for quality reporting and carry US journalism's most prestigious jobs –

❏ An estimated 770,000 US college graduates move to New York annually. ❏

The stage
Those intent upon a career in the performing arts ignore New York at their peril. A major early boost is being one of the thousand accepted every year into the city's highly rated Juilliard School of Music and Performing Arts.

For thespians, there is no disputing New York's place at the heart of US theatre, be it with Broadway blockbusters or the dozens of Off-Off Broadway productions. New York offers acting opportunities away from live audiences, too: the majority of TV soap operas and commercials are cast in Manhattan, even though most TV and film work is centred in Los Angeles.

New York's ballet, orchestras and opera companies, meanwhile, are among the world's most highly rated.

■ **Everybody knows, or thinks they know, New York long before they arrive there, having seen the city depicted – be it lovingly or with loathing – in innumerable movies. Here is a highly selective list of the most revealing, or simply the most enjoyable, films set in New York. (Woody Allen's New York films are detailed on page 188) ...■**

Crossing Delancey (1988). Woody Allen gets a sideways acknowledgement in this tale of an unlikely Manhattan romance between an Upper West Side literary aide and a Lower East Side pickle-seller, engineered by the former's archetypal Jewish grandmother.

The Crowd (1928). Two years after the futuristic *Metropolis* came King Vidor's expressionistic study of the ordinary man's struggle in the seething city: memorable New York scenes abound.

Escape from New York (1981). There are those who think present-day Manhattan should be declared a federal prison as it is in this futuristic thriller. Ironically, the movie was filmed in St Louis, real Manhattan streets being deemed unsafe for night-time filming.

King Kong (1933). The conflict between man and nature reaches its climax as the giant ape of the title swats planes while flirting with Fay Wray beside the then infant Empire State Building.

The Lost Weekend (1945). Believe it or not, the bar in which Billy Wilder's red-eyed long weekend began still exists – PJ Clarke's, Third Avenue at 55th Street.

Mean Streets (1973). Martin Scorsese had a bigger hit three years later with *Taxi Driver*, but this convincingly contrasts the New York of hippies and flower-power with the macho traditions of young Italian-Americans on the make.

Metropolis (1926). Director Fritz Lang claimed his first sight of the Manhattan skyline as the inspiration for this classic study of the alienation of modern industrial society.

Portrait of Jennie (1948). A lovely and appropriately haunting film in which a troubled artist is enchanted by a young girl in Central Park, and later discovers that she is a ghost.

Q – The Winged Serpent (1982). Witty, low-budget piece in which a giant bird flies out of Aztec mythology to terrorise sunbathing New Yorkers. It lays an egg inside the tower of the Chrysler Building, only to be discovered by a hoodlum who tries to cash in on his amazing find.

The Refrigerator (1992). Flawed but enjoyable low-budget comedy in which a yuppie couple from the mid-West move into a seedy Lower East Side apartment and discover their refrigerator to be the gateway to hell – and a metaphor for the changes the

❏ Thomas Edison may have electrified the city but a combination of factors – royalties due on Edison-patented cinematic equipment, the demands of actors' unions, and inclement weather – encouraged fledgling film-makers to leave New York (where movies were a natural offshoot of Broadway theatres) in the early 1900s for the sunshine of southern California. ❏

The city's best-known screen moment: King Kong and Fay Wray in 1933

neighbourhood brings to bear on their relationship. The wife runs off with a Bolivian plumber.

Saturday Night Fever (1977). A product of 1970s disco mania, but giving a taste of the culture of young Italian-Americans in Brooklyn's Bensonhurst neighbourhood.

Serpico (1973). In real life, Frank Serpico was an honest cop whose efforts to stamp out corruption in the New York police force met with intimidation and violence. Serpico's stand eventually led to a massive clean-up campaign – and to Al Pacino playing him in this highly charged thriller, which has great location shots.

Seven Year Itch (1955). Probably Marilyn Monroe's finest screen moment, this film is known for one of her most enduring images: her skirt is lifted by air rising from the subway grille at the junction of 52nd Street and Lexington Avenue.

Sweet Smell of Success (1957). A brilliant Tony Curtis stars as the sleazy press agent currying favour with a powerful and sinister Broadway gossip columnist, played by Burt Lancaster.

When Harry Met Sally (1989). Katz's Deli on the Lower East Side was a New York legend even before this film's fake orgasm scene was shot there; an enjoyable but lightweight comedy romance in which the Metropolitan Museum of Art's Temple of Dendur steals a scene.

❑ An unknown 18-year-old actress called Lauren Bacall was crowned Miss Greenwich Village in 1942. ❑

Saturday Night Fever *in Brooklyn*

racial tensions.

Due to it's mixed population, New York City has more daily reports of cultures working together than any other city in America.

■ Beneath its veneer of glamour and afflu-ence, New York is a city wrenched asunder by social problems – chiefly stemming from racial intolerance, homelessness and drug abuse. Despite constant media attention and the endless rhetoric of politicians, New York's troubles seem unlikely to go away ...■

Racial tensions New York's 7 million inhabitants span a multitude of nationalities, colours and religions, but while it may appear to be the world's greatest melting-pot, racial tensions frequently surface here and often escalate into violence.

In 1986, 23-year-old black Michael Griffiths was killed after being chased by a white mob wielding baseball bats. The car Griffiths had been travelling in had broken down in a white area – Howards Beach, Queens – and he had left the vehicle to find a public telephone to call a mechanic.

Three years later, a black youth, Yusuf Hawkins, was shot dead by young Italian-Americans in the white, middle-class suburb of Bensonhurst in Brooklyn. Along with three friends, Hawkins was in the area to look over a bike which he had seen advertised.

The Bensonhurst incident contributed to the election of New York's first black mayor, David Dinkins, in the hope that he could quell the city's racial strife.

Dinkins' first test came a few months later, when years of feuding between the predominantly black residents of the depressed Crown Heights district of Brooklyn and the neighbourhood's ultra-strict, political-ly active Lubavitcher Jews exploded after a black child was killed by a car driven by a member of the sect. Soon after, black protesters killed a rabbinical student and four days and nights of violence ensued.

Mayor Dinkins' hesitancy at order-ing police to quell the disturbance brought the charge that he was showing favour to blacks, outrag-ing the city's Jewish com-munity and his political oppo-nents.

Harlem riots in 1964 and (below) hope for the future?

DINKINS

Sheraton Ce   'el

Police tactics have often inflamed racial tensions

In 1992 the police shooting of a suspected drug dealer in the Hispanic Washington Heights area incited more street violence, and allegations of racism in the city's police force came under scrutiny.

❏ New York schools are no strangers to violence. In one Brooklyn high school, the 1991–2 academic year finished with three students killed and a teacher critically injured, all from shootings. ❏

Homelessness Numbering approximately 100,000, New York's homeless population was swelled by the razing of single-occupancy hotels – sleazy establishments occupied by single, poor people on a long-term basis – and the mass discharge of mental hospital patients in the 1960s.

As the homeless became increasingly visible and the phrase 'bag lady' entered New York's vocabulary, public pressure led to the creation of large city-funded hostels. These brightly lit (and sometimes rat-infested) structures proved unpopular with the homeless themselves. An estimated 5,000 homeless people have taken refuge in the subway system, living either on the platforms or along the tunnels in sidings. Some homeless people earn enough for a meal by spending their days collecting tin cans, earning 5¢ a can by doing so.

Others earn a few dollars by selling the newspaper *Street News*, launched in 1989.

Despite a $14-million initiative from City Hall and the fact that New Yorkers are, on the whole, fairly sympathetic towards Aids victims, New York provides woefully inadequate care for sufferers, many of whom have been forced to joined the ranks of the homeless over recent years.

Drugs Used for a long time by New York's rich and fashionable, drugs also provide a means of escape from the drudgery of life in the city's slums – either by consuming them or by dealing in them.

In 1985, the city's drug problems worsened with the arrival of crack cocaine. Easier and cheaper to make and supply than heroin, crack brought immense profits to dealers, some of whom started as schoolchildren carrying bags of the drug to users.

An estimated 70 per cent of the city's 5,000 prostitutes are thought to be crack addicts. They are also the fastest-growing group found to be HIV-positive.

17

❏ To prove how easy it was to buy crack cocaine on New York's streets, Senator Alfonse D'Amato went undercover in 1986 and, watched by a TV crew, bought a $20 bag of the drug in Washington Heights. ❏

■ **Few areas of New York stay the same for long. Not only do entire districts undergo staggering transformations within just a few years – socially, architecturally and commercially – but sometimes a whole new neighbourhood can rise up where previously there was nothing but a hole in the ground ...■**

Battery Park City The newest and sleekest testament to New York's powers of metamorphosis is Battery Park City, a $4-billion project combining commercial, residential and recreational areas on a 92-acre land-fill site on the western edge of the Financial District.

Conceived in the 1970s, Battery Park City gave a new lease of life to an abandoned stretch of Hudson River waterfront while finding a use for the thousands of tons of earth and rock excavated during the building of the World Trade Center. Like the Rockefeller Center (to which it is frequently likened), Battery Park City is evolving through the labours of several architects working within a single design plan, intended to re-create the atmosphere of an elegant and traditional Manhattan neighbourhood.

Of the commercial architecture, Cesar Pelli's World Financial Center, completed in 1986, was well received for its palm-decorated Winter Garden atrium, but encountered a mixed response overall.

More universally appreciated is the mile-long Esplanade, restoring public access to this section of the Hudson River for the first time in decades. Victorian-style lamp-posts and wooden benches heighten the leisurely ambience. The 19 residential buildings are luxury apartments, mostly inhabited by Financial District high-flyers and their families.

Times Square and 42nd Street The 1970s saw busy Times Square and the adjacent stretch of 42nd Street – on the borders of the Broadway theatre district – being taken over by porno cinemas, massage parlours and adult bookshops. Drug dealers and prostitutes plied their trade, and homeless people were a common sight, while pedestrian congestion made the area ideal for pickpockets.

A $2½-billion programme of demolition and construction in the Times Square area began in the mid-1980s. The aims were to create new hotels

Will Times Square lose its pizazz?

The Esplanade along the Hudson

and office buildings, to facilitate the restoration of several historic but decaying theatres, and to update Times Square's subway station.

The police have steadily clamped down on local street crime as work continues apace on Times Square Center – four high-rise buildings, one on each corner of the junction of Broadway, Seventh Avenue and 42nd Street – designed by architects Philip Johnson and John Burgee.

> ❏ 'A sobering effect' – the architects' intended impact of Times Square Center on seething Times Square. ❏

Many New Yorkers are sceptical about the scheme's chances of success, happy to lose the sleaze but fearful at the same time of trading Times Square's legendary vitality for a sterile landscape of modern towers.

SoHo and TriBeCa In the late 1960s, the abandoned factories of SoHo (see page 175) provided dirt-cheap, light-filled studios for scores of aspiring artists. A few years later, when opposition to a proposed freeway focused attention on the neighbourhood's 19th-century architecture and the artists' presence had stimulated the opening of successful galleries, the area became the most fashionable in the city, and a plethora of trendy, expensive restaurants and bars appeared. The fortunes of TriBeCa (see page 182), another neglected former industrial area, also rose simply through its proximity to SoHo.

East Village As Greenwich Village moved out of the price range of all but the most established writers and artists, the city's creative spirits crossed Broadway into the less characterful but less costly East Village. Unlike former commercial areas such as SoHo and TriBeCa, however, the East Village already had its own population with deep roots. This prevented the area moving headlong into gentrification – despite rising rents and the surge of interest spearheaded by its avant-garde artists in the early 1980s.

> ❏ The continuing eastward migration of New York's unknown and lesser-known artists from Greenwich Village, through SoHo and the East Village, now finds them across the East River, creating loft studios in the former factories of Brooklyn's Williamsburg. Here they form a striking contrast to the area's concentration of ultra-orthodox Satmarer Jews. ❏

■ **Thanks to a unique combination of ultra-wealthy collectors and a wartime influx of modern European artists, New York has not only amassed some of the world's finest pieces of art – displaying them in several world-class museums – but has also evolved into a renowned showcase for new artistic ideas and directions ...■**

First collections Founded in 1804, the **New-York Historical Society** became the city's first repository for art, acquiring a singular collection of early American works, including many originally commissioned by Robert Lehman, a New Yorker who opened part of his town house as a gallery and brought American artists such as Thomas Cole to public attention.

The paintings collection of New York's **Metropolitan Museum of Art** (pages 142–8) began with a modest purchase of 174 Dutch and Flemish canvases in 1870 and grew – aided by bequests and donations – into a world-class stock, including many major pieces by Van Gogh, Turner, El Greco and Vermeer.

Businessmen become collectors
With more money than they knew what to do with, and newly built Fifth Avenue mansions in need of decoration, New York's 19th-century millionaires began raiding the art collections of Europe. One such hard-headed industrialist was Henry Clay Frick, who acquired the phenomenal hoard now known as the **Frick Collection** (see page 110).

Patrons Many affluent New Yorkers indulged themselves by commissioning artists to paint their portraits but one who did much more to encourage the creativity of American artists was Gertrude Vanderbilt Whitney. Displaying and promoting emergent artists such as Edward Hopper and John Sloan, Whitney also established an influential Parisian-style salon during the early 1900s. Her legacy, the **Whitney Museum of American Art** (page 191), continues to champion the country's unknown artists regardless of prevailing fashions, and has many of the

The Metropolitan Museum of Art

Art for Sale – a private SoHo gallery

❑ New York is said to be home to 90,000 artists and to hold 500 art galleries. A new and controversial form of New York art emerged in the 1970s complex and colourful graffiti began appearing in public places, such as subway trains, created with paint sprayed from cans and signed by its makers only with a distinctive symbol or 'tag'. ❑

finest American artists of the 20th century represented among its permanent stock.

As Gertrude Whitney was furthering appreciation of American art, wealthy industrialist Solomon R Guggenheim was discovering the art and artists of modern Europe. Guggenheim's purchases of early Cubist and abstract canvases were displayed on the walls of his suite at the Plaza Hotel, and later became the basis of the **Guggenheim Museum** (pages 122–4).

An international art centre As war loomed in Europe, New York found itself acquiring not only European art but European artists as well. By the 1940s, many of modern art's major names were resident in the city. They were to have a colossal impact on the New York art scene.

New York surpassed Paris (then under Nazi occupation) as the centre for international art dealing and the city's pre-eminence was confirmed by the emergence of abstract expressionism (see pages 128–9). Meanwhile, the **Museum of Modern Art** (see pages 158–60), founded in 1929, was evolving into the world's most prestigious modern art museum.

New York now New York spawned pop art, op art and minimalist art during the 1960s, and by the late 1970s the shabby warehouses of SoHo (see page 175) had been transformed into pristine galleries showcasing new trends and new talents.

In the economically buoyant 1980s, New York art became big business as new buyers sought inflation-proof investments to hang in their new apartments. The artists in vogue then – Julian Schnabel, David Salle and Eric Fischl – could expect poverty to be a thing of the past.

For a few years, unconventional artists challenged the status quo by setting up their own galleries in the low-rent East Village and Lower East Side. Typically for New York, the result was the seeds of gentrification being sown in the East Village and the adoption of the best of the artists by the SoHo galleries.

❑ Among the most remarkable of New York's many plaza sculptures is Jean Dubuffet's *Group of Four Trees*, in the Chase Manhattan Bank in the Financial District. ❑

■ **Not only is New York the centre of US publishing, it is also a city which has provided more material for 20th-century writers than perhaps any other. Literary landmarks are liberally strewn about, and several New York neighbourhoods have carved out special places for themselves in the annals of literary achievement ...■**

A publishing capital Geography made New York the publishing capital of the US in the 1850s. Before the US recognised international copyright laws in 1891, any book (usually British fiction) could be copied, printed and sold, earning its US publisher fat profits as no royalties were due.

To maximise earnings, American publishers vied with one another to be first with the latest foreign manuscripts. As New York became the nation's major seaport, the city's publishers could get their hands on new books and pirate them faster than rivals elsewhere.

The city observed New York has long provided rich pickings for observant writers. From a barstool vantage point in the early 1900s, O Henry (the pen name of William Sydney Porter) produced short stories drawing on the seamy side of city life. In a similar vein a few decades later,

Damon Runyon

❏ Born in Manhattan in 1783, Washington Irving might well be considered New York's first home-grown writer. His satirical *A History of New York* was written under the memorable pseudonym of Diedrich Knickerbocker. ❏

Damon Runyon described the characters on the fringes of Broadway theatreland. The dark side of the jazz age was illustrated by F Scott Fitzgerald's *The Great Gatsby*, while Truman Capote's *Breakfast at Tiffany's* was fine-tuned to the nuances of 1950s New York high life.

The stresses of 1980s New York underpinned Tom Wolfe's rambling comic novel, *Bonfire of the Vanities*, and the same decade saw the emergence of the so-called Brat Pack authors: young writers whose ambivalent prose dwelt on the selfishness and conceits of contemporary New York.

Among them, Tama Janowitz's *Slaves of New York* had the distinction of being marketed with a promotional video, although a title garnering far more publicity was *American Psycho* by Brett Easton Ellis, notable less for its literary qualities than for its graphic depictions of the violence perpetrated by an archetypal New York yuppie.

Literary neighbourhoods In the mid-1880s, New York literary life revolved around the fashionable drawing-rooms of Greenwich Village town houses, where heavyweights like James Fenimore Cooper rubbed

Washington Square and (below right) Henry James

shoulders with the publishers of literary journals. Such times were described in Edith Wharton's *The Age of Innocence*, and by Henry James in *Washington Square*.

As Greenwich Village rents fell, the area drew a host of talented but impoverished writers – as diverse as Willa Cather, John Reed, Theo Drieser, John Dos Passos, Robert Frost, Eugene O'Neill and Thomas Wolfe – who between them created the first American Bohemia and helped Greenwich Village become filled with literary landmarks (see pages 112–18).

The East Village and the Lower East Side began attracting impecunious scribes from the 1950s, when Beat writers like William Burroughs and Allen Ginsberg moved in alongside émigrés such as W H Auden. Another arrival was Norman Mailer, who had earlier written *The Naked and the Dead* at his parents' house in Brooklyn Heights.

Mass African-American migration into Harlem helped stimulate the Harlem Renaissance of the 1920s, bringing black writers such as Langston Hughes and Zora Neale Hurston to public notice. In the 1950s, Harlem-born James Baldwin created a stir with *Go Tell it on the Mountain*, though not before leaving Harlem for Europe. More recently, Chester Himes used Harlem as the setting for a series of thrillers.

❏ Rejected writers in New York have included some notable names. Born in Lower Manhattan in 1819, Herman Melville worked as a customs officer on the East River after his *Moby Dick* received scathing reviews. Only after his death was it acclaimed as a masterpiece. Edgar Allan Poe's poems and short stories were admired in Europe but in New York he scraped a living from journalism before dying drunk in a gutter. Walt Whitman penned eulogies to Manhattan and the Brooklyn Bridge in the 1840s, but every publisher in the city turned down *Leaves of Grass*, eventually acknowledged as one of the great works of American poetry. ❏

23

■ **For architecture enthusiasts, the Manhattan skyline is the stuff of dreams. The city's colonial structures may have almost completely vanished, but extant buildings are a thrilling mixture, encompassing styles from formative years to the most contemporary adventures in post-modernism ...■**

The Federal style From 1760 to 1830, the Federal style became the first genuine American building style, though it drew heavily on British Georgian and treated public buildings to columns and domes reminiscent of ancient Rome: **City Hall** (see page 89) is a prime example.

Federal-style residential architecture was distinguished by semi-detached houses of brick and wood, with fanlights above the entrances and dormer windows. The **Gracie Mansion** (see page 111) is one example. A grander specimen is the former James Watson residence, now the **Shrine of Elizabeth Bayley Seton** (7 State Street).

❏ Unless you are rather well connected socially or happen to be making a business call to an office inside one, your chances of seeing the interior of a brownstone – other than staring through the window – are very limited. Two brownstones are open to the public, however: the reconstructed birthplace of Theodore Roosevelt (page 182), and the residential section of the Pierpont Morgan Library (page 169). ❏

Revivals As New York enjoyed an economic surge during the 19th century, the Greek revival style – bringing porticos and floral-patterned ironwork to the facades of the new rows of town houses, such as those facing **Washington Square Park** – was the first of a spate of revivals, which included Italianate, Renaissance and Gothic. Examples of all these are widely found.

Brownstones A cheap form of sandstone quarried in New Jersey, brownstone was used to build swiftly and cheaply in the mid-1800s, and brownstone town houses became the main residences of the middle classes. Held in little affection at the time, brownstones enjoyed a surge of popularity from the 1950s and the many that remain – especially in Midtown – are highly prized, both as residences and offices.

Luxury apartment blocks By the turn of the century, property prices in Midtown Manhattan had risen beyond the pockets of the middle classes, who began colonising the new luxury apartments on the Upper West Side. Sumptuously appointed and with anything up to ten rooms, the apartments also boasted futuristic extras such as built-in fridges and pneumatic mail-delivery systems. The still-standing **Dakota** (see page 96) was the first such block, and several others remain near by.

Early skyscrapers The 1902 **Flatiron Building** (see page 106) was the city's first 'world's-tallest' structure, and was also the first to be supported by a steel frame – a technique which showed the way for creating even taller buildings. A 1920s build-

ing boom gave Manhattan the **Chrysler** and **Empire State** buildings, both of which not only reached record heights but bore the hallmarks of art deco (see pages 162–3).

The international style The towers of steel and glass which rise above Manhattan and form most people's image of the city's architecture resulted from the arrival in New York of Europe's most creative architects, who fled Nazism and brought with them the anti-traditional ideas of the international style.

The **Museum of Modern Art** (see pages 158–60) became the city's first international-style building. Among the many that followed was Mies van der Rohe's 1958 **Seagram Building** (Park Avenue between 52nd and 53rd streets), which gave New York its first plaza – an open space where the public could stroll, sunbathe and eat a snack. By the late 1970s, plazas were incorporated into every high-rise plan, some being enclosed to form atriums.

❑ The richly decorative beaux-arts style arrived in New York in 1890 and is exemplified by Carrère and Hastings' **New York Public Library** (see page 168), by Cass Gilbert's **US Custom House** (see page 190), and in numerous works by the firm of McKim, Mead and White. ❑

The 1980s boom With the 1980s construction boom, Manhattan gained its first modern buildings not bearing the international-style stamp. Philip Johnson's **AT&T Building** (on Madison Avenue between 55th and 56th streets) became known as the Chippendale skyscraper for its similarity to a piece of furniture; **Trump Tower** (see page 183) rose as a shrine to vulgar consumerism, and the **World Financial Center** filled its atrium with palm trees.

The Chrysler Building and its futuristic neighbours

■ **Rare is the visitor who manages to be in New York when there is not some kind of festival taking place, be it a traffic-stopping parade along Fifth Avenue or a low-key neighbourhood get-together. These are just a few highlights from an exceptionally busy festivals and events calendar. For precise dates and details, read the New York newspapers or contact the New York Convention and Visitors' Bureau (festivals hotline tel: 397 8200) ...■**

January
Chinese New Year (Date depends on the lunar cycle; sometimes takes place in early February.) Celebrated by dragon and lion dances and by firecrackers in the streets of Chinatown. Festive banquets are offered by the neighbourhood's restaurants.

❑ With a 150-year history, the St Patrick's Day Parade (along Fifth Avenue between 44th and 86th streets) is by far the biggest of New York's street parades. Much of the city, including the Empire State Building, is decked out in green to mark the day's celebration of Irish-American identity.

The parade became the centre of controversy in the early 1990s, however, when the Irish Gay and Lesbian Organisation were denied a place in the parade by the organisers, the staunchly Catholic Ancient Order of Hibernians. ❑

Winter Antiques Fair At Seventh Regiment Armory, Park Avenue at East 66th Street. Upmarket antiques and their dealers; well-heeled members of the public are also welcome (see also page 226).

February
Black History Month Lectures and exhibitions on African-American themes held throughout the city.
Lincoln's Birthday and **Washington's Birthday** Each celebrated with sales in shops and local department stores.

March
Greek Independence Day Parade On Fifth Avenue between 59th and

Chinese New Year celebrations: the Lion Dance

79th streets. Honours the regaining of Greek independence in 1821: a sea of blue and white as school bands and Greek-Americans in national costume march jovially along the route.

Parade of Circus Animals Creatures from the Ringling Bros and Barnum & Bailey Circus trek from a railway siding at Twelfth Avenue and 34th Street to Madison Square Garden.

The St Patrick's Day Parade is New York's largest street parade

❏ The Puerto Rican Day Parade, along Fifth Avenue between 44th and 86th streets on the first Sunday of June, brings New York's huge Puerto Rican population on to the streets to celebrate their nation's Independence Day; red, white and blue Puerto Rican flags are everywhere, traditional foods are sold from stalls, and live bands playing on floats provide a non-stop soundtrack of salsa music to wildly appreciative audiences. ❏

St Patrick's Day Parade (see box opposite).

April
Easter Day Parade Along Fifth Avenue, beginning near St Patrick's Cathedral. On the Saturday before Easter, a children's egg-rolling contest takes place on Central Park's Great Lawn.
Japanese Cherry Blossom Festival In Central Park's Conservatory Garden and at the Brooklyn Botanic Garden.

May
Memorial Day parades In many locations around the city.
Martin Luther King Memorial Day Parade Along Fifth Avenue from 44th to 86th streets.
Ninth Avenue International Food Festival A two-day feast of the city's ethnic cuisines, on Ninth Avenue between 37th and 57th streets.
SoHo Festival Along Prince Street.
Ukrainian Festival In the East Village along 7th Street on the weekend closest to 17 May, the anniversary of Ukraine's adoption of Christianity: traditional foods, crafts and folk dancing.
Washington Square Outdoor Arts Show A gathering of local artists showing and selling their wares over three successive weekends.

June
American Crafts Festival Lincoln Center. Over two successive weekends, exhibitors from all over the US show their skills at creating jewellery, sculpture, and all forms of decorative arts.
Feast of St Anthony of Padua Little Italy. More restrained than the neighbourhood's Feast of St Gennaro (see September), with food stalls along Sullivan Street and an image of the saint carried through the streets after dark.
Puerto Rican Day Parade See box.
Lesbian and Gay Pride Day Parade Along Fifth Avenue to Washington Square Park and around Greenwich Village. New York's gay and lesbian community splits into many factions but they band together for this assertion of strength through unity.

Museum Mile Celebration The museums of Fifth Avenue's Museum Mile hold special events and stay open later than usual.

The Metropolitan Opera Free performances in city parks, including Central Park.

Shakespeare in the Park Works by the bard staged for free at Central Park's Delacorte Theater.

July

Feast of O-Bon Japanese music and dance in the Upper West Side's Riverside Park, marking the full moon.

Independence Day celebrations Including Macy's firework display from barges moored on the Hudson River.

Mostly Mozart Festival At the Lincoln Center's Avery Fisher Hall (see page 235).

The horrors of Hallowe'en

August

Harlem Week A two-week celebration of Harlem's history and culture.

New York Philharmonic Open-air concerts in city parks.

September

Labor Day Parade Along Fifth Avenue. Ostensibly to celebrate the American worker, really just an excuse to mark the end of summer with a parade.

New York is Book Country Fifth Avenue between 48th and 59th streets. All the major – and many minor – publishers are represented at stalls; many well-known authors give readings and signings.

New York Film Festival At the Lincoln Center (see page 234).

Feast of St Gennaro Lasts ten days along Little Italy's Mulberry Street. Makeshift kitchens serve sausages and hunks of pizza, while a shrine to the saint is carried through the streets and showered with dollar bills. (See also page 135.)

Washington Square Outdoor Art Show Stands with locals' artworks and ethnic food sold from stalls.

October

Columbus Day Parade Fifth Avenue between 44th and 72nd streets. As awareness of indigenous American cultures grows throughout the US, this parade to commemorate Christopher Columbus' 'discovery' of the New World has become increasingly controversial. Many Native American and Hispanic groups – and others – oppose the event.

Hallowe'en, Make-believe witches and wizards parade through Greenwich Village to Washington Square Park Memorial Arch.

New York Marathon Run from Verrazano-Narrows Bridge to Central Park's Tavern on the Green (occasionally this may be held in early November).

November

Macy's Thanksgiving Day Parade Along Central Park West and Broadway with helium-filled balloons; the huge balloons can be seen in the evening before the parade being filled with gas beside the American Museum of Natural History.

December

Rockefeller Center The lighting of the Rockefeller Center Christmas Tree marks the start of the city's Christmas festivities. Over the Christmas period, many shops mount fantastic window displays.

❏ Thousands of New Yorkers gather in Times Square to see in the New Year. As midnight approaches, an illuminated ball (disguised as a big apple) slides down Times Tower. ❏

NEW YORK WAS

■ **During the 16th century, the eastern seaboard of North America was steadily explored by European seafarers, not with the expectation of locating the site of the future world's greatest metropolis, but in the hope of finding the North West Passage – a short cut to the spice islands of the Pacific. Many years were to elapse between the European discovery of the land that now holds New York and its eventual settlement ...■**

Early explorers The first European sighting of what became New York was made in 1524 by Giovanni da Verrazano, a Florentine merchant in the employ of the French. Verrazano described the land he found as having 'commodiousness and beauty' and its native inhabitants uttering 'loud cries of wonderment' as they spotted the vessels of the Europeans.

It was not until 1609 that a more thorough navigation of the area was made, this time by Hendrick (Henry) Hudson, an Englishman working for the Dutch East India Company. He sailed up the river that now bears his name, as far north as present-day Albany.

New Amsterdam (New York), 1673

❏ Before European settlement, the New York area was inhabited by several Native American groups, most being of the Algonquin tribe. The Native Americans, who lived by farming, hunting and fishing, did not share the European concept of land ownership – the root of many future disputes – but they did share the European enthusiasm for trading, which helped keep early relations fairly cordial.

A sustained series of Dutch-led attacks eventually forced the natives away from the settled areas. European diseases, to which Native Americans lacked immunity, also took their toll. ❏

Like Verrazano, Hudson failed to find the fabled North West Passage, but he did note that the Native Americans were rich in beaver, mink and otter pelts and were also eager to trade them.

The first New Yorkers Attracted by the prospect of commerce with the Native Americans, the Dutch West India Company was founded in Amsterdam and launched several North American settlements. In 1625, one such settlement – named

The arrival of Henry Hudson in 1609 at the mouth of what is now the Hudson River

New Amsterdam – was founded in what is now Lower Manhattan. It was made up of Dutch and French-speaking Walloon families and their African slaves.

In 1626, the leader of the Dutch colony, Peter Minuit, bought Manhattan Island from a native tribe for a box of tools and trinkets worth the equivalent of $24.

■ **Though established as a colonial trading base, Dutch New Amsterdam – soon to become British New York – quickly acquired a character of its own, partly through the ethnic and religious diversity of its inhabitants and partly through the fact that many of them quickly came to share a desire to rid themselves of their Old World links for good ...■**

New Amsterdam – success and failure

Much to the delight of the Dutch West India Company, New Amsterdam soon began to flourish as a trading centre. New settlers arrived, taking advantage of the company's generous land grants. Some came here to escape religious persecution in their homeland, seeking the freedom of worship that the company had promised.

New Amsterdam was far from being the tranquil replica of a Dutch town that the company might have hoped for, however. Violence and lawlessness were rife, unmarried couples cohabited, pigs ran wild in the streets, and – with a tavern for every 12 adults – many of the population spent their spare time drinking to excess.

A new governor

In 1647, the corrupt governor was dismissed and the job of bringing order to bear on the wayward colony was given to Peter Stuyvesant, a noted disciplinarian. Under his iron rule, and with a new city charter providing for elected officials, New Amsterdam doubled in population and in size, gaining its first hospital, prison, school and post office, and its first proper commercial institutions.

The colony also gained a protective wall to its north, which would later prove ineffectual at halting British advances but did give rise to the thoroughfare named Wall Street.

Peter Stuyvesant

The British arrive

Stuyvesant's unpopularity, coupled with excessive tax demands by the Dutch West India Company, caused the population of New Amsterdam to offer no resistance when four British warships blockaded the harbour in 1664. Under British rule, the colony was renamed New York, after James, Duke of York, brother of King Charles II.

Sited between the major British bases to the south and north, and at the mouth of the strategically important Hudson River, it is not surprising that New York became a prominent seaport. Nonetheless, the British proved no more able to stamp their authority on the everyday life of the colony than had the Dutch, and New York remained as socially robust as ever.

By 1700 New York had acquired a population numbering 20,000, composed of an almost unchartable mix of nationalities and religions.

The American Revolution

After the 1763 Treaty of Paris confirmed their dominance over the 13 American colonies, the British imposed a series of punitive taxes on the settlements. Previous anti-colonial uprisings had been violently quashed by the British, but with the world entering a post-colonial age and the theories of republicanism being universally discussed, the idea of independence

❑ When the Declaration of Independence was publicly read at New York's Bowling Green in July 1776, the excited crowd overturned the green's equestrian statue of King George III. Legend has it that the lead statue was melted down and turned into bullets, subsequently used against the British. ❑

became increasingly attractive to the 13 by now economically thriving colonies.

Following the Declaration of Independence in 1776, George Washington mounted a revolutionary war against the British. Many British troops were billeted in New York, where they commandeered food supplies, terrorised locals, and imprisoned captured rebel prisoners on board ships in which hunger and disease were rife.

New York was to remain the last toehold of British rule in the New World. Although the 1783 Treaty of Paris formally ended the war, not until Washington's march from Harlem into the Bowery in November of that year were the remaining British troops withdrawn. Their final act was to grease the flagpole to hinder the raising of the Stars and Stripes.

■ **As the country's major seaport, New York was the gateway to the New World. Through the 19th century it was on the receiving end of the largest migration in human history; a mass movement of people which not only transformed the city but shaped the future of the entire US ...■**

34

New York's population had been markedly cosmopolitan from the earliest days of settlement and a steady influx of immigrants continued after the American Revolution.

Some new arrivals were attracted by the prospect of shaping the first democratic mixed-nationality society, others were radical intellectual rebels driven into exile by governments who feared them, and a few were simply adventurers or fortune-seekers.

In the mid-19th century, however, came the great waves of mass immigration which were to change the city completely.

Mass migrations Three major factors contributed to the mass waves of European migration into New York during the first half of the 19th century: the social upheaval caused by the Napoleonic wars, the potato famines in Ireland and Germany, and the industrial revolution, which spread across Europe and robbed many skilled craftsmen and smallholding farmers of their livelihoods.

On the receiving end of a mass movement of people on a scale never

Arriving in the New World: an engraving of 1892

Immigration into
19th-century New York:
1820s 150,000
1840s 1.7 million
1850s 2.5 million

before known, New York's over-stretched Castle Garden (now Castle Clinton) immigrant processing centre was replaced in 1890 by the federally funded Ellis Island complex. The new receiving centre – a pristine, state-of-the-art affair – was a far cry from what awaited most new arrivals once they set foot in New York as US citizens.

While not all of the new arrivals stayed in New York, many did, and they placed a massive burden on the city's resources. In order to fit more people into a single plot, the 1860s saw the creation of tenement blocks – five- or six-storey buildings where an entire family would sometimes occupy a single windowless room and earning the nickname 'lung blocks' for the high incidence of tuberculosis among their inhabitants. Inadequate drainage and sewerage systems made diseases such as yellow fever and cholera a constant threat.

In a city of immigrants, a mix of guile, initiative and extremely hard work in appalling conditions usually bore rewards, and the major ethnic groups became assimilated (particularly as child immigrants reached adulthood fully conversant with the ways of the New World) and began climbing the city's social ladder comparatively swiftly.

The northward spread of Manhattan's grid-style streets was matched by a steady northward flow of wealth. As the city's rich occupied the newest, most northerly homes, their previous dwellings were occupied by prospering ethnic groups while the poor – the latest immigrants – were housed in the south, usually in the tenements of the Lower East Side.

Anti-immigration laws Fearing loss of jobs, the spread of disease and the decline of Anglo-Saxon supremacy (after the American Revolution, 60 per cent of Americans were of English origin), established and powerful groups campaigned for tighter immigration controls.

In 1882, the Chinese Exclusion Act had banned further Chinese immigration into the US – an effect of the tide of anti-Chinese feeling which led to the creation of New York's Chinatown. The US entered the 20th century as the world's richest industrial power, and calls for protecting what had been created grew stronger.

The outbreak of World War I encouraged the isolationist stance which paved the way for the immigration curbs of the 1920s (although the granting of US citizenship to all Puerto Ricans was an exception). Mass immigration as seen in earlier decades came to an end.

❑ While the mass migrations of the 19th century are unlikely ever to be repeated, immigration into New York is by no means a thing of the past. Easing of immigration restrictions in the 1960s caused a dramatic expansion of Chinatown (where many inhabitants are actually Vietnamese or Cambodian) and enabled Indians, Koreans, West Indians, Filipinos, Latinos (people of Latin American origin or descent) and Middle Eastern nationals to feature prominently among the 90,000 people who still settle in New York every year. ❑

■ **Seldom has the entrepreneur (or the rogue) had such opportunities to make a name and a fortune for himself as in 19th-century New York. At that time the city, rapidly evolving from an outpost to a metropolis, was alive with speculation, sharp dealing and money-making. From these heady times, a handful of names are remembered – be it fondly or fretfully – into the present day ...■**

John Jacob Astor (1763–1848) A fur-trade millionaire, John Jacob Astor switched his attentions to property in 1834, buying New York land while currying favour with city politicians and ingratiating himself into New York high society. Profits from slum housing helped Astor become the country's richest man by the time he died in 1848. In a rare act of generosity, however, Astor bequeathed $400,000 for the creation of the US's first public library, now the Joseph Papp Public Theater.

Andrew Carnegie (1835–1919) Andrew Carnegie started in industry as a cotton-factory worker and rose to become a magnate with interests spanning iron, coal, steel, ships and railways. Believing in the motto 'a man who dies rich, dies disgraced', Carnegie financed numerous trusts, some 2,000 libraries, and gave $2 million for the building of Carnegie Hall – yet still had $23 million when he died in 1919. The Carnegie mansion on Fifth Avenue is now the home of the Cooper-Hewitt Museum, (see page 95).

From mill-worker to multimillionaire: Andrew Carnegie

❑ When Caroline Schermerhorn married into the Astor family in 1853, she became the fabled 'Mrs Astor', a New York high-society legend for her annual balls, regarded as the city's definitive social barometer. The 400 people invited (400 being the number of people in New York who, it was thought, fitted into a ballroom) could consider themselves 'in'; those not invited – which included anyone who worked for a living or who had made their millions through railways – were definitely 'out'. ❑

Henry Clay Frick (1849–1919) A partner of Andrew Carnegie in the Carnegie Steel Company, Henry Clay Frick was credited with few redeeming qualities. He instigated the blackest event in the history of US labour relations: hiring a mob to bring a steel-mill strike to a violent and murderous end. Some of Frick's fortunes went into acquiring the great stash of European art that now forms the Frick Collection, housed in the hated man's former Fifth Avenue mansion (see page 110).

Jay Gould (1836–92) Robber baron, swindler and socialite, Jay Gould made his first pile at the age of 21. He would bet on the outcome of Civil War battles, having first heard the result by tapping telegraph lines. The most spectacular of Gould's many underhand dealings netted $11 million on the gold market and brought about the calamitous 'Black Friday' financial crash of 1868.

John Pierpont Morgan (1837–1913)

Much of the European money invested in the US during the 19th century was channelled through banker and financier John Pierpont Morgan. Able to wield influence on every new project that needed money, Morgan gained considerable wealth and importance. He had a finger in every entrepreneurial pie, and oversaw the creation of the US Steel Corporation, which became the world's first billion-dollar business in 1901.

Along with the US Treasury, Morgan spent $25 million buying gold to save New York – and the nation – from bankruptcy in 1907. He also founded the Pierpont Morgan Library (see page 169).

Cornelius Vanderbilt (1794–1877)

Beginning with a ferry service between Staten Island and Manhattan in the early 1800s, Cornelius Vanderbilt built a steamship empire which dominated transportation across New York Bay and plied routes as far afield as Latin America and – at the height of the Gold Rush – to California.

In 1864, Vanderbilt diverted some of his $20 million into railways, laying the tracks that linked the steel-producing factories of Pittsburgh and the dairy farms of rural New York state to the city's docks – where his cargo ships awaited loading.

When he died in 1877, Vanderbilt was worth $105 million.

> ❏ J P Morgan fully deserved his reputation as a hard-headed businessman but he regularly consulted society astrologist Evangeline Adams before making decisions. Evidence of the banker's interest in astrology is easy to find at the Pierpont Morgan Library, where symbols of the zodiac are incorporated into the lavish décor. ❏

37

An early wheeler-dealer: investment banker John Pierpont Morgan

■ **Unusually for a major city, the pattern of New York's expansion is easy to trace. The city's growth was a simple case of the long, narrow island of Manhattan being smothered with urban development, starting at one end and working systematically towards the other ...■**

The European settlement of Manhattan began at the island's southern tip, the easiest place for ships to berth. Here the first businesses and homes became established. As the settlement grew, it could only expand northwards. In the process, it acquired the haphazard street pattern which remains largely intact in today's Financial District.

The grid plan In 1811, the city's Board of Commissioners ratified a rectangular, grid-style street plan formulated by a surveyor, John Randel. Ignoring all existing streets except for Broadway – a track that followed an ancient Native American route northwards – the design called for numbered streets (intended for residence) running east–west and numbered avenues (intended for

The new Brooklyn Bridge must have seemed a miracle in its day

commerce) running north–south.

The grid plan provided a much-needed blueprint for Manhattan's development. In 1820, with a population of 123,000, New York was already the US's largest city, despite barely extending beyond Canal Street. North of Canal Street, a few villages had taken root in what are now Chelsea and Greenwich Village, and the areas now comprising the Upper East Side and the Upper West Side were a mixture of farms, wasteland, and squatters' camps.

When the Erie Canal opened in 1825, it linked New York to the Great Lakes and the agriculturally productive mid-West, and left the city unchallenged as the major American seaport – the gateway to lucrative international trade. This, coupled with the waves of mass immigration which began in the 1840s, set the scene for New York's rapid expansion throughout the 19th century.

elite. By the 1860s, several hundred millionaires were calling Manhattan home. Many of them occupied the luxury apartment blocks recently erected along Fifth Avenue, facing the newly created Central Park – and the Upper East Side became the lasting domain of the rich.

A metropolis is born Steadily, the city gained an infrastructure worthy of the metropolis it was becoming. In 1868, the first 'El' (or Elevated) train went into service. Two years later the first subway line was drilled. Work on the Brooklyn Bridge – the engineering miracle of its day – began in 1870, and was completed in 1883. Thomas Edison's company began the electrification of the city, opening its first generating station in 1882.

In 1898, the creation of Greater New York linked the five boroughs – Manhattan, Brooklyn, the Bronx, Queens and Staten Island – under a single municipal government. New York City's population was now 3.8 million, making it the second largest city in the world.

Harlem was speedily developed by 19th-century speculators

Money moves north Property developers wasted little time in moving northward through Manhattan, flattening hilly land and erecting new buildings. Around the mid-1800s, the first of the city's handsome brownstone town houses appeared, providing comfortable accommodation for New York's expanding moneyed classes on the city's northerly fringes.

In the Lower East Side, meanwhile, the first tenement blocks arose, housing penniless migrants and swiftly maturing into desperate slums.

As its poor toiled in sweatshops, New York generated incredible wealth for its already well-heeled

❏ When work began on New York's City Hall in 1803, the building stood on what was then the city's northern edge. Marble was used for the building's front and sides, but the north-facing rear was made from cheap red sandstone in the expectation that nobody would ever see it. Such was the rate of New York's expansion, however, that by the time of its completion in 1812, City Hall was already ringed by new buildings. ❏

■ **The early years of American independence were coloured by frequent financial uncertainties, but none of the early banking hiccups quite prepared the city for the Wall Street crash of 1929, which dragged the country – and the world – into the Depression ...■**

New York lasted only a year as the capital of the US, but the financial institutions on and around Wall Street – most notably the US Stock Exchange, which began as a trading place for the $80 million-worth of bonds created to pay Revolutionary War debts – remained at the heart of the nation's monetary system.

As unscrupulous investors played on the insecurities and inexperience inherent in the new nation's financial systems, crashes were numerous. The panic of 1837 wiped $60 billion dollars off the value of shares and left 50,000 people without jobs; 20 years later, another crash put 40,000 out of work. A further stock-market tumble occurred in 1873, and in 1907 New York's banks had to be saved from insolvency by the wealthy financier J P Morgan.

The booming twenties As federal government replaced independent financiers and the US emerged from World War I as a rich and powerful nation, financial uncertainties seemed very much a thing of the past.

The US economy boomed and rumours of fortunes being made overnight caused the stock market to trade faster than ever before, its ticker-tape machines struggling to keep up with developments.

Even economically irrelevant events, such as Charles Lindbergh's successful first solo flight across the Atlantic in 1927, were enough to quicken dealing. Trading levels regularly broke new records during 1928.

The crash of 1929 Although warning signals had been observed – industrial production was declining and the economy was beginning to stagnate – few people paid any heed until the third week of October 1929 when everyone began selling at once. Millions of shares were traded at a loss, causing 11 dealers to kill themselves and 29 October 1929 to go down in history as 'Black Tuesday' – the day the Depression began.

❏ 'Sooner or later a crash is coming, and it may be terrific' – financial expert Roger W Babson, speaking in September 1929. ❏

By 1932, the Depression's bleakest year, more than a third of New York's 29,000 manufacturing firms had closed down, leaving a quarter of the city's work force idle. Those with part-time jobs could consider themselves fortunate. Many others, unable to afford rent, were living in the shanty towns which appeared in Central Park (dubbed 'Hoovervilles' after the incumbent US president, Herbert Hoover) and queuing for free food provided by soup kitchens set up in Times Square.

Many of the city's most enduring skyscrapers had appeared through the buoyant 1920s, but now the building boom ground to a halt. The Empire State Building, opened in 1931, had to pay for its upkeep on the proceeds of tourist visits rather than office rents.

La Guardia leads recovery For New Yorkers, the woes of the Depression were made worse by the incompetence of their mayor, Jimmy Walker, better known for his songwriting skills than for his political abilities. Not the first – nor the last – city mayor to be embroiled in a corruption scandal, Walker departed from office in 1932 and fled to Europe.

Walker's replacement was Fiorello La Guardia, a young, credible politician pledged to ending corruption and leading the city out of the Depression. With New Deal federal funds provided by the nation's new president Franklin D Roosevelt, La Guardia instigated the largest low-cost housing construction programme seen in the US, providing work as well as affordable homes. Another city official, Robert Moses, presided over major park, bridge and road-building schemes.

Staged in Queens, the 1939 World's Fair was intended to symbolise New York's emergence from the Depression, but it was the US's entry into World War II in 1941 which really restored the city's finances, as tens of thousands of soldiers and streams of tanks, trucks and planes passed through New York bound for the European theatre of war.

❑ In 1940, the capital budget of New York City was $1. ❑

Below: The drama of the Wall Street crash, as illustrated by an Italian magazine of the day

BROOKLYN DAILY EAGLE
And Complete Long Island News

WALL ST. IN PANIC AS STOCKS CRASH

Attempt Made to Kill Italy's Crown Prince

■ **Police being paid off by criminals and the mayor using public funds for private gain are enduring images of New York – and with good reason. Corruption was part and parcel of New York life from the city's earliest days and has proved a hard vice to shake off, even in recent times ...■**

The Tweed Ring A former volunteer fireman and street-gang member, William Marcy 'Boss' Tweed got himself elected in 1851, aged 21, as assistant alderman to a council body popularly nicknamed 'the 40 Thieves'.

By promising (and delivering) jobs and money to people – often freshly arrived immigrants – in return for votes, Tweed quickly rose to the top of the thuggish faction of New York's Democratic Party called Tammany (after a Native American chief). The city's administration was soon under the thumb of the 'Tweed Ring', a coterie of corrupt officials who, during their brief reign, are estimated to have helped themselves to $300 million of public money.

As commissioner of public works, Tweed was able to extract fat commissions from construction companies as a reward for giving them lucrative contracts, and extort large sums from businesses in return for providing essential services. A share of the ill-gotten gains was earmarked for bribes to police, bureaucrats and others, to prevent them spilling the beans.

Tweed's most spectacular swindle involved the construction of the New York County Courthouse (known as the Tweed Courthouse). Started in 1862 with a budget of $250,000, the courthouse eventually cost New York taxpayers $14 million, of which the Tweed Ring creamed off around $12 million.

Eventually, an angry City Hall clerk (said to have been offered a $500,000 bribe to keep quiet) passed incriminating documents to the *New York Times*. In jail, Tweed was allowed out each day for lunch and escaped to Chile before being recaptured. Again imprisoned, he died in 1878 in a jail which his corrupt regime had commissioned.

THE "BRAINS"

The secret of success: one 1871 cartoonist's view

❏ Since most of the people who voted for him were illiterate, Tweed claimed to have little interest in what newspapers wrote. He considered the satirical cartoons – which he called 'them damn pictures' – published in Harper's Bazaar to be more damaging to his career than reports on his dirty dealings documented in words. ❏

Mayor William O'Dwyer at his desk in City Hall (below)

Mayors Quaker Fernando Wood was viewed as the man to end corruption at City Hall in 1844, despite previous accusations of fraud and the fact that he was elected mayor with more votes than there were voters. In fact, Wood sold the job of city commissioner for $50,000 and provided guarantees of naturalisation to immigrants in return for their electoral favours.

A symbol of the booming 1920s, songwriter and playboy Jimmy Walker was elected mayor in 1925. Walker dressed in white suits, frequented nightclubs, and never arrived for work until the afternoon. After raising his own salary from $25,000 to $40,000, Walker skipped town in 1932 as the news broke that he had taken $1 million in pay-offs for city contracts.

After the term of the admired mayor Fiorello La Guardia, it was dirty business as usual at City Hall. The subsequent incumbent, William O'Dwyer, made a swift exit to Mexico in 1951 as his links with organised crime were about to be exposed.

The Police In a city corrupt from head to toe, it was little surprise that 19th-century New York police similarly veered off the straight and narrow. Patrolmen routinely acted as paid

lookouts for illegal gambling dens and brothels, while higher ranks improved their salaries with bribes and the proceeds of bank robberies. Crimes were liable to 'disappear' in return for payments, and many robberies were investigated only if a reward was offered.

Actual arrests were usually intended to improve the appearance of the city for its affluent classes, removing any 'lewd women', beggars or homeless people from well-to-do areas.

Within the force, payments secured a popular 'beat' and would bring promotion. According to a newspaper report of 1892, a fee of $300 was required to become a patrolman, while $14,000 was the asking price for a precinct captain's job.

■ **It may be a bastion of big business, high finance, the media and the arts, but New York's lofty position in the hierarchy of world cities is largely due to the simple matter of possessing an outstanding natural harbour. This stroke of geographical good fortune made possible its rise from an obscure colonial trading post to the world's greatest port ...■**

Early days New York's discovery by Europeans stemmed from the search for the North West Passage, a short cut to the spice islands of the Pacific. Early explorers did not find the short cut, but they did record that New York Bay provided a safe, sheltered anchorage in an area which enjoyed a comparatively mild climate and was relatively free of fog. With the Hudson River, the bay also provided access to a navigable route inland.

Even so, New York was but one of several moderately busy ports on the continent's east coast and was fortunate when the British – then ruling over the American colonies – chose it in preference to Boston as the main recipient of their exports.

The Erie Canal The trigger of New York's phenomenal rise as a seaport – and its subsequent emergence as a major world city – was the building of the Erie Canal. The Hudson River provided a transport route between the city and the upstate farms (and the important towns of New England),

❑　New York's waterside streets were traditionally among the dirtiest, most dangerous and crime-ridden in the city. The glamour accorded to Fifth Avenue partially derived from its geographical position: plumb in the centre of Manhattan and as far from the rivers as it was possible to be.　❑

but the Erie Canal – begun in 1817 and completed in 1825 at a cost of $7 million – connected the Hudson to Lake Erie and thereby opened a swift, direct line of communication between New York and, via the Great Lakes, the newly settled farmlands of the American mid-West.

Using the canal, the 500-mile journey between Buffalo (on Lake Erie's shores) and the city could be completed in 10 days. With the American

Manhattan and several of its numerous busy piers in the 1860s

The 20th-century port: South Street Seaport today (above) and (right) the Queen Mary *at 51st Street Pier*

heartland opened up, ships from almost every nation converged on New York bearing products destined for the interior.

The port expands By the turn of the 20th century, the southern end of Manhattan was lined by 22 miles of docks, with 270 piers extending along the East River and the Hudson River.

The advent of railways did more to improve New York's transport links. Many rail freight lines ran directly to the docks, while Grand Central Station (now Grand Central Terminal) became the country's foremost rail passenger station.

By the 1930s, 'the freighter, the river boat, the ferry and the soot-faced tug' plied the city's rivers – making the Hudson River itself barely viewable below 23rd Street. They were among the 3,500 vessels that berthed in New York each month.

Ocean-going luxury Cargo may have been the bread-and-butter of the New York docks but the city's place among the world's great ports was symbolised by the graceful ocean liners of the 1910s to the 1940s. Greeted by low-flying planes and water jets, the *Queen Mary* arrived in New York for the first time in 1936 and was just one of several vessels regularly ferrying the rich and famous between Europe and the US, where New York welcomed them in a blaze of publicity.

Gradual decline As patterns of international trade changed, New York was eclipsed as the world's leading port. Simultaneously, the rising popularity of air travel reduced the demand for ocean-going liners. One by one, the great passenger ships made their final farewells to New York (although the QE2 remains a regular visitor).

Nonetheless, New York is still a busy port, handling a vessel every 28 minutes and annually unloading cargo valued at $50 billion. Meanwhile, the fall in passenger routes failed to deter the construction, at a cost of $40 million, of a new passenger ship terminal on the Hudson River in 1974.

■ After three centuries of almost constant growth had made it one of the world's most affluent cities, nobody could quite believe the news that New York was on the verge of bankruptcy. In 1975, however, that was exactly the position as New York teetered on the verge of an economic abyss ...■

The 1960s was a decade of turmoil and change throughout the US. In New York, violence erupted in the black ghettos of Brooklyn and Harlem, tens of thousands of Puerto Rican immigrants settled in East Harlem and the Lower East Side, and the so-called 'White Flight' – the movement of around a million Anglo-American families, and many businesses, out of New York – was in full swing.

Strained resources The exodus of the affluent middle classes and of many profitable companies (600,000 jobs disappeared in the six years from 1969) eroded one of the city's main sources of revenue at a time when the cost of its welfare services, then among the most liberal in the country, was spiralling.

The incumbent mayor, John Lindsay, insisted that there would be no cuts in welfare services. Through Lindsay's intransigence, a strike by 34,000 transit workers, which brought the city to a standstill in 1966, ended up by costing the city $70 million and gave

❑ 'Saving New York is like making love with a gorilla – you don't stop when you're tired, you stop when the gorilla's tired' – Felix Rohatyn, Chairman of MAC. ❑

the green light to other unions to demand high pay increases.

Meanwhile, the number of people employed by the city had grown by nearly a third in five years, and their wages – plus increased pensions and other benefits – put further strain on the city's finances.

The city administration resorted to ever more creative accountancy in order to maintain its levels of expenditure, at one stage even creating a 364-day year to enable debts to be passed on to the next 12-month period. This short-term planning had the effect of increasing interest levels on money borrowed by the city – and simply postponed an inevitable crisis.

Brink of disaster This state of financial disorder was inherited by Abe Beame, elected mayor in 1974. An accountant by profession, Beame was nonetheless unable to balance the city's books and in 1975 New York was $2 billion in the red.

❑ 'Ford to City: Drop Dead!' – *Daily News* headline encapsulating President Ford's attitude to New York's financial crisis. ❑

Strikes dogged 1960s New York

Queues at Grand Central Terminal in the 1966 transit workers' strike

As Wall Street financiers warned that municipal bonds would soon be worthless, Beame made cuts in public expenditure on a scale not seen since the Depression. Panic took hold, and trade unions agreed to wage freezes.

With no money to pay for rubbish collection or water supplies – and with President Ford refusing federal aid – New York's entire infrastructure seemed about to collapse, and the prospect of one of the world's greatest cities going broke was becoming ever more likely.

Rescue The governor of New York injected state funds into the city and set up the Municipal Assistance Corporation (popularly known as the Big MAC) to control expenditure at City Hall, but it took an eleventh-hour loan from the city's sanitation workers' union to finally pull New York back from the brink. Being advised that the future of the world economic system depended on New York's survival, the White House eventually agreed to a $2.3 billion federal loan.

Having survived the crisis, the city effectively came under the control of the MAC, whose primary concern was to retain the confidence of bankers. New York's under-funded services continued to decline – most notoriously its subway system – and welfare benefit levels were frozen for seven years.

Recovery and Ed Koch Elected in 1978, Ed Koch had a larger-than-life style which made him a popular mayor and he presided over years of steady recovery. Federal loans were repaid ahead of schedule, and a mid-1980s building boom – encouraged by tax breaks and low-interest loans – saw the creation of new high-rises such as Trump Tower and the AT&T Building.

Koch's reign was to end ignominiously, however. As Wall Street buzzed with yuppies, a 1985 survey found that more than 23 per cent of New Yorkers were living below the poverty line.

Ed Koch

NEW YORK CITY

Fonthill Castle
Wave Hill

Hackensack
Englewood

PALISADES INTERSTATE PARKWAY

Bronx Community College (Hall of Fame)

TREMONT

Clifton

Garfield

BERGEN - PASSAIC EXPRESSWAY

E

Cedar Grove

Passaic

Leonia
Fort Lee

GEORGE WASHINGTON BRIDGE

Yankee Stadium

Caldwell

Bloomfield

Ridgefield

Verona

Montclair

Nutley

Meadowlands Sports Complex (New York Giants)

GARDEN STATE PARKWAY

Lyndhurst

Secaucus

North Bergen

Hudson

HUDSON

D

West Orange

Belleville

Weehawken

Central Park

Isamu Noguchi Garden Museum

Orange
East Orange

Kearny

Union City

MANHATTAN

LONG ISLAND CITY

American Museum of the Moving Image

Passaic

Hackensack

LINCOLN TUNNEL

HENRY HUDSON

ROOSEVELT DRIVE

FRANKLIN

NEW JERSEY TURNPIKE

Hoboken

Irvington

Newark

PULASKI SKYWAY

HOLLAND TUNNEL

GREENPOINT

QUEENS

78

Jersey City

EAST River

BROOKLYN EXPRESSWAY

Union

Hillside

Museum of Migration
American Immigrant Wall of Honor

Ellis Island

East River

BROOKLYN HEIGHTS

WILLIAMS BURG

RIDGEWOOD

BUSHWICK

C

Newark International Airport

78

Statue of Liberty

SOUTH BROOKLYN

Brooklyn Academy of Music (BAM)

Elizabeth

Newark Bay

Bayonne

Upper New York Bay

Prospect Park

Brooklyn Children's Museum

Brooklyn Museum

Brooklyn Botanic Garden

Linden

95

BAYONNE BRIDGE

Kill Van Kull

Staten Island Children's Museum

QUEENS EXPRESSWAY

FLATBUSH

GOETHALS BRIDGE

PORT RICHMOND

Snug Harbor Cultural Center & Botanic Garden

NEW BRIGHTON

The Narrows

Shore Road Park

BROOKLYN

Rahway

Staten Island Zoo
Clove Lakes Park

278

Alice Austen House

Harbor Defense Museum, Fort Hamilton

BERGEN BEACH

NEW JERSEY TURNPIKE

Willow Brook Park

CLIFTON

VERRAZANO NARROWS BRIDGE

Marine Park

William T Davis Wildlife Refuge

STATEN ISLAND EXPRESSWAY

Garibaldi-Meucci Museum

SHORE PARKWAY

SHEEPSHEAD BAY

Sheepshead Bay

B

Carteret

Fresh Kills Park
La Tourette Park

STATEN ISLAND

High Rock Park
SOUTH BEACH

Jaques Marchais Center of Tibetan Art

Lower New York Bay

Norton Point

Astroland

New York Aquarium

BRIGHTON BEACH

WEST SHORE EXPRESSWAY

Richmond Town Historic Restoration

Staten Island Historical Museum

CONEY ISLAND

Clay Pit Pond Park

OAKWOOD

Great Kills Park

Gateway National Recreation Area

Rockaway Point

RICHMOND PARKWAY

ANNADALE

OUTERBRIDGE CROSSING

Arthur Kill

PRINCESS BAY

Crookes Point

TOTTENVILLE

Conference House

A

Wards Point

Raritan Bay

1   2   3

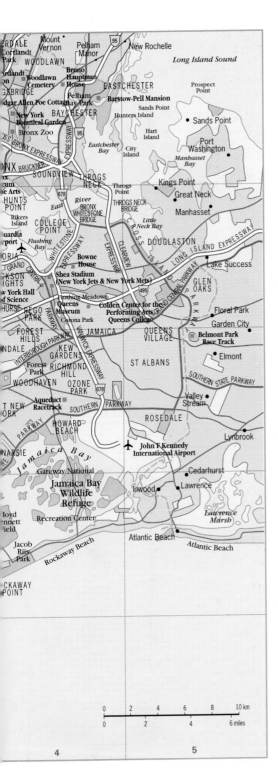

RDALE
Mount Vernon
Pelham Manor
New Rochelle
Cortlandt Park
WOODLAWN
rdlandt
on
Woodlawn Cemetery
Bruno Hauptman House
Long Island Sound
BBRIDGE
Pelham
Pelham Bay Park
EASTCHESTER
Prospect Point
dgar Allen Poe Cottage
BAYCHESTER
Barstow-Pell Mansion
Sands Point
Hunters Island
New York Botanical Garden
Bronx Zoo
95
Eastchester Bay
City Island
Hart Island
• Sands Point
Port Washington
Manhasset Bay
SS EXPRESSWAY
EXPRESSWAY
NX BRUCKNER
SOUNDVIEW
THROGS NECK
Throgs Point
Kings Point
um
e Arts
678
East River
BRONX WHITESTONE BRIDGE
THROGS NECK BRIDGE
• Great Neck
HUNTS POINT
Rikers Island
COLLEGE POINT
Little Neck Bay
Manhasset
uardia
port
Flushing Bay
WHITESTONE EXPRESSWAY
CLEARVIEW EXPRESSWAY
DOUGLASTON
LONG ISLAND EXPRESSWAY
ORIA
GRAND
Bowne House
Lake Success
KSON
GHTS
Shea Stadium
(New York Jets & New York Mets)
495
GLEN OAKS
w York Hall
of Science
HURST
Flushing Meadows
Queens Museum
Corona Park
Colden Center for the Performing Arts,
Queens College
PARKWAY
Floral Park
REGO PARK
Garden City
FOREST HILLS
JAMAICA
QUEENS VILLAGE
Belmont Park Race Track
NDALE
KEW GARDENS
VAN WYCK EXPRESSWAY
ST ALBANS
• Elmont
INTERBOROUGH PARKWAY
Forest Park
RICHMOND HILL
SOUTHERN STATE PARKWAY
WOODHAVEN
OZONE PARK
678
Valley Stream
T NEW
ORK
Aqueduct Racetrack
SOUTHERN PARKWAY
ROSEDALE
PARKWAY
HOWARD BEACH
Lynbrook
NARSIE
Jamaica Bay
John F Kennedy International Airport
Cedarhurst
Gateway National
Jamaica Bay Wildlife Refuge
Inwood
Lawrence
loyd
ennett
ield
Recreation Center
Lawrence Marsh
Jacob Riis Park
Atlantic Beach
Atlantic Beach
CKAWAY
POINT
Rockaway Beach

0   2   4   6   8   10 km
0   2   4   6 miles

4   5

Browsing in Greenwich Village makes good entertainment: shops here range from the mildly quirky to the completely outlandish

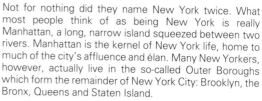

Rufus Newton on New York
'Vulgar of manner, overfed,
Overdressed and under-bred,
Heartless, Godless, hell's delight,
Rude by day and lewd by night.'

Not for nothing did they name New York twice. What most people think of as being New York is really Manhattan, a long, narrow island squeezed between two rivers. Manhattan is the kernel of New York life, home to much of the city's affluence and élan. Many New Yorkers, however, actually live in the so-called Outer Boroughs which form the remainder of New York City: Brooklyn, the Bronx, Queens and Staten Island.

Manhattan As far as the rest of the world is concerned, the island of Manhattan holds everything that defines New York: towering skyscrapers, teeming streets, cease-less noise, and giant neon advertisements which turn night into day. Yet only a fraction of Manhattan - just over 12 miles long and for the most part 2½ miles wide – actu-ally fits this image. The island divides into a number of separate areas, each with its own distinctive history, looks, atmosphere, and residents.

Lower Manhattan At Manhattan's southern extremity, the modern high-rise towers of the **Financial District** rise above the oldest part of New York. It was here that the first Dutch settlement took root and, while few markers to the colonial days remain, the entrepreneurial spirit with which the colony was founded remains very much alive – from the floor of the New York Stock Exchange to the street-side ethnic food-stands dispensing plates of steaming noodles to power-dressed brokers.

Pressed hard against the Financial District's northern edge, the short busy streets of **Chinatown** make up one of New York's longest-established ethnic areas. Lately, Chinatown's banks, bakeries and dim sum houses have spread across the traditional boundaries of **Little Italy**: a tiny area, but one where freshly made cappuccino can still be consumed at sidewalk tables.

Continue north and the ethnic atmosphere gives way to

artiness in the compact areas of **SoHo** and **TriBeCa**, trendy locations which, not long ago, were derelict industrial sites – prime examples of the neighbourhood transformations which are a New York speciality.

By contrast, the elbow of land jutting towards the East River is consumed by the **Lower East Side**, a long-time first base of newly arrived immigrants and a place without a fashionable loft apartment to be found. But in the cut-rate shops and street markets, the work-hard-and-prosper ethos which built the city stays strongly in evidence.

Many New Yorkers never venture deeper into Lower Manhattan than **Greenwich Village** and then only after dark, when the neighbourhood's plentiful bars, cafés and music venues are in full swing. Nightlife apart, Greenwich Village has great character, some fine houses, intriguingly narrow streets and a knack of attracting the writers and artists who, historically, have shaped American culture.

Across Broadway – which runs the length of Manhattan – the **East Village** is a gritty counterpart to Greenwich Village: its clubs and bars are fewer and less polished, while a preponderance of quirky shops and offbeat cafés serves the area's modern-day Bohemians, lured by the district's comparatively inexpensive rents and its earthy, uncommercialised nature.

H G Wells on New York
'To Europe, she was America, to America she was the gateway of the earth. But to tell the story of New York would be to write a social history of the world.'

Choose from several skyscraper viewing galleries to contemplate the almost unbelievable panorama of Manhattan and beyond

51

The WPA Guide to New York City (1939)
The guide – commissioned during the Depression to create jobs for writers – gave this description of the scene around the Hudson River docks: 'A surging mass of back-firing, horn-blowing, gear-grinding trucks and taxis'.

52

Leon Trotsky on New York
'New York impressed me tremendously because, more than any other city in the world, it is the fullest expression of our modern age.'

Little Italy – one of several ethnic areas that make up New York's complex cosmopolitan patchwork

Midtown Manhattan Unlike Lower Manhattan, where the streets tend to have names and to be short and crooked, Midtown Manhattan finds the city's grid-plan system getting into top gear. Its numbered streets and avenues make a visitor's life a simple one.

With the exception of the Statue of Liberty (which holds its flame aloft off Manhattan's southern tip), everybody's favourite symbol of New York is to be found in Midtown Manhattan, be it the Empire State Building, the United Nations complex, Rockefeller Center, St Patrick's Cathedral, the Chrysler Building, Grand Central Terminal, the Broadway theatre district, department stores like Macy's or Bloomingdale's, or just broad, busy thoroughfares packed with people and reverberating to the wail of police sirens.

Midtown Manhattan's northern border is defined by the southern perimeter of Central Park, an imposing and precisely rectangular chunk of greenery intended to re-create a piece of the country in the heart of the city. At this, Central Park succeeds admirably but to see it safely, pay heed to the tips on page 84.

Upper Manhattan To the east of Central Park, gaining much of its long-lasting prestige from the mansions and apartment blocks erected to face the bucolic expanse, the **Upper East Side** is far and away Manhattan's wealthiest neighbourhood, a fact borne out by its exclusive clothes stores, gourmet restaurants and sizeable gathering of up-market art galleries.

Even visitors without money to burn or a passion for window-shopping will find the Upper East Side has much of appeal. Three of the city's major art museums are located here: the Metropolitan Museum of Art, the Guggenheim Museum and the Whitney Museum of American Art. To enjoy art in a luxurious setting, it is hard to beat the Frick Collection, still housed in Henry Clay Frick's 19th-century mansion.

Across Central Park, the **Upper West Side** can only offer the Lincoln Center, the American Museum of Natural History and the Cathedral of St John the Divine as

The Wollman Memorial Rink in Central Park

Le Corbusier on New York
'A hundred times I have thought New York is a catastrophe and fifty times: It is a beautiful catastrophe.'

major attractions, but its tall apartment blocks were the height of luxury living at the turn of the century and are still coveted addresses in what has grown into a vibrant neighbourhood favoured by young professionals.

Stretching across the northern reaches of Upper Manhattan, **Harlem** has played a key role in the history and culture of black America from the turn of the century, though through recent decades it has been plagued by the poverty and crime common to deprived inner-city areas. **East Harlem**, too, above the Upper East Side and the centre of the city's enormous Puerto Rican population, has more than its share of social problems.

The Outer Boroughs Locals would quickly disagree but, unless time is no object, the Outer Boroughs probably merit no more than day-trip excursions from Manhattan.

Brooklyn, with the exceptional Brooklyn Museum and the enjoyable Brooklyn Heights neighbourhood, has most in its favour. On the coast, Brooklyn also has Coney Island. Its glory days are long gone but the pleasure park remains a curious piece of Americana and neighbours the lively Russian community of Brighton Beach.

Staten Island is also worth a visit, partly for the fun of the ferry ride to reach it, but also to enjoy the refreshingly pastoral pace of the surprisingly large island, and its scattering of low-key museums.

In the largely suburban **Bronx**, the Bronx Zoo (now called the International Wildlife Conservation Park) may be the highlight of a New York trip for children. A more sombre relic is the cottage in which neglected author Edgar Allan Poe resided for two troubled years.

Like the Bronx, **Queens** is expansive suburbia and its worthwhile features tend to be far-flung and barely repay the effort needed to reach them. If you are eager for the challenge, however, dotted about Queens you will find everything from thriving ethnic areas to remnants of the early New York film industry.

ADMISSION TICKET

Richmondtown Restoration

New York City's Historic Village

■ **Everyone will tell you that New York is a dangerous place. Like many cities, it can be. But for every New York visitor who gets mugged (or worse), there are many hundreds more who leave with nothing but good memories – and millions live there without becoming crime victims. Unless you are very unlucky, surviving New York simply means being prepared – so heed the tips below …■**

Night-time no-go areas
Wherever you go in Manhattan at night, you will need to be even more cautious than by day. Several areas that you might visit with comparative nonchalance in daylight (most of which are described in the A to Z section of this book) should be regarded as off-limits at night: Alphabet City past Avenue C (Avenues A and B are fine), Central Park, the western edge of Greenwich Village along the Hudson River, Harlem and most of Midtown Manhattan west of the theatre district.

Arriving With bewildered expressions and more luggage than they can carry, newly arrived tourists uncertain of their next step bring a gleam to every mugger's eye.

However long you spend in New York, rarely will you be as vulnerable as you are on arrival. Airports are comparatively safe havens, but be sure to check transport routes into the city *before* leaving the terminal building.

If you take a taxi from the airport, look for the uniformed guide who will show you to the official taxi rank. Be wary of unlicensed cab drivers who may approach you. Most unlicensed drivers are simply trying to make a living, but some have other ideas. The safest course is to stick to official operators.

Arriving at Manhattan's train and bus terminals can be more problematic, especially late at night. Although taxis can usually be hailed immediately outside, it is worth taking the trouble to plan your route from the terminal in advance. It cannot be stressed enough that you must not let a stranger carry your bags for you. If you are planning to walk to your hotel, be warned that the area around the Port Authority Bus Terminal is very seedy.

Walking in the city Before venturing out, stash your valuables in the hotel safe (some hotel rooms have built-in safes of their own) and carry only enough cash to get you through the day. If you are embarking on a major shopping expedition, use credit cards or travellers' cheques to

The city's self-styled (and controversial) 'Guardian Angels' aim to keep the streets and subways free from crime and violence

The subway – much maligned, but better than driving

pay for your purchases rather than wads of cash.

Stick to the crowd, avoid deserted alleys, and do not flash expensive jewellery around. Women should not hang bags on the backs of chairs in restaurants and men should carry their wallets in their front pockets.

Plan your route before setting out. Manhattan's grid system makes navigation easy (though Lower Manhattan can be confusing). Even for lifelong New Yorkers, no street is perfectly safe, so never carry anything that can be easily snatched. Do not be taken in by anyone who approaches you with a hard luck story, and beware that if you buy watches or jewellery in the street they are likely to be fakes.

At night, again stick to the crowds on the major north-south thoroughfares, such as Broadway and Fifth Avenue, and on the main streets of Greenwich Village. If you need to walk east-west, go along a major traffic-bearing street rather than risk a short cut along a quiet one. Walk near the kerb.

Riding the subway While many people regard going down into New York's subway system as akin to a descent into hell, the system is by no means the Dante's Inferno that it is made out to be. Certainly there is no speedier way to get about the city.

By day your biggest problems are likely to be in mastering the network (see page 257 for how to do this). If you find yourself at the wrong station in an unsavoury neighbourhood, simply take the next train back as soon as you can.

Subway travel becomes far more unnerving at night. At this time, aim to board the middle cars, where one of the conductors usually sits, or look for occupied cars. If you are waiting on a near-deserted platform, look for the supervised 'off-hours' waiting area.

Once on board, some comfort might come from the fact that everyone else is likely to be as nervous as you are.

The mugger's tax
The odds are astronomical against your being mugged in New York but should a figure leap from the shadows and demand money, it is a good idea to have some cash ready to hand over. Many New Yorkers have got into the habit of carrying a small sum (sometimes contained in a spare wallet), usually around $20, partly to avoid losing a larger amount and partly to save time: the longer a mugger has to wait, the more unstable he may become.

Itineraries

You could spend your entire life in New York and never feel you had seen the whole city. Nonetheless, these suggested itineraries will provide as balanced a view of New York as is possible within their limited time spans.

Weekend itinerary
Day one In the morning, visit the Empire State Building and continue on foot to the New York Public Library, Rockefeller Center and St Patrick's Cathedral. Have lunch in Midtown Manhattan and spend the afternoon at the Museum of Modern Art.

Day two Take an early-morning ferry from Battery Park to the Statue of Liberty and Ellis Island. After returning, have lunch at the World Trade Center and spend the afternoon exploring Greenwich Village.

More than 20 years after losing its world-record status, the Empire State Building is still a magnet for visitors

One-week itinerary
Day one As day one of weekend itinerary.

Day two Take an early-morning ferry from Battery Park to the Statue of Liberty and Ellis Island. After returning, have lunch at the World Trade Center and spend the afternoon exploring the Financial District and South Street Seaport.

Day three Spend the whole day at the Metropolitan Museum of Art. If a whole day seems too long, spend part of it shopping for clothes in the top-name stores of Midtown Manhattan and Madison Avenue, or in the second-hand and discount outlets of Lower Manhattan.

Day four In the morning, explore Central Park. Travel to Greenwich Village for lunch and spend the afternoon exploring Greenwich Village, SoHo, Little Italy and Chinatown.

Day five On the Upper East Side, tour the Frick Collection and the Cooper-Hewitt Museum. After lunch, continue to the Guggenheim Museum and the Whitney Museum of American Art.

Day six Travel by subway to the Brooklyn Museum. Spend the morning at the museum and eat a picnic lunch in Brooklyn Botanical Gardens. Spend the afternoon exploring Brooklyn Heights and return to Manhattan by crossing the Brooklyn Bridge on foot (avoid the rush hour as several muggings have taken place).

Day seven Tour the Lower East Side and the East Village. After lunch, explore the Gramercy Park area of Midtown Manhattan and conclude at the Pierpont Morgan Library.

The Statue of Liberty is essential viewing, even for those on a flying visit to the Big Apple

Two-week itinerary

Day one As day one of weekend itinerary.

Day two As day two of week itinerary.

Day three As day three of week itinerary.

Day four In the morning, explore Central Park. Have lunch on the Upper West Side before visiting the American Museum of Natural History.

Day five Spend the whole day at Staten Island.

Day six Tour the Lower East Side and Chinatown. Have lunch in Chinatown and spend the afternoon exploring Greenwich Village.

Day seven As day six of week itinerary.

Day eight On the Upper East Side, tour the Frick Collection and the Cooper-Hewitt Museum. After lunch, continue to the Museum of the City of New York and the Puerto Rican market on 116th Street.

Day nine Visit the Forbes Galleries and idle away the rest of the morning in Washington Square Park. Have lunch at a café in Greenwich Village and then continue to the East Village and on into the Gramercy Park area of Midtown Manhattan, concluding at the Pierpont Morgan Library on 36th Street.

Day ten Explore Harlem and the museums of the Audubon complex. After lunch, tour the Columbia University campus and the Cathedral Church of St John the Divine.

Day eleven Spend the day in the Bronx or Queens.

Day twelve Divide the day between the Whitney Museum of American Art and the Guggenheim Museum.

Day thirteen Explore Bloomingdale's store in the morning and then travel by subway to Coney Island and continue to Brighton Beach.

Day fourteen Spend the morning at the Cloisters, returning to Midtown Manhattan for lunch and to visit the Museum of TV and Radio, and the American Craft Museum – and any landmark building you have yet to view at close quarters.

Guided tours of Harlem
Harlem is one of New York's most celebrated areas but can be intimidating for the first-time visitor. One way to see Harlem without worries is with a guided tour. Harlem Spirituals, Inc (tel: 757 0425) offer a choice of three: a Sunday tour which combines a gospel church service with a tour of historic Harlem, a weekday tour which offers a soul-food lunch and a local history commentary, and an evening fling based around several hours of jazz at the Cotton Club.

■ **From the top of the World Trade Center to the decks of the Staten Island Ferry, New York has views that no other city can match. Public observation decks are a feature of many Manhattan skyscrapers – several of which had the prestige, in their day, of being the tallest building in the world. The Empire State Building and the Woolworth Building are two that can now be viewed from the top of even taller towers – an angle their architects never imagined possible.**

If heights are not your strong point, then leave Manhattan to view it from afar. And do not give up on New York views as night falls – a panorama of Manhattan by night is a sight you'll remember for years ...■

58

HG Wells on New York views, 1906
'Suddenly as I looked back at the skyscrapers of lower New York a queer fancy sprang into my head. They reminded me quite irresistibly of piled-up packing cases outside a warehouse. I was amazed I had not seen the resemblance before.'

Empire State Building This is the star of virtually every Manhattan view except those from its own 86th-floor observation level. On a clear day, the beady-eyed can see through the anti-suicide wire mesh into Massachusetts and Pennsylvania, and peer down at jets swooping into New York's airports. Come after dusk to see night-time Manhattan: the building is open until midnight.

World Trade Center The twin towers are only eight storeys taller than the Empire State Building, but their sheer sides make them seem far higher. From the southernmost tower's observation level, the long-distance views are not significantly different from those of the Empire State Building. From the open-air rooftop level, however, there is an unequalled vista of Financial District rooftops and the copper-domed 1913 Woolworth Building.

Rockefeller Center From the 65th-floor windows of the Rainbow Room in the GE (formerly RCA) Building, the Empire State Building rises to the south as the World Trade Center looms to its rear. Look north, and the great green rectangle of Central Park cuts between the stately apartment blocks of the Upper East Side and the Upper West Side towards Harlem.

Above the East River From its terminal at the junction of Second Avenue and 60th Street, the cable-car that crosses the East River to Roosevelt Island gives clear views of the island's former lunatic asylums and hospitals. The best – and much less ghoulish – aerial views, however, can be enjoyed on the return journey. They take in a lengthy swathe of riverside Manhattan from Midtown's United Nations complex northwards, far into the Upper East Side.

Fort Tryon Park Close to the northern tip of Manhattan, Fort Tryon Park offers not only the unexpected sight of a reassembled medieval European monastery (the

Cloisters) but also, from the hilltop site of the fort itself, views across the Hudson River to New Jersey's Palisades Park and, on the other side of Manhattan, the Harlem River.

The Outer Boroughs Some of the most rewarding views of Manhattan are found by leaving it. From Brooklyn Heights Promenade, the eastern edge of the Financial District – the so-called Water Street corridor, a heady mix of glass, steel, limestone and marble – walls the East River. Behind this immediate forest of high-rises, you should be able to pick out two of the world's one-time highest buildings, the Woolworth Building and the World Trade Center, while two more, the Chrysler Building and the Empire State Building, are visible in the cluster of skyscrapers marking Midtown Manhattan.

Be sure not to use up all your film on the Promenade: returning to Manhattan on foot across the Brooklyn Bridge reveals the same scenes from continually shifting perspectives behind the struts of the bridge, providing endless scope for inventive photographers.

Look across the harbour from Brooklyn Heights to see the green hills of Staten Island rising to the south. You might also spot the Staten Island Ferry as it plies between the island and the southern tip of the Financial District.

Riding the ferry is much more interesting than looking at it, however. From the vessel are dramatic views of Manhattan's skyline (best on the return leg, when the skyscrapers appear to grow bigger and bigger), and slightly less dramatic ones of Governors Island (occupied by the US Coast Guard), the Statue of Liberty, and the world's longest suspension bridge, the Verrazano-Narrows Bridge, which links Staten Island to Brooklyn.

In the Bronx, the hills holding the Hall of Fame at the Bronx Community College provide a bucolic site for savouring the view across the East River into Upper Manhattan. The Bronx's best-kept secret, though, is the Upper Manhattan panorama visible from the steep streets that hold its richest neighbourhood, Riverdale.

Statue of Liberty views
If you are visiting the Statue of Liberty, which sits on an island between Manhattan and New Jersey, you will find the outlook from it to be a stirring one. Across the Hudson River, Battery Park City and the World Trade Center are prominent. In the foreground, scores of yachts, tugs and pleasure boats skim by on the water, while helicopters zip past overhead.

59

The Tompkins Square Park riot

In the heart of Alphabet City, Tompkins Square Park was the scene of a heavy-handed police operation on a steamy August night in 1988, when 12 mounted police, soon joined by 400 reinforcements, battled for four hours to clear the 16-acre park of the homeless people who were occupying it.

The incident was recorded on video by a local artist and the police brutality which the playback showed triggered outrage across the city and nightly violence at the park. Mayor Dinkins closed the park for major renovations, posting police guards to keep out anyone but dog-walkers and basketball players. Reopened, the park is now fairly peaceful during the day.

Tompkins Square Park, in Alphabet City, has seen its share of problems, but it is now a fairly safe and peaceful place in daylight

▶ **Abigail Adams Smith Museum**   *151D3*
61st Street at York Avenue
Subway: 59th Street

Neither Abigail Adams, daughter of John Adams, the second president of the US, nor her husband, William Stephens Smith, an aide to George Washington, ever lived in what is now the Abigail Adams Smith Museum. Instead, the ashlar stone building – a characterful structure enclosed by less distinguished modern blocks – was the carriage house of their intended 23-acre country estate on the banks of the East River.

Financial decline caused the couple to move on in 1799, however, and the stables were converted first to an inn and then to a private residence before being purchased in 1924 by the Colonial Dames of America, an organisation pledged to preserving the history of the revolutionary period. The building was gradually equipped with the Federal-period furnishings and objects which are now displayed throughout nine of its rooms, making for an entertaining half-hour's viewing.

Alphabet City   *IFCB2*
Subway: Second Avenue

A decade ago, nobody visited Alphabet City for fun. An area east of First Avenue between Houston and 14th streets, with lettered rather than numbered avenues, Alphabet City was synonymous with the worst aspects of urban blight: drug-dealing, poverty and homelessness. Anyone who unwittingly strayed on to these mean streets could consider themselves lucky to emerge with nothing worse than a mugging to complain about.

Since then, efforts by the local community (and a major police initiative) have lessened the drug trade and improved the area's general safety, though social problems clearly remain. Another change has been an influx of yuppies and other invaders spilling over from the adjoin-

The Abigail Adams Smith Museum occupies an elegant 18th-century carriage house – a refreshing antidote to New York skyscraper architecture

ing East Village, bringing a rash of trendy restaurants and watering holes to the fringes of the area.

Nonetheless, Alphabet City is still a place that is hard to visit without feeling at least slightly intimidated; the safest course is to venture no further east than Avenue B.

► **American Academy and**   *IFCD5*
   Institute of Arts & Letters

Broadway at 155th Street
Subway: 155th or 157th streets
Two august cultural bodies – the National Institute of Arts, founded in 1898, and the American Academy, founded in 1904 – unified in 1977 and jointly honour American achievements in art, writing and music. They share an Italian Renaissance building marked by the inscription 'All arts are one, all branches on one tree... hold high the flaming torch from age to age'.

Although much of its activity may appear to be little more than mutual back-slapping, the organisation also administers grants to deserving artistic causes, and stages temporary seasonal exhibitions highlighting the work of individual members. If your favourite author, painter or composer is being featured it could be worth a visit. For details, tel: 368 5900.

► **American Bible Society**   *151D1*

Broadway at 61st Street
Subway: 59th Street
A 1960s cast-in-place concrete structure a bagel's throw from busy Columbus Circle makes an unlikely home for the American Bible Society, founded in 1816 in order to circulate the Bible 'without note or comment'.

The bibles the society has distributed are less notable than the bibles that it has collected, however. Over the years, historic bibles from near and far have been collected to form the society's extensive library and archive. It includes an illustrated Armenian account of the Four Gospels dated to the early 1400s, and a 16th-century bible translated by a New England preacher into Massachusetts (an Algonquin Native American dialect).

A few changing selections are displayed on the first-floor level, alongside a reconstruction of a Gutenberg printing press and a feature on the Dead Sea Scrolls.

Audubon Terrace
The American Academy and Institute of Arts & Letters occupies one section of Audubon Terrace, a Renaissance Revival complex planned in 1908 and intended to provide a suitably imposing setting for several venerable national institutions – others among them including the American Numismatic Society (see page 65) and the Hispanic Society of America (see page 126).

Situated between Riverside Drive and Broadway and 155th and 156th streets, the scheme was never entirely successful: not only a poor architectural job, it also left its tenants in a humdrum residential area far removed from the ebb and flow of New York life.

The terrace was built on a part of the estate of John James Audubon, the eminent American naturalist of the late 1800s.

61

AMERICAN CRAFT MUSEUM

Changing exhibitions of pottery, textiles, furniture and other artefacts can be viewed in spacious surroundings at the American Craft Museum, which showcases the work of contemporary craftspeople

Museum of American Illustration

Within a few steps of the American Federation of the Arts, the Society of Illustrators (63rd Street between Lexington and Park avenues), established in 1875, holds the small but interesting Museum of American Illustration. Through lively temporary exhibitions, the museum highlights the contribution made to Americans' self-image through cartoons, advertising, book and magazine drawings and much more. The museum is free and open Tuesday, noon–8pm; Wednesday to Friday 10am–5pm; Saturday noon–4pm; closed Sunday and Monday. For the latest exhibition details, tel: 838 2560.

▶▶ **American Craft Museum** *151C2*

53rd Street between Fifth and Sixth avenues
Subway: Fifth Avenue

Be they teapots or tapestries, baskets or brooches, the exhibits of the American Craft Museum are always stimulating. Chosen from the museum's own vast hoard or using loaned pieces, the displays illustrate design trends and techniques, and often feature the work of the most artistic and skilful 20th-century American craftsmen and women.

The museum is run by the American Craft Council, whose purchase of a brownstone house on this site in 1959 turned out to be a wise investment. A 1980s property speculator eager to erect a high-rise block here agreed to give the museum a spacious chunk of the new building's ground floor, enabling the displays to be mounted around a lovely three-storey atrium – and partially viewed for free through the museum's impossibly large front window.

▶ **American Federation of the Arts** *151D2*

65th Street between Park and Madison avenues
Subway: 68th Street

The American Federation of the Arts collects and arranges travelling exhibitions for the small museums of the US, often finding time to display some of them in its own galleries. It is pot-luck what might be on display, but a look inside also reveals the building's lavishly decorated interior, a 1960s restoration of what was originally the home of a successful stockbroker, built around 1910.

▶▶ **American Museum of Natural History** *IFCF3*

Central Park West and 79th Street
Subway: 79th Street or 81st Street

With 36 million exhibits, this is one of the world's best-stocked museums. Whether you are gazing at a stuffed sabre-toothed tiger or an ancient inscription from Guatemala, there is every chance it will be among the foremost examples of its kind on show anywhere in the world.

Darwin's theory of evolution and Mendel's law of heredity were two of the natural science breakthroughs that provided the stimulus for the museum's founding in 1869. Within a decade, the collections had acquired a purpose-built home, a stately Romanesque structure beside Central Park intended to be the 'largest building on the continent'. Unfortunately, its grandeur has been steadily eroded by uninspired additions, creating an imposing but unsatisfying architectural mish-mash.

Inside, however, the story is quite different. Greatly improved by a $30 million restructuring, the museum's fossil collection – already among the best in the world – now forms part of a six-room, state-of-the-art complex revealing the intricacies of the evolutionary relationships as far back as the Jurassic period (180–120 million years ago). The climax of this section are the two Dinosaur Halls, which feature magnificent skeletons of Tyrannosaurus Rex and Apatosaurus.

Native American life, and the evolution of North American animal and bird species, are outlined by comprehensive but fairly dreary habitat dioramas. Much more enjoyment

Carl Akeley
The Akeley Gallery at the American Museum of Natural History is named after Carl Akeley, a naturalist, explorer and inventor. Akeley twice narrowly escaped death by dangerous animal. In 1911, he was gored by an elephant but saved himself by swinging beneath the creature's body; on another occasion, he ran out of bullets while confronted by an angry leopard and saved himself by strangling it. Among his many technical innovations was a new taxidermy technique, which he employed on the seven elephants that stand in the gallery. Ironically, Akeley died in 1926 from complications arising from a gnat bite.

63

Massive exhibit in a massive museum – the Barosaurus at the Museum of Natural History

is to be found in the excellently arranged anthropological collections on Africa, Asia and Central and South America. This last section is particularly strong, including thousands of curious religious, ceremonial and everyday objects. Look for the Aztec musical instruments made from human bones, the 17th-century sheet-metal ornamental llamas from the Andes, and shrunken heads from the Amazon rainforest – and be ready for intriguing insights into Mayan astronomy.

The museum unveiled a new permanent exhibition in 1993, the Hall of Human Biology and Evolution. It studies the workings of the human body, traces ancestors over the centuries, and features a computerised archaeological dig and an electronic newspaper on human evolution.

Measuring 94ft in length and weighing 10 tons, what is thought to be the world's largest museum exhibit replicates the world's largest mammal – the blue whale – above the Hall of Ocean Life and Biology of Fishes. The fibreglass whale steals the show, although the room's dioramas and fish skeletons do a commendable job in unravelling the mysteries of reproduction, feeding and self-defence far beneath the ocean's waves.

Moving on, even the mindbogglingly priced gems of Midtown Manhattan's jewellery stores pale into insignificance when compared with the contents of the museum's Hall of Minerals and Gems, a collection valued at $80 million. A great chunk of crystal-impregnated copper and scores of darkened display cases filled with sparkling, spellbinding stones are just part of a cleverly planned

The gorilla diorama at the American Museum of Natural History. Few aspects of the world's wildlife are left untouched by the museum's vast collections

exhibition focusing on the natural forces that create the world's most prized pieces of rock. Some of the stones are the size of a pinhead, others are as big as your fist; the 21,000-carat Brazilian Princess Topaz weighs a quarter of a ton and is the world's largest uncut gem.

Should the celestial fragments in the impressive Hall of Meteorites give you a taste for outer space exploration, venture into the **Hayden Planetarium**, adjoining the museum, for state-of-the-art astronomy exhibitions and guided tours of the night-time sky.

Also entered directly from the museum, the **Naturemax Cinema** has screenings on natural history themes using the giant-screen IMAX system. If you have ever wanted to inspect a lion's dental set at close quarters, this is the safest way to do it.

► **American Numismatic Society** *IFCD3*

Broadway at 156th Street
Subway: 155th or 157th streets
A vast hoard of coins and medals that is unsurpassed anywhere in the world, the collections of the American Numismatic Society are primarily intended to aid the research of devoted coin-collectors and academics. There are, however, two surprisingly engaging ground-floor exhibitions open to the public. The first is a spirited documentation – using maps, photographs and many remarkable specimens of very ancient money – of the origins of, and the spread of, coins throughout the world.

After viewing the coins, you may not have sufficient energy left to do justice to the extensive display of medals housed in the second exhibition. Upstairs, there is a public inquiry counter at which you can find out whether the foreign coin you have just found in your change is likely to improve your lifestyle dramatically.

►► **Asia Society** *151D3*

Park Avenue at 70th Street
Subway: 68th Street
Founded in 1956 and pledged to improving understanding between Asia and America, the Asia Society hosts conferences, concerts, workshops and film shows, and mounts stunning temporary exhibitions of Asian art drawn from the world's foremost collections. Also on display are selections from the society's own collections, which include Chinese ceramics from the 11th century BC, some very fine pre-Angkor Cambodian sculpture, and wonderful Japanese Edo-period prints, all donated by John D. Rockefeller III. The decorative lion above the entrance to the eight-storey red granite gallery building, incidentally, is the motif of the society and is based on an 18th-century bronze of a Nepalese guardian lion.

St James Church
A short walk from the Asia Society, the Sunday services at St James Episcopal Church (861–3 Madison Avenue) draw many of New York's better-bank-rolled believers from their Upper East Side homes. Drop in during the week to admire the church's impressive stained glass and reredos, and to ponder on the possibility that few of its rich congregation are aware that the poor and homeless are nourished by St James' lunchtime soup kitchen.

65

The bright interior of St James Church on Madison Avenue – one of several notable places of worship on the Upper East Side

BATTERY PARK

St Elizabeth Bayley Seton
The well-preserved Federal-style building at 7 State Street – its columns said to be cut from ship's masts – was erected in 1783 for the prominent Watson family, but has found longer-lasting fame as the shrine of Elizabeth Bayley Seton. She founded the Sisters of Charity, the first order of nuns in the US, in 1812 and in 1975 she became the first native-born American woman to be canonised by the Roman Catholic Church. This was her home from 1801 to 1803.

▶ **Battery Park** 104B1

Subway: Bowling Green

A welcome open space on the edge of the Financial District, Battery Park provides 22 acres of greenery with outstanding harbour views. Historical texts are pinned to its lamp posts, leaving you with no excuse for not discovering something of early New York simply by strolling the tree-lined pathways.

The park took its name from the row of cannons that the British stored during the 17th century along State Street, which now borders the park but which then marked the Manhattan shoreline. The park attained its present form as a result of mid-1800s landfill.

If you are taking the ferry to the Statue of Liberty and Ellis Island you will enter Battery Park's most interesting possession to reach the ticket booth, which is situated on the one-time parade ground of **Castle Clinton**. This circular fortification, finished in 1811, was built to repulse British attack.

Though there is little evidence of the fact today, Castle Clinton has enjoyed a prominent place in New York life. As its defensive importance waned, the fort was planted with floral gardens and became the scene of well-attended concerts and exhibitions; later it pre-dated Ellis Island as a landing and processing point for immigrants, almost 8 million of whom came ashore here between 1855 and 1889. The castle also served a 46-year stint as the city aquarium, the target of many New Yorkers' Sunday afternoon outings.

The rest of Battery Park is dotted with statues and memorials of minor interest – not to be confused with the concrete slabs shielding the air vents of the Brooklyn-Battery Tunnel (which runs beneath the park). Giovanni da Verrazano, the first European known to sail into New York harbour, is one notable honoured, while the pint-sized Peter Minuit Plaza is named after the Dutchman who bought Manhattan from its Native American inhabitants for the equivalent of $24.

Left and below: Aspects of Battery Park

Boat trips

■ **On manic streets beneath the towering skyscrapers, it is easy to forget that Manhattan is an island. One of the best ways to get a grasp of its size and shape is from the water that surrounds it, on a guided boat trip ...■**

Most boat-tour operators seem to be offering much the same thing – a sightseeing trip along the Hudson River and the East River which includes a stop at the Statue of Liberty and a view of any New York landmarks visible from the water. There are variations, however, so consider all the options to find the trip that suits you best.

In-depth sightseeing The most comprehensive sightseeing cruise is run by **Circle Line** (tel: 563 3200), although some find it rather boring. This comprises a three-hour narrated circumnavigation of Manhattan Island, passing beneath 20 bridges on the way. The same company operates a two-hour cruise after dark

Even on a short stay, sightseeing by boat can make a pleasant change from hot pavements and traffic jams

(Manhattan at night is not a sight to be easily forgotten) and periodic 'celebrity cruises', which feature notable New Yorkers giving their own view of the city.

Other options Typical of other operators, **Spirit of New York** (tel: 727 2789) offers a more condensed sightseeing tour, concentrating on Lower and Midtown Manhattan landmarks (and the Statue of Liberty) on a two-hour trip; there are also brunch cruises on Saturdays and Sundays and a Moonlight Party Cruise on Fridays and Saturdays, which casts off at 11.30pm for drinking, dancing and moonlit Manhattan views lasting into the small hours.

If time is tight, the catamaran of **TNT Express** (tel: 800–BOAT RIDE) has the swiftest tours, zipping from the Statue of Liberty to the United Nations in 75 minutes. By contrast, **Seaport Line** (to book, tel: 233 4800) harks back to bygone days using a replica 19th-century river boat to complete 90-minute sightseeing trips, with two-hour lunch cruises and one-hour evening cocktail spins as other options.

For the serious eater
Visitors love to sightsee but New Yorkers love to eat, and they are the people most in evidence on the lunch, brunch and dinner cruises offered by World Yacht (tel: 630 8100). These are not calorie-watching affairs: lunch and brunch are lavish buffets, and dinner is a four-course treat followed by dancing.

Broadway's first bend

Broadway's angular scythe through Manhattan's otherwise largely grid-style street plan gave rise to squares such as Union, Madison and Times. Its first bend – after travelling for 3 ruler-straight miles north from Bowling Green – was due to the refusal of a Dutch landowner, Jacob Brevoort, to allow it to cross his property, a site now occupied by Greenwich Village's Grace Church.

Broadway's nerve centre: the theatre district near Times Square

Backstage on Broadway

By making an advance reservation (tel: 575 8065) and provided you are in a group of 8 or more people, you can be shown the various processes involved in launching a Broadway show, from the first rehearsals to the set design and the first-night nerves. The guides are usually 'resting' actors.

▶▶ **Broadway** *151C2*

The story of Broadway is the story of New York. This is the city's oldest and longest thoroughfare – in one guise or another, Broadway not only runs south–north through Manhattan but continues for 140 miles to Albany. It has witnessed every good, bad and indifferent phase in the city's growth, while its internationally famous theatre district around Times Square is, for many, what New York is all about.

Originally part of a Native American trail, Broadway was known to early Dutch settlers as De Heere Straat, or Main Street. It has remained New York's major (and perhaps most famous) artery ever since.

Broadway acquired the city's first numbered housing in 1793 and was also the first New York street to see its residential properties put to commercial uses. The commerce came in contrasting forms, with seedy bars, brothels and gambling dens alongside the city's finest retail outlets. In the 1880s, a popular saying held that if you fired a shotgun in any direction at the junction of Broadway and Houston Street, you would not hit an honest man.

In the days before traffic lights and one-way streets, Broadway was bedlam. Holding the city's major businesses and being the main route north, Broadway's sidewalks were thronged with pedestrians and its centre was a crush of handcarts and horse-drawn wagons. At times, police had to physically intervene to prevent the thoroughfare becoming completely blocked.

Walkers took their lives in their hands when attempting to cross Broadway. The junction with Fulton Street was so infamously hazardous that, in 1867, the authorities erected a footbridge – only for it to be torn down at the insistence of shop-owners fearful of losing their side's share of captive pedestrians.

What evolved into New York's theatre district began in Broadway's southern reaches and steadily moved north, one of the first theatres opening in 1798 at the junction with what is now Park Row. Broadway's theatres quickly forged a reputation for entertaining the city's well-to-do classes with productions of artistic merit and were considered a cut above their Bowery counterparts, popularly regarded as offering low-brow titillation for the consumption of the masses.

By the 1880s, the heyday of vaudeville and the age of stars such as Lillie Langtry, the Broadway theatres had pushed north to Union Square. Around this time, however, the Metropolitan Opera House opened on an unlikely site 26 blocks north and began drawing the city's elite to an area then dominated by livery shops and stables. Broadway crossed this area at Longacre Square.

Ten years passed before a theatre opened at Longacre but by then a section of Broadway around 34th Street had famously been labelled 'the Great White Way' on account of its giant advertising hoardings lit by hundreds of electric light bulbs.

Soon, **Times Square** – as Longacre Square was renamed after the publisher of the *New York Times* got permission to build an office tower above it – was similarly illuminated. Once joined to the subway system, it quickly became the heart of the city's theatre district.

Broadway continued north but the theatre district stayed put. By the 1920s most of the theatres were showing movies and, 50 years on, the oldest of them were demolished in a spate of office building.

As if to echo the sleaziness of an earlier Broadway, Times Square degenerated into porno shops, prostitution and drug dealing, though the sheer gaudiness of the place and the many genuine theatres still operating in its vicinity failed to stem the tide of tourists.

Over recent years, efforts to make Times Square safe and restore some of its lost grandeur have made headway – but this is still an area to be approached with caution, especially after dark.

The night-time neon of Broadway – less stunning than in its heyday perhaps, but still dazzling visitors a century after the first electrically lit sign was switched on

Bronx Zoo practicalities
The closest subway stop to the Bronx Zoo is Pelham Parkway, which leaves a short walk to the zoo's Bronxdale entrance. An alternative route from Manhattan is with the Liberty Lines Express Bus (BxM11), which runs from Madison Avenue to the Bronxdale entrance (for details, tel: 718/652 8400).

Summer is the best time to visit. During the winter (November to April) many of the zoo's open-air sections are closed and the animals moved indoors. From Tuesday to Thursday admission is by voluntary donation, though there are always additional charges for some individual sections, such as the ape and reptile houses, and a charge for using the monorails.

For general information on the zoo, tel: 718/367 1010.

▶   **The Bronx**   *49D4*

The Bronx has fewer admirers than any other New York borough. The portion closest to Manhattan, the **South Bronx**, has become an enduring symbol of the most extreme forms of urban decay: abandoned buildings stripped clean of their fittings and the night-time sky regularly illuminated by the handiwork of arsonists. President Carter visited the South Bronx and spouted platitudes in 1977, but it has been left to local community groups to bring about the improvements which are very slowly changing its character.

The rest of the Bronx is quite different. Off **Grand Concourse**, a stately thoroughfare laid out in 1892 and still (though no longer deserving of its title) scything south-north through the borough, lie safe and tidy residential areas, pockets of history, immense parks, and the **Bronx Zoo.**

In the South Bronx, **Yankee Stadium** (161st Street and River Avenue) has been the home of the New York Yankees baseball team since its completion in 1923. A $100-million renovation programme carried out in the mid-1970s was intended to improve the area as much as the building. If you visit the stadium, continue to the **Bronx Museum of the Arts** (1040 Grand Concourse). Opened in 1971, the museum has exhibitions of local art and Bronx-related cultural topics.

If they are not fans of the Yankees, most New Yorkers brave the Bronx for just one thing: the **Bronx Zoo**▶ (now officially called the Wildlife Conservation Society's Bronx Zoo), the largest city zoo in the US. Spanning 265 acres, the zoo puts its emphasis on herds and flocks rather than single animals and on re-created natural habitats rather than cages. The indoor rainforest of Jungle World, for

example, finds gibbons and monkeys leering at their human visitors from across artificial rivers. You should also spot a few Indian gharials, a type of alligator whose ancestry goes back 180 million years. Rare snow leopards are the star turn of the Himalayan Highlands, while World of Darkness – where day is transformed into night – allows glimpses of foxes, aardvarks, bushbabies, bats (including the vampire variety who receive a daily ration of blood) and other nocturnal species.

The zoo's principal open space, Wild Asia, can only be viewed on a 25-minute narrated monorail ride. The open-sided carriages glide above a plain roamed by antelopes, elephants, rhinoceroses and sika deer – a species now extinct in its native habitat.

More traditional exhibits include the ape and reptile houses, and the less common Mouse House, its cages inhabited by a mighty stock of tiny furry things. There is also a separate Children's Zoo, intended to provide young minds with an insight into animal behaviour, and offering plenty of cute and cuddly creatures for stroking.

Beginning across Fordham Road from the zoo, the **New York Botanical Garden▶** is a wonderful mixture of formal gardens, rock gardens and rugged woodlands – including a 40-acre hemlock forest. In the northwest cor-

A monorail ride (left) is a good way to see some of the 4,000 inhabitants of the Bronx Zoo

The Bruno Hauptman house
The house at 1279 East 222nd Street, east of the Bronx's Woodlawn Cemetery, looks like any other but it was here in 1934 that police arrested Bruno Hauptman on the charges of abducting and holding to ransom (and subsequently murdering) the baby of flying-ace Charles Lindbergh.

The celebrated case galvanised the media and popularised the term 'kidnapping'. Hauptman was found guilty and executed, but doubts over the verdict rose with the discovery that the police had kept vital pieces of evidence from the jury.

The site where the $50,000 ransom was paid is also in the Bronx: St Raymond's Cemetery, between East Tremont Avenue and Eastern Boulevard, just south of Throg's Neck.

71

ner, the Enid A Haupt Conservatory is filled by a glorious array of banana plants, palm trees, cacti, and other vegetation seldom seen in these northern climes.

The **Edgar Allen Poe Cottage▶** (off Grand Concourse at East Kingsbridge Road) is where the writer lived for two years during the 1840s, moving here in the hope that the country air would improve his wife's health. In the unheated dwelling, however, Poe's tubercular spouse resorted to hugging the cat for warmth and died during the first winter. Holding a few of the Poes' sparse furnishings, the cottage is an aptly bleak memorial to a man whose short life was seldom a happy one.

In the grounds of the **Bronx Community College▶** (181st Avenue and University Avenue) is the Hall of Fame for Great Americans. Here the bronze busts of

THE BRONX

Riverdale

When New Yorkers mention the Bronx, they are not usually thinking of Riverdale, an extremely wealthy enclave of enviable homes reaching from the eastern edge of Van Cortlandt Park to the Hudson River – a world apart from the poverty of the South Bronx. The area is difficult to explore by car: many of the streets are not only narrow and hilly but are also riven with potholes – the locals aiming to preserve their exclusivity and save money on road repairs at the same time.

One place worthy of a visit is the 1846 **Fonthill Castle**, a Gothic Revival structure modelled on an English folly and originally the home of actor Edwin Forrest. It now serves as the admissions office for the College of Mount St Vincent, at Riverdale Avenue and 263rd Street.

around 100 prominent Americans are lined up along an open-air colonnade. Though the Hall of Fame is every bit as pompous as it sounds, its neo-classical style is noteworthy, and is replicated across the campus, much of which is credited to the prominent turn-of-the-century New York architect Stanford White.

Predating the college, and most other buildings in the Bronx, the **Van Cortlandt Mansion**▶ (off Broadway between 240th and 242nd streets) was built in 1748 for a family prominent in politics and farming, their land holdings consuming what are now the wild expanses of **Van Cortlandt Park**. The mansion, Georgian-style with Dutch adornments, also provided a part-time base for George Washington, who marched from here into Manhattan to celebrate the signing of the Paris Peace Treaty in 1783, ending the Revolutionary War. The mansion shows off its English, Dutch and Colonial furniture, and a few other 18th-century odds and ends.

Strange as it may sound, a more intriguing stop than the mansion is **Woodlawn Cemetery**▶ (East 223rd Street and Webster Avenue). Rather than raid the art collections of Europe or finance Manhattan skyscrapers, some ultra-rich early New Yorkers spent their fortunes on extravagant mausoleums. Among those buried here in ostentatious style are shop-founders Richard H Macy, J C Penney, and F W Woolworth – whose sphinx-guarded, pseudo-Egyptian palace defies belief. Other more discreet tombs remember cultural figures such as writer Herman Melville and jazz giant Duke Ellington.

The New York Botanical Garden

■ **People of African origin have lived in New York from the city's earliest days, and their struggle for civil rights has been a long, uphill battle. New York's first black migrants were slaves who arrived with the Dutch, by whom they were treated with comparative benevolence. A change for the worse occurred during the British era, when the colony's new rulers showed no respect for people whom they regarded as chattels. Their response to slave uprisings was public hangings and burnings ...■**

Racism continues After the Revolutionary War, a few freed slaves attained respectable social positions but others were illegally transported to the Deep South. All were subject to racist hostility.

By the early 1800s, New York's African-Americans encountered segregation in public places and were prevented from obtaining the necessary work skills to be employed as anything other than labourers and servants.

The rise and fall of Harlem In response, the first black churches and mutual aid societies were formed and, after years of enduring racism in the city's slums, it was amid the stylish brownstones of Harlem (originally built for wealthy whites) that New York's blacks first felt they had found a secure and self-supporting enclave.

Harlem's population doubled during the 1920s, a period when its art, music and literature flowered into the 'Harlem Renaissance'. Swiftly, however, the Depression made Harlem a ghetto and its problems, along with those of black areas in the Outer Boroughs, were never tackled by the authorities.

Civil rights and riots A few black faces were beginning to be seen in the corridors of power but it took the Civil Rights Movement and the Harlem speeches of Malcolm X to bring racial issues into the public spotlight during the 1960s. Since then, the African-American community's monetary riches may not have matched its cultural ones, but various self-help ventures have improved areas that once saw some of New York's most desperate living.

The raising of black consciousness in the 1960s was helped by public campaigners such as Malcolm X, seen here addressing a Muslim meeting in Harlem. He was assassinated in 1965

BROOKLYN

Green-Wood Cemetery
Henry Pierrepont, the man who developed Brooklyn Heights, was not only concerned with providing homes for the living. With Green-Wood Cemetery (main entrance at Fifth Avenue and 25th Street), he created a 478-acre landscaped plot to be enjoyed by some of the most prominent New Yorkers on their earthly demise.

The cemetery drew 100,000 visitors a year in its Victorian heyday to wander its 20 miles of footpaths, take in the views over New York harbour, and contemplate the many richly (and often tastelessly) decorated tombs. Richard Upjohn's remarkable Gothic Revival gate and gatehouse, at the Fort Hamilton Parkway entrance, is just the start.

Brooklyn – a city within a city

▶▶▶ Brooklyn   48C3

Brooklyn was once a fully fledged city in its own right, with an affluent population and revered cultural institutions. In 1898, buoyed by the opening of the Brooklyn Bridge spanning the East River, it decided (by a narrow majority) to become part of New York City.

The decision has been cursed by Brooklynites ever since. Post-independence humiliations have been many: the Depression and a huge influx of immigrants turned many of Brooklyn's stylish neighbourhoods into slums and created breeding grounds for organised crime; the naval shipyards were closed down; Brooklyn's award-winning *Daily Eagle* newspaper bit the dust after a strike. Perhaps most galling of all, the Brooklyn Dodgers baseball team moved to Los Angeles in 1955.

Despite these setbacks, Brooklyn remains the most distinctive and enjoyable of the Outer Boroughs, with its own unique personality. The moderate tempo of its streets comes as a welcome relief after the bustle of Manhattan.

If it were still a city, Brooklyn would be the sixth most populous in the US. Within its metropolitan sprawl are four pockets of special interest. Downtown Brooklyn and the historic Brooklyn Heights lie closest to Manhattan. Just to the north, Fort Greene is gaining a reputation as the home of the new black artistic community. South of Downtown, the elegant Parkway leads to the massive Brooklyn Museum and the Botanic Garden; further south, on the coast, is the fabled but faded Coney Island amusement park and Russian-dominated Brighton Beach.

From the Brooklyn Bridge, any turning to the right leads into the short leafy streets of **Brooklyn Heights▶▶▶**. The 1814 invention of the steam-powered ferry made this district, set on bluffs above the East River, a residential plot coveted by the bankers and speculators active in Manhattan's Financial District, just across the water.

Continued on page 76.

Brooklyn-by-the-Sea

■ **Where Brooklyn meets the Atlantic Ocean you will find not only a coastline but two contrasting images of New York life: Coney Island amusement park, world-famous but a pale shadow of its former self, and Brighton Beach, a declining seaside resort energised and transformed since the 1970s by a massive influx of Russian émigrés ...■**

Coney Island For 30 years up until the mid-1940s, this was many New Yorkers' idea of heaven. For a nickel subway fare they could swop their over-crowded, over-heated city streets for a day of fun beside the ocean, munching candyfloss and sending themselves dizzy on the roller-coasters, or lurking around the peep-shows. Coney Island is undoubtedly a legend but today it is also – in every sense – history.

In the amusement park area between Surf Avenue and the Boardwalk and West 8th and West 16th streets, little more than run-of-the-mill fairground rides suggest the old days, though a rickety 1927 roller-coaster, the fearsome Cyclone, is still in business, as is the even older wooden Wonder Wheel.

Another survivor is Nathan's Famous, a fast-food outlet at the corner of Surf and Stillwell avenues. The claim that Nathan himself invented the hot-dog may or may not be true, but it is a fact that Coney Island nostalgia is best experienced while eating one. Let the ketchup drip over your fingers as you walk around the site where a million people a day once found contentment.

On summer days, Coney Island's beach still gets plenty of users, and the Boardwalk beside it – which passes the performing sea lions and captive sharks of the Aquarium for Wildlife Conservation – is as atmospheric as ever.

Coney Island's name
The most plausible of many theories as to how Coney Island acquired its name is that it derives from the Dutch *Konijn Eiland* – Rabbit Island.

Brighton Beach Continue east along the Boardwalk to reach this revitalised area where between 10,000 and 20,000 ex-Soviet immigrants form the largest Russian community in the US, beneficiaries of the USSR's relaxing of restrictions in the years before its collapse. With caviar and ice-cold vodka advertised in Cyrillic script, and the riotous restaurants along Brighton Beach Avenue known to round off the evening with frenzied dancing and the occasional drunken punch-up, so-called Little Odessa (many settlers arrived from the Black Sea port) is fast becoming one of the most unique and celebrated areas of New York City.

Maxim Gorky on Coney Island
'Fabulous and beyond conceiving, ineffably beautiful, is this fiery scintillation'

BROOKLYN HEIGHTS

Stroll along Brooklyn Heights Promenade for classic views of Manhattan across the East River. In the middle distance is South Street Seaport

Stroll: Brooklyn Heights
An enjoyable way to walk off a good lunch is with a stroll along Brooklyn Heights Promenade. Also called the Esplanade, this wide pathway above the East River offers views of Manhattan strong enough to draw Brooklyn office workers with picnic lunches, and to push the prices of west-facing penthouse apartments along nearby Columbia Heights into the realms of the phantasmagoric.

Continued from page 74.

Brooklyn Heights subsequently became covered with brownstone dwellings which, be they Gothic, Greek or Romanesque in style, largely survive intact in an area which became a National Historical Landmark in 1965.

The Heights can be enjoyed on a directionless amble, but structure your explorations sufficiently to include Orange Street and its **Plymouth Church of the Pilgrims▶**. It was here during the 1800s that minister Henry Ward Beecher delivered eloquent and impassioned sermons against slavery and made the church a platform for the leading abolitionists. He is remembered by a statue in the adjoining garden. Another worthwhile stop is at 128 Pierrepont Street, where the **Brooklyn Historical Society▶** mounts exhibitions of local memorabilia.

Below the Heights, Downtown Brooklyn spills along Fulton Street, which bends around the unappealing Greek Revival Borough Hall, erected in 1848. Of far greater interest, the **New York Transit Museum▶▶▶** occupies a former subway station at the junction of Boerum Place and Schermerhorn Street. Inside, art deco air-vent coverings and mosaic-tiled station name plates indicate the care that went into the early years of what became the world's second largest mass transit system.

Downstairs along the one-time platforms stand subway carriages from 1904 to 1964: step aboard and wonder how passengers avoided being scalped by the vicious-looking fans that preceded air-conditioning.

Between Downtown Brooklyn and the former naval dockyards, **Fort Greene▶** is another district well endowed with leafy streets and brownstones. After they were vacated by their wealthy white owners, many of Fort Greene's elegant homes were bought by Brooklyn's more affluent blacks. Many became rooming houses during the Depression, causing the area to fall into neglect.

Though signs of inner-city poverty remain apparent, Fort Greene is very much on the rise. African-Americans still make up 70 per cent of the district's population, a significant number of them being successful in the arts. Jazz singer Betty Carter and artist Ernest Critchlow are long-established locals; another is film-maker Spike Lee, who resisted the lure of Hollywood and located his production company here. Lee grew up in Fort Greene and his 1986 movie, *She's Gotta Have It*, made use of a local landmark: **Fort Greene Park**, designed by Olmsted and Vaux (better known for Manhattan's Central Park) in 1860. The Doric column was added later in memory of the 12,000 American patriots who died on British prison ships during the Revolutionary War and lie buried beneath the park.

Be cautious when visiting Fort Greene: though not unduly dangerous, its streets see comparatively few tourists. Keep to the area south of the park, where you will find the most impressive of the brownstones.

There are many more brownstones in the residential streets between Flatbush Avenue and Sixth Avenue, an upmarket section of the Park Slope neighbourhood. A much more spectacular sight in this area, however, stands at the centre of Grand Army Plaza (on Flatbush Avenue by the main entrance to Prospect Park, described

Born in Brooklyn
Woody Allen (1935), Clara Bow (1905), George Gershwin (1899), Mickey Rooney (1922), Barbra Streisand (1943), Mae West (1892).

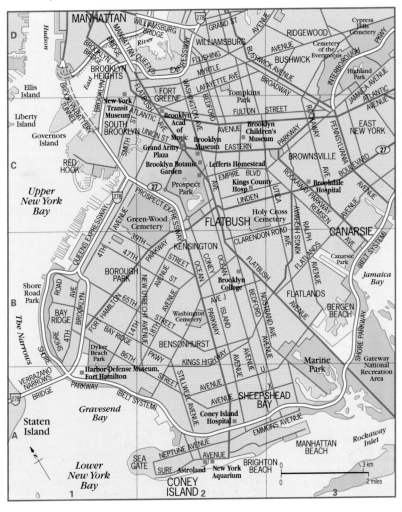

BROOKLYN

The Satmarer Jews
Since the 1940s, Brooklyn's Williamsburg district (north of Downtown) has been a base of the ultra-strict Satmar sect, a branch of Hassidic Judaism which originated in Hungary. Satmarer males sport beards and side curls, and wear dark frock coats and hats; the heads of married women are shaven and covered by a wig. Satmarers adhere rigidly to an ultra-strict glatt kosher diet, and members typically eschew TV and radio. The heart of the community is along Lee Avenue while the sect's schools and synagogues are on neighbouring Bedford Avenue.

on page 79): the wildly oversized Soldiers' and Sailors' Memorial Arch, raised in 1892 to commemorate the Union forces who died during the Civil War.

This Brooklyn version of an imperial Roman arch was designed by John H Duncan, who was also responsible for the similarly grandiose General Grant Memorial (see pages 110–11). The memorial's sheer size makes it much more of an architectural curiosity than a fitting shrine to the dead. The sense of pomposity is compounded by the heroic sculptures added to the memorial in 1898, though some amends is made by the finely detailed bas-reliefs which decorate the walls on the inside of the arch.

The grand streets and landscaped open spaces – as well as the triumphal monuments – that Brooklyn acquired during the late 19th century were the hallmarks of a city very much on the rise. In keeping with the optimism of the times – and in an effort to create a symbol of Brooklyn's cultural superiority over Manhattan – the **Brooklyn Museum**▶▶▶ (200 Eastern Parkway) was founded in 1897 with the intention of becoming the largest museum in the world. Such great ambitions were never fulfilled, however, and this fine museum has undeservedly been playing second fiddle to the better-known museums of Manhattan for decades.

Brooklyn Heights. Not all of the city's best skyscrapers are in Manhattan

The museum's fifth floor reveals an exceptional collection of 19th-century American portraiture, including Gilbert Stuart's iconographic image of George Washington. Elsewhere, Francis Guy's light and airy *Winter Scene in Brooklyn* of 1817 stands out, and a quality selection from the Hudson River School culminates in Albert Bierstadt's *Storm in the Rocky Mountains, Mt Rosalie*, an intense landscape of rugged, exposed granite beneath brooding storm clouds.

The fourth floor of the museum has colonial-period ceramics and interiors ranging from 17th-century farmhouses to 1920s art deco lounges. Note the Moorish Room: a dreamy conglomeration of patterned tiles, gold-brocaded walls, oak panels and thick velvet drapes, which once graced John D Rockefeller's Manhattan mansion.

Other storeys are filled by comprehensive Asian art collections, while the ground floor holds pottery, figurines and votive objects from Africa, Oceania and Central and South America. Most striking among the latter is perhaps the Paracas Textile, a 2,000-year-old Peruvian burial cloth.

The Native American collections, on the same floor, feature diverse tribes and exhibits ranging from buckskin jackets to totem poles. A newer section of the museum is now the resting place for the world's third largest stock of ancient Egyptian artefacts, a remarkable stash dating from pre-dynastic times to the Roman conquest.

Should you be feeling drained after exploring the museum, head for the 52 divinely landscaped acres of the **Brooklyn Botanic Garden▶▶**, just to the rear, where soft colours and wondrous fragrances will revive your senses. The garden is across Flatbush Avenue from **Prospect Park▶**, a broad and bucolic open space completed in 1874. With none of the restraints that were imposed with Central Park, their most famous project, architects Olmsted and Vaux gave their imaginations free rein here and considered Prospect Park their finest work.

The quiet charm still to be found in parts of Brooklyn Heights contrasts with the frenetic streets of Manhattan, just across the East River

Literary Brooklyn Heights
Brooklyn Heights has strong literary associations. Poet Hart Crane and novelist John Dos Passos both lived at 110 Columbia Heights during the 1920s (Crane also resided briefly at 77 Willow Street). Henry Miller spent a short time at 91 Remsen Street during the 1920s, and Truman Capote wrote *Breakfast at Tiffany's* in the basement of 70 Willow Street. Norman Mailer wrote *The Naked and the Dead* while living with his parents at 102 Pierrepont Street. At the same address Arthur Miller wrote his play *All My Sons*, before moving to 155 Willow Street, where he is remembered by a plaque – though he wrote *Death of a Salesman* at 31 Grace Court.

BROOKLYN BRIDGE

Ill luck and the Brooklyn Bridge

In its early years, the Brooklyn Bridge saw more than its share of tragedy. Its designer, John A Roebling, died following an accident before his bridge was complete. His son, Washington, took over, but became paralysed and had to supervise the construction work from his sick bed. Twenty of the 600-strong workforce died during the construction of the bridge. Six days after the bridge opened, the screams of a woman who tripped on the approach caused a panic in which 12 people lost their lives, mistakenly believing the bridge was about to collapse. In 1884, however, circus-owner P T Barnum led 21 elephants across it; since then there have been few doubts as to the bridge's strength.

The pedestrian walkway on the Brooklyn Bridge. The towers of Manhattan's Financial District gleam behind the intricate web of suspension cables

▶▶ Brooklyn Bridge   77D1

Subway: Brooklyn Bridge

Completed in 1883, the Brooklyn Bridge was the world's first steel suspension bridge, and, for 20 years, the longest. It formed the first fixed link between the then separate cities of Brooklyn and Manhattan.

Enhanced immeasurably by its two Gothic 272ft-high stone arches (when they were finished, only the spire of Trinity Church rose higher into the New York sky), the bridge is an aesthetic as well as an engineering masterpiece. It has inspired many writers, including Brooklyn-based Walt Whitman, to wax lyrical over its beauty.

Cyclists, skaters, joggers and muggers (at the Brooklyn end during rush hour) – and sometimes high winds – can be a hazard to walkers on the bridge's pedestrian path, easily the best way to appreciate the structure. From Manhattan, the views used to be of Brooklyn's busy shipyards, a scene re-created by one display beside the footpath, while another recounts the bridge's origins.

▶ Carnegie Hall   151C2

57th Street at Seventh Avenue

Subway: Seventh Avenue or 57th Street

Financed by a $2 million gift from steel magnate Andrew Carnegie, Carnegie Hall opened to the public in 1891 and quickly gained an international reputation for its outstanding acoustics. Its horseshoe-shaped auditorium is modelled on those of Italian opera houses.

A recent refurbishment has restored the hall to the sumptuous appearance of its younger days – best appreciated by attending a concert or taking a guided tour.

Even if you fail to see inside the hall, look around the **Carnegie Hall Museum** which records the hall's origins and the long list of famous names that have graced its boards. Besides Benny Goodman's clarinet and Arturo Toscanini's baton, look in the bookings diary for 1964 for the handwritten entry recording the first New York appearance of 'The Beetles'.

►► **Cathedral Church of
St John the Divine**

IFCB5

Amsterdam Avenue at 112th Street
Subway: Cathedral Parkway (110th Street)
The cornerstone of the Cathedral Church of St John the Divine was laid in 1892, marking the beginning of what is now an immense episcopalian edifice spread across 11 acres – the largest church in the US, and the largest Gothic church in the world, yet still years short of completion more than a century later.

The original plans were for a church of Byzantine/Romanesque design, but delays caused by engineering problems and lack of finance meant that only the choir and four stone arches were completed in the first 25 years. Changing tastes (and the death of the project's original architect) saw the structure remodelled in French Gothic form, gaining a facade reminiscent of Notre-Dame in Paris.

The nave, covering a staggering 32,000 sq ft, was completed in a comparatively swift ten years but the US's entry into World War II again halted progress, as did a decision during the 1960s to divert building money to the needs of the community. The current building programme did not get under way until 1978, when funds were available to import a master stonemason from England to cut the Indiana limestone used in the towers and to train a small army of local apprentices.

As its towers still rise, enclosed by scaffolding, the cathedral's exterior takes on a surreal appearance. Inside, the scale is breathtaking. The clash of Gothic and Romanesque/Byzantine styles is most apparent from the unfinished crossing, where the structure's anatomy is revealed and above which the red-tiled dome, installed as a 'temporary' shelter during 1909, remains in place.

Foremost among the cathedral's decorations are two sets of religious tapestries: the Mortlake Tapestries, woven in England during 1623 from cartoons by Raphael; and the 17th-century Barberini tapestries, which were woven on papal looms.

**New York Public Library:
115th Street branch**
The main branch of the New York Public Library on Fifth Avenue (see page 168) is one of the city's greatest architectural delights, and the 115th Street branch (between Seventh and Eighth avenues) is no mere pile either. Dating from 1908, the library was the work of the revered firm of McKim, Mead and White, and its imposing Renaissance style was intended to match the grandeur of early Harlem.

CENTRAL PARK

Map of Central Park showing:

CENTRAL PARK NORTH

Harlem Meer

Great Hill — Conservatory Garden — MADISON AVENUE

The Pool — The Loch

North Meadow

FIFTH AVENUE

E 96TH ST

Reservoir

E 86TH ST

Great Lawn — Metropolitan Museum of Art

Shakespeare Garden

Belvedere Lake

The Lake — The Ramble

Bethesda Terrace

Strawberry Fields — The Mall

Sheep Meadow

EAST DRIVE

Dairy — E 65TH ST — FIFTH AVENUE

Zoo

The Pond

CENTRAL PARK SOUTH

0   500 m

CENTRAL PARK WEST / WEST DRIVE / CENTRAL PARK WEST

82

▶▶▶ **Central Park**   *1FCF3*

From almost any high point in Manhattan, what holds the eye longest is not the Empire State Building or the Statue of Liberty but the great rectangle of greenery in the heart of the urban jungle. Central Park fills 843 acres and runs for 50 city blocks between the Upper East and Upper West sides.

The candidates in New York's mayoral campaign of 1850 were agreed on just one issue: the need for a large public park of the kind civic leaders and journalists had been advocating since poet and newspaper editor William Cullen Bryant raised the idea in 1844. At that time, property developers were breaking all records in their northward streak across Manhattan.

In 1856, the city paid $5.5 million for a tract of land – an area well to the north of the city as then established, dotted with pig farms and squatter camps and mostly used as a garbage dump. Two years later work began on the park, to the plans of Frederick Olmsted (a farmer-turned-engineer-turned-journalist-turned-landscape architect) and English architect Calvert Vaux.

The park's design emphasised the natural form of the land: glades, copses and rock outcrops were developed, and some 5 million trees planted. Bridges linked the park's internal thoroughfares and – a revolutionary concept at the time – cross-park traffic was carried by sunken roads to keep the pastoral view intact.

With tree-lined driveways for the wealthy to parade in horse-drawn carriages, and footpaths for the working classes (who typically at the time toiled in sweatshops and lived in filthy tenements) to experience, as Olmsted expressed it, 'a specimen of God's handiwork', the park was an instant success.

Though now fully enclosed by buildings and with far more monuments than Olmsted would have liked, Central Park is still a great escape from the city streets. The Fifth Avenue and Upper West Side apartment buildings that appear above the tree-tops simply add to the park's country-in-the-city effect.

Getting lost temporarily in Central Park is surprisingly easy. Be sure to pick up a map from one of the information kiosks before you enter.

From the south, the first place to make for is the **Dairy**. In pursuit of a romantic rural vision, the Gothic-style Dairy was built here in 1870 as a place where traditionally attired milkmaids would serve fresh milk (a luxury at the time) to mothers and young children. The quaint building now holds the park's main Visitor Center, with displays and several leaflets describing park walks.

North of the Dairy, across the 65th Transverse, the 22-acre **Sheep Meadow** did indeed hold sheep during the park's earliest years, the resident flock being led across the park's West Drive twice a day to the Sheepfold, which occupied the site of the present Tavern on the Green. Oddly enough, given Olmsted and Vaux's obsession with re-creating the country in the city, the Sheep Meadow was originally intended as a military parade ground.

Just east of the Sheep Meadow begins the **Mall**, one of the first completed sections of the park and its only formal area. Many 19th-century New Yorkers got their first taste of European-style promenading along this tree-lined avenue, and some also gained their first experience of donkey- and goat-cart riding, both of which were on offer here.

Olmsted initially resisted attempts to have statuary in the park but eventually agreed to the memorials of writers – Shakespeare, Robert Burns and Sir Walter Raleigh among them – which are grouped around the Mall's southern end to form the **Literary Walk**.

Continuing north, the Mall leads into the **Concert Ground** and the **Naumberg Bandshell**, the scene of free live music on most summer weekends.

Cross the 72nd Street Transverse and you enter **Bethesda Terrace**. At its heart is the elegant *Angel of the Waters* statue. One of the few pieces commissioned especially for the park, the statue was unveiled in 1873 to commemorate the opening of the aqueduct which gave New York its first regular supply of fresh water.

There is more water directly north of Bethesda Terrace, in the form of the **Lake**. A leisurely paddle along this imposingly calm body of water is a fine way to round off a park visit. Boats can be hired from the Loeb Boathouse, on the eastern banks of the lake.

New York's 'green lung' and the Plaza Hotel

Stroll: Strawberry Fields
From the Upper West Side, entering Central Park on 72nd Street leads into Strawberry Fields, a 3-acre section maintained by an endowment from Yoko Ono, as a memorial to her late husband John Lennon.

Overlooked by the Dakota Apartment building, where the Lennons lived (see page 96), Strawberry Fields is planted with 161 species of plant, representing 161 nations of the world. The Imagine mosaic on the pathway was a gift from the City of Naples. Incidentally, the New York authorities were not unanimous in agreeing to the tribute: conservative elements argued instead for a memorial to Bing Crosby.

83

CENTRAL PARK

Central Park in style
One way of seeing the park is as the city swells of the 1880s did: by horse and carriage. Buy a ticket from the kiosk at Grand Army Plaza (at the junction of 59th Street and Fifth Avenue) and climb aboard. Prices have risen over the last hundred years, however: expect to pay around $15 per person for a half-hour trot.

If you are determined to do something more energetic, cross the lake on foot by way of the Bow Bridge – one of Central Park's seven original cast-iron bridges – to **The Ramble**. Comprising 33 acres of painstakingly re-created rurality, complete with rustic bird-houses and beehives, The Ramble is ripe for exploration and is also an excellent location for birdwatching. Do not ramble alone, however, as this is an isolated and dangerous area.

Across the 79th Street Transverse from The Ramble, a replica Scottish castle, **Belvedere Castle**, was erected in 1869 for no reason other than fun. It was occupied for many years by a weather station.

To the left, a path leads to the **Shakespeare Garden**, planted with trees and plants mentioned in the bard's

A sedate tour or (left) the more energetic pastime of rollerblading – two of many ways to relax in the park

works, and continues to the **Great Lawn**. Nowadays covered more by concrete sports courts than grass, the Great Lawn attracted half a million people to hear a Simon & Garfunkel concert in 1981; slightly fewer attend free summer concerts given here by the New York Philharmonic.

The northerly section of the park (north of the reservoir) is the least visited and consequently the most dangerous. If you do want to explore here – the lure is a landscape far rockier and much more hilly than that to the south – it is wisest to enter and leave the park at its Fifth Avenue and 105th Street entrance. Doing this will lead directly into the park's **Conservatory Garden** and allow you to pass through the lavish wrought-iron gates that once fronted the mansion of Cornelius Vanderbilt.

Central Park has had its share of well-publicised crimes: muggings are far from uncommon, and murders are not unknown. Despite this, much of the park is no more dangerous than the average New York street, though there are many isolated areas where a person wandering alone will be viewed as an easy target. Never visit the park after dark.

The Chelsea Hotel

■ **When the Chelsea opened in 1888 at 222 West 23rd Street, it was the first apartment block in New York to be topped by a penthouse. Its façade featured wrought-iron balconies with sunflower motifs. Converted to a hotel in 1905, it did not become famous through its architecture, however, but as a haunt of writers, painters and composers, who gave it a Bohemian ambience unmatched by any other hotel in the world ...■**

Painter John Sloan, and writers Mark Twain and O Henry (the pen name of William Sydney Porter), were among the Chelsea's early guests but the hotel got into its artistic stride during the 1930s, after poet Edgar Lee Masters eulogised it in verse and novelist Thomas Wolfe took up residence.

Impressed by the size of his suite, Wolfe dubbed his bathroom the 'Throne Room' and kept 4,000 loose pages of prose strewn across his floor. Selections from these would be assembled and supplied to his publisher as finished works.

The 1950s and 1960s Its literary links were already established by the time Dylan Thomas made the Chelsea his New York base during the early 1950s. His last conscious hours, after claiming to have downed 18 whiskies in a Greenwich Village bar, were spent in room 205, and he died a few days later in St Vincent's Hospital.

A decade later, Brendan Behan took shelter at the Chelsea and begged to be commemorated by a plaque – as he now is. Besides Behan, Beat writers William Burroughs and Gregory Corso, expatriate Russian novelist Vladimir Nabokov, and abstract expressionist painter Jackson Pollock were among the renegades who gathered at the Chelsea's bar (now a Spanish restaurant).

Pop and punk The hotel provided a backdrop for Andy Warhol's rambling split-screen film *Chelsea Girls* (which starred Warhol acolyte Edie Sedgwick, a Chelsea resident) and through the 1960s its guests included many pop-music icons – among them Bob Dylan, who wrote his epic song 'Sad Eyed Lady of the Lowlands' in one of its rooms. The hotel's most ignominious night came in 1978, when punk rocker Sid Vicious allegedly stabbed his girlfriend to death in their suite – the film *Sid and Nancy* actually featured the hotel.

Step into the Chelsea's lobby and you will find plaques commemorating its most illustrious residents, and many works donated by artist guests. Should you be tempted to stay, the Chelsea's rooms are among the least costly in Midtown Manhattan. Many of them are occupied by eccentric long-term guests.

Its decorative design may once have been ahead of its time, but the Chelsea has long been known not as an architectural landmark, but as a cultural one

The choking mayor
One regular visitor to Chinatown's restaurants was former New York mayor, Ed Koch. One day in 1981, Koch was enjoying lunch at Sun Lok Kee (13 Mott Street), when a piece of food lodged in his throat. As the mayor leapt to his feet mouthing the words 'I'm choking', his dining partner performed the Heimlich manoeuvre whereby he grabbed the mayor, gripped him tightly from behind and forced the food to be ejected from his throat.

What the food actually was is disputed. The mayor claimed it was watercress; others suggest it was really a piece of pork and that the mayor, with an election due that year, did not want to upset the Orthodox Jews (who are forbidden to eat pork) among his supporters.

Frenetic but fascinating, Chinatown's streetlife never takes a break

▶▶▶ Chinatown   *IFCB2*

New York streetlife enters a new dimension on the tightly clustered, densely crowded pavements of Chinatown, enclosed by the Civic Center, Little Italy and the Lower East Side. Stalls are laden with seafood, vegetables or fruit; herbalist shops dispense wondrous remedies; bakeries concoct tooth-shatteringly sweet cakes; and rows of gaudy neon signs advertise (in English and Chinese) the noodle shops, tea parlours and dim sum houses that bring most non-Chinese New Yorkers to the area.

There has been a Chinese presence here since the 1850s, but only with the relaxing of immigration laws in 1965 did Chinatown truly begin to expand. Spilling beyond its traditional boundaries, Chinatown now holds around half of New York's 300,000 Chinese population and still it expands, further swelled by new arrivals from Vietnam and other parts of South East Asia.

The imminent hand-over of Hong Kong to Beijing has also been felt. Hong Kong banks have opened here and brightly lit shopping malls, stuffed with jewellery and electrical goods, have spread along Canal Street.

Tumultuous they may be, but Chinatown's streets are some of the safest in New York. Local businesses – including more than 300 restaurants – depend on New Yorkers in search of food and visitors in search of the exotic, so they play their part in keeping things quiet. Chinatown's crime is not on the streets but behind closed doors: the feuds between rival gangs, or the fresh arrivals who toil for subsistence wages in Canal Street's garment factories, are facets of Chinatown outsiders never see.

In fact, beyond business and people, there is not a lot for visitors to see in Chinatown. A few places of interest are noted in the Chinatown Walk opposite, but the neighbourhood cries out for a decent historical collection.

約 界慶祝中華民國八十二年雙十國慶

THE CHINESE COMMUNITY OF NEW YORK CELEBRATES THE 81ST "DOUBLE TEN" ANNIVERSARY OF THE FOUNDING OF REPUBLIC OF CHINA

CHINATOWN

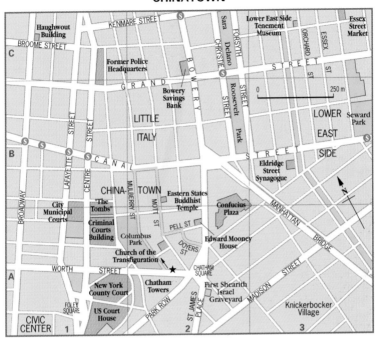

KENMARE STREET

Haughwout Building
BROOME STREET

C

Former Police Headquarters

GRAND

Bowery Savings Bank

LITTLE

ITALY

CANAL

CHINA-TOWN

City Municipal Courts

"The Tombs"

Criminal Courts Building

Columbus Park

Church of the Transfiguration

WORTH STREET

New York County Court

Chatham Towers

FOLEY SQUARE

US Court House

CIVIC CENTER

Sara Delano
FORSYTH STREET
CHRYSTIE STREET

Lower East Side Tenement Museum

ORCHARD STREET
ESSEX STREET
Essex Street Market

STREET

Roosevelt Street

Park

LOWER

EAST

SIDE

Eldridge Street Synagogue

Eastern States Buddhist Temple

Confucius Plaza

MOTT ST

PELL ST

DOYERS ST

Edward Mooney House

CHATHAM SQUARE

First Shearith Israel Graveyard

MADISON STREET

MANHATTAN BRIDGE

Knickerbocker Village

Seward Park

0   250 m

N

BROADWAY
LAFAYETTE STREET
CENTRE STREET
MULBERRY ST

PARK ROW
ST JAMES PLACE

1   2   3

Walk Chinatown streetlife

Effervescent streetlife is the main attraction of Chinatown, which holds few specific sights. This walk covers the main sights and captures the atmosphere of the area – leaving scope for independent meandering.

Begin at **Columbus Park**, which replaced a notorious slum and red-light area of the mid-1800s. Today, noisy ball games and the rumble of traffic along Mulberry Street rob the park of any peacefulness. Cross on to **Canal Street** and you will pass Chinatown's biggest and brightest shopping emporiums before reaching Mott Street.
   At 64 Mott Street, the **Eastern States Buddhist Temple** is a genuine temple but also sells souvenir Buddha figures, arranged in eye-catching rows. Built in 1801, the Georgian **Church of the Transfiguration**, at 25 Mott Street, predates Chinatown. Close by, **Doyers Street** was once

the domain of opium dealers and prostitutes, and its bend was used as an ambush point during 19th- and early 20th-century Tong Wars, when rival Chinese gangs fought over the control of drug-trafficking, prostitution and gambling. Nowadays perfectly safe, Doyers Street is lined by restaurants.

The Chinese

■ **Chinese faces were rare in early 19th-century New York, but today the Chinese community is expanding fast in both size and importance. Whether in academia or business, Chinese-Americans are frequently among New York City's most spectacular achievers ...■**

Chinese in the US

Although only a few Chinese were present in New York prior to the late 1800s, they were already established in California where 25,000 had arrived in 1852. Most of them worked in the California gold mines and, subsequently, on the transcontinental railroad that linked the West Coast to the rest of the US. The Chinese gained a reputation as dependable labourers, but in the economic depression that followed the Gold Rush, they found themselves prevented from opening businesses or owning land. Banding together, the Chinese settled in what became the 'Chinatown' districts of many California communities, some making the cross-country trip to the less hostile atmosphere of New York.

The 75 Chinese immigrants estimated to be living in New York in 1870 were mostly individuals who had jumped ship and assimilated themselves as best they could into established ethnic groups. By 1890, however, New York's Chinese population had rocketed to 12,000. Many of the new arrivals came here from California, where they had provided labour for the transcontinental railway.

With their looks, language and culture at odds with European New York, the lone Chinese males (denied the company of their relatives by an anti-immigration law of 1896) rarely strayed from Chinatown. Aided by family-based self-help organisations, they toiled in shops and laundries, sending any spare money back home.

The seamy side The popular imagination saw Chinatown as a neighbourhood of incredible exotica. Rich tourists were given guided tours by opportunistic locals, failing, of course, to see the axe murders, the slavery, the gambling and the opium dens described in lurid press accounts.

Gambling, prostitution (provided by white women) and opium dens did in fact exist, but usually in upstairs rooms or basements. These activities were overseen by the Tongs – a form of Chinese secret society which originated in Imperial China to fight the Manchu Dynasty.

Acceptance and expansion The Japanese invasion of China in 1937 helped unite warring factions in the Chinese community and the subsequent US-Sino military alliance reduced anti-Chinese feeling among New Yorkers. A bigger change came in 1965, when limitations on Chinese immigration were lifted and waves of new arrivals from Taiwan and Hong Kong came to Chinatown.

The new Chinese were eager to embrace American ways. They quickly made their presence felt in mainstream New York life – though some younger elements embraced briefly notorious criminal gangs such as the Ghost Shadows and the Flying Dragons – and many left the inner city for suburbia as soon as they could.

Chinese food 'to go'. Chinatown's eateries cover a vast range of styles and regional cuisines

*The unmistakable
Chrysler Building –
New York art deco at
its finest, and every-
one's favourite
skyscraper*

▶▶ Chrysler Building   151B3

42nd Street at Lexington Avenue
Subway: 42nd Street/Grand Central
The definitive symbol of New York art deco and briefly the
world's tallest building, the 1,045ft Chrysler Building was
completed in 1930. Its tower is still among the city's most
recognisable landmarks. More impressive than the exteri-
or view, however, is the lobby, retaining its walls of red-
veined African marble and a mural by Edward Trumbull
depicting the glories of world transportation. The lifts,
too, still have their original decor of plush, laminated
woods, and the entire 77-storey building is studded by
automobile motifs.

▶ Civic Center   104C2

Subway: City Hall
The Civic Center is a convenient name for the cluster of
municipal buildings near the foot of the Brooklyn Bridge.
   The oldest among them, the **City Hall**, a mix of Federal
and French Renaissance styles dating from 1811, is still in
use. The barriers which line the front of the building are
intended to prevent the frequent demonstrations in City
Hall Park from blocking councillors' access to the building. Inside, a circular staircase winds beneath the eye-
catching rotunda to the first floor, where the **Governor's
Room** is lined by portraits of early New York notables and
items of furniture mostly contemporaneous with the
building, but also including a writing table used by George
Washington.
   Immediately north stands the **Old New York County
Courthouse**, an intended shrine to justice but a building
whose financing was one the biggest swindles in New
York history (see page 42). It is now used as municipal
offices. Across Centre Street, the present **New York
County Courthouse** enjoys a hexagonal shape and a
magnificent Corinthian portico.

Inside the Chrysler Building
As a partner to their Energy
Museum (see page 149), the
Consolidated Edison power
company opened the
Conservation Center inside
the Chrysler Building. The
mildly engaging and
interactive exhibits focus on
themes of efficient energy
use and recycling.

Police riots
In 1857, City Hall Park was
the scene of violence
between New York's two
rival police forces, the dis-
credited Municipal and the
newly formed
Metropolitan. Their battles
continued into City Hall and
ended only when National
Guardsmen drew their bay-
onets.
   In September 1992, New
York's finest again
disgraced themselves in
the park, when a poorly
planned demonstration
against Mayor Dinkins culminated in officers (some
of them clearly the worse
for drink) stepping over the
barricades and blockading
the entrance to City Hall.

■ **Sport has a stranglehold on the American mind, and New Yorkers – represented by two professional teams in each of the nation's most popular sports – are no exception. Loyalties and rivalries run deep, even though the closest most people get to actual matches is the couch facing the TV in their living rooms. This is not just due to laziness: tickets, especially for American football matches, tend to be both expensive and scarce ...■**

The New York Marathon

What began in 1970 with 127 runners making four laps around Central Park is now the world's largest urban marathon. Its 26-mile course is contested by some 22,000 runners and watched by over 2 million spectators. Held on the third or fourth Sunday in October (or occasionally on the first Sunday in November), the New York Marathon begins on Staten Island at the Verrazano-Narrows Bridge. Its route passes through each of the city's five boroughs on the way to the finishing line at Central Park's Tavern on the Green.

Baseball In recent years, the more successful of the city's two baseball teams has been the New York Mets, who play at Shea Stadium in Queens (tel: 718/507 8499). Ticket prices range from around $6 for the deck chair area (known as the bleachers), where you will hear the New York crowd at its most witty but also get the worst view, to around $14 as you move up into the tiered seating.

Beset by off-the-field problems through the early 1990s, the New York Yankees are hoping to put their troubles behind them and emulate their glory days. The Yankees play at Yankee Stadium in the Bronx (tel: 718/293 4300), and ticket prices are similar to those for the Mets.

The baseball season runs from April to October.

Basketball From autumn to spring, basketball fans can watch the New York Knicks (short for 'Knickerbockers') playing their matches at Madison Square Garden (tel: 465 JUMP). The Knicks had an all-win 'dream' season in the

One of the great events of New York's sporting year

early 1970s but their form has been patchy since. Match tickets cost around $10–$15 and are difficult to get only if the Knicks have qualified for the end-of-season play-offs.

College basketball should not be underestimated. Many collegiate players are embryonic professionals and most of the best appear at the inter-college tournaments staged at Madison Square Garden during November and March.

Ice-hockey The incredible lack of success of the city's New York Rangers was dramatically ended by their winning of the Stanley Cup in 1994. The Rangers puck off at Madison Square Garden (tel: 308 NYRS) in a season which lasts from late autumn to spring. New Yorkers who want to see a local ice-hockey side win are more inclined to travel to Uniondale in Long Island, where the New York Islanders play at the Nassau Coliseum (tel: 516/794 9300).

American football Neither of New York's two professional football teams plays within the city's boundaries, opting instead for Giants' Stadium, Meadowlands, East Rutherford, New Jersey (tel: 201/935 8222). In recent years, the New York Giants have been much more successful than their rivals, the New York Jets.

The football season runs from August to December and the cheapest tickets for the Jets are around $23. Particularly for the Giants' fixtures, however, tickets are virtually impossible to obtain without booking many months (if not years) in advance.

Horse-racing At daily meetings held from May to July and from September to mid-October, thoroughbreds can be seen stampeding along the turf at Belmont Park, Elmont, Long Island (tel: 516/488 6000), and from late October to May at the Aqueduct Racetrack, Ozone Park, Queens (phone number as for Belmont Park). During August, the state's equine fanciers move upstate to the Saratoga Raceway (tel: 518/584 6200), for a month-long series of meetings.

Betting on horse races If your interest in horses extends only as far as betting on them, aim for one of the many branches of New York City Off-track Betting, where bets can be placed and races watched on TV simulcast. Other venues for a flutter are The Inside Track, Second Avenue between 53rd and 54th streets (tel: 752 1940), a sports bar in the style of an English pub with two giant screens and 15 TV monitors, or the elegant Select Club, 165 Water Street (tel: 425 0052).

Tennis Early in September, the big event in the national tennis calendar, the US Open, takes place at Flushing Meadows, Queens (tel: 718/641 4700). Tickets for the Open's later rounds are snapped up many moons in advance, though it is often possible to see international stars during the first few days' play at short notice. Alternatively, aim for the springtime Tournament of Champions, which features many of the sport's top names and is held at the West Side Tennis Club in Forest Hills, Queens (tel: 718/271 5100).

Sports bars
If you feel like drowning your sorrows after failing to get a ticket for the sporting event that you have travelled all the way to New York to see, do so in one of the city's innumerable sports bars. Not only do such places provide alcohol, they also have gigantic TV screens tuned to seemingly every sports event anyone could possibly have an interest in. If a New York side is involved, you can also be sure of loud and frequent partisan comments and suggestions.

Informal basketball

THE CLOISTERS

The George Washington Bridge

Look southwards from any high point in or around the Cloisters and you will be able to admire the elegant form of the George Washington Bridge, spanning the Hudson River from 178th Street, and once described by famed modernist architect Le Corbusier as 'the most beautiful bridge in the world'.

▶▶ **The Cloisters**   IFCF6

Fort Tryon Park, Washington Heights

Subway: 190th Street

Manhattan and medieval European monasteries may seem an unlikely partnership, but venture to **Fort Tryon Park**, close to Manhattan's northern tip, and you will find – perched on a spectacular site above the Hudson River – parts of five 12th- to 15th-century monastic buildings from France and Spain brought together to form the Cloisters, a fitting home for a large portion of the Metropolitan Museum of Art's medieval collection.

Although much of the Cloisters' architecture is new disguised as old, the genuinely historic bits and bobs – assorted columns, cloisters, chapels, apses and much more – were gathered by sculptor George Gray Bernard as he roamed the back roads of Europe during the early 1900s. Bernard grabbed all the forgotten religious art and architecture he could lay his hands on. Some of his pieces were discovered lying in pigsties and ditches near old churches, others were being used as garden ornaments. Bernard put the haphazard collection on show in

Altarpieces and chapel furnishings at the Cloisters

Manhattan and it was brought to the Met in 1925 with funds provided by John D Rockefeller, who subsequently commissioned the construction of the Cloisters to put it on permanent show.

Arranged more or less chronologically, each section of the Cloisters highlights particular aspects of medieval creativity. The Romanesque Hall, for example, is entered through one of three sculptured church doorways, demonstrating the stylistic shift from 12th-century Romanesque to 13th-century Gothic. Most impressive of the three is the latest: a High Gothic masterpiece from Burgundy which shows Christ crowning the Virgin, flanked by Clovis, first Christian ruler of France, and his son, Clothaire. The two men are so realistically sculptured they seem ready to reach forward and shake your hand.

Off the Romanesque Hall you will find the apse of the 12th-century Fuentidueña Chapel, which survived as its

Two for the price of one

If you visit the Metropolitan Museum of Art and the Cloisters on the same day, a single ticket is valid at both. During the summer there is also a direct bus link between the two museums, which is quicker though more expensive than public transport.

A 'medieval' home for medieval treasures: the Cloisters

church crumbled around it: note the frescoes, and the statues of St Martin and the Annunciation of the Virgin, both of which remain highly impressive despite the ravages of age.

Next door, stroll around the cloisters of the Benedictine Saint-Guilhem Monastery admiring the 12th-century carved capitals before passing through the Romanesque room for the Langon Chapel. During the 12th century, few places produced better wood sculpture than Autun, in Burgundy. Gaze long enough at the chapel's major piece – an Enthroned Virgin and Child – and its many subtleties of form and texture gradually become clear.

Beyond the Langon Chapel are several Gothic rooms and the Cuxa Cloister, its pink arches and columns built in 1188 for a Pyrenean monastery. Across the cloister are the amazing Unicorn Tapestries, probably 16th-century and of Flemish origin. Depicting the hunt for the mythical unicorn as an allegory for Christ's Incarnation, the Unicorn Tapestries are vivid in colour and rich in detail. Pick out the images of love and fertility (within the flora and fauna), which mingle with the Christian symbols and suggest that the series may have been commissioned to celebrate a wedding.

The beauty of the tapestries tends to outshine everything else in the Cloisters, except for the six glorious stained-glass lancet windows in the adjoining Boppard Room. Produced during the 1400s, the panels originally stood in the Carmelite Church of St Severinus in Boppard-on-Rhine in Germany. With stunning artistry and craftsmanship, the glass shows several saints occupying canopied niches around the central figure of the Virgin.

Another important exhibit is a few steps away: Robert Campin's *Annunciation* altarpiece, an early Flemish triptych pioneering the use of oils on wood panels and also breaking new ground by using a contemporary domestic setting.

Fort Tryon Park
This park, in which the Cloisters stands, was the site of the Battle of Washington Heights during the Revolutionary War. The fort that stood here then was renamed Tryon by the victorious British, after the last British governor of New York. Subsequently, its 66 acres were divided into private estates which, one by one, were later purchased by John D Rockefeller. Rockefeller gave the land to the city in 1930 and the Olmsted Brothers (descendants of Frederick Olmsted, architect of Central Park) were commissioned to landscape the lawns, terraces and picnic grounds that stand here now.

COLUMBIA UNIVERSITY

Riverside Church
Just to the south of the Columbia University campus, the Cathedral of St John the Divine rises in its monumental and still unfinished form (see page 81).

Another substantial slab of religious architecture sits just to the north, between 120th and 122nd streets off Riverside Drive, in the very imposing French Gothic form of Riverside Church.

Since its inception, the church – now interdenominational – has championed the underprivileged, and radical liberal views have frequently been aired from its pulpit. A lift runs to the tower's 20th-storey observation level for blustery views across the Hudson River and over Upper Manhattan Go after the Sunday morning service for an earful of the world's largest carillon, housed in the tower.

Alma Mater, *Daniel Chester French's statue, outside Columbia University's Low Library*

▶ **Columbia University**   *IFCB5*

114th–120th streets between Amsterdam Avenue and Broadway
Subway: 116th Street

Founded in 1754 with a charter from the British king George III (it was originally named King's College) on a site in Lower Manhattan, Columbia University was intended to raise New York's cultural profile at a time when the fast-growing city was regarded as an uncouth, money-crazed upstart by the comparatively refined communities of Boston and Philadelphia, where the universities of Harvard and Yale were well established.

The campus occupied various locations in Manhattan. Through its steady movement northwards, Columbia acquired ownership of the land which was later occupied by Rockefeller Center; it sold the prized plot during the mid-1980s for $400 million. The university arrived at its present location in 1897.

The specially designed campus (on the grounds of a former lunatic asylum) placed the academic buildings around a series of fountain-dotted plazas at the heart of which stands the majestic **Low Library**, based on Rome's Pantheon. This was the gift of Seth Low, university president and briefly, from 1902, mayor of New York.

An elegant three-tiered stairway leads up to the library's colonnaded entrance. Inside, you will see 16 green marble columns supporting an impressive octagonal rotunda. What you will not see is students poring over weighty tomes: the library is used only for ceremonies and exhibitions. On the first floor, the Columbiana Collection charts the history of the university with a mass of drawings, documents, paintings and assorted paraphernalia.

On the library's steps you will pass Daniel Chester French's symbolic sculpture, *Alma Mater*, which was covered in gold leaf until 1962 and which formed an

unlikely rallying point for the anti-Vietnam War demonstrations which spread across the campus in 1968. Just east of the library is the Italian Renaissance **St Paul's Chapel**, which has a masterly vaulted interior.

Free guided tours of the campus operate most weekdays; tel: 857 1754.

▶▶ Cooper-Hewitt Museum 187C1

91st Street at Fifth Avenue
Subway: 86th or 96th streets
Inspired by their 1897 visit to London's Victoria and Albert Museum, the three Hewitt sisters set about creating a visual library of design that would inspire new ideas.

From their motley assortment of wallpaper, keys and unusual jewellery, the Cooper-Hewitt Museum has grown into a collection of more than 250,000 items. It includes ceramics, wall coverings, textiles, decorative arts, drawings and prints, plus encyclopaedic reference and picture libraries devoted to design matters.

Selections from the eclectic stocks make up the museum's thematic shows and whether they feature 17th-century French needlework, contemporary Italian typewriters, Middle Eastern embroidery, American hatboxes or three centuries' worth of maps (to mention a few past shows), here you will find New York's most imaginative, and sometimes most controversial, exhibitions.

The kudos of the museum rose greatly in 1967 when its collections, previously displayed in Lower Manhattan, were put into the care of the prestigious Smithsonian Institution and later moved to their present home, the former residence of industrialist, Andrew Carnegie.

Carnegie was one of the world's richest men by the time he announced his intention to have built the 'most modest, plainest, and roomiest house in New York'. Not exactly plain, the 1901 Georgian mansion, in red brick and limestone, sits amid extensive gardens and has 64 rooms – for Carnegie, his wife, daughter, and their 19 servants.

As you wend your way around the exhibitions, look out for the vaulted ceilings, the Tiffany glass windows, and the Louis XVI music room furnished with French antiques and with a set of bagpipes moulded into the decorations – a reminder of Carnegie's Scottish origins. (A major renovation of the building is currently underway and may affect public admittance.

Peter Cooper
The fortunes of inventor and philanthropist Peter Cooper, grandfather of museum founders Sarah, Amy and Eleanor Hewitt, were built on glue and iron. The Cooper foundry, in New Jersey, was where the tracks of the US's first great railways were forged. Recognising that his riches stemmed from the 'co-operation of the masses', Cooper founded the first free college, the Cooper Union, which still stands in what is now the East Village (see pages 98–9).

▶ Daily News Building 151B3

220 East 42nd Street
Subway: Grand Central Terminal/42nd Street
Created by Raymond Hood, who with it established his credentials as the father of New York skyscraper architecture, the 1930 Daily News Building (now properly called the News Building) is a landmark, a no-frills structure of thrusting verticality. Inside the largely original lobby, a frieze recounts the rise and rise (though a question mark hangs over its immediate prospects) of New York's biggest-selling newspaper – a legend for its punchy headlines and salacious stories. An immense revolving globe sits at the centre of displays on meteorological themes. If the building seems familiar, you may be remembering the 1980s *Superman* films, in which it starred as the offices of the *Daily Planet*.

The Dakota in the movies
Plenty of the Dakota's residents have had leading roles in films. So, too, has the building. With years of grime darkening its brickwork and lending a Gothic spookiness to its turrets, towers and gables, the Dakota provided a suitably unsettling location for Roman Polanski's 1968 story of demonic possession, *Rosemary's Baby*.

The spookily grim Dakota Apartments – home of the stars, and a screen star itself

▶ **Dakota Apartments** 151D2

1 West 72nd Street
Subway: 72nd Street
Wealthy New York house-owners of the 1880s had yet to be convinced that apartment living was the lifestyle of the future when Edward S Clark, heir to the Singer sewing machine fortunes, commissioned a luxury apartment building in what is now the Upper West Side but was then wild, open land dotted by shanty dwellings and not even linked to the city's power supplies.

So far out was the site that critics suggested it may as well be in the Dakota territories – which is how the building got its name and the ears of corn, arrowheads and the Native American head that decorate its entrance.

As the city spread northwards and Midtown Manhattan house prices rocketed, there were suddenly lots of takers for the Dakota's marble floors and oak- and mahogany-panelled dwellings. The building quickly became – and continues to be – a prestigious address, with a roll-call of rich and famous residents including Leonard Bernstein, Lauren Bacall, Judy Garland and John Lennon – who was murdered while entering the building in 1980. Lennon's widow, Yoko Ono, still lives here.

■ **More inspired by Manhattan's celebrity-filled soirées than by its art museums, the ever-quotable Andy Warhol might be the one world-famous artist New York can truly call its own ...■**

Born Andrew Warhola to Czech immigrant parents in Pittsburgh, Andy Warhol moved to New York in 1949 and within seven years was among the city's most sought-after commercial artists, much of his work appearing in high society magazines.

Fame in a soup can Warhol loved the party-going life of New York but found his own fame – and artistic vocation – after a trip to a supermarket in 1962. As the artists of the pop art explosion created collages of consumerist images, Warhol began painting soup cans, according the gravity of serious portraiture to each one.

Be it depictions of dollar bills, electric chairs, or Brillo boxes, Warhol relished the publicity that his work aroused. A reviewer wrote that Warhol's silk-screened images of Marilyn Monroe were 'as sentimental as Fords coming off the production line'. In reply, Warhol declared 'I want to be a machine' and named his studio the Factory.

In the mid-1960s, Warhol's Factory became filled by every oddball character in New York, many of whom starred in the underground movies that the artist began making, including *Chelsea Girls*, described by one critic as 'an image of the total degeneration of American society'.

Getting rich The Factory's excesses ended in 1968, when Warhol narrowly survived an assassination attempt and found his financial affairs under scrutiny. Feeling he should be earning more money, the guru of pop art became a society portrait painter, charging $25,000 a time, while his revamped *Interview* magazine began providing lucrative advertising alongside its celebrity gossip.

Warhol's wealth and fame became greater than his creativity. After moving to an expensive Upper East Side house in 1975, he squandered time and money on several ill-fated projects and appeared happiest during his daily shopping expeditions.

Shortly before his death in 1987, Warhol opined 'getting rich isn't as much fun as it used to be'.

Andy Warhol said
'In the future, everybody will be famous for 15 minutes.'
'I don't think my art has any lasting value.'
'I never wanted to be a painter. I wanted to be a tap dancer.'

'Little Ukraine'

In an area of the East Village around Second Avenue between 4th and 14th streets is New York's 'Little Ukraine'. Ukrainians began settling here from the late 1800s and, though their numbers have been greatly depleted, are still much in evidence among the neighbourhood's many Slavic restaurants and shops selling traditional Ukrainian crafts – such as painted Easter eggs. The tiny Ukrainian Museum, 203 Second Avenue, has changing exhibitions on past and present Ukrainian life in New York and in the homeland.

► **East Village** *IFCC2*

In the 1950s, rising rents in Greenwich Village began pushing New York's more radical artists and writers across Broadway into the East Village. Here they took cheap apartments in tenement buildings otherwise inhabited by hard-up eastern European immigrants, many of them from the Ukraine.

The heart of New York hippiedom in the 1960s and the epicentre of its 1970s punk rock scene, the East Village is regularly in the vanguard of alternative culture – despite increasing signs of gentrification, expect to see at least one person dressed head-to-toe in leather and sporting bright green hair. Bizarre one-of-a-kind shops, ethnic eateries and a vibrant street scene are the things the East Village does best, although a handful of historical sights are also worthy of attention.

Astor Place carries the name of John Jacob Astor, one of early 19th-century New York's wealthiest men. Like the similarly deep-pocketed Cornelius Vanderbilt, Astor owned one of the series of marble-fronted houses that became known as **Colonnade Row**. Once the grandest residences in New York, those that survive, now looking rather shabby, are on Lafayette Street (numbers 428 to 434).

Across Lafayette Street, Astor financed the city's first free public library in a brownstone building which, since the 1960s, has been the **Joseph Papp Public Theater**, a venue for varied theatrical, cinematic and other arts events.

Another 19th-century remnant is the **Cooper Union Building**, just south of Astor Place. Founded in 1859 by millionaire railway tycoon Peter Cooper to provide free education for all, the college was the first of its kind in the US and also became an airing place for political views: Abraham Lincoln was among the famous orators who spoke here.

East of Astor Place is St Mark's Place, where the unprepossessing building at number 77 was home to Anglo-American poet W H Auden from 1953. This was also where, four decades earlier in the basement, Leon Trotsky had plotted the Russian Revolution.

Near by, the church of **St Mark's-in-the-Bowery** arose on the estate of New York's Dutch governor, Peter Stuyvesant, in 1799. Its original body was later topped by a spire and fronted by a cast-iron portico. The church serves its eccentric East Village congregation with episcopal services, poetry readings and performance art. On the church's eastern side, Stuyvesant and six generations of his descendants lie buried.

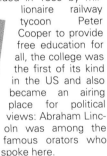

he Public Theater
: Films Du Losange
Little REGULAR 7.00
GA 007
KESPEARE FESTIVAL PRODUCTION

THE JOSEPH PAPP PUBLIC THEATER
425 Lafayette Street
N.Y.C. 10003

NEW YORK SHAKESPEARE FESTIVAL

Walk East Village stores and sights

This walk touches historical sites and also highlights the contemporary flavour of the East Village.

Begin at the 1799 church of **St Mark's-in-the-Bowery** and continue along Stuyvesant Street to the **Cooper Union Building** (1859), which was the US's first free college.

Directly ahead, the Astor Place subway station is marked by a fetching beaux-arts-style kiosk. **Cooper Square Books**, just across Fourth Avenue, is one of the largest independent bookstores in New York.

Along East 6th Street you will find a variety of intriguing shops selling unusual clothing, antiques and ornaments. On East 7th Street, **Caffè della Pace**, number 48, draws the East Village's fashionable faces for espresso and snacks. **McSorley's Ale House**, at number 15, has been a local landmark since 1854.

Unusual shop in the East Village

EAST VILLAGE

ELLIS ISLAND

*Ellis Island, where
the future of many a
would-be American
was determined.
Museum displays
now bring to life the
hopes, fears and dis-
appointments of
those newly arrived
immigrants*

▶ ▶ ▶ **Ellis Island**   48C3

Around 100 million present-day Americans have ancestors who passed through Ellis Island, a modest speck of
land in the shadow of the Statue of Liberty in New York's
Upper Bay. From 1892 to 1924 this was the country's
busiest immigration centre.

Later serving as an army hospital and as an enemy alien
detention centre, Ellis Island was closed in 1954 and suffered total neglect until a $160 million refit reopened its
major building as the Ellis Island Immigration Museum in
1990.

Those who arrived at Ellis Island hoping to become
Americans were drawn from Europe's underclasses
(immigrants of means were processed elsewhere and
allowed immediate entry into the US). The elation they
experienced on seeing the Statue of Liberty quickly dissi-
pated as they reached the place nicknamed the 'Island of
Tears' and faced the bureaucracy that stood between
them and American citizenship.

Would-be Americans were screened for contagious diseases and signs of insanity, and questioned about their
relatives and their work skills. Any sign of sickness, or giving the wrong answers, could mean being detained and
perhaps deported (as two per cent of the new arrivals
were). Some also got their first taste of American corruption at Ellis Island: among the many scams were bribes
for immigration officers and over-priced rail tickets for
onward travel in the US.

From statistics projecting the country's future ethnic
make-up to trunks and string bags that carried treasured
possessions, the museum has many eye-opening
exhibits. The jail-like dormitories where detainees were
quartered are singularly depressing, but the taped oral
histories of former arrivals do most to suggest the hopes,
the fears, and the sheer sense of bewilderment that most
of the would-be immigrants experienced as they stepped
into this building.

▶ ▶ ▶ **Empire State Building**   151B2
34th Street at Fifth Avenue
Subway: 34th Street
The World Trade Center may be taller and the Statue of
Liberty a more potent national symbol, but New York's
best-loved and most enduring emblem is the Empire State
Building, over 60 years old and still rising above Midtown
Manhattan with a gracious, ageless aplomb.

As construction mania swept through New York during

The lobby of the Empire State Building

Empire State Building facts
Height: 1472ft.
Weight: 365,000 tons.
Number of bricks:
10 million.
Budget: $60 million.
Actual cost: $40,948,900.
Tallest visitor: King Kong, 1933
Greatest tragedy: Plane crashing into the 79th storey in 1945, killing 14.

Guinness World of Records Exhibition
The Empire State Building may deserve a place in the Guinness Book of Records, but it is debatable whether the Guinness World of Records Exhibition deserves its place on the Empire State Building's concourse level. Inside, the inevitable tourist scrum mills around displays and dioramas on record-breaking achievements that range from the courageous to the grotesque.

the booming 1920s, the Empire State Building was the winner in the financiers' race to create the world's tallest building, snatching the title in 1931 from the Chrysler Building, and holding it until the first World Trade Center tower was finished in 1973.

Although the building rose to 1,250ft (gaining a further 222ft with a TV mast in 1951), it was constructed within only two years. The zoning laws (building regulations) of the time resulted in the tiered design that tempers the

Federal Hall National Memoral. The statue of George Washington commemorates his inauguration as president, which took place in an earlier building on the site

impact of the structure's bulk and contributes greatly to its elegant profile.

Conceived in an economic boom, the building was topped out amid the gloom of the Depression, the Wall Street crash occurring as the 2-acre site – which held the original Waldorf-Astoria Hotel – was being cleared. Consequently, much of the office space remained unrented for years, and most of the building's early income was from tourists visiting for the views.

Admire the art deco fittings of the lobby before descending to the concourse for a ticket and the express elevator to the 86th-floor observation level (the enclosed 102nd-floor level hardly justifies the additional elevator ride to reach it). On a clear day you see for 80 miles.

► **Federal Hall National Memorial** 104B2

Wall and Nassau streets
Subway: Broad Street

Its finely proportioned flight of steps and smart Doric columns impose themselves grandly in the heart of the Financial District, but a sense of history is disappointingly missing from the echoey interior of the 19th-century Federal Hall. Built as the first US Custom House, it later served as a bank before being declared a national memorial in 1939.

If you are exploring the Financial District, Federal Hall ought to be on your itinerary but do not expect anything spectacular. Inside, only a short film and a rather tame collection of exhibits record events that took place on the site: a glass-encased section of balcony railing, on which Washington leaned when addressing the crowds after his inauguration, and a pair of the great man's belt-buckles form the highlights.

► **Film Center Building** 151C1

Ninth Avenue between 44th and 45th streets
Subway: 42nd Street

You may not want to visit any of the 75 film companies who have offices here, but the Film Center Building justifies a call for one of the city's most stunning art deco interiors: its lobby, vestibule and entrance hall – the work of Ely Jacques Kahn. Already an outstanding modernist architect, by the late 1920s Kahn also had a reputation for his distinctive interior decoration based on inter-linked geometric forms – employed here to wondrous effect.

►► **Financial District** IFCA1

The nation's monetary institutions took root in Lower Manhattan from the early 1800s, and as the city grew so did its Financial District, quickly becoming a global centre of trade and commerce. Side by side in this compact area stand grandiose neo-classical buildings, whose form signified their status as repositories of wealth, and the high-rise glass and steel blocks that are the contemporary towers of mammon.

These days, a sombre mood hangs over the Financial District. The exuberant 1980s saw Wall Street (just one of several thoroughfares here, but internationally synonymous with the highest of high finance) yield millions and give birth to the yuppie. But the party was over by the end of the decade, when a succession of scandals put the

The original Federal Hall
The historic significance of the present Federal Hall is eclipsed by that of its predecessor, which housed the first US government and which was where, in April 1789, George Washington was sworn in as the country's first president.

Despite its role in US history, the original building reached such a dilapidated state that it was sold for scrap in 1812.

overly greedy behind bars and heralded the economic uncertainties of the 1990s. Now, besuited wheeler-dealers are as likely to be seen queuing for a felafel from a street vendor as consuming an expense-account lunch.

Facing Wall Street from Broadway, the striking neo-Gothic form of **Trinity Church** has been reminding the Financial District's power-brokers of a force greater than money since the 1840s. Note the bronze doors and the reredos, and continue into the small church museum to look at drawings showing a Manhattan skyline dominated by church spires rather than high-rise towers. In the graveyard, which has been receiving the dead since 1681, lies Alexander Hamilton, the first US treasurer.

Pre-dating Trinity Church by almost a century is Manhattan's only surviving pre-revolutionary church, **St Paul's Chapel**, which faces Fulton Street from Broadway. Laid out in a graceful Georgian style with a surprisingly bright interior, the chapel was regularly visited by George Washington, and dutifully maintains the Washington Pew, where the nation's first president sat during the service marking his inauguration in 1789.

Wall Street's name
An oaken barricade erected by Dutch governor Peter Stuyvesant in 1653 to mark the northern boundary of New Amsterdam and deter British invaders was the 'wall' that gave the world-famous street its name. The wall never quite fulfilled its promise, because its planks were steadily removed to build and repair the wooden homes of settlers. In 1699 its remains were finally demolished by the then well-entrenched British.

Now dwarfed by skyscrapers several times as high, Trinity Church began life as the city's tallest building, at 264ft

FINANCIAL DISTRICT

Map showing the Financial District with labeled locations:

- Civic Center and City Hall
- City Hall Park
- Pace University
- Wall Street Synagogue
- Woolworth Building
- CHURCH STREET
- PARK ROW
- BROOKLYN BRIDGE
- PEARL STREET
- World Financial Center
- WEST STREET
- World Trade Center
- St Paul's Chapel
- BROADWAY
- FULTON STREET
- Fulton Fish Market
- MAIDEN LANE
- Federal Reserve Bank
- Equitable Building
- Chase Manhattan Bank
- South Street Seaport
- Pier 17
- LIBERTY
- TRINITY PLACE
- GREENWICH STREET
- Dow Jones
- St Nicholas Greek Orthodox Church
- Trinity Church
- NASSAU STREET
- Federal Hall National Memorial
- WALL STREET
- BATTERY PARK CITY
- New York Stock Exchange
- BROAD STREET
- WATER STREET
- ELEVATED HIGHWAY
- Hudson
- Museum of American Financial History
- BROADWAY
- Bowling Green
- BEAVER STREET
- U S Customs House (Nat Mus of the American Indian)
- Fraunces Tavern
- Jeanette Park
- BATTERY PLACE
- STATE ST
- WHITEHALL
- Battery Park
- Castle Clinton
- BROOKLYN BATTERY TUNNEL
- Shrine of St Elizabeth Ann Seton
- East River
- Verrazano Statue
- Staten Island Ferry Terminal
- N
- 0 — 400 m
- 1   2   3
- A / B / C

Walk Financial District architecture

OUR NATIONAL DEBT:
1,005,561,484,000
OUR Family share $ 52,048
THE NATIONAL DEBT CLOCK
...ONAL DEBT INCREASE PER SECOND $ 13,000

Encompassing historic churches, and financial and architectural landmarks, this walk is a good way to explore the varied facets of the Financial District.

Begin at **Trinity Church** (page 103) and continue along Wall Street, stopping at **Federal Hall** and detouring along Broad Street for the **Stock Exchange** (page 182). Continue along

Nassau Street for **Chase Manhattan Bank**, the first international-style structure in Lower Manhattan.

Across Maiden Lane, you can gaze (advance reservations essential, tel: 720 6130) over 11,000 tonnes of gold – the wealth of many nations – stored below ground at the **Federal Reserve Bank**. Otherwise, examine the richly decorative ironwork of the enormous building's façade.

On the corner of Broadway, the much-detested 1915 **Equitable Building** rises for 40 sheer storeys; this was the first high-rise office block and the first to plunge its neighbouring buildings – and much of the street – into darkness.

Continue along Broadway for **St Paul's Chapel** (page 103) and finish the walk at the **World Trade Center** (page 193).

■ **Tussles during the 19th century among Eastern Europe's Slavic peoples – Poles, Ukrainians and Russians – and the totalitarian suppression of more recent times, helped create two of New York's most stridently nationalistic communities: the Poles and the Ukrainians, who now co-exist peaceably alongside their former foes, the Russians …■**

Polish-Americans Struggles against colonial oppression in their own country made New York's Poles natural allies of the Americans in the revolutionary battles with the British. Later, New York offered refuge to those who had led an unsuccessful Polish republican uprising in 1830. The 234 who arrived were among Poland's finest minds and gave New York its first Polish cultural institutions.

By contrast, the mass Polish migrations of later years were drawn from the peasantry, who found jobs in the industrialised Greenpoint area of Brooklyn. Some ran the shops and restaurants which became community focal points, and by the 1930s Polish-Americans were visible in every sphere of New York life.

The Ukrainians Enforced military service in the Tsar's army caused many Ukrainians to flee their Russian-dominated homeland during the 1800s. Arriving in New York with their families, they turned a section of what is now the East Village into the world's largest urban Ukrainian community by 1919.

Russian immigrants The bulk of Russian immigration into New York was formed by Jews fleeing persecution under the Tsar (see page 139). More symbolic of the effect of European political upheavals, though, were the Russian aristocrats who arrived in New York as Leon Trotsky (here since the abortive 1905 revolution) left for Moscow to help the Bolsheviks seize power. Typical of moneyed immigrants, the newly arrived Russians quickly became integrated into New York high society and married into the establishment – a far cry from the ex-Soviet Russians who settled in Brighton Beach during the 1970s and 1980s (see page 75).

The Pulaski and Kosciuszko bridges
Two of the bridges – the Pulaski and the Kosciuszko – linking Brooklyn and Queens bear the names of Poles who aided the American cause in the Revolutionary War. Cavalry expert Casimar Pulaski was noted for his bravery in battle (he died in an attack on the British); the engineering skills of Thaddeus Kosciuszko were crucial in preparing the anti-British fortifications at West Point and Saratoga.

105

Founded in the 1920s by emigrés who were missing their native Russia, the famous Russian Tea Room is now favoured by New York high society. Ethnic specialities, from caviar to tea from the samovar, can be enjoyed in elegant surroundings

FLATIRON BUILDING

23 Skidoo
A story goes that in the days when well-dressed ladies had skirts to their ankles, high winds would find voyeurs lingering outside the Flatiron Building on 23rd Street hoping to spot female legs exposed by the breeze. The shouts of the police when moving the gentlemen on are thought to be the origin of the term '23 skidoo'.

The Flatiron Building – an unmistakable Fifth Avenue landmark

▶   **Flatiron Building**   *151A2*
Broadway and Fifth Avenue at 23rd Street
Subway: 23rd Street
Architect Daniel H Burnham solved the problem of fitting a building into the triangular plot of land where Broadway crosses Fifth Avenue with the most logical solution: a triangular building. It was the world's tallest (285ft) on its completion in 1902, and was one of the first to be erected around a steel frame – the basic support of every subsequent skyscraper.

Nowadays, it is not height or building techniques that make the Flatiron Building one of New York's most-loved structures but its pretty French Renaissance features and the fact that its limestone body tapers to an impossibly slender 6ft-wide corner curve on 23rd Street.

▶ **The Forbes Galleries** *113C2*

Fifth Avenue between 12th and 13th streets
Subway: 14th Street
Even in New York, few magazine publishers have broken the speed record for ballooning across the US or have hurtled along Fifth Avenue on a motorbike. Malcolm S Forbes did both of those things, and a lot more, in a career which began by accident and left him with wealth estimated, at his death, to be in excess of $700 million.

Born in 1919, two years after his father had founded *Forbes*, a ground-breaking magazine of investigative financial journalism, Forbes had turned the ailing title into a thriving concern by the time he took it over in 1964. One of the secrets of his success was a genius for garnering maximum publicity for himself and the magazine. Through the 1970s the media doted on Forbes and his colourful activities, which ranged from lavish parties and his mania for motorbikes and balloons to his offbeat collecting interests.

The Forbes Galleries bear the fruits of Forbes' quirky collecting passion. They occupy the ground floor of the Forbes Magazine building. Among the displays are 500 model boats and submarines (some of them in bathtubs) viewed to the accompaniment of what purports to be the sound of the Battle of Jutland. Some 12,000 model soldiers are arranged in battle-ready poses, and there is an extraordinary room of trophies awarded for achievements such as having the best pure-bred bull of 1878 and the best 5 acres of swedes grown with Bradburn's manure.

The Presidential Papers room holds less eccentric material, drawn from the Forbes collection of 3,000 historical documents, while another special room displays gem-encrusted Easter eggs – and scores of other priceless *objets d'art* – made by master jeweller-goldsmith Peter Carl Fabergé for the last two Tsars of Russia.

▶▶ **Fraunces Tavern** *104A2*

54 Pearl Street
Subway: Bowling Green, South Ferry or Broad Street
A Federal-style brick building which looks like a dolls' house beneath the glass-and-steel high-rises of the Financial District, the original Fraunces Tavern (what stands here now is a re-creation) was a hotbed of subversion during the 18th century, when its customers included George Washington and his revolutionary friends.

At the successful completion of the Revolutionary War, Washington made a famously emotional farewell to his officers here after a meal in the Long Room – a scene re-created with period furnishings on the tavern's second floor, while other objects and paintings from the revolutionary period are displayed on the third floor.

Hard to believe it may be, but the tavern became the unofficial seat of several government bodies during the earliest days of nationhood, and spent three years as the recognised base of the Department of Foreign Affairs, the War Department and the US Treasury, before being unceremoniously sold to a Brooklyn butcher.

Visit the tavern around lunchtime, when the atmosphere is enhanced by the smell of food wafting up from the ground-floor restaurant, a cosy niche favoured by Financial District wheeler-dealers with clients to impress.

107

A bomb at the Fraunces Tavern
George Washington was not the last revolutionary to make a point at the Fraunces Tavern. In January 1975, the building was rocked by a bomb which killed four Wall Street businessmen and left 55 people injured. Responsibility was claimed by an underground group called the FALN, in revenge for the US's resistance to Puerto Rican independence.

■ **For those with money, and preferably a well-known face (or name) to go with it, New York can easily become the ultimate playground. What follows is a very selective Manhattan list for the well-heeled person about town. For those visitors who need to budget carefully for every cab ride, a peek inside one or two of these establishments might at least offer a brief glance of the good life ...■**

Café des Artistes (67th Street at Central Park West, tel: 877 3500). A mural of frolicking nymphs, painted in 1934 by Howard Chandler Christy, contributes to the Café des Artistes' reputation as New York's most romantic dining spot. The nymphs have yet to lose their allure, and the café's rural French cuisine is divine. Expect to spend from $80 to $120 for dinner for two. A less costly alternative is the café's bar, the scene of much refined chit-chat and cocktail imbibing.

Afternoon tea at the Pierre (Fifth Avenue at 61st Street, tel: 838 8000). Even if they are lodging elsewhere, discriminating visitors to New York seeking a taste of the high life should try afternoon tea at the Pierre Hotel. This long-established ritual takes place beneath the Pierre's striking rotunda, its two-storey-high walls decorated by Edward Melcarth's remarkable mural which appears to be a potted documentation of mankind's history. The hotel's doting staff offer you a choice from a dozen or so fine teas and bear plates of melt-in-the-mouth scones. This slightly decadent treat costs around $20.

Getting around luxury New York

When money is no object, the hurly-burly of Manhattan can be avoided – or at least temporarily forgotten – by travelling between expensive stops in a chauffeur-driven stretch limousine. Equipped with VCRs, telephones and bars – and other features that make Manhattan's traffic-stopping gridlock almost seem attractive – stretch limos can be hired from around $50 per hour. Carey Limousines (tel: 599 1122) and VIP Prestige (tel: 868 8999) are among the operators awaiting your call.

Four Seasons (East 52nd Street between Park and Lexington avenues, tel: 754 9494). Architecture buffs and art fans will find something to please them at the Four Seasons, though the serious trade here is power-lunching corporate executives – plus a sprinkling of lawyers, politicians and publishers – with bottomless expense accounts. On the ground floor of Mies van der Rohe's landmark Seagram Building, this Philip Johnson-designed restaurant features a large Picasso tapestry and other noted modern pieces. The lunch menu is designed to be good but simple, so it does not detract from the deals being struck across the tables. At dinner, the chef excels himself with exceptional Continental creations, some of which are prepared at your table. A full dinner here is liable to cost $100 per person; lunch should be a comparatively modest $40.

The 21 Club (West 52nd Street between Fifth and Sixth avenues, tel: 582 7200). A row of cast-iron model jockeys simulate a horse-race along the exterior of the 21 Club, which opened on New Year's Eve 1929 and was – in those Prohibition times – just one of scores of speakeasies lining 52nd Street. The others quickly disappeared but the 21 Club endured, maturing into a favourite watering hole of the New York establishment.

Despite a complete refurbishment in the 1980s, the 21 Club's dark, wood-panelled walls and deep-pile carpets offer a picture of old-style luxury New York that is rarely found today. Although appearances suggest otherwise, the 21 Club is not a club, although you should not show up without a reservation. Many regulars come here to confirm their place in the New York social pecking order as much as to dine: the food tends to vary in quality. You might try the '21 Burger' at $25, or the pre-theatre *prix-fixe* dinner at around $40.

Rainbow Room (30 Rockefeller Plaza, 50th Street between Fifth and Sixth avenues, tel: 632 5100). With a big band playing the music of Gershwin and Cole Porter, and a 65th-floor view of the Manhattan skyline, you will experience New York's romantic side when you spend an evening at the Rainbow Room.

When it opened in 1934, the Rainbow Room was a glamorous crown atop the new Rockefeller Center. A $20-million facelift in the 1980s has brought back some of the grandeur, although the serious Manhattan socialite might well consider the place overly tourist-oriented.

Perhaps the best order of doing things at the Rainbow Room is drinks, dinner, shaking a leg on the revolving dance-floor, and finally returning to your table for a dessert of baked Alaska. Reservations need to be made six weeks in advance.

Sightseeing by helicopter
One way to beat the crowds at the Statue of Liberty or the World Trade Center is to view such attractions, and the rest of Manhattan, from a helicopter. Sightseeing helicopter flights are operated day and night by Island Helicopter Sightseeing (tel: 683 4575) and Liberty Helicopter Tours (tel: 800/542 9933 or 967 6464).

109

Tea at the opulent Pierre is a good way to experience luxury New York without breaking your budget

Having made his fortune in Pittsburgh, the notoriously ruthless and unpopular industrialist Henry Clay Frick moved to New York, where he had this elaborate mansion built to house his superb collection of European art

Moving pictures
Each summer, Henry Frick had his fantastic art collection packed into crates and transported in a special railway carriage so he could enjoy it while staying on his estate in Massachusetts. Asked if he was worried about losing the priceless canvases through an accident in transit, Frick allegedly replied, 'No, they're insured'.

▶▶ **Frick Collection**   151D2
70th Street at Fifth Avenue
Subway: 68th Street
In his day, Henry Clay Frick was a little-loved union-busting robber baron who made a fortune through coke, steel and mean-minded business practices. Ironically, the Frick Collection of 14th- to 19th-century European art, housed on the ground floor of the French-style mansion in which Frick spent the last five years of his life (he died in 1919) is perhaps the most loved of New York's many art troves.

The absence of ropes, descriptive texts, and other museum trappings is intended to make seeing the collection akin to visiting a private house, though guards hover in every nook and cranny. The collection is a triumph of quality over quantity and there is not a single painting in the 19 rooms that does not deserve its wall space.

Highlights are many, and naturally vary according to individual taste. Few could fail to be impressed, however, by Gainsborough's *The Mall in St James's Park*, a refined vision of privileged promenaders that stands out in a dining room lined by 18th-century English portraiture.

The living hall has two particularly potent canvases: Titian's *Portrait of a Man in a Red Cap* and El Greco's *St Jerome*. But it is on the walls of the west gallery that the cream of the collection is hung: two of Turner's studies of northern European ports resonate on facing walls, close to Rembrandt's 1658 *Portrait of a Young Artist – Self-Portrait* and the same artist's much debated (its authenticity is disputed) *Polish Rider*.

After leaving the final room, take a break in the garden court before starting through the collections once again, this time concentrating on the outstanding sculptures, tapestries and decorative arts exhibits.

▶ **Fulton Fish Market**   104C3
South and Fulton streets
Subway: Fulton Street
If you are an insomniac or a very early riser, be at the Fulton Fish Market (tel: 669 9416) at 6am on the first or third Thursday of each month for a behind-the-scenes tour of the 1907 'Tin Building'. Here truckloads of squirming fish and creeping crustaceans are unloaded and prepared for sale to the city's classiest restaurants.

Assuming you survive the smell, it is unlikely that the sight of all those dismembered fins and discarded fish guts will make you hungry – but if it does, there are plenty of early-morning seafood eateries nearby.

▶ **General Grant Memorial**   IFCC5
Riverside Drive at 122nd Street
Subway: 116th Street
The largest mausoleum in the US, its grey granite form rising 150ft beside the Hudson River and its entrance fronted by six Doric columns, the General Grant Memorial (commonly known as Grant's Tomb) holds the remains – in 9-ton marble sarcophagi – of Ulysses S Grant and his wife. As commander-in-chief of the victorious Union forces in the Civil War, Grant achieved enormous fame: an estimated million people lined the route of his funeral procession in 1885. This over-ambitious attempt to copy the great European mausoleums was completed in 1897.

Inside, a chilled atmosphere prevails and your footsteps echo as you walk around reading the brief accounts of Grant's distinguished military service and his much less successful eight-year tenure as the US's 18th president.

► **Gracie Mansion** 187C2

East End Avenue at 88th Street
Subway: 86th Street
The official residence of the mayor of New York since 1942, Gracie Mansion was built in 1799 as a country retreat for shipping magnate Archibald Gracie. Following the collapse of his business, Gracie sold the mansion and it spent an ignominious period as a refreshment stand before being purchased by the city. Despite the numerous modifications made over the years, recent renovations have made the mansion a finer example of Federal architecture (the first architectural style considered distinctly American) than it ever was in its infancy. The house can only be fully appreciated on guided tours, usually conducted on Wednesdays from April to October (reservations necessary; tel: 570 4751).

The grandiose mausoleum of Civil War general Ulysses S Grant was inspired by Napoleon's tomb in Paris

Henderson Place
In a cul-de-sac on the north side of 86th Street, close to the Gracie Mansion, stands the lovely row of 24 Queen Anne style houses that constitute the Henderson Place Historic District. The houses were commissioned during the 1880s by fur-hat manufacturer, John C Henderson, to provide homes for 'persons of moderate means'.

Greenwich Village second-hand shops may not offer such good bargains as less fashionable areas of the city, but they are hard to beat for sheer variety

Grace Church
One of the few things in Greenwich Village likely to bring to mind the European Middle Ages is the 1846 Grace Church, on Broadway between 10th and 11th streets. The church's finely proportioned Gothic Revival design – among the earliest examples of the style in the US – helped its architect, James Renwick, win the commission for the larger, grander St Patrick's Cathedral in Midtown Manhattan. Set on Broadway's first curve, the church's spire could originally be seen from as far south as what is now Battery Park.

▶ ▶ ▶ Greenwich Village

IFCC1

No place in New York has a greater cultural aura than Greenwich Village. For almost 100 years this has been a breeding ground and rallying point for the nation's most inventive and imaginative minds.

From its earliest days, Greenwich Village has kept its distance from mainstream New York life. Its first homes were built to enable the wealthy to escape the outbreaks of disease which were common in the 1790s, pushing back the boundaries of the city which, until then, had been contained within present-day Lower Manhattan.

By the late 1800s, the rich were moving north again and their Greenwich Village town houses were being converted into shops, factories and rooming houses for foreign immigrants. By the turn of the 20th century, Greenwich Village's diverse ethnic mix had fostered an atmosphere of tolerance which, coupled with low rents, attracted the unconventional elements that gave birth to the country's first, and eventually most celebrated, Bohemian enclave.

Over three decades, writers and artists from Walt Whitman to Edward Hopper were to turn American culture upside down from their Greenwich Village bases. During the 1950s, the earliest Beat writers began taking Greenwich Village still further away from the materialist values of middle America, but rents were soon on the rise as new transport links made Greenwich Village the target of moneyed professionals in search of a well-placed characterful neighbourhood.

Living in Greenwich Village today certainly requires financial security, but the lawyers and investment bankers who have flocked here have certainly not dampened the community spirit or Greenwich Village's rebellious streak. A Bohemian mood still percolates through its innumerable Italian cafés and restaurants, even though today most Greenwich Village visitors are more likely to be partying suburbanites than impoverished souls at creativity's cutting edge.

Continued on page 116.

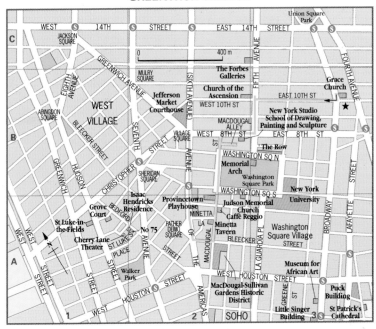

GREENWICH VILLAGE

Walk The heart of Greenwich Village

From Grace Church in the east, this walk passes through the heart of Greenwich Village, concluding at the foot of Christopher Street.

Leaving Grace Church, walk along 10th Street to the 1840 **Church of the Ascension**, a Gothic brownstone designed by English architect Richard Upjohn, also responsible for Trinity Church in the Financial District.

Shop-lined 8th Street holds the New York Studio School of Drawing, Painting and Sculpture, first home of the Whitney Museum. This was founded in 1931 by Gertrude Vanderbilt Whitney; her own studio was a converted stable at 17½ MacDougal Alley.

In business since 1785, **Caffè Reggio** is the oldest of many cafés lining MacDougal Street; its dark interior has been seen in films such as *Godfather II* and *Serpico*.

On Sixth Avenue, Village Square is dominated by the gables, turrets and towers of the 1877 **Jefferson Market Courthouse**, now a library. Off the square runs **Christopher Street**; bars, shops and eateries make this one of the Village's liveliest thoroughfares.

Washington Square Park

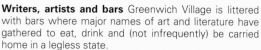

■ **Like delis and subway stations, bars are an essential facet of New York life. From crusty Bohemian hangouts to elegant hotel cocktail lounges, New York bars come in all shapes, sizes and forms. Miss them and you are definitely missing New York. (For guidance on New York bar-going etiquette, see pages 223–5) ...■**

Writers, artists and bars Greenwich Village is littered with bars where major names of art and literature have gathered to eat, drink and (not infrequently) be carried home in a legless state.

On his New York stays, poet Dylan Thomas held court at the **White Horse Tavern** (567 Hudson Street). One night in 1953, a drunken Thomas spluttered 'I've had my 18th whisky, and I think that's the record'. Within a few days he was dead. It was Norman Mailer who turned the White Horse Tavern into a writers' watering hole, but he chose the **Lion's Head** (59 Christopher Street) as his campaign headquarters when he ran for mayor in 1959. Now, as then, the Lion's Head is a haunt of journalists and authors, whose book jackets line the wall.

No longer in its original location, the **Cedar Tavern** (82 University Place) was a meeting place for the painters of what became the New York School of Abstract Expressionism. As Jackson Pollock and others loudly lamented the state of art, Beat writers such as Allen Ginsberg and William Burroughs eavesdropped from neighbouring tables.

Bars for beer-drinkers Beer connoisseurs will welcome the 200 imported varieties sold at the **Peculier Pub** (145 Bleecker Street). The wooden bench tables here often overflow with New York University students. For New York's best brewed-on-the-premises beer, head for the **Manhattan Brewing Company** (42 Thompson Street), which boasts a fine selection of invigorating ales.

Bars with a view The Manhattan skyline looks better than ever when viewed with a cocktail in your hand. At **City Lights**, on the 107th floor of the World Trade Center, a pianist tinkles the ivories, smartly dressed dancers glide across the floor, and the views stretch for miles. In Midtown Manhattan, try the 39th-floor **Top of the Sixes** (666 Fifth Avenue), where the drinks are accompanied by free snacks and a splendid panorama.

Bars for the good-looking New York's singles bars are no longer dominated by hopeful lone souls arranged along bar stools. These days, the accent is on having fun while seeking new friends. Investigate the **Coffee Shop** (29 Union Square West), favourite stamping ground of the young and beautiful, with a long, snaking bar, Brazilian food and loud music. Alternatively, try the equally hip **Fez** (downstairs from the Time Café on Lafayette at Great Jones Street), with its good jazz and basement dance

New York's oldest bar
In business since 1854, McSorley's Old Ale House (15 East 7th Street) is justified in its claim to be New York's oldest surviving bar. For years a men-only establishment patronised by career drinkers from the Bowery's Skid Row, McSorley's began admitting women in 1970 and now pulls a young, mainly student crowd.

floor. Mingle among fashionable faces at **Live Bait** (14 East 23rd Street), a bar and southern-food eatery decked out as a fishing shack.

Real bars A basement bar with absolutely no frills, **The Dugout** (Third Avenue between 13th and 14th streets) is a serious drinker's delight, but might be a bit too real for many New York first-timers. A more comfortable option is **Costello's** (225 East 44th Street), the best of several Irish-flavoured Midtown Manhattan bars. On the Upper West Side, the **All State Café** (250 West 72nd Street) is a dimly lit, wood-panelled saloon with few equals as a place for a long evening's drinking in the true New York style.

Hotel bars It is by no means only guests who imbibe in hotel bars. Many are favoured by locals for their elegant surroundings and the fact that you do not have to shout to hold a conversation. The **Gramercy Park Hotel Bar** (2 Lexington Avenue) is one of a dying breed: a piano bar with a well-turned-out clientele and knowledgeable bar staff. For spotting celebrity guests, try the **Round Bar** of the **Royalton** (44th Street between Fifth and Sixth avenues), or the Conservatory Bar at the **Mayflower Hotel** (Central Park West at 61st Street).

Marie's Crisis Café
Few places symbolise changing New York better than Marie's Crisis Café (59 Grove Street). Nowadays, do not be surprised to find this lively bar packed by gay men singing hit songs from famous Broadway shows. Two centuries ago it was a home of Thomas Paine, whose publication, *Crisis*, helped fuel the American Revolution.

115

Conviviality, Irish-style, at McSorley's Old Ale House

GREENWICH VILLAGE

Greenwich Village writers
James Agee, James Baldwin, Willa Cather, James Fenimore Cooper, Hart Crane, Theodore Dreiser, e e cummings, Henry James, Ruth McKenney, Herman Melville, Edna St Vincent Millay, Eugene O'Neill, Anaïs Nin, John Dos Passos, Edgar Allan Poe, John Reed, William Styron, Mark Twain, Tennessee Williams, Edmund Wilson, Thomas Wolfe.

Tex-Mex food, margaritas and tequila are the specialities at the Caliente Cab Company on Seventh Avenue

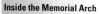

Inside the Memorial Arch
In 1916, maverick artist Marcel Duchamp and friends forced their way through the locked door of Washington Square Park's Memorial Arch and climbed the 110 steps to the top. Once there, they hung balloons, Chinese lanterns and banners proclaiming Greenwich Village as the independent republic of New Bohemia. After eating a picnic, Duchamp and company were forced down by militiamen.

With somewhat less spectacle, a man is thought to have lived in the arch for seven months during World War II. He was noticed only when he hung his washing out to dry.

Continued from page 112.

There is no better place to begin exploring Greenwich Village than **Washington Square Park**▶▶▶ where jugglers, unicyclists and chess-players put on a show for the families, visitors and street urchins who promenade along the park's pathways.

On the park's northern side, the triumphal **Washington Memorial Arch**▶▶ stands at the foot of Fifth Avenue, 77ft high and erected by Stanford White in 1892 on a spot where he had earlier raised a wooden marker to celebrate the centenary of George Washington's inauguration.

What the white marble arch does not commemorate, however, are the 22,000 people who were buried beneath the park when it served as a mass cemetery during epidemics. There is also no reminder of the fact that during the early 1800s some of the park's trees were used for public hangings.

Besides ending hangings and covering over the burial ground, the creation of the park in 1827 greatly increased the social *cachet* of the immediate area. Smart terraces of town houses rose around it, the only survivors being **The Row**▶▶ on the north side: note their porticos, shuttered windows and elongated stoops – steps up to the front door, emphasising the distinction between the owner's entrance and the servants' entrance at ground level.

To the park's south and east are a few of the buildings of New York University. With 14 separate schools scattered throughout Greenwich Village, the university is one of the city's major landowners.

Continued on page 118.

■ With the exception of San Francisco, there is probably no better city than New York in which to be a homosexual man or woman. Whether quietly absorbed into mainstream life or visible through a host of information and support organisations, gay men and lesbians are now a firmly established feature of New York's social landscape ...■

Homosexuality has been around in New York for a long time, but has not always found the acceptance it enjoys today. The census of 1880 found five men in prison for 'unspeakable crimes against nature' – a euphemism of the time for homosexual activity .

The early gay community By the 1930s, a small network of gay rendezvous points had spread across Manhattan; places where discretion was uppermost and which remained invisible to the heterosexual world.

In the period following World War II, when the values of family life were extolled to the hilt, gays and lesbians increasingly felt the backlash. Sexual minorities were pilloried in the press and the police were urged to clamp down on what was perceived as a menace to society.

The Stonewall riot and after In June 1969, a police raid on the Stonewall Inn in Greenwich Village was resisted by the customers and met with a hail of missiles from the patrons of other gay nightspots near by. The two days of rioting that followed became a turning point in gay history: for the first time, the community had risen up to defend itself, and its new-found solidarity led to the founding of the Gay Pride movement.

The movement's many achievements are celebrated annually by the Gay Pride Parade (see page 27), while the gay community has been at the forefront in raising public awareness of Aids and condemning the US government's inadequate response to the crisis.

Anti-violence helpline
Homophobic violence is increasingly common in the city, and it seems that New York's gays and lesbians will need to muster all the strength they can to protect, and build on, the hard-won freedoms of the last 25 years. An emergency telephone line is available to victims of such violence (tel: 807 0197).

117

Specialist shops aimed at the gay community find a ready market in New York. This gay clothing store is in Greenwich Village

Stroll: Greenwich Village

The maze of side streets off Christopher Street holds some of Greenwich Village's quietest and prettiest corners. Take time to admire the lovely row of brick and brownstone Italianate houses on St Luke's Place, and venture into Bedford Street for the Isaacs-Hendricks Residence (see page 130) and the 9ft-wide house at number 75½. Its dainty dimensions did not deter writer John Barrymore, playwright Edna St Vincent Millay or screen star Cary Grant from living in it at various times.

Its subway station may have preserved its original handsome blue tiles (above), but Bleecker Street today (right) has little to recall its importance in the 1950s and 1960s. At that time its cafés and folk clubs reverberated with the pioneering ideas and developing sounds of a whole new postwar subculture, kicking off with the Beat writers and later including folk singers who were to become household names all over the world

Continued from page 116.

Not content with his Memorial Arch, Stanford White also erected the **Judson Memorial Church►**, on the park's south side, in largely Romanesque style. More noteworthy than the architecture are the church's stained-glass windows, the work of Hudson River artist John LaFarge.

A block away, on MacDougal Street, the unremarkable exterior of the **Provincetown Playhouse** does nothing to suggest that the group based here forged new ground in American drama in the 1910s, helped in no small measure by the talents of Eugene O'Neill. Just south, on the corner of Minetta Lane, the **Minetta Tavern►** displays photos and mementoes from the dawn of Greenwich Village Bohemia.

Running across MacDougal Street, **Bleecker Street►►►** holds the best of Greenwich Village's bars and clubs, though nothing these days matches the stirrings of the early 1960s when local folk clubs spawned talents such as Bob Dylan, Judy Collins and Arlo Guthrie. A decade earlier, the Bleecker Street cafés had reverberated to the performance poetry and drunken debates of embryonic Beat writers like Gregory Corso, Jack Kerouac, Allen Ginsberg and William Burroughs (see page 119).

More restaurants, bakeries and cafés line Bleecker Street as it continues westwards across Sixth Avenue into the West Village, the main artery of which, Christopher Street, cuts westwards from Village Square and the extraordinary **Jefferson Market Courthouse** (see page 113), towards the Hudson River.

On Christopher Street and in its vicinity are numerous gay bars, clubs and bookshops. At number 53 was the **Stonewall Inn**, which gave its name to the 'Stonewall Riots', which united the local gay community in 1969 (see page 117).

The Beats

■ A handful of characters frequenting the bars around New York's Columbia University and Greenwich Village in the 1940s evolved into what became the Beat Generation, the country's first post-war subculture and one that used drugs, jazz and Eastern religion to inspire the new forms of writing which, for a brief time in the 1950s, seemed set to tear American society to pieces ...■

If the Beat Generation had a starting point it was the West End Café (on Broadway between 113th and 114th streets) in the mid-1940s. Here teenaged student Allen Ginsberg, 30-year-old William Burroughs and 22-year-old Jack Kerouac swopped ideas, later adjourning to an apartment at 421 West 118th Street to hold animated discussions to the sound of the newly emerged bebop jazz.

Beat writing Ginsberg began writing 'serious' poetry, Kerouac worked on his breathless prose style, and Burroughs steadily assembled the pieces that would evolve into his novels. By the end of the 1940s, the chief hangouts were the San Remo (189 Bleecker Street) and the Cedar Tavern (then at 24 University Place).

Success and notoriety Ginsberg was living in San Francisco in 1956 when, besides working for an advertising agency and studying Buddhism, he wrote his epic poem, *Howl*, describing characters and ideas from the last few years. The poem was published to enthusiastic reviews – and an obscenity trial which greatly increased the notoriety of 'the Beats', as did *On the Road*, Kerouac's novel published the next year.

When Ginsberg and Kerouac returned to New York, the *Village Voice* proclaimed 'Witless Madcaps Come Home to Roost', and the events of a decade earlier quickly became, and continue to be, a source of legend.

Why 'Beat Generation'? Ginsberg and another writer, John Clellon Holmes, conceived the term 'Beat Generation', partly from the 'Lost Generation' of the 1920s, and partly from a Times Square junkie who always described himself as 'beat'. When Holmes' novel *Go* was published in 1952, the New York Times reviewer seized on the handy phrase, but this did not help Ginsberg, Burroughs or Kerouac find publishers for their work.

119

Allen Ginsberg (left) listens to a speaker at a 1960s anti-Vietnam War rally near Tompkins Square Park

■ **For every major religious edifice such as St Patrick's Cathedral or the Cathedral Church of St John the Divine, New York has dozens more places of worship which seldom receive a visit from passing travellers. Many of these are mentioned in the A to Z section of this book, but those described below are especially notable for illustrating the city's many forms of church architecture or for highlighting New York's endless ethnic and religious diversity ...■**

120

Same church, different religion
Indicative of the changing ethnic make-up of the Lower East Side, the 1895 Russian Orthodox Cathedral at 4th Street between Avenues C and D is now San Isidro y San Leandro Orthodox Catholic Church of the Hispanic Rite, serving the Lower East Side's now predominantly Puerto Rican population.

The statue of Shinran-Shonin outside the New York Buddhist Church

Greek Orthodox Just one of many churches in the Financial District which predate the high-rise glass towers and embody something other than materialist values, the **St Nicholas Greek Orthodox Church** (155 Cedar Street) is New York's earliest Greek church. The compact interior is decorated with brass chandeliers, icons, and the model ships which are reminders of its original seafaring congregation (St Nicholas being the patron saint of sailors). As the Greek community prospered and moved northwards, the **Greek Orthodox Cathedral of the Holy Trinity** (74th Street near First Avenue) became its religious focal point, in 1931. The interior of the stylish Romanesque church holds another trove of icons.

Jewish Also in what is now the Financial District, New York's first Jews established the city's earliest synagogue some 300 years ago on what became William Street. A replica of their 20-seat shrine can be seen on the fourth floor of the **Wall Street Synagogue** (47 Beekman Street). As Jews from many parts of Europe became established in New York, the city's first Jewish architect raised the **Central Synagogue** (Lexington Avenue at 55th Street). Its rough-hewn Moorish facade, complete with onion domes and banded arches, was intended to reflect the experience of Jews in Moorish Spain. With a colourful interior decorated in shades of red, blue and ochre, the synagogue was completed in 1872.

Roman Catholic Just north of the Central Synagogue, architect Bertram Goodhue produced an accomplished and imposing façade for the **Church of St Vincent Ferrer** (Lexington Avenue at 66th Street) in 1918, but saved his best touches for the interior. Note the reredos and Charles Connick's exceptional stained-glass windows.

Russian Orthodox The seat of the Russian Orthodox Church in North America is in New York's Upper East Side, where the **St Nicholas Orthodox Cathedral** (97th Street near Fifth Avenue) was erected at the turn of the century, financed by donations collected across the Tsarist Russian empire. The cathedral's splendidly ornate style – red brick patterned with blue and yellow tiles and five bulging onion domes – is based on the church architecture of 17th-century Moscow.

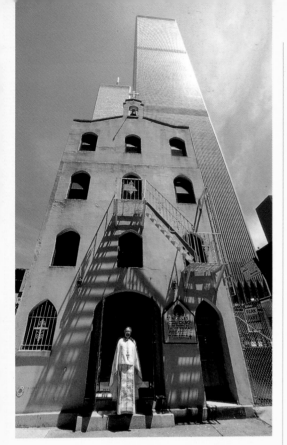

An embarrassed church architect
With Grace Church (see page 112) and St Patrick's Cathedral (page 150), church architect James Renwick made his name. Among his less acclaimed works, however, was the 1846 **Calvary Church** (Park Avenue at 21st Street). The church still stands but without its steeples, which Renwick allegedly tore down through embarrassment in 1860.

Be they Greek Orthodox (above left) or Buddhist (above), the city's places of worship mirror its diverse ethnic make-up

Muslim The design of St Nicholas is strikingly different from the drab buildings around it, as is that of the **Mosque of the Islamic Culture Center** (Third Avenue at 96th Street), which also deviates from the usual grid-style alignment of Manhattan buildings by being pointed towards Mecca. The first permanent place of worship for New York Muslims, the $12-million mosque was largely financed by the government of Kuwait.

Buddhist On the other side of Central Park, you might easily go right past the **New York Buddhist Church** (Riverside Drive between 105th and 106th streets) without realising the fact – were it not for the unmistakable bronze statue of Shinran-Shonin, the 13th-century founder of a Buddhist sect, which stands outside.

Abyssinian Baptist Harlem's **Abyssinian Baptist Church** (138th Street near Lenox Avenue) was founded in 1808 by, and to serve, New York's black community and quickly acquired the largest black congregation of any church in the US. Past ministers include Harlem's first black member of congress, Adam Clayton Powell. His struggles to end racial discrimination and raise African-American living standards made him a nationally controversial, but locally revered, figure from the 1940s. The present Gothic-style church dates from 1923 and has a display recording Powell's achievements.

Sarabeth's Kitchen
It may sound like an honest-to-goodness coffee shop, but Sarabeth's Kitchen's prestigious address (Madison Avenue and 92nd Street) can only mean one thing: gourmet food to delight the palates and lighten the wallets of Upper East Side residents. It all began with marmalade, made to a recipe passed down through eight generations of Sarabeth's family. Now Sarabeth's Kitchen (with another branch on the Upper West Side; see page 281) is where many locals start their day, breakfasting on home-made muffins, waffles and pancakes. Lunch and dinner are also served, and Sarabeth's Kitchen even bakes gourmet dog biscuits for the pooch with class.

▶▶▶ **Guggenheim Museum** 187C1

Fifth Avenue between 88th and 89th streets
Subway: 86th Street

A member of an ultra-wealthy New York family whose fortunes were founded on copper and silver mines, Solomon R Guggenheim followed the usual track of an Upper East Side millionaire with more money than he knew what to do with by dabbling in art. Guggenheim's first purchases were unremarkable Old Masters, but his tastes and his acquisitions were changed radically in 1927 when he met Baroness Hilla Rebay von Ehrenwiesen, an outspoken and energetic enthusiast of the European abstract art scene.

Through the baroness, Guggenheim met artists such as Robert Delaunay, Fernand Léger and Albert Gleizes, and quickly amassed a superb stock of their work, and works by other contemporary artists, particularly Wassily Kandinsky, hanging them on the walls of the rooms he occupied with his wife at New York's Plaza Hotel. At the suggestion of the baroness, Guggenheim commissioned architect Frank Lloyd Wright to design and build a museum to be called (with an ideological correctness insisted on by the baroness) the Museum of Non-Objective Painting.

Guggenheim had been dead for 10 years by the time Wright's extraordinary achievement opened in 1959, its name changed to the Solomon R Guggenheim Museum. By this time, Guggenheim's initial collection of abstracts had been swelled and greatly broadened in scope by purchases and bequests, particularly the Thannhauser Collection of impressionist and post-impressionist paintings.

The best way to see the collection is to take the elevator to the top level and slowly work your way down the museum's remarkable spiral ramp. This means that you can study the exhibits, look over the parapet to the lobby below, and finish up where you began without ever losing your way. Precisely what will be on show when you visit has been scheduled years in advance; the museum stages several special exhibitions each year, often focusing on the work of an individual artist. What you can be fairly certain of seeing, however, is the Thannhauser Collection, displayed in comparatively orthodox fashion in several galleries reached off the second level of the ramp.

Highlights of the Guggenheim's permanent collections include works by Kandinsky, Modigliani, Klee, Mondrian, Braque and Malevich, though if your favourites are not on display you might concentrate your energies instead on the quality selections of the Thannhauser Collection.

Among these, Van Gogh's *Mountains at Saint-Rémy* is outstanding, its vibrant swirls of colour painted in 1899 as the artist recovered from one of his bouts of mental illness. Works by Cézanne include *Still Life: Flask, Glass, and Jug*, and *Bibémus*, a shimmering pre-abstract landscape, and the slightly mystifying *Man With Crossed Arms*, described as a 'proto-Cubist' piece, whose figure has been thought to embody the spirit of

1071 Fifth Avenue · New York, NY 10128 · 212 423 3500

The Guggenheim Museum SoHo Opens July 1.

Sunday, Monday, and Wednesday 11am–6pm
Thursday, Friday, and Saturday 11am–10pm

Complimentary NY V.I.P. pass SRGM 2
81682 1:41PM

GUGGENHEIM MUSEUM

SAT
9/1

quiet resignation which the artist himself possessed during the last years of his life.

A couple of paintings by the enigmatic Henri Rousseau are amusing and defiantly odd. In *The Football Players*, five handlebar-moustached and ludicrously attired figures strike up absurd poses while frolicking with a ball in a wood; similarly handlebar-moustached but more correctly attired soldiers form the core of *The Artillery Men*.

The earliest of several canvases by Picasso, *Le Moulin de Galette*, was painted in 1900 when the artist was 19, and was inspired by his first visit to Paris. The gloomy but angular figure of 1904's *Woman Ironing* is a product of the latter stages of Picasso's Blue Period; from a year or two later, *Fernand with a Black Fortilla* marks a change of style – and perhaps the first step towards Cubism.

The most striking piece in the Thannhauser Collection is also the earliest: *The Hermitage at Pontoise*, an 1867 landscape by Camille Pissarro. The artist later became a leading impressionist but here uses a realist style that goes hard against the grain of traditional French landscape painting – and seems to make the idyllic rural scene radiate from the canvas.

Raymond Hood
Architecture buffs impressed by his subsequent Daily News Building and Rockefeller Center's RCA Building (or GE Building, as it is now more correctly known) may care to cast an eye over Raymond Hood's 1928 apartment block at 3 East 84th Street, bearing many of the features – such as pressed-metal spandrels – that later appeared in refined form on his more famous works.

The vertiginous interior of the Guggenheim

■ It has been called a doughnut, a snail, and an insult to art, but Frank Lloyd Wright's Guggenheim Museum is one of the outstanding contributions to New York architecture – even though there is plenty of truth in the accusation that it often steals the show from the art that it exhibits. Wright inserted the inscription 'let every man practise the art he knows' in bronze on the entrance floor – intended perhaps as a lasting riposte to the building's critics ...■

124

The Guggenheim in the 1990s
Renovation work completed in 1992 has left the Guggenheim looking almost as good as new. The recent addition of an 11-storey tower, welded to the rotunda, has provided much-needed extra office and exhibition space, leaving Wright's original building uncluttered by the trappings of gallery administration, and making more of the collection permanently viewable.

More than 30 years after it opened, the Guggenheim remains a controversial and unique feature of the New York landscape

'Organic architecture' The originator of the 'Prairie style', Wright's best architecture blended buildings into the organic, natural forms around them. The Guggenheim's predominantly curving exterior is totally out of step with the vertical lines of the neighbouring Upper East Side apartment blocks, but has plenty in common with the trees and shrubbery of Central Park, directly across Fifth Avenue.

With the Guggenheim Museum, his only major New York commission, Wright also made a radical departure from the traditional room-by-room gallery style. The exhibits here occupy partitioned spaces off a quarter-mile-long spiral walkway that rises six storeys high, steadily growing wider as it climbs.

Controversy and restoration The architect's persistent battles with the city authorities and his disagreements with the museum's director over the structure's supposed failure to meet the practical needs of an art museum contributed to the delays that caused 16 years to elapse between Wright's finished plans and the Guggenheim's opening in 1959, the year of his death. The aesthetic debate has raged ever since, though the museum is now very much part of the Upper East Side landscape.

▶ Harlem

Seldom mentioned in tourist brochures, but a vital and distinct component in New York's character, Harlem begins north of 110th Street and splits into two sections.

Above the Upper West Side, West Harlem (or Harlem proper) is the longest-established home of the city's African-American population. Above the Upper East Side, East Harlem – or **El Barrio** ('the Neighbourhood') – is New York's largest Spanish-speaking area, the majority of its residents having Puerto Rican origins.

Eager to repeat the success of the Upper West Side, property speculators covered West Harlem with brownstones and elegant apartment blocks during the 1890s. The anticipated rush of 'up-market' buyers never materialised, however, and Harlem's homes were let out to black tenants. Rents were inflated because of housing pressure at the time – thousands of African-Americans were arriving in New York and the competition for housing was great.

Tens of thousands of the nation's blacks fled the Deep South for Harlem, seen by them as the promised land. By the 1920s, the Harlem Renaissance was in full swing: a flowering of African-American culture through art and literature as jazz and blues percolated through Harlem nightclubs such as the **Cotton Club**.

Although Harlem has endured many typical inner-city problems, things have improved since the raising of black consciousness in recent decades. West Harlem

125

Fidel Castro in Harlem
Arriving to address the United Nations in 1960, Cuban leader Fidel Castro and his entourage spent several nights in a Midtown Manhattan hotel, reputedly running up a $10,000 bill for damage before being asked to leave. No other hotel was eager for Castro's patronage, but Harlem's Teresa Hotel (272 West 125th Street), long known as a radicals' meeting place, filled the breach. During their week-long stay, the Cuban contingent were cheered by locals and were visited by Soviet leader Khrushchev. In 1971, the Teresa became an office block.

Few people visit Harlem for its architecture, but the buildings can be just as lively as the atmosphere

Marcus Garvey in Harlem
Arriving in Harlem from Jamaica in 1914, Marcus Garvey pre-empted the Black Panthers of the 1960s by encouraging black pride and assertiveness. Winning many followers through his brilliant powers of oration, Garvey founded the Universal Negro Improvement Foundation, published the *Negro World* newspaper and purchased two ocean liners to carry out his promised repatriation of America's blacks to Africa.

Eventually, Garvey was arrested on trumped-up charges and deported. He died in London in 1940. Garvey's doctrines became crucial elements in Rastafarianism, and in 1973 the Harlem park that straddles Fifth Avenue between 120th and 124th streets was re-named in his honour.

Sadly, the park, which holds a curious fire-watch tower of 1856, is nowadays a drug-users' meeting place and is best left unvisited.

Harlem gospel choir

today is no paradise, but with leafy boulevards neighbouring its low-rent housing projects, it is quite safe if you stick to daylight hours and the main thoroughfares.

Along the main commercial strip, West 125th Street, you will find the **Apollo Theater** (number 253), legendary for its amateur talent nights and for showcasing every African-American jazz, blues and soul act, from Billie Holiday in the 1930s to James Brown in the 1960s. Brown's *Live at the Apollo* album was recorded here in 1962 and captures some of the venue's raw excitement. You will also find the temporary exhibitions and photographic archive of the **Studio Museum in Harlem** on West 125th Street (number 144), and more soul-food restaurants than anyone could wish for.

For the best of early Harlem architecture, explore the **St Nicholas Historic District** on 139th Street. The stylish 1890s town houses between Seventh and Eighth avenues were occupied by successful blacks from 1919 and hence earned their lasting nickname 'Striver's Row'.

Further north, on Broadway between 155th and 156th streets, is the **Audubon Terrace** complex of museums (see page 61). Aside from location, the complex has little to do with Harlem, but it does house the American Academy and Institute of Arts & Letters, the Hispanic Society of America, and the American Numismatic Society.

Always shabbier than its westerly counterpart, East Harlem was first settled by working-class Italian and Irish families but, from the 1920s, steadily evolved into the city's major Puerto Rican neighbourhood. The **Museum of the City of New York** and El Museo del Barrio (see pages 156–7) stand on its fringes, but the place to make for is **La Marqueta**, under the Park Avenue viaduct between 110th and 116th streets, where market stalls bear sugar cane, yams and papaya, and stands dispense snacks of pork rinds and mashed plantains – all to the sounds of salsa pumping from ghetto-blasters.

▶ **Hispanic Society of America**
Broadway at 155th Street
Subway: 157th Street
Paintings by Velázquez, El Greco and Goya are among the most prized possessions of the Hispanic Society of America, founded in 1904 by Archer M Huntington, aesthete son of transportation magnate Collis P Huntington. However, this substantial gathering of Spanish and Portuguese art, archaeology, tilework and tomb decorations is overall less impressive than its setting: a sumptuous two-storey Spanish Renaissance interior, decorated with ruby-red terracotta.

■ **An automatic right to US citizenship has made it possible for Puerto Ricans to settle freely in New York, where they have become the biggest and longest-established of the city's Spanish-speaking communities ...■**

Early 19th-century New York drew Puerto Ricans active in the sugar and coffee trade. Others, inspired by the American Revolution, came here hoping to use the city as a base to plot the overthrow of their Spanish colonial masters.

The US in Puerto Rico In 1898, however, Puerto Rico was deeded by Spain to the US, which established a military government on the Caribbean island and allowed American interests to rule its economy. In return, Puerto Ricans were made American citizens (although not until 1917), so were able to settle freely in the US.

The profiteering of American companies encouraged Puerto Rican migration and, by 1930, around 45,000 Puerto Ricans had settled in New York. Many were employed in jobs given up by upwardly mobile Jews and Italians; others worked in traditional trades such as cigar-making.

El Barrio Although there were Puerto Rican neighbourhoods across Manhattan, the majority colonised the low-rent apartments of East Harlem. This area soon became *El Barrio*, base of Puerto Rican cultural institutions and Spanish-language cinemas and publications. Future mayor Fiorello La Guardia recognised the political power of the Puerto Ricans by encouraging them to register to vote.

In the 1950s, when cheap flights began operating between New York and San Juan (the Puerto Rican capital), the Puerto Rican population in New York soared to 600,000, some spilling from El Barrio into the Bronx. The majority of the new arrivals were uneducated farm labourers, unable to find work or adjust easily to city life.

Now a major part of the city's ethnic jigsaw, with representatives in every sphere of life, Americans of Puerto Rican descent still encounter discrimination. While it is fêted among trendy New Yorkers for its spicy foods and for its salsa music, El Barrio (like the Puerto-Rican dominated Alphabet City) has continued to struggle with every contemporary inner-city problem.

Rum, produced from Puerto Rican sugar cane and imported into the US, is one of the better-known ethnic specialities

127

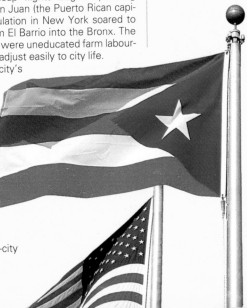

■ **At an exhibition in Los Angeles in 1956, the phrase 'the New York School' was first coined. It became the lasting name for the group of artists who, in New York a decade or so earlier, had spearheaded the country's first modern art movement – and one that was to create a worldwide audience for American art – abstract expressionism ...■**

The Cedar Tavern

Rare is the major art movement that was not influenced to some degree by drunken debate. Abstract expressionism was no exception. The favoured gathering place of many of the artists who became the New York School was the Cedar Tavern, then at 24 University Place, between Greenwich Village and the East Village. Here, discussions would rage into the night and sometimes culminate in an inebriated rearrangement of the furniture.

Fans of abstract expressionism who also like a drink may be pleased to know that the Cedar Tavern still exists (though it has moved to 82 University Place). These days, however, it is a very plain and rather uninteresting bar.

The Armory Show of 1913 (see page 149) not only brought modern European art to the US for the first time, but also made it plain that the country had no modern style to call its own. Dadaist Marcel Duchamp summed up America's contribution to world art as 'her plumbing and her bridges'.

Even if they viewed it only as a stop on the way to Paris, however, New York was still a magnet for young American artists. They arrived to escape humdrum rural towns, to take classes at the city's Art Students League, and to paint in spacious light-filled loft studios available for cheap rents.

European influences As Europe moved towards war, many of the continent's most innovative and influential artistic minds fled across the Atlantic. When the Nazis marched down the Champs Elysées, New York eclipsed Paris as the nerve centre of international art.

In the late 1940s, as the conclusion of the war seemed to present a world free of the shackles of traditionalism and filled with new possibilities, the abstract expressionists emerged.

Jackson Pollock A farmer's son from Wyoming, Jackson Pollock had arrived in New York in the 1920s and was later employed briefly at the embryonic Guggenheim Museum.

In 1947, Pollock seized one of his paintings from its easel, fixed it to the floor, and started applying paint directly from the can in great sweeping arcs across the canvas. Soon after, Pollock dispensed with easels and brushes entirely, pouring paint on to the flat canvas and manipulating it with 'sticks, trowels or knives'.

As the final product depended entirely on the act of Pollock dripping and throwing paint (likened to a western cowboy's lasso skills), the technique gave rise to the term 'action painting' (sometimes called 'gestural painting').

De Kooning, Gottlieb and Rothko Another key abstract expressionist was Willem de Kooning. While de Kooning used figures much more than Pollock – often formed by white contours on black – he was every inch the action painter, attacking his canvas with an energy that sent specks of paint flying in every direction.

A major influence on the abstract expressionists was the *Pictographs*, a series of paintings by Adolph Gottlieb, each of which was divided into compartments holding a mythological figure or symbol.

The abstract expressionists sought to transmit primal emotional states through their work – a goal which went beyond what was possible within traditional painting and which the horrors of the war had helped awaken.

Mark Rothko, an associate of Gottlieb's, became the foremost figure of what was termed the 'color field' branch of abstract expressionism. As the full terrors of the Nazi concentration camps emerged, there was a special poignancy when Rothko, the Latvian-born son of Russian Jewish émigrés, asserted that 'human incommunicability' had rendered figurative painting obsolete. Rothko's work evolved into floating rectangles of colour which, he said, provided 'a spiritual basis for communion'.

Barnett Newman and after Barnett Newman likened the color field artists' work to that of 'primitive' cultures, keen to reach a 'metaphysical understanding'. In the late 1940s, Newman produced the first of his 'zip paintings', their flat field of colour split by a narrow vertical line.

Perhaps ironically, it was a misinterpretation of Newman's work that influenced later artists such as Jasper Johns, who paved the way for the break from the mentally wrought canvases of abstract expressionism to the recasting of familiar images practised by the 1960s pop art movement.

Perhaps in keeping with the anguished soul-searching of their work, the lives of abstract expressionism's two major figures both ended prematurely: Jackson Pollock died after driving his car into a tree in 1956, and Mark Rothko committed suicide in 1970.

Abstract expressionism on display
The Museum of Modern Art (see pages 158–60) has an excellent collection of abstract expressionist works, and besides those mentioned on these pages also features work by other highly influential members of the movement such as Robert Motherwell, Franz Kline and Arshile Gorky.

The Guggenheim Museum (pages 122–4) has a fair number of abstract expressionist canvases in its possession (sometimes on display in temporary exhibitions), and important works by Pollock, de Kooning and Rothko usually turn up in the Highlights Gallery of the Whitney Museum (page 191).

129

One, *a huge canvas of 1950 by Jackson Pollock, now in the MoMA*

Photography House
One of the most handsome neo-Georgian mansions on the Upper East Side is home to the International Center of Photography. The four-storey red-brick building was completed in 1914 by the firm of Delano & Aldrich for Willard Straight, a wealthy ex-diplomat who founded the influential *New Republic* magazine. The International Center of Photography also has a midtown branch – called simply **ICP Midtown** – at 1133 Sixth Avenue, at 43rd Street.

▶▶ International Center of Photography   187D1

Fifth Avenue at 94th Street
Subway: 96th Street
One of the world's few museums entirely devoted to photography, the International Center of Photography has four galleries mounting changing exhibitions of both internationally established names and lesser-knowns beginning to make their mark.

One gallery is usually filled with selections from the center's permanent collection, which holds prints by almost every notable photographer you can think of: Henri Cartier-Bresson, Ernst Haas, Weegee, and Robert Capa to name a few.

▶ Intrepid Sea-Air-Space Museum   151C1

West end of 46th Street
Subway: 42nd Street, then take crosstown bus
Pacifists may well feel like throwing themselves overboard from the flight deck of the *Intrepid*, a US Navy aircraft carrier which is the star turn of this entirely militaristic museum. Permanently moored on the Hudson River, the *Intrepid* saw action in the Pacific during World War II and served in an anti-submarine role during the Vietnam War.

Now de-commissioned, the vessel is stuffed with exhibits from its own wartime exploits – its aircraft shot down 650 enemy planes and destroyed 289 ships – and from its peacetime role retrieving Mercury and Gemini space capsules. Armed forces' hardware abounds, not least the several dozen fighter and bomber planes which sit on the flight deck with their cockpits open for inspection.

Moored alongside the carrier are a destroyer, the *USS Edson*, which also served in Vietnam, and the more menacing *USS Growler*, the first guided-missile submarine to be put on public display. Its contents include an (unprimed) nuclear cruise missile.

▶ Isaacs-Hendricks Residence   113A2

77 Bedford Street, Greenwich Village
Subway: Christopher Street
You could be forgiven for walking right past the Isaacs-Hendricks Residence without noticing it. Alterations in 1836 and 1928 have detracted from its Federal style, of which it is one of the earliest surviving examples, having been erected in 1799. The clapboard wall on the side with Commerce Street is the main clue to the house's pedigree.

▶ Jan Hus Presbyterian Church   187B2

74th Street between First and Second avenues
Subway: 77th Street
Named for the Czech martyr of the Reformation, the Jan Hus Presbyterian Church was founded in 1914 to serve Czech settlers in an area that was known as 'Little Bohemia' into the 1930s. The church, whose bell-tower was modelled on the Powder Tower in Prague, is better patronised for its secular activities than for its services. Musical and dramatic events are regularly staged at the church's hall, which also makes an unlikely headquarters for an improvisational comedy group.

Only a fraction of New York's Czech-American population now lives in Little Bohemia and, besides the church, there are only a couple of notable reminders of the Czech presence. One is the run-down Bohemian National Hall, on 73rd Street between First and Second avenues, raised in 1895. The other is the Vasata restaurant, two blocks north on 75th Street, still a purveyor of traditional Czech cuisine.

► **Jewish Museum**   *187D1*
Fifth Avenue at 92nd Street
Subway: 96th Street
An imitation French Gothic *château* might seem a strange home for the largest stock of Judaic ceremonial art and historical objects in the US, but the fine collections of New York's Jewish Museum have been housed in just such a place since 1944. It was then that the premises were bequeathed by the widow of their original owner, banker Felix M Warburg.

The museum's permanent collection contains, perhaps, exactly what you might expect. Some of the tremendous stash of coins, household objects and religious pieces dates back to Roman times; much more is representative of Jewish life from medieval times into the present century.

However, it is with its lively and sometimes provocative temporary exhibitions – exploring the Jewish experience from new and challenging perspectives – that the institution does most to excite the jaded New York museum-goer.

Czechs in New York
The first significant group of Czechs in New York arrived in 1848 to practise the free thinking denied them by the ruling Hapsburg Empire. Nicknamed the '48ers', they founded many of the institutions that were to provide assistance to the second wave of Czech immigrants – mostly peasants who arrived in the 1870s.

The Nazi invasion, the Soviet coup and the failure of the 1968 Prague Spring also brought fresh waves of Czech migration, most of the newcomers becoming quietly assimilated into suburban American life.

131

The Intrepid Sea-Air-Space Museum

■ From the major TV networks to the loony public-access channels and from the venerable *New York Times* to free magazines packed with ads for tarot-readers, media is a big part of New York life and information oozes from every pore of the city ...■

What's on TV?
Vacationing couch-potatoes will be pleased to know that all New York's daily newspapers carry full listings of TV programmes, as does the news-free *TV Guide*, available from most supermarkets and newsstands, and free with the Sunday *New York Times*. With so many channels to choose from (most of which operate around the clock), however, deciphering US TV listings is a skilled art.

New York's radio stations provide up-to-the-minute travel news

Television The major American TV networks – ABC, CBS and NBC – are as alike as their initials, with a format of quiz shows and chat shows interspersed by early and late evening news programmes, all of which start on the hour or half-hour and are interrupted by commercials every few minutes.

Things improve dramatically with PBS (Public Broadcasting Service), the output of which includes quality dramas, documentaries and current affairs coverage. Cable TV brings further options, though most hotels are equipped with only a few of the many available cable stations.

Widely found cable channels include CNN (a round-the-clock news channel that becomes boring if the day's news is dull), MTV (endless rock videos), the Weather Channel (continuously updated weather information), and several movie channels such as HBO, which shows selected new films but fills its spare time-slots with its own specially produced rubbish.

Sadly, you will rarely find a hotel TV equipped with Manhattan's public-access cable channels, on which people pay to make a half-hour show – be they crazed astrologers or self-styled sex therapists.

Radio New York's radio stations are almost too many to number and possess call signs usually too complicated to remember. Music fans should scan the FM frequencies for an ear-boggling choice of stations, each with its own speciality, be it round-the-clock hip-hop, soul, funk, jazz, country, heavy rock, or classical sounds. The AM waveband has music too and is where the liveliest phone-ins are found. Listen to these for an hour or two (the newspapers give programme listings) and you will soon be getting to grips with the intricacies of the New York accent.

Newspapers Of New York City's four daily newspapers, the *New York Times* is unmatched for in-depth coverage of international and national affairs, while its Metro section delivers the New York news that matters. The *Times'* special features can provide intriguing insights into city life, and the Friday edition is invaluable for its listings of weekend events and activities.

Reading the *Times* can be a challenge, however, partly because the large amount of advertising causes stories to be run across several pages and partly because it is written virtually without humour. It also lacks cartoon strips.

While the *Times* is regarded as liberal, the tabloid *New York Post* is the home of conservative reaction, despite having some sharp columnists. New Yorkers who hate the *Post's* politics but love tabloid headlines turn instead to the *Daily News*. The best-selling newspaper in the US, though experiencing a sharply declining circulation, the *Daily News* has built its reputation on well-written racy stories to match its famously racy headlines. It can be relied upon to reveal the most heinous of crimes and the juiciest of scandals.

Facing the increasingly strong challenge of *New York Newsday* – a Long Island-based tabloid which boasts a colour front page – the future of the *Post* (recently re-acquired by media tycoon Rupert Murdoch) and the *Daily News* currently hangs in the balance.

The weekly *Village Voice* began as an alternative paper (author Norman Mailer was one of its co-founders) in the mid-1950s and is now as much a part of the city as the Empire State Building. It explores city politics and fringe issues with relish and carries comprehensive arts and entertainment listings. Reading its 'lonely hearts' ads can put a whole new perspective on your view of New Yorkers.

Magazines Appearing in weekly editions, *New York* is a glossy celebration of the New York lifestyle and has a strong events-listing section. The staid *New Yorker*, also published weekly, is said by some to have become more lively and colourful since the appointment of an English editor in 1992. Noted for long articles written by the country's literary heavyweights, the *New Yorker* is hardly subway-ride reading, although there are many who buy it solely for its well-considered film reviews.

Free publications
All manner of free publications are to be found in New York's shops, restaurants, bars, hotel lobbies, and in special bins around the city. Whether they specialise in pet-care, advancing your career, or the beliefs of the New Age, many such organs are simply vehicles for advertising. Others, such as *Manhattan Spirit*, *New York Perspectives*, *New York Press*, and *Upper West Side Resident*, are also packed with advertising, but are worth reading for their reviews and listings.

133

A sense of occasion is never lacking at the Metropolitan Opera House, whose glittering interior is certainly the grandest feature of the Lincoln Center

Guided tours of the Lincoln Center
Hour-long guided tours depart from the Lincoln Center's concourse level fairly frequently between 10 and 5 on most weekdays. The anecdote-packed tours weave their way through all the complex's major buildings (except the Metropolitan Opera House – see below), visiting the backstage areas and often catching rehearsals in progress. For details, tel: 875 5350. Tours of the Metropolitan Opera House leave from the entrance foyer of the Met from Monday to Friday at 3:45 and on Saturday at 10:30 (tel: 769 7020).

▶   **Lincoln Center for the
         Performing Arts**   *151D1*
62nd to 66th streets between Columbus and Amsterdam avenues
Subway: 66th Street/Lincoln Center
What takes place inside their walls is of an impressive standard, but the buildings and plaza of the Lincoln Center for the Performing Arts do little, in themselves, to encourage appreciation of life's finer things.

The complex arose in the 1960s as part of a Utopian plan to give New York's highbrow culture vultures a single rendezvous point. One element in the Lincoln Center's genesis was the decision of the New York Philharmonic, faced with what seemed likely to be the imminent destruction of Carnegie Hall, to seek a home of its own. Philharmonic Hall was completed here in 1962, changing its name in 1973 to Avery Fisher Hall in honour of the man who parted with $10 million to improve its atrocious acoustics.

The Philharmonic's search for new premises coincided with that of the Metropolitan Opera; the 10-storey **Metropolitan Opera House** now rises boldly (many would say vulgarly) above the plaza, two enormous Marc Chagall murals visible through its windows. What putting your nose against the glass fails to reveal, though, are the crystal chandeliers above the auditorium, which are sucked into the gold-leafed ceiling before a performance.

Architecturally the most successful building, Eero Saarinen's **Vivian Beaumont Theater** has ironically endured poor reviews for its cultural offerings. Next door, the **New York Public Library for the Performing Arts** holds 50,000 tomes and finds room for three separate galleries hosting temporary exhibitions.

On the north side of the complex, the world-famous **Juilliard School** numbers violinist Itzhak Perlman and actor William Hurt among its alumni. Beside the school, the **Alice Tully Hall** provides a refreshingly intimate and acoustically brilliant home for the Lincoln Center Chamber Music Society – and for free concerts given by students, usually on Wednesday lunchtimes.

►► Little Italy 87B2

Both Italian and little, Little Italy has had its boundaries steadily eroded by the expansion of Chinatown and by the drift of its original inhabitants to Italian enclaves in the Outer Boroughs. Between 1890 and 1924, however, 145,000 migrants from Sicily and southern mainland Italy settled here, in an area between Houston and Canal streets.

After years of decline (the area's tenement buildings are just beginning to show signs of gentrification), only a few thousand Italians remain in the neighbourhood. Many of them are employed in the restaurants, cafés and bakeries along Grand and Mulberry streets, which provide Little Italy's main appeal. The food is good but far from cheap and the cost-conscious way to imbibe Little Italy's atmosphere is with a cappuccino at an outdoor table.

The closest the district comes to a genuine Italian landmark is **Umberto's Clam House** (129 Mulberry Street), which acquired fame for all the wrong reasons in 1972, when, in settlement of a gangland feud, 'Crazy' Joe Gallo was shot while tucking into a seafood supper.

The local Irish, who predated the Italians, had their spiritual needs fulfilled by what is now **'Old' St Patrick's Cathedral** at 264 Mulberry Street. The city's earliest Gothic-style building, the cathedral lost its original facade in an 1866 fire and was demoted to a parish church when a new St Patrick's Cathedral was consecrated in Midtown Manhattan in 1879.

On the fringes of Little Italy, take a look at the **Old Police Headquarters** at 240 Centre Street. This Renaissance palace, topped by a green dome, was an immeasurably imposing symbol of law and order when it arose in the midst of one of the city's most crime-ridden districts in 1909.

Walk on to the **Puck Building** at 295–307 Lafayette Street. This was completed in 1886 to house the *Puck* satirical magazine and, with its deliriously complex red brickwork, was instantly revered as a prime example of New York commercial design.

Festival of San Gennaro
Each September, Little Italy's Mulberry Street is lined by makeshift stalls selling home-made sausage, calzone and other Italian specialities (plus an increasing number of Chinese ones), and jumps to the sound of marching bands in a two-week celebration of the Feast of St Gennaro. The religious aspect of the festival, honouring the patron saint of Naples, is evident as a likeness of the saint is carried along the streets and showered with dollar bills.

The tenements of Little Italy. Many of them have a restaurant or a café at street level – worth a stop at any time for a cappuccino, an ice-cream or a pizza

The Italians

■ No ethnic group has had a greater impact on New York than the Italians, who first arrived in large numbers during the 1880s. Through a combination of hard work, traditional values and business acumen, the Italian community had prospered enough to take the helm of the city by the 1940s ...■

A refuge for Italian liberals and revolutionaries through the 19th century, New York's first Italian neighbourhood was on Bleecker Street during the 1860s. Its population was chiefly made up of sophisticated northerners. By contrast, the grinding poverty of rural southern Italy triggered the massive influx of the late 1800s, and 145,000 people were soon packed into the tenements of what became, and still is, Little Italy.

Many Italians work in the catering industry, providing New Yorkers and visitors alike with pasta, pizza and other universally popular specialities

Exploitation and after Speaking little or no English, these new arrivals were exploited not least by their fellow countrymen who had been in the US long enough to learn the language and who knew enough about traditional Italian values to be sure that the recently arrived immigrants could be overworked and underpaid with minimal complaint.

Little Italy's men built New York's sewers and subways and its women worked in garment industry sweatshops. Any spare money was sent home to their villages. Many Italians had escaped Little Italy for East Harlem by the 1910s, and by the 1940s were wealthy enough to move to surburban areas in the Outer Boroughs.

Rising fortunes It was from East Harlem that Fiorello La Guardia emerged. This Protestant Italian son of a Jewish mother was destined to be remembered as the best mayor New York ever had. La Guardia's rise was a symbol of the assimilation of Italian-Americans into city politics, a sphere where they replaced the Irish as the dominant ethnic group.

With descendants of the first Italian-Americans excelling in every walk of New York life, a new wave of immigrants appeared almost unnoticed during the 1980s. In contrast to the Italian arrivals of a century earlier, affluent and stylish Italians moved into the exclusive Upper East Side and opened the up-market boutiques and gourmet Italian restaurants that won over the hearts and the wallets of rich Upper East Siders.

▶ ▶ ▶ Lower East Side IFCB2

Don't come to the Lower East Side expecting epoch-making architecture, fashionable faces, glamorous boutiques or expense-account restaurants. This is downbeat New York with no pretensions, traditionally the first stop for newly arrived immigrants whose priority is to work hard and earn enough money to move on.

The history of the Lower East Side is a far cry from the usual New York tales of millionaire indulgences and high-society fripperies. The first to arrive here were the Irish, fleeing their homeland's famine in the mid-1800s. They were followed by successive waves of German and Eastern European immigrants, including the 2 million Jews who turned the Lower East Side into the world's largest Jewish community.

Living in windowless rooms in overcrowded tenements and often working in sweatshops for breadline wages, the immigrants nonetheless founded cultural institutions and places of worship and established the educational organisations that were to make their children's lives easier than their own.

The 1924 tightening of immigration laws slowed the European influx into the Lower East Side, although by then its more successful inhabitants had moved on and established ethnic pockets elsewhere, and it was to these new districts that new arrivals headed.

With land here yet to become valuable, many Lower East Side tenements remain, as do the delis, the garment shops and the jewellery stores on which the first locals made their money. Nowadays, the owners are likely to be Indian or Korean, representing the latest waves of immigration.

Less immediately obvious to outsiders are the Lower East Side's Caribbean immigrants, including the many Puerto Ricans who dominate a broad area east of Essex Street and spill north across Houston Street into Alphabet City (see page 60).

It is the shops and their heavily discounted prices that bring most visitors to the Lower East Side. The area is at its busiest and best on Sundays when bargain-hunting

Tenement life:
the annual move
Few Lower East Siders ever stayed in a particular tenement for longer than they had to, and the offer of a free month's rent in return for a year's tenancy was usually sufficient inducement for tenement dwellers to up sticks and move every 12 months. It also became common for entire families to move back and forth across the same street, often moving in and out of the same tenements many times over at yearly intervals.

For vast stocks of cut-price clothing, the stores and stalls of Orchard Street, at the heart of Jewish New York on the Lower East Side, are hard to beat

LOWER EAST SIDE

Walking tours
The Lower East SideTenement Museum organises various walking tours, each concentrating on a specific facet of Lower East Side life – such as ethnic heritage, the lives of women, tenement architecture, and the exploits of New York's ear-liest street gangs. The walks are not cheap but they are enjoyable and incredibly informative. They leave on Sunday afternoons from outside the museum. For details and reservations, tel: 431 0233.

Typical Lower East Side tenements on Delancey Street. Blocks like these sprang up in the 19th century to house newly arrived immi-grants – often in very overcrowded and unhealthy conditions

New Yorkers descend on the narrow streets off Delancey Street for some of the biggest clothing discounts to be found in the city. The crush is fiercest outside the gar-ment stores lining **Orchard Street►**. When the crowds become overwhelming, explore the marginally less busy neighbouring streets such as Allen, Grand and Essex.

The tumult of Sundays is not repeated during the week, when the streets are much quieter – and actually rather dull. An exception to this is the **Essex Street Market►**, where Lower East Siders buy their fresh meat, vegeta-bles and fruit. The current ethnic mix of the area is evinced by the conversations carried out here in Yiddish, Spanish and Chinese – and by the plantains and bean sprouts sitting alongside the Jewish staples. The market is closed on Sundays. Bear in mind also that many shops will be closed on Saturdays in observance of the Jewish Sabbath.

Beyond shopping, imbibing the atmosphere and sam-pling fresh-made knishes (doughy pastries filled with meat or potatoes) from one of several dozen Jewish bak-eries, the Lower East Side has little to hold attention. Before leaving, however, be sure to visit the **Lower East Side Tenement Museum►►►** at 97 Orchard Street (closed on Sat). It is housed in a six-storey tenement, built in 1863, and which, believe it or not, housed 11,000 peo-ple over a 70-year period.

The museum provides a fascinating background to Lower East Side life and reveals countless illuminating facts about the deprivations of tenement living. The upper floors have been re-created to show the conditions that the house's tenants – including Irish, Germans, Russian Jews and Italians – endured.

■ **Since 1654, when 23 Sephardic Jews deported from Brazil landed in New York and resisted the Dutch governor's attempts to remove them, Jews have become deeply ingrained in the fabric of the city's life. They have played a vital role in shaping its character with everything from bagels to Irving Berlin ...■**

Established and respected in the commercial life of colonial New York, Sephardic Jews continued to flourish after the American Revolution. In the 1830s German Jews began to arrive, looking for new opportunities in the city.

Germans and Russians Assisted by mutual aid societies, the Germans settled in the Lower East Side and were soon establishing the area's jewellery and garment industries. Such businesses provided employment for the Russian Jews who arrived during the late 1800s, escaping the pogroms of Tsar Alexander III. For the most part, the Russians shunned the charity offered by the German Jewish aid societies and formed their own self-help organisations. In the garment industry sweatshops, the Russians formed powerful labour unions.

The Russian Jews also brought a rich cultural life to the Lower East Side, particularly with the Yiddish theatres in an area which became known as the 'Yiddish Rialto'. Although the Yiddish theatre began with vaudeville and farce, the arrival of Jacob Gordin, a leading Russian playwright, helped it develop serious drama and stage works by the likes of Ibsen and Gorky. Future stars such as Walter Matthau and Edward G Robinson cut their teeth before the lively Yiddish theatre audiences. Meanwhile, smoke-filled Lower East Side cafés became centres of political and literary debate, as well as venues for closely fought chess matches.

Some anti-Semitism was encountered, but New York Jews never suffered the hostilities which had been their fate in Europe and Jewish culture soon became deeply embedded in New York life.

Later arrivals The Lower East Side was still the first area of settlement when poor Sephardic Turkish, Greek and Syrian Jews arrived during the Balkan Wars of the 1910s. By the 1930s, however, the better-educated Jews fleeing the rise of Nazism were able to move directly into comfortable Jewish enclaves established in the Upper West Side and the Outer Boroughs.

In the 1970s, a few ex-Soviet Jews began settling in Brooklyn's Brighton Beach – an area which (as Soviet emigration rules loosened) quickly became swamped with ex-Soviet citizens seeking economic rather than religious freedom.

Today, the most conspicuous aspects of New York's Jewish community are seen in areas dominated by ultra-orthodox sects, such as Williamsburg's Satmar Jews (see page 78).

Black hats (fur trimming denotes a rabbi) and matching long coats make men belonging to the rigidly orthodox Satmar sect instantly recognisable

■ **Many visitors come to New York for no reason other than to shop. Once the designer outlets and the big-name department stores have been exhausted, however, the attention of the serious shopper turns to the city's flea-markets and second-hand shops – where the quest for that elusive item at a giveaway price can bring hours of pleasure ...■**

140

Thrift stores
The intrepid bargain-hunter will not want to leave New York without delving into at least a few of its thrift stores. Often linked to a church and run by volunteer labour with the proceeds going to charity, thrift stores are filled by cast-off clothing, household objects, books and other items. For a full list, consult the *Yellow Pages*.

Flea markets Wherever the New York pavement is wide enough you are likely to find an impromptu flea market. The merchandise will probably range from out-and-out junk to stolen goods (often with fake designer labels). Resist temptation, and instead visit one of the city's four main official flea markets, where better fare turns up.

At weekends, the **Canal Street Flea Market** (western end of Canal Street) offers a very large choice of cheap and often ugly and useless objects, though some handy clothing accessories might be unearthed.

Every weekend between March and December, the **Annex Antiques Fair and Flea Market** (Sixth Avenue between 24th and 26th streets) features a varied stash of bric-a-brac, clothing and jewellery. The quality tends to be low, but a browse can be worthwhile.

Prices are higher at the Saturday **Greenwich Village Flea Market** (Greenwich Street at Charles Street), though this small market merits a call if you are exploring the neighbourhood.

The **PS 44 Flea Market** (Columbus Avenue between 76th and 77th streets) is a larger and classier affair, with clothing, jewellery, ornaments, and large pieces of furniture that would not disgrace even the most design-conscious home.

Books Not only do they love bargains, New Yorkers also love to read. This explains the massed ranks of browsers to be found perusing the latest acquisitions of the city's second-hand bookstores.

Spend a whole day browsing in the **Strand Book Store** (Broadway at 12th Street) and you will barely make an impression on its 8 miles of shelves; the stocks range from dog-eared paperback best-sellers to discarded review copies of pristine hardbacks – all sold for a fraction of their original price.

Much smaller but equally interesting, the intimate **Gryphon** (Broadway between 80th and 81st streets) carries general-interest subjects but specialises in history. By contrast, a massive, unclassified clutter of paperbacks fills **Ruby's Book Sale** (119 Chambers Street), where you might also be tempted by piles of vintage magazines.

Clothing The city's more affluent elements may shop for clothes among the designer-name stores that proliferate in Midtown Manhattan, but the sartorially adventurous – and those in search of a bargain – hit the vintage clothing stores of Lower Manhattan.

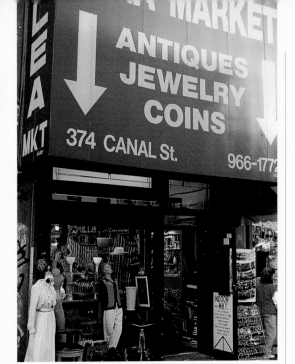

The Post Office Auction
Once a month, the General Post Office (33rd Street between Eighth and Ninth avenues) auctions off the contents of parcels that have been undelivered and unclaimed for a year. Even if you do not intend to buy anything, it is worth turning up for the viewing to see the sometimes weird and wonderful (but mostly mundane) objects that pass through the New York postal system. For details, tel: 330 2932.

Left: You will find plenty of junk (and, just possibly, a bargain or two) on sale in Canal Street

The enormous stocks of **Antique Boutique** (712–14 Broadway) have plenty to keep the vintage-clothes fanatic engaged, although dedicated bargain-hunters might be better served by a ferret through the racks at **Andy's Chee Pees** (16 West 8th Street), or **Cheap Jack's** (Broadway between 13th and 14th streets).

Clothes of the 1950s are the specialities – though far from the total extent – of the reasonably priced stock at **Love Saves the Day** (Second Avenue at East 7th Street) and **Rose's** (East 9th Street between Avenue A and First Avenue). **Panache** (Hudson Street between 10th and Charles streets), meanwhile, carries a mouthwatering assortment of 1920s and 1930s garb, much of it of excellent quality.

Another happy hunting-ground is **Alice Underground** (two branches: Broadway between Broome and Grand streets, and Columbus Avenue at 78th Street). Here you will find great collections of very classy – but attractively priced – togs.

CDs and Records New York has a massive audience for all kinds of music, but predominant on the second-hand racks are indie rock and classical rarities.

Underground rock music and hot dance cuts are found at **St Mark's Sounds** (20 St Mark's Place). **Rock's In Your Head** (157 Prince Street) specialises in alternative rock and carries a large stock of British imports. At **Smash Compact Discs** (17 St Mark's Place), you will find heaps of everything that ever rocked, from the 1950s to the present.

Fans of classical music should explore the used records section of **Academy Records** (10 West 18th Street), and seek out the many rarities sold for princely sums at **Gryphon Records** (251 West 72nd Street) and **G&A Rare Records** (139 West 72nd Street).

It is hard not to be overwhelmed by the sheer volume of print at the Strand Book Store, which claims to be the world's largest second-hand bookshop

The Met's imposing neo-classical entrance

The original building
Few New York facades are as overwhelming in their grandeur as that of the Metropolitan Museum of Art, even though the exuberant neo-classical features which greet visitors to the Met's Fifth Avenue entrance are but one of many additions made to the museum's original body.

In 1880, in an effort to blend the planned museum into its setting on the edge of Central Park, its original architects Jacob Wrey Mould and Calvert Vaux (one of the park's co-designers) devised a High Gothic form for the main facade, which then faced the park.

As its collections grew, so too did the museum building. In 1902 it gained the Fifth Avenue entrance which remains in place today. Only a segment of Mould and Vaux's work can still be seen, inside the much more recent Robert Lehman Wing.

▶▶▶ **Metropolitan Museum of Art** 187C1

Fifth Avenue and 82nd Street
Subway: 86th Street

Founded in 1870, the Metropolitan Museum of Art is now among the world's most important art museums. Over the years, the collection has been greatly swelled by donations from some of America's richest people. The Met will exhaust you long before you exhaust it. The best way is to think of it as a dozen or so separate museums.

If you cannot decide where to begin, aim first for the European paintings on the second floor. Rows of aristocratic English portraits line most of the first room, where works by Reynolds, Gainsborough and Lawrence provide much to admire in their technical virtuosity. Of the Met's English paintings, however, it is two landscapes which are most likely to hold your gaze: Turner's *Grand Canal, Venice*, capturing the artist at the height of his powers, and Constable's radiant *Salisbury Cathedral*.

Moving on, the French rooms reveal choice works spanning three centuries. Among many striking pieces, George de la Tour's *The Penitent Magdalen* has a rare ability to draw the viewer into its dark corners, and Rousseau's *The Forest in Winter at Sunset* seems to resonate with the primaeval forces of nature.

The galleries of French impressionists and post-impressionists include wonderful contributions from Manet, Monet, Cézanne, Gauguin and Renoir but winning the day are the canvases of Van Gogh, among them *Self Portrait with a Straw Hat* and the stunning *Cypresses*.

The Dutch galleries include almost a whole room of Rembrandts and five of Vermeer's 40 extant paintings. Among the Spanish contributions, focus on El Greco's *View of Toledo*, a striking depiction of the 16th-century religious centre beneath menacing storm clouds.

Continued on page 144.

■ **The detailed explanatory displays are an essential aid to comprehending the Met's Egyptian collections, an otherwise overwhelming stash of 40,000 objects that stretch from pre-dynastic times to the arrival of the Romans ...**■

Mercifully, you need not be a scholar to enjoy the collections or the lasting impression they provide of one of the world's greatest civilisations. Some of this colossal stock of treasures were donated by individuals but many come from the Met's own 30-year excavation programme. The single biggest exhibit, the Temple of Dendur (see panel), was a gift from the government of Egypt to the United States in the 1960s.

Although the walk-through Tomb of Perneb – a structure which draws attention as soon as you enter the Egyptian galleries – is a reconstruction, most of the objects on show are originals in excellent states of preservation, making them seem far younger than they really are and allowing their imagery, and their often extravagant use of colour, to be surprisingly forceful.

The trappings of death The most powerful examples are the numerous brightly decorated coffins, that of the 12th-dynasty (1897–1843 BC) Khnumnakht being particularly notable for its painted eyes – intended to allow the dead to look into the land of the living – which still stare forth with intensity.

The smaller items, too, can be striking. From the Ptolemaic period (332–30 BC) are a sculptured Anubis, the jackal-headed god of embalming who watched over the dead, and the erect and disconcertingly alert bronze likeness of a cat, hollowed out and used as a coffin for the animal regarded by some ancient Egyptians as sacred.

The Temple of Dendur stands in its own huge gallery

The Temple of Dendur
Destined to be submerged following the construction of the Aswan Dam, this 2,000-year-old temple was packaged up and transported to the museum from its original site on the banks of the Nile. The sandstone temple, a monument to Isis and two Egyptian brothers who drowned in the Nile, was constructed around 15 BC in an effort by the Roman emperor Augustus to win the hearts of the conquered locals. It manages to be both spectacular and disappointing, overwhelmed by its purpose-built modern gallery and overlooked, through a vast glass wall, by the trees of Central Park and the penthouses of Fifth Avenue.

METROPOLITAN MUSEUM OF ART

Continued from page 142.

The American Wing holds an outstanding collection, defining the development of art and design in the US as European traditions were by stages mimicked, absorbed and finally submerged, as American styles developed

Foremost among the paintings are the the finely detailed landscapes of the Hudson River artists, many of which captured the continent's natural breadth and diversity as white settlers steadily forged westwards. A series of period rooms shows the progress of the decorative arts, from Queen Anne armchairs and Philadelphia Chippendale chests of drawers to the unique art nouveau glasswork of Louis Comfort Tiffany, who worked in Long Island, and a large living-room which brilliantly expresses the vision of Frank Lloyd Wright's Prairie-style architecture, intended to replicate the wide open spaces of the American heartland in a domestic setting.

Compared with their American counterparts, the European period rooms seem vulgarly stuffed with finery – they include Venetian bedrooms, English interiors by Robert Adam, and a Louis XIV state bedchamber – while the phenomenal collection of clocks, mirrors, and *objets d'art* lining the adjacent passageways is enough to bring tears to the eyes of any passing antique dealer.

Just a few steps away, a flamboyantly decorated 16th-century Spanish patio leads to the stairwell and the main entrance to the museum's cache of medieval art. Should medieval art be your abiding interest, make this your first call. Only with a clear head are the 4,000-odd exhibits – from the fall of Rome to the dawn of the Renaissance and from a tiny 3rd-century Alexandrian medallion to a three-storey-high wrought-iron choir screen from 17th-century Spain – likely to fall into a comprehensible pattern.

Continued on page 146.

More medieval art
After a thorough rummage through the Met's main collections, true medievalists might consider forsaking the remainder of the museum for New York's second batch of medieval treasures, displayed at the Met's Cloisters wing (see pages 92–3). Admission tickets are valid at both locations on their day of issue.

144

One of the less well-known and more restful corners of the labyrinthine Met: the Petrie Sculpture Court

■ Documenting the origins and spread of Islam through the highly skilled and often beautiful art and craft works which it inspired, the Met's Islamic Art collections fill 10 richly laden galleries on the second floor. Though these are among the Met's lesser-known exhibits, they make up one of the finest such displays in the world ...■

After a bright introductory room describing the founding of Islam by Muhammad in 622 and the religion's steady outward spread from Mecca, the initial galleries are lined by dozens of well-stocked display cases revealing a wonderful assortment of gold and silver pieces such as beads, pendants and plaques from the craftsmen of Egypt, Iran and Syria during the 9th, 10th and 11th centuries.

A side room is even more copiously stocked, holding the enormous collection of ceramics unearthed during the Met's own excavations in Nishapur during the 1930s and 1940s. The Iranian town was a 10th-century centre of Islamic creativity.

Calligraphy and ceramics Flanked by exquisite mosque lamps and perfume sprinklers, another gallery holds a series of leaves from the Koran, demonstrating the development of calligraphy from angular kufic scripts on parchment from 9th-century Egypt to the final refinement of cursive scripts achieved by the oblique cutting of the pen nib in 13th-century Iraq. (Chairs are thoughtfully provided for close scrutiny.) In the same room stands a 14th-century prayer niche (Mihrab), each of its tiny ceramic tiles individually fired to maximise the glaze and heighten the floral decoration. Since it showed the direction of Mecca, the Mihrab was (and still is) the most important item in a Muslim place of worship.

Small is beautiful Many exquisite examples of 14th-century miniature painting, used in text illustration and characterised by pure and harmonious colours and a strong sense of patterning, are displayed in rotation. The influence of miniature artwork was carried over into Islamic carpet design through later years, and carpets and prayer rugs are the prize exhibits of subsequent galleries. Look especially for the lavish textiles – some decorated with gold leaf – with which Mogul emperors lined their tents.

Finally, peer into the Nur ad-Din Room, a reassembled winter reception room typical of a wealthy Syrian home of the early 1700s: heavily decorated wood-panelled walls rise from a patterned marble floor and reach up to stained-glass windows and a sumptuous beamed ceiling.

A 14th-century gilded and enamelled glass mosque lamp

METROPOLITAN MUSEUM OF ART

Continued from page 144.

Prints and photographs
As comprehensive and as engrossing as any other section of the museum, the Met's collections of prints and photography includes everything from Rembrandt etchings to Russian constructivist photography. Every print-maker and shutter-clicker that you have ever heard of – and many less familiar – are represented.

Unlike the tightly packed rooms of the main museum, the recent Lila Acheson Wallace Wing holds spacious, light-soaked galleries and makes an excellent setting for the museum's 20th-century art.

Picasso's portrait of Gertrude Stein is a piece that stands out, though the bulk is provided by Americans – de Kooning, Lichtenstein, Pollock and O'Keeffe among them. This is not the greatest trove of modern art in New York (for that, see the Museum of Modern Art, pages 158–60), but the side room holding selections from the Berggruen collection of Paul Klee drawings is a definite plus. So, too, is the rooftop sculpture garden, reached by elevator. Its views across Central Park tend to draw your attention away from the sculpture, which is taken from

Changing exhibitions of sculpture and sweeping views over Central Park are two good reasons to visit the Met's rooftop

Met practicalities
Faced with the Met's abundance of riches, it is essential to plan your visit (or visits) and establish priorities. When doing so, bear in mind that some galleries close in rotation at certain times on certain days. Schedules are available from the desk, or for recorded information tel: 535 7710.

the permanent stock in the museum and exhibited on a rotational basis.

Another recent addition to the museum is the Michael C Rockefeller Wing, named after the collector who went missing (presumed drowned) on a trip to Papua New Guinea in 1961. This wing now houses the art of Africa, Oceania and the Americas. Of a large, wide-ranging and constantly intriguing assemblage, items from the Asmat tribe of Irian Jaya are perhaps the most absorbing. The Asmat people believe that death is never natural but caused by an enemy; when too many deaths occur, it is necessary to seek vengeance. The Asmat *mbis* ceremony culminated in enemies being tracked down and killed; their heads were then placed on the *mbis* poles, covered with carved ancestral figures and other symbols. Several 20ft-high examples tower over visitors.

Continued on page 148.

■ **Bequeathed by a millionaire banker who allegedly spent his youth roaming Europe tracking down masterpieces and telegramming his father for the money to buy them, the Robert Lehman Collection – housed in a modern pavilion attached to the main building – makes a relaxing break from the museum's more crowded rooms ...■**

The Lehman Collection's more important paintings, chiefly 14th- and 15th-century Italians, are hung on the first floor in reassembled period rooms from the Lehman town house at West 54th Street. Other paintings vie for attention with the temporary exhibitions of drawings at ground level, including work by Dürer and Rembrandt.

Botticelli Modest in size but immense in its importance, the highlight of the collection is perhaps Botticelli's *Annunciation*, revealing the achievements of late 15th-century Florentine art in the use of perspective. The painting sets a row of classical pillars between a resonant Virgin and the Archangel Gabriel. God's message arrives as light through a doorway, the rays cutting a diagonal path, splitting the painting's horizontal and vertical lines and linking the two figures.

Venetian painters The Bellini family is represented with a Madonna and Child by Jacopo Bellini, and an early work by his more famous son, Giovanni, placed at around 1460 and depicting the Madonna and Child in intense poses before an eerily still landscape. From a few years later, another Venetian, Jacometto Veneziano, contributes two portraits: *Alvise Contarini* and *Nun of San Secondo*, intriguing works pre-empting the Venetian portrait style which came to prominence during the 1500s.

Giovanni da Paolo Among a strong complement of Sienese works, da Paolo's *Expulsion from Paradise* stands out, not least for its lively use of colour. The painting shows God soaring above an intensely vibrant constellation, pointing a finger at a barren Earth – the destination for a spindly Adam and Eve as they are shooed out of Eden by a nervous angel.

Another interesting Sienese contribution is *Temptation of Saint Anthony Abbot*, credited to the Osservanza Master, placing the founder of monasticism in what looks like a devastated, post-nuclear holocaust landscape.

French works
The collection's 19th-century French paintings are less inspired despite bearing famous names: Monet's unusually airy *Landscape near Zaandam* is worth a look, as are *Promenade among the Olive Trees* (above) by Matisse, and Cézanne's *House behind the Trees on the Road to Tholonet* and *Girl Bathing*.

147

Jacopo Bellini's
Madonna and Child

METROPOLITAN MUSEUM OF ART

Continued from page 146.

The Met has a couple of offbeat departments which – though not designed for the purpose – might well come as a godsend if you have young minds to keep occupied.

The Musical Instruments galleries house 4,000 weird, wonderful and sometimes priceless tune-making devices. Among the displays, look for the remarkably unattractive legs of the world's oldest extant piano – dated to 1720 and a product of the workshops of Bartolommeo Cristofori – and a Stradivari violin made in 1691 and restored to its original appearance.

Strange instruments are plentiful, such as the 19th-century Indian mayuri, a kind of bowed sitar in the shape of a peacock, and a Native American shaman rattle, its carved animal emblem intended to symbolise the transfer of magical power from the spirits to the shaman.

Though it gets comparatively scant attention from the public, the Met's Arms and Armour collection is, predictably, among the best of its kind to be found. Close study of the massed rows of suits of armour, from the 15th century onwards, reveals the high level of artistic flair and craftsmanship which went into the creation of such battle apparel.

One example, thought to have been worn by Sir George Clifford in the late 1500s, shows a mass of interwoven Tudor Roses and fleurs-de-lis. Some of the weapons are no less ornate, be they engraved flintlock pistols or short-swords, or an emerald- and diamond-decorated sabre.

Explore just a few of the sections mentioned above and you will easily have filled a day without even touching on the Met's Greek and Roman art, the Chinese and Japanese galleries (which feature a dazzling display of painted scrolls), the Asian art, or the arts of the Ancient Near East. Be sure to return – but after several days' rest.

Figures and figurative art: visitors and exhibits at the Metropolitan Museum of Art

Eating and drinking at the Met

A thorough exploration of the Met calls for great stamina, and even if you have consumed a hearty breakfast before arriving, you will be in need of further nourishment well before it is time to leave.

On the museum's ground floor, near the entrance to the Michael C Rockefeller Wing, a spacious atrium holds a self-service cafeteria, with a choice of hot and cold dishes at reasonable prices, and a slightly more expensive waiter-service restaurant.

If you are only pretending to visit the museum – or its size simply becomes too much to bear – you could while away the day over a glass or two of something at the atrium's bar.

▶▶▶ Midtown Manhattan

Midtown Manhattan is the New York of popular imagination: a place where battalions of power-dressed office-workers march along packed sidewalks to the sounds of wailing police sirens and bumper-to-bumper traffic, as street-stands dispense hot-dogs and knishes (meat- or potato-filled dough pastries) in the shadows of the world's most striking high-rise architecture.

In reality, such scenes are only found between 42nd and 59th Streets, an area with many highlights, most of which are detailed elsewhere in this book and explored by the walks on page 150. To New Yorkers, Midtown is usually the section bounded on the north by 59th Streeet and on the south by 34th Street. The Midtown map on page 151, however, extends the area south to 14th Street.

Where Broadway crosses 14th Street, busy **Union Square ▶** was ringed by elegant homes and became the centre of the city's theatre district in the late 1800s. By the early decades of the 20th century, the social life had moved north and Union Square had become a left-wing rallying point. In 1927, police hoisted machine-guns on to nearby rooftops during a demonstration. Three years later, a 35,000-strong protest against unemployment ended in pitched battles between police and protesters.

The domain of drug addicts in the early 1980s, Union Square has regained some of its dignity with two new art deco subway entrances and the **Farmers' Market,** where fruit, cheeses, vegetables and home-made bread are sold from stalls on Wednesdays, Fridays and Saturdays.

Just east along 14th Street, the offices of Consolidated Edison – the firm responsible for providing New York's power supply – fill a building notable at night for its illuminated facade and clock-tower and by day for its **Energy Museum▶**, which records the triumph of Thomas Edison in electrifying the city. Audio-visual displays explain the vine-like entwinements of pipes and cables beneath a typical New York street.

Continued on page 152.

The Venetian-style Metropolitan Life Insurance tower, once the world's tallest building, dominates the Midtown skyline near Madison Square Park

The Armory Show
The 69th Regiment Armory on Lexington Avenue between 25th and 26th streets is not the only National Guard barracks to be modelled on a medieval fortress, but it is the only one to have staged the legendary Armory Show of 1913, the first exhibition of modern European art in a country then still obsessed with traditional landscapes and portraiture. The work of Marcel Duchamp and others shocked critics and public alike and the Armory Show's effect on American art was profound. A small plaque on the armory's façade notes the historic event.

Walk Midtown Manhattan landmarks

Beginning at the Empire State Building and finishing at the United Nations complex, this walk passes seven decades worth of landmark New York architecture.

After visiting the **Empire State Building** (pages 100–2), continue north along Fifth Avenue to the **New York Public Library** (page 168), its entrance set back from the street and guarded by sculptured lions. Walk east along 42nd Street to Grand Central Terminal (pages 166–7) and the **Philip Morris Headquarters**, on Park Avenue, a modern building with

a gallery holding exhibits from the Whitney Museum of American Art.

Further east on 42nd Street, pass through the cast bronze doors of the 1923 **Bowery Savings Bank** (now the Home Savings Bank of America) to see the lavish Romanesque interior. Close by, note the stunning art deco bas-reliefs by Edward Trumbull on the exterior of the **Chanin Building**. Ahead are the unmistakable **Chrysler Building** (page 89) and **Daily News Building** (page 95), while turning north on First Avenue reveals the **United Nations** complex (page 184).

Walk Midtown churches and museums

View of St Patrick's Cathedral and the Olympic Tower

Beginning and ending at Rockefeller Center, this walk includes several Midtown churches and also passes the **Museum of Modern Art** (pages 158–60) and the **American Craft Museum** (page 62).

Facing **Rockefeller Center** (pages 173–4) across Fifth Avenue, the twin-spired **St Patrick's Cathedral** was completed in 1888 in richly carved Gothic form. Inside, the chapels and shrines glow with candlelight.

On East 50th Street, the art deco **Waldorf-Astoria Hotel** has accommodated kings, queens, emperors and every US president since its opening in 1931: join the well-heeled travellers lounging in the lobby. Near by, the slim octagonal brick tower of the **General Electric Building** is another art deco landmark. A contrast is provided by the Byzantine-style **St Bartholomew's Church**, remodelled in 1919 and boasting a splendid triple-arched entrance portal.

Back on Fifth Avenue, a single corner tower gives **St Thomas' Episcopal Church** a disjointed look, but do not miss the striking reredos inside.

MIDTOWN MANHATTAN

UPPER WEST SIDE · WEST 72ND STREET · Dakota Apartments · St James Episcopal Church · EAST 72ND STREET · Asia Society · UPPER EAST SIDE

Strawberry Fields · Frick Collection

American Museum of Folk Art · AMSTERDAM AVE · BROADWAY · CENTRAL PARK WEST · The Mall · Central Park · AVENUE · Temple Emanu-El · AVE · AVE · Church of St Vincent Ferrer · Rockefeller University

WEST END AVENUE · HIGHWAY · COLUMBUS · American Federation of the Arts · EAST 64TH STREET · MADISON · PARK · LEXINGTON · THIRD · YORK · AVE

Lincoln Center for the Performing Arts · American Bible Society · Dairy · Wollman Memorial Rink · Zoo · FIFTH · Museum of American Illustration · Abigail Adams Smith Museum

COLUMBUS CIRCLE · N Y Coliseum · CENTRAL PARK SOUTH · Bloomingdale's · QUEENSBORO BRIDGE

Trump Tower · EAST 57TH ST · SECOND

WEST 57TH STREET · New York Convention & Visitors Bureau · Carnegie Hall · Museum of Modern Art · EAST 55TH STREET · Central Synagogue · FIRST

WEST 53RD ST · AVENUE · St Thomas' Episcopal Church · EAST 53RD STREET

De Witt Clinton Park · American Craft Museum · Museum of TV & Radio · St Bartholomew's Church · General Electric Bldg · ROOSEVELT DRIVE

WEST 49TH STREET · SEVENTH AVE · Radio City Music Hall · St Patrick's Cathedral · EAST 50TH ST · Waldorf-Astoria Hotel · ROOSEVELT River

THEATER DISTRICT · Rockefeller Center · EAST · Former Pan Am Building · 47TH ST

WEST 45TH STREET · (SIXTH) · Grand Central Terminal · Chrysler Building · United Nations

Intrepid Sea-Air-Space Museum · WEST 42ND STREET · Times Square · Philip Morris · E 42ND ST · QUEENS

Port Authority Bus Terminal · Bryant Park · HQ · Chanin Building · Daily News Building · MIDTOWN TUNNEL

LINCOLN TUNNEL · WEST 39TH STREET · New York Public Library · Pierpont Morgan Library · Bowery Savings Bank · FRANKLIN · East

Jacob Javits Convention Center · WEST 37TH STREET · WEST 34TH STREET · GARMENT DISTRICT · Macy's Store · Madison · EAST 37TH STREET · MURRAY HILL · EAST 34TH STREET · Heliport

General Post Office · Madison Square Garden · Empire State Building · LEXINGTON · AVENUE · AVENUE · NYU Medical Center

WEST 30TH STREET · Penn Station · Little Church Around the Corner · EAST 28TH STREET · THIRD · SECOND · FIRST · Bellevue Hospital Center

Tin Pan Alley · Chelsea Park · AVENUE · AVENUE · Madison Square Park · Metropolitan Life Building

WEST 26TH STREET · CHELSEA · OF THE AMERICAS · EAST 23RD STREET

WEST 23RD STREET · Flatiron Building · National Arts Club · GRAMERCY · Gramercy Park

General Theological Seminary · WEST 20TH STREET · Theodore Roosevelt Birthplace · Players Club · Police Academy Museum · EAST 20TH STREET

WEST 18TH STREET · TENTH · NINTH · EIGHTH · SEVENTH · AVENUE OF · FIFTH · Stuyvesant Square · STUYVESANT TOWN

Hudson · WEST STREET · WEST 14TH STREET · 0 · 2 · 1 km · Energy Museum · EAST 14TH STREET

MILLER · TWELFTH AVENUE · ELEVENTH AVENUE

151

Madison Square Park

Continued from page 149.

During the mid-1800s, the city's élite relocated from Greenwich Village into the new areas of **Gramercy**▶ and **Murray Hill**▶. Favoured by more prominent citizens were the brownstone town houses around **Gramercy Park**▶▶, between 20th and 21st streets, part of a residential plot laid out in imitation of the grand squares of London.

An aura of wealth and understated elegance still lures well-heeled but publicity-shy New Yorkers to Gramercy, where Gramercy Park is the city's only private park: keys are given to local residents in return for a steep annual rent. Look through the park's high railings and you will see statues which include a likeness of actor Edwin Booth in the role of Hamlet. In 1888, Booth founded the influential **Players Club**▶ in a building of 1845 at 16 Gramercy Park South. Two ornamental theatrical masks decorate its entrance, which was designed by Stanford White.

The co-designer of Central Park, Calvert Vaux, added the Ruskin-influenced Gothic features to the building next door, now the **National Arts Club** but earlier occupied by Samuel Tilden, governor of New York State from 1874. Tilden's stand against corruption in New York public life did not alleviate his fears of public insurrection: he had a secret passageway set under the house to hasten his escape if angry mobs barricaded the entrance.

A few blocks east, at 235 East 20th Street, the **Police Academy Museum**▶▶ has many intriguing exhibits, among them Al Capone's machine-gun and a stash of terrifying weaponry collected during amnesties.

Heading west, 20th Street holds the **Theodore Roosevelt Birthplace** (see page 182) while shop-lined 23rd Street leads into **Madison Square Park**. On the southern side stands the **Flatiron Building** (see page 106) and, on the eastern side, the 1893 **Metropolitan Life Building**, which gained its tower in 1909.

Baseball's birthplace
Baseball as a sport had been introduced to the US in 1842, but not until 1845 did a group of enthusiasts – who had been playing the game regularly at what later became Madison Square Park – band together to create a fixed set of rules and the first baseball club, the Knickerbocker Club. As baseball spread in popularity across the US, it was known at first as the 'New York Game'.

When asked to provide a funeral for an actor in 1870, one Murray Hill church representative said 'we don't accept actors but there's a little church around the corner that does'. From then on, the 1849 Church of the Transfiguration, on 29th Street just off Fifth Avenue, became better known as the **Little Church Around the Corner►►**, serving New York thespians in spiritual need. A picturesque garden fronts the church and the intimate interior holds several memorials to actors.

Chelsea►, west of Fifth Avenue, is one of the least easily categorised New York neighbourhoods, and has little of obvious appeal. Make your way, though, to the **General Theological Seminary►**, between Ninth and Tenth avenues and 20th and 21st streets. This is among the city's earliest examples of Gothic Revival architecture. The oldest sections date from the 1830s and overlook a placid wooded square in the heart of the **Chelsea Historical District►**, an easily strolled area revealing the diverse residential styles of 19th-century New York.

Moving north, McKim, Mead and White's monumental 1913 **Post Office►**, on Ninth Avenue at 33rd Street, stands between Chelsea and the **Garment District** – powerhouse of the city's fashion industry. It dissolves into the **Theater District**, near Times Square.

The Algonquin Hotel
In the Oak Room of the Algonquin Hotel at 59 West 44th Street stands a round table which, from 1919, became *the* Round Table. Around it a legendary coterie of critics, playwrights and journalists engaged in sparkling wit and repartee. The exchanges were reported in Franklin P Adams' widely read column in the *New York World* magazine.

Cheek-by-jowl Midtown skyscrapers – with a view!

153

■ It was an Irishman, Thomas Dongan, who gave his name to the charter of 1686 which created New York's modern system of administration. As governor of a British colony, however, Dongan probably never expected that in years to come his country-men would flock to New York to free themselves of British oppression and take a controlling grip on New York life ...■

154

Under British rule, Protestant and Catholic Irish were established in professional life in New York, but – mindful of British treatment of the Irish at home – both groups embraced the American Revolution and saw their chance to build a truly democratic, self-governing society.

Fall and rise The potato famines brought tens of thousands of Irish into New York during the 1800s, arriving on the 'Irish berths': cramped, airless sections of ships where disease was rife. Once ashore, the penniless Irish – faced with growing anti-Catholic feeling – were forced to occupy crowded rooms, often in atrocious conditions.

By 1860, Irish Catholics made up a quarter of the city's population and were the backbone of the police force, fire-fighting teams and building trades. Irish organisational skills created powerful unions and paved the way for Irish domination of New York's entire administrative machine from the 1870s to the 1940s.

Church and tavern One symbol of the Irish Catholic ascendancy in New York was the building of St Patrick's Cathedral in 1888. But while the church was important in Irish immigrant life, so too was the tavern. A first stop for new arrivals, taverns were informal clearing-houses for jobs. Some served free lunches to Irish workmen.

Irish-Americans are still strongly represented in New York public office although Irish culture – as portrayed in some bars – is often highly romanticised. New York's last outpost of authentic Irish culture is Bainbridge, in the Bronx. First settled in the 1840s by Irishmen who saw its enticing greenery while working on the Harlem Railway, Bainbridge's bars are the genuine article, without an ornamental leprechaun or bottle of green beer in sight.

St Patrick's Day (17 March) sees the city's biggest street parade, along Fifth Avenue

▶ **Museum for African Art** *116A3*

Broadway between Houston and Prince streets
Subway: Prince Street or Spring Street
Arts and crafts from sub-Saharan Africa form the core of the temporary exhibitions staged in this highly respected museum, one of the US's major spaces for African art, along with the Smithsonian Institution. Far from being static displays, the shows frequently take provocative directions. In 1995, for example, a display titled 'Exhibitionism' studied the approach taken to African art by western museums.

▶ **Museum of American Financial History** *104B2*

Broadway at Bowling Green
Subway: Bowling Green
This one-room collection need not detain you long, but it is an appropriate stop when touring the Financial District.

Visitor Information Center
On the ground floor of what looks vaguely like a Middle Eastern mosque facing Columbus Circle (the main junction between Midtown Manhattan and the Upper West Side, and a short distance from the Museum of American Folk Art), the Visitor Information Center provides free maps and information to New York visitors and has many shelves of free leaflets describing the city's attractions.

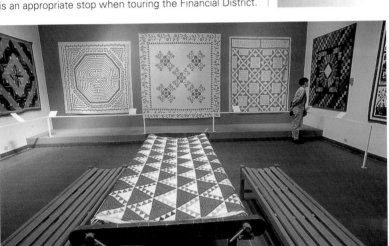

Inside the former Standard Oil Building, once presided over by multimillionaire John D Rockefeller, the changing exhibitions explore diverse historical avenues in the US economy.

Woven hangings at the Museum of American Folk Art – a showcase for the talents of craftspeople from all over the Americas

▶ **Museum of American Folk Art** *151D1*

2 Lincoln Square (but moving soon to West 53rd Street)
Subway: 66th Street
From toys and weather vanes to carved walking sticks and gravestone rubbings, the collections of the Museum of American Folk Art are drawn from the output of artists and craftspeople – many of them revered figures within their own communities – from all over the Americas. Be it Mexican wooden animal figures or Navajo blankets, the work on display is frequently of an exceptionally high standard and decorated with symbolic detail which only becomes apparent with close inspection.

In a city which falls over itself to honour the art of Europe, these exhibitions of indigenous American culture – a mix of permanently shown items and pieces chosen to form special temporary shows – are very welcome indeed.

MUSEUM OF THE CITY OF NEW YORK

The Museum of the City of New York, whose dignified grand entrance on Fifth Avenue is the gateway to a mixed collection charting aspects of the Big Apple through the ages

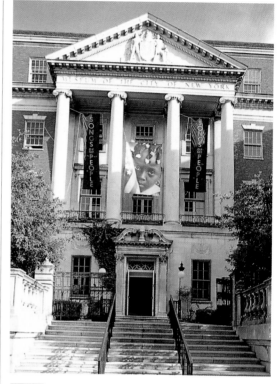

▶ **Museum of the City of New York** *IFCA5*

Fifth Avenue at 103rd Street
Subway: 96th Street

Chronicling the rise and rise of one of the world's most diverse and colourful cities is no easy task, and while the Museum of the City of New York has its share of interesting bits and pieces from the formative years of the great metropolis, it struggles to bring them together with any cohesion. Many of the museum's exhibits seem lost in the spacious innards of the neo-Georgian building that houses them.

The devoted history buff will find plenty here to mull over, however. Chronologically, things begin on the second floor with staid dioramas of Native American life in the years leading up to European discovery. Far more intriguing are the first maps of the New York area, and drawings and paintings from the mid-1600s, thought to be the earliest depictions of what was then the Dutch trading post of Nieuw Amsterdam.

Six undistinguished period interiors give a very general impression of the furnishings – from simple Dutch tables to ornate English colonial cabinets – that stood in New York drawing-rooms from the 17th to the early 20th century. Close by, several cases hold a glittering array of New York-made silver tea caddies, tankards and cutlery that graced the kitchens of the city's most illustrious residents from the late 1700s.

A few figureheads and many model ships and boats are the principal pieces in a forgettable room intended to document the city's growth into a major seaport. Take care, though, to look at the paintings – such as Alonzo Chappel's simple but expressive *Bowery on a Rainy Day*, painted in 1849, and another that shows ice-skaters in Central Park during 1865 – which hang on nearby walls and do more to evoke the New York of their period than many of the more valuable exhibits around them.

The museum enjoys its finest moment on the third floor, where a glorious collection of toys (some dating to the mid-1700s) includes a room filled by elaborate three- and four-storey dolls' houses. The dolls, too, are as impressive as the houses, and include a specimen of almost every type produced in the US from the late 18th to the mid-19th centuries. The oldest doll is a French-made import dating from 1724.

The Rockefeller Rooms (which may be closed because of financial cutbacks) on the museum's fifth floor comprise the master bedroom and dressing room from the mansion purchased in 1884 by John D Rockefeller at West 54th Street – a site now consumed by the garden of the Museum of Modern Art. A wealth of intricately carved woodwork with mother-of-pearl inlays inspired by English designer Charles Eastlake, the rooms were the height of fashion in Victorian New York. What you will not see here is the mansion's wonderful Moorish room, now held in the Brooklyn Museum (see page 78–9).

Temporary exhibitions fill the ground-floor rooms, while the museum's basement is occupied by poorly arranged memorabilia from New York's earliest fire-fighters. The centrepiece is a well-maintained hose-carriage of 1865, but smaller and more revealing pieces fill the surrounding display cases. Among the helmets, lamps, model fire-appliances, and press cuttings detailing New York's most famous fires and the men who put them out, look for the fire-fighters' ear trumpet – a device intended to improve communication in blazing buildings. When plugged at one end, it also served as a beer-drinking vessel and a handy weapon for when the 'fire laddies' (as they were known) gathered for an evening in a tavern.

El Museo del Barrio

A few strides across 104th Street from the Museum of the City of New York, El Museo del Barrio is very much a product of its East Harlem environment, evolving from a local school classroom into a museum devoted to the cultures of Latin America, particularly that of Puerto Rico. The small permanent collection of pre-Columbian objects is regularly eclipsed by temporary exhibitions which span paintings, sculpture, video and more, reflecting diverse aspects of Latin American life, past and present.

157

Times change: one of the museum's dioramas shows what New York's East River waterfront would have looked like in the 1850s

Queuing for a special MoMA exhibition

The MoMA building
In 1939, the MoMA acquired not only its current home but also what would, on completion, be one of the first international-style buildings in the US. Architects Philip Goodwin and Edward Durrell Stone interrupted West 53rd Street's row of brownstones with a facade of marble, tile and glass. The very term 'international style' had been coined at a MoMA exhibition in 1932, by Philip Johnson, later to oversee several additions to the building, most notably the Sculpture Garden.

Van Gogh's Starry Night

▶▶▶ **Museum of Modern Art**   *151C2*

53rd Street between Fifth and Sixth avenues
Subway: Fifth Avenue or Seventh Avenue

This really is *the* Museum of Modern Art. Nowhere in the world will you find a museum so well stocked or so aptly designed to illustrate the principal movements and trends, and showing so many of the major works, of the last 150 years of artistic achievement.

Paintings and sculpture form the core of the museum's permanent stock, but there are also excellent collections of photography, drawings, prints and illustrated books, a section on architecture and design and an encyclopaedic film and video archive.

It may seem hard to imagine today, but when MoMA (as it is known) staged its first exhibition in 1929, the artists it featured – Cézanne, Gauguin, Seurat and Van Gogh – were not represented in any other New York museum. The otherwise all-encompassing Metropolitan Museum of Art was just one which considered such names to be too much of a risk. Nonetheless, 47,000 people visited the MoMA exhibition in a single month.

A decade later, MoMA acquired its present plot (a gift of the Rockefeller family) and through the energy of its young director, Alfred H Barr Jnr, and the benevolence of a host of millionaire benefactors, it steadily became the world's primary repository for modern art's most influential works, acquiring a prestige all of its own.

The museum itself is a stimulating place, with escalators linking the multi-level galleries and natural light in abundance, enabling visitors to enjoy its contents without suffering exhaustion or eye strain. The painting and sculpture galleries are arranged broadly in chronological sequence across the second and third floors, starting with a room of post-impressionists richly hung with canvases by Cézanne, Toulouse-

Lautrec, Seurat and notable others. It is Van Gogh's mighty *Starry Night*, however, that stands out, arguably the museum's most celebrated possession.

Given a corner of its own just outside the post-impressionist galleries, Monet's *Water Lilies*, painted in 1920, is a remarkable study of the subtleties of light and shadow on water and land, the ripples of colour appearing to undulate before your eyes.

The next sequence of galleries picks out some of the seminal works of cubism – pioneering pieces like Picasso's *Three Women* and Braque's *Man With a Guitar*, which can be contrasted with offerings from the genre's other leading proponents, such as Gris and Léger.

Moving on, you will pass prime examples of expressionism and futurism, before entering a room dominated by Mondrian's colourful geometric grids – the New York-influenced *Broadway Boogie-Woogie* being prominent.

In a later gallery, you will find the pick of MoMA's extensive Matisse holdings (where *Dance* holds centre stage). Beyond it, a single room is devoted to Klee paintings and drawings. Finally, you will reach an entire wall covered by

The Sculpture Garden
Directly opposite the lobby, and a great place to pass an hour on a sunny afternoon after viewing the interior exhibits, MoMA's Abbey Aldrich Rockefeller Sculpture Garden is filled with an excellent and diverse collection of sculpture. Highlights include Henry Moore's *Family Group*, Picasso's *She Goat* – and Rodin's striking *Memorial to Balzac*, a towering bronze that was rejected by its Parisian commissioning committee in the 1890s.

159

an imposing selection of works by Picasso. Dating from the 1930s, some of these arresting images show the impact on Picasso of Europe's slide into war. They include the hauntingly grim *Charnel House*.

A wealth of works by Miró – who had tremendous influence on New York artists in the 1940s – dominates the surrealist rooms, though it is the arguably less accomplished pieces by Dali (*The Persistence of Memory*) and Magritte (*The False Mirror*), that provide instantly familiar, if no less surreal, images.

Also on the second floor are temporary photographic exhibitions, drawn from a permanent stock which ranges from Cartier-Bresson to Diane Arbus.

The third floor is detailed on page 160. Taking the escalator to the fourth floor, you will pass beneath an aluminium-bodied Pinin Farina sports car and a 1945 Bell helicopter as you enter the architecture and design exhibitions. These feature architectural models and drawings from Frank Lloyd Wright, Le Corbusier and others. The permanent design collection covers everything from Tiffany lamps to state-of-the-art Italian saucepans.

Inside the MoMA building – New York's earliest piece of architecture in the international style, and a fitting home for some of the most famous paintings and sculptures of the 20th century. Clever design, using plenty of natural light, and with space to stand back and relax, allows unhurried appreciation of the exhibits

■ **The Museum of Modern Art's third-floor galleries hold some of the most influential works in modern American art, from seminal abstract expressionist canvases to the latest mixed-media experiments ...■**

Temporary exhibitions at MoMA
It hardly need be said that a museum of MoMA's standing has no trouble in attracting temporary exhibitions of international repute. This is great news for art-loving New Yorkers, but not so good for visitors who may have travelled to New York only to find that their favourite artworks have been stored away to make room for a blockbusting temporary show. To avoid this, contact the museum (tel: 708 9480) or the New York Convention & Visitors' Bureau (tel: 397 8222) before making travel plans.

European influences Many items here reveal the influence of Europeans such as Matisse and Miró, both of whom have later works displayed here. An entire room, in fact, is devoted to Matisse's wonderful *The Swimming Pool*, a large-scale paper mural which originally decorated a wall of his home.

The New York School The most important galleries chart the development of abstract expressionism and the New York School (see pages 128–9). The influence of the surrealists' concern with the subconscious and universal myths is seen in early works by Jackson Pollock (*The She-Wolf* and *Gothic*), and Willem de Kooning.

Similar themes are explored by the so-called gesture artists, among them Franz Kline and Robert Motherwell, who used large blocks of black and white. By contrast, the color field artists such as Barnett Newman and Mark Rothko used shimmering bands of luminous colour to evoke emotional states.

Move through the chronologically arranged galleries and the abstract expressionist canvases grow steadily bigger and bolder, reaching their apotheosis in Pollock's monumental *One*.

Recent works After the draining and intense works of the abstract expressionists, it comes almost as light relief to enter the galleries of contemporary art, including Jasper Johns' *Target with Four Faces*, Robert Rauschenberg's study in mutating forms, *Bed*, the comic-strip paintings of Lichtenstein, and Claes Oldenburg's enjoyable oversized papier-mâché models of America's favourite foods.

Painting from the Museum of Modern Art's excellent third-floor galleries

►► **Museum of Television and Radio**   *151C2*

25 West 52nd Street
Subway: Fifth Avenue or Seventh Avenue
For serious media students and couch-potatoes alike, the
Museum of Television and Radio is the stuff that dreams
are made of. For almost anyone else, a visit here can be a
highly entertaining experience – and a perfect antidote to
sightseeing. This is quite unlike other museums. Over
40,000 American television and radio broadcasts from the
1920s to the present are stored here, all of them available
to the public at little more than a flick of a switch. Several
thousand new programmes are added to the collection
every year.

Each day, several small screening rooms show selections from the museum's televisual archive (schedules
are available from the lobby, or tel: 621 6800), while the
headphones in the cosy radio listening room can be
switched to one of five separate channels, each exploring
a different area of broadcasting history – anything from a
landmark Metropolitan Opera transmission to a wartime
comedy show.

*A TV addict's dream
come true – the
Museum of TV and
Radio offers your own
choice of viewing at
one of around 100
individual video con-
soles*

More demanding visitors can rifle through the library's
computerised cataloguing system and make their own
selections from the entire collection. Not only listing television programme titles, the database also carries details
of the personnel involved in each production – a handy
resource if you have forgotten who played Thing in *The
Addams Family*, or want to discover the real-life identity
of your favourite *Batman* villain.

Once you have made your choice (restricted to two
hours of viewing time) leave the library for the viewing
room, where your selection will be made ready almost
immediately (though there may be a three-day wait for
particularly obscure items) for watching at a video con-
sole.

Commercials – of which the museum has 10,000 in
stock – also feature among the daily screenings, as do
television shows from other countries, be they heavy-
weight documentaries or vintage episodes of *Monty
Python's Flying Circus*.

The museum building
You may be too eager to
renew your acquaintance-
ship with Perry Mason or
Lou Grant to notice, but the
building that houses the
Museum of Television and
Radio is a curious blend of
classical and modern
styles from architects
Philip Johnson and John
Burgee. With its 16-storey
limestone-clad tower, the
structure has been
described as the world's
first vertical museum.

■ **The advent of art deco coincided with the skyscraper boom which gripped New York during the 1920s, and the new decorative style was seen as the natural accompaniment to the world's most adventurous architecture. From world-famous buildings to fine details of decoration, walk around the city and you will find the art-deco influence everywhere ...■**

162

Zoning laws

In 1915, when the Financial District's Equitable Building rose straight up in the air, robbing adjacent streets and buildings of their sunlight and breezes, the city authorities responded with the US's first set of building regulations – or zoning laws.

The Zoning Law of 1916 divided New York into commercial and residential plots and insisted that future high-rise buildings were constructed with cutbacks as they rose above the street. This greatly affected the architecture of the city for the next 50 years.

Art deco first emerged in 1925 at the Paris Exposition Internationale des Arts Décoratifs, a show intended to highlight the fine skills of French craftsmen at a time when the German Bauhaus was revolutionising the world of the decorative arts.

New York was already aware of art deco, however, as the Metropolitan Museum of Art had amassed a collection of the finest European work and inadvertently aided the creation of an American bastardised art-deco style dubbed 'moderne'. With the emphasis on overall effect rather than individual craftsmanship, moderne art deco was tailor-made to the needs of the American market. Mass-produced terracotta and bronze friezes covered with geometric and floral designs, available by mail order, soon began appearing on buildings all over the country.

The new style began to affect interiors too. Some of New York's finest art-deco entranceways and lobbies, such as the Film Center Building (see page 102), are the work of the talented architect Ely Jacques Kahn.

One of the many fine art-deco sculptures in the Rockefeller Center

New York Telephone Company One of the city's earliest art-deco buildings was the New York Telephone Company (also called the Barclay-Vesey Building, 140 West Street), described by one critic as 'Mayan art deco'. To get around the constraints imposed by the narrow street, designer Ralph Walker gave the building a series of pedestrian arcades decorated by a cast-concrete frieze cluttered with depictions of bunches of grapes, rabbits, elephant heads, bells and much more.

Chrysler Building The single most spectacular and lastingly impressive art-deco building in New York, the Chrysler Building (see page 89) was one of the first buildings to use exposed metal. It rises in a series of cutbacks with each new level marked by a different type of decoration, be it a brickwork frieze of car wheels or immense winged radiator caps. Its most distinctive feature, however, is the seven-storey dome which takes the form of a tiered arch with triangular dormer windows encased in chrome steel.

Empire State Building The Chrysler Building was soon eclipsed as the world's tallest building by the Empire State Building. Built purely for commercial renting, every inch of the Empire State Building was critical and consequently the decoration was kept to a minimum – allowing the structure to emerge as a specimen of skyscraper art deco at its most restrained and dignified.

Chanin Building Sculptor René Chambellan's façade for the Chanin Building (122 East 42nd Street), drawing the eye away from the nearby Chrysler Building, depicts swooping birds on a bronze band which winds around the building below a terracotta frieze of geometric animal forms. Inside the bronze- and marble-dominated lobby, further bas-reliefs depict the 'City of Opportunity' – or New York as it was for the building's owner, Irwin Chanin, a property developer who struck lucky.

Raymond Hood Destined to become one of the leading architects of the Rockefeller Center, Hood used black brick and gold terracotta to emphasise the upright form of the **American Radiator Building** (40th Street between Fifth and Sixth avenues). He later developed this idea with vertical columns of windows and spandrels for the **Daily News Building** (see page 95). In the former **McGraw-Hill Building** (42nd Street between Eighth and Ninth avenues), with its green and gold terracotta, Hood continued his move towards the international style but the building's lobby retains its impressive art-deco interior.

With the **Rockefeller Center** (pages 173–4), New York art deco had its greatest day. Raymond Hood had a large hand in the center's showpiece RCA (now GE) Building. At the building's foot, Paul Manship's *Prometheus* is the first of scores of art-deco items decorating the entire complex. Meanwhile, the Rockefeller Center's **Radio City Music Hall** takes art deco into another dimension. Its vast and theatrical interior is intended to be as much a part of the evening's entertainment as the performers appearing on stage.

The Chrysler Building, resplendent with eagle gargoyles

▶   **National Academy of Design**   187C1

Fifth Avenue at 89th Street
Subway: 86th Street
Founded in 1825 by a group of accomplished artists, architects, sculptors and engravers – their ranks included luminaries such as the artist/inventor Samuel Morse, and the creator of Washington Square's handsome town houses, Ithiel Town – the National Academy of Design was established with the intention of becoming an artist-run school and museum to uphold and encourage 'the highest standards in the arts'.

Selections from the permanent collections are shown in the upstairs galleries, but one piece you can be certain of seeing is the sculptured figure of Diana by Anna Hyatt Huntington, which pivots at the foot of an elegant staircase leading up the Academy's galleries.

▶▶   **National Museum of the**   104A2
       American Indian

US Custom House, Bowling Green
Subway: Bowling Green
For many years, the US's major collection of Native American artefacts was housed in the Audubon Terrace complex in Harlem, where its geographical distance from most of the city's major museums caused it to be neglected by the majority of visitors. In the early 1990s, much of the collection was moved to the Smithsonian Institution in Washington, DC, but the city retained enough to fill several floors of the US Custom House (see page 190).

As the rights of indigenous peoples are slowly being recognised by the US's powers that be, some items for-

A focal point at the National Academy of Design: Anna Hyatt Huntington's statue of Diana

Early equipment on display at the Fire Museum

merly in the museum's possession have been returned to Native American tribes. Nonetheless, the museum retains a colossal hoard. Baskets, quilts and pottery drawn from the many and diverse cultures of North, South and Central America are among objects displayed, as are some of the infamous treaties which paved the way for European colonisation of Native American lands.

▶ New York City Fire Museum IFCB1
278 Spring Street, SoHo
Subway: Spring Street
It may not be at the top of every New York visitor's itinerary, but the New York City Fire Museum fills three floors with the buckets, hand-pumps, and horse-drawn fire-appliances that saved the city from near-total destruction on more than one occasion.

The antiquated carriages are the most spectacular exhibits but the bulk of the museum is made up of a mind-boggling collection of hose-pipe nozzles, ladders, axes, tools, fire alarms and extinguishers, and uniforms and helmets of shapes and sizes diverse enough to suggest that fire-fighters were rarely of similar size.

▶▶ New-York Historical Society IFCS3
Central Park West at 77th Street
Subway: 81st Street
Predating all the city's other museums, the New-York Historical Society was founded in 1804 (its hyphen dates from that time) and was uniquely placed to receive the bequests of wealthy New Yorkers. Consequently, the society is able to boast a substantial collection of works that range from early portraits of significant New Yorkers to important canvases from the country's first home-grown art movement, the Hudson River School. The society also holds a substantial collection of glassworks by Louis Comfort Tiffany and all extant watercolours in John James Audubon's *Birds of America* series.

The Great Fire of 1835
The temperature in New York City on 16 and 17 December 1835 was well below freezing, but that did not stop one of the most destructive fires in the city's history from razing 674 buildings on a 13-acre site in and around the Financial District.

Crowds arriving from the notorious Five Points slums looted the burnt-out buildings and helped the flames engulf many more. With insurance companies enduring the same losses as many of their clients, many of the city's banks and financial institutions were unable to reopen and as a result New York endured galloping inflation for the next two years.

■ In the 1930s, passengers boarding the New York–Chicago early evening service from Grand Central Terminal were, quite literally, given the red carpet treatment. Few who trod the venerated carpet, however, would have thought that just a few decades later the terminal – an architectural *tour de force* that was dubbed 'the gateway to the nation' – would be threatened by cheap air travel and by the rising value of the land on which it stands ...■

Grand Central Station? Many people, including life-long New Yorkers, often erroneously refer to Grand Central Terminal as 'Grand Central Station'. In fact, as trains can only begin or end their journeys there, 'terminal' is the correct word to use. The confusion was not helped by an enormously popular radio drama series which began in 1937, set in New York and titled *Grand Central Station*.

In the 1960s the Penn Central Railroad (the company in charge of Grand Central Terminal, and previously responsible for the demolition of the original and much-loved Pennsylvania Station) proposed to raise a 55-storey office tower above the terminal, but these short-sighted plans were thwarted by public pressure, and the building eventually became an official New York City landmark, gaining lasting protection.

Grand Central Terminal was completed in 1913 on a plot of land which then marked New York's northern edge. The land had been purchased by transportation magnate Cornelius Vanderbilt (see page 37), who had gained control of all rail routes into New York. After a ten-year period of construction, the station was unveiled to wide public acclaim both as an engineering marvel and as a delight to the eye.

Architectural elegance The terminal's construction was a joint effort. One architectural firm devised the innovative split-level design which allowed for a smooth flow of traffic – be it train, subway or pedestrian – into and through the station; another firm focused their energies on creating the terminal's graceful beaux-arts style. Since it was the arrival and departure point for millions of travellers (by 1939, as many people were passing through Grand Central Terminal each year as lived in the entire US), shops, hotels, restaurants and offices opened up in close proximity to the terminal, making the site a prime Midtown Manhattan plot.

Many side entrances and maze-like tunnels link the terminal with its surrounding streets and adjacent office towers such as the former Pan Am Building (now the Metropolitan Life Building, see panel on page 183), immediately to the north.

On the terminal's southern façade you will first see Jules-Félix Coutan's 48ft-high figures of Mercury, Hercules and Minerva, draping themselves around an American eagle. There is also a bronze likeness of Cornelius Vanderbilt – seemingly counting potential railway passengers as they pass.

The interior Once inside, head for the terminal's second storey and look upwards. On the 150ft-high vaulted ceiling, French artist Paul Helleu used 2,500 electric lights to

replicate the zodiacal constellations. The design is based on a medieval manuscript illustration and the debate continues as to whether or not Helleu was aware that medieval illustrators commonly depicted the heavens reversed – giving God's view.

Lower your gaze slightly and you will see the glass-walled catwalks along which pedestrians pass swiftly through and high above the heart of the terminal. The second storey of the terminal holds the now disused long-distance platforms – most trains today are used by commuters, the cross-country services running from the renovated Pennsylvania Station across town. Disappointed train-spotters might seek solace in the welcoming bar, which also provides an excellent view of the Main Concourse, below.

The quiet grandeur of the **Main Concourse** is often obliterated by the pounding of half a million pairs of commuters' feet each day and a ring of gaudy shop signs. Nonetheless, try to find a slow moment to descend the marble flight of steps on to its floor and seek out a quiet corner to contemplate its 75ft windows, its claim to be the world's largest room, and the once serious suggestion to develop the concourse into three separate bowling alleys.

A pearl of a restaurant The terminal's lower levels provide access to the subway system and also to a number of restaurants, including the legendary **Oyster Bar**. Besides serving a diverse selection of crustaceans – plus a wide variety of other seafood – the Oyster Bar has a low, vaulted ceiling, covered by tan-coloured Guastavino tiles. The restaurant also has unusual acoustic properties; the quietest whisper across one table can easily be audible across the room. There are few better places for listening in on the lunchtime gossip of New York executives (prices here can hit the expense-account bracket), although the suggestions that fortunes have been made on the Stock Exchange by inspired eavesdropping are apocryphal at best.

The huge scale and grand style of the Main Concourse (said to be the largest room in the world) affirm Grand Central Terminal as a monument to the halcyon days of rail travel

Guided tours
For a more detailed exploration of Grand Central Terminal, join the guided tour run by the Municipal Art Society (tel: 935 3960) which begins at 12:30 pm each Wednesday from outside the branch of Chemical Bank on the Main Concourse.

The imposing main entrance to New York Public Library on Fifth Avenue

The library's treasures

The New York Public library has an extraordinary stock of rare and valuable books and prints, some of which may be on display. These include a Gutenberg bible; a 1493 folio edition of a Christopher Columbus letter describing his American discoveries; the first full folio edition of Shakespeare, from 1623; the 1640 Bay Psalm Book (the first English book published in America); a handwritten copy of George Washington's farewell address; and an early draft of Jefferson's Declaration of Independence.

► ► ► **New York Public Library**   *151B2*

Fifth Avenue and 42nd Street
Subway: 42nd Street

You cannot borrow a book at the New York Public Library (the 3 million or so tomes are for reference only), but you can explore one of the city's finest expressions of public-use architecture, a beaux-arts temple created by the legendary firm of Carrère and Hastings and opened in 1911.

Just approaching the building is a treat. Its terrace and elegant steps are decorated by twin sculptured lions, fountains fronting statues symbolising Truth and Beauty, and bronze flagpole bases cast at the Long Island studios of Louis Comfort Tiffany.

The triple-arched portico entrance leads into the exquisitely proportioned Astor Hall – named after John Jacob Astor, founder of the US's first library (one of the three which combined to create the present library's original holdings).The information desk here dispenses floor plans and marks the starting point for free tours (Monday to Saturday 11am and 2pm).

Immediately ahead, Gottesman Hall stages some of the library's temporary exhibitions, but turn left for the De Witt Wallace Periodical Room at the end of the corridor. Publisher De Witt Wallace spent many hours in this room scanning periodicals and abridging their contents for his fledgling venture, the *Reader's Digest*. His considerable profits financed the room's 1983 restoration: its brass lamps and walnut chairs regained their original glory, and were joined by Richard Haas' splendid murals of New York magazine and newspaper offices.

Climb the marble stairway to the third floor, noting the original lamps and the lions'-head drinking fountains along the corridors on the way to the vaulted McGraw Rotunda, decorated in 1940 by Edward Laning's murals depicting the development of reading. This marks the entrance to the public catalogue room, where researchers beaver through computer databases. Across the corridor, the Edna Barnes Salomon Room displays the library's paintings and selections from its stock of printed treasures.

▶▶▶ Pierpont Morgan Library   151B2

36th Street at Madison Avenue
Subway: 33rd Street

Born into wealth and educated in Europe, J Pierpont Morgan had become one of New York's leading financiers by the closing decades of the 19th century but, unlike his *nouveau-riche* contemporaries, trusted his own taste and judgement as he lavished a fortune on European cultural treasures, acquiring rare books, manuscripts and drawings which by 1890 had become one of the finest private collections in the US.

In 1902, Morgan commissioned the leading architect of the day, Charles F McKim, to create the Renaissance-style Pierpont Morgan Library. The Palladian porch which marks the library's original entrance on 36th Street merits a special look, though the present entrance is on the Madison Avenue side, and enters a 1928 annexe on the site of Morgan's son's brownstone residence.

The temporary exhibitions filling the immediate rooms could hold your attention for hours, but look first around the library itself, starting at the West Room, where Morgan's study is preserved as it was on the fabled financier's death in 1913. Once described as 'the most beautiful room in America', the study is lined by Italian Renaissance paintings and dominated by Morgan's immense wooden desk.

From the study, free-standing columns of green-veined marble mark the way to the imposing rotunda and the East Room. In a nutshell, the East Room is the plushest reading room you are ever likely to see. Three tiers of bookcases, fashioned from bronze and inlaid walnut, rise to a ceiling covered by colourful murals of artists and scholars (and signs of the zodiac), while above the fireplace hangs a 16th-century Flemish tapestry.

Sumptuous though it certainly is, the East Room is never overbearing and you could spend a long time here, poring over priceless letters and manuscripts.

The Pierpont Morgan collections
The following are just a few items from the vast collections of the Pierpont Morgan Library: three Gutenberg bibles; a Shakespeare first folio; an autographed manuscript of Milton's *Paradise Lost*; manuscripts and early editions of Rudyard Kipling, Oscar Wilde and Gertrude Stein bearing the authors' doodles and changes; musical scores from the hands of Bach, Brahms and Beethoven; etchings and prints by Rembrandt, Rubens and Degas; and a huge selection of pre-19th century paintings and *objets d'art*.

Space for the studious: the reading room of New York Public Library. Choose your tome from the library's many miles of shelving and consult it here

QUEENS

*The interior of
Bowne House, the
oldest building in
Queens*

▶   **Queens**   48C3
An almighty slab of suburbia holding 2 million people and
spreading across 119 square miles of western Long
Island, Queens is completely incomprehensible unless
you think of it as its residents do: a network of separate
and self-contained communities, many of which are eth-
nically distinct and have nothing except geography in
common with the neighbourhood that happens to be
found next door.

While much of Queens fits the bungalow-and-two-car-
garage image of the typical American big-city bedroom
community, many portions reflect New York's immigration patterns. Large communities of Koreans, Indians and
Japanese nestle beside other areas long dominated by
Greeks or Puerto Ricans.

Even though you probably failed to realise it at the time,
if your arrival point in New York was **La Guardia** or **JFK**
airport, you have already had a brief taste of Queens. Both
airports are sited in the borough. Planes into JFK swoop
above the 20 square miles of marshlands comprising the
Jamaica Bay Wildlife Refuge, a place much more interesting to migrating birdlife than to all but the most ornitho-
logically obsessed humans.

You will need a car and a very detailed map to explore all
of Queens but the main points of interest – seeing which
will also give a broad flavour of the borough's ethnic mix –
are slotted into a handful of key areas, easily reached by
public transport from Manhattan.

Take the subway from Manhattan to **Flushing**, for
example, and you will soon see why the route is unoffi-
cially dubbed the 'Orient Express'. What Flushing's
Japanese supermarkets, Korean restaurants, and
Chinese dim sum houses do not suggest, however, are
the town's 17th-century links with Quakers.

At 137–16 Main Street, a Friends' Meeting House has
stood since 1694 and, on a nearby corner, the 1661
Bowne House▶▶ has further connections with the
Society of Friends. The house's owner, John Bowne, was
exiled for defying the ban imposed by Peter Stuyvesant –
New York's iron-fisted Dutch governor – on Quaker
meetings. However, he persuaded the Dutch West India
Company – who did not want to risk losing any would-be
settlers – to insist that all religious groups would be toler-
ated in the new colony: a step towards the religious freedoms later enshrined in the US constitution.

The house holds some of Bowne's colonial furnishings,
plus those of his descendants, resident here until the
1940s. Tours of the small modest dwelling wend their
way into the kitchen, where the clandestine Quaker
meetings took place.

A short walk from the Bowne House, the 1774
Kingsland Homestead is an example of the Dutch and
English architectural mix which was typical of Long Island
farmhouses of the period. Otherwise, the house is only of
interest because the Queens Historical Society has its
offices inside, where an informative historical guide to the
borough is available.

A mile east of Flushing, **Flushing Meadows-Corona
Park▶▶** began life as a swamp and was later a rubbish
dump but by 1939 it was drawing millions to the World's
Fair which symbolised New York's emergence from the

The United Nations in Queens
The City Building, which houses the Queens Museum in Flushing Meadows-Corona Park, was used by the United Nations as the organisation awaited the completion of its purpose-built site in Manhattan. Among the motions carried here was the 1947 one that paved the way for the creation of the state of Israel.

Depression. A few ruins from the 1939–40 fair remain, as do many more from a second World's Fair held here in 1964–5. Among these are Philip Johnson's **New York State Pavilion Building** – the architectural highlight of the 1960s show, but these days in a much crumbled condition which reflects poorly on the construction ideas of the time – and the 140ft-high **Unisphere**, intended to represent the Earth and its satellites. Another 1960s survivor, the **New York Hall of Science▶**, is these days crammed with hands-on computer exhibits designed to explain the rudiments of science to young minds.

More modest-sized memorabilia from both world fairs is displayed inside the **Queens Museum▶**, housed in a structure which dates from the 1939–40 fair. What fascinates most here is the Panorama: a scale model of New York City which covers 18,000 square feet and includes every building in the city. Created for the 1960s fair, the Panorama is updated regularly.

The park is also home to the **Queens Wildlife Conservation Center**, a small zoo featuring North American animals in their natural habitat.

A busy street in New York's largest borough

Roosevelt Avenue, in the Jackson Heights neighbourhood of Queens, is known for its bakeries and restaurants

Baseball fans and devotees of the Fab Four might care to note that Shea Stadium, home of the New York Mets and the venue of a now legendary concert by the Beatles in 1965, stands in the northerly section of the park.

On the borough's northern side, facing the Bronx across the East River, Astoria▶ is one of the world's largest Greek communities. Lining 31st Street and Ditmars Boulevard are countless Greek bakeries, cafés and restaurants, and even the graffiti on the walls is in Greek.

Not remotely Greek, though, and failing to live up to its grand title, is Astoria's **American Museum of the Moving Image**▶, 36–11 35th Avenue, which occupies part of a working studio complex. During the 1920s, Paramount shot silent movies here with legendary figures such as Rudolph Valentino, Clara Bow, Gloria Swanson and the Marx Brothers before they – along with the rest of the American film industry – relocated to Hollywood.

The museum presents selected cinematic classics and carries temporary exhibitions on various aspects of movie history. On permanent display is a large but only mildly interesting collection of props, costumes, film-making equipment, fan magazines and vintage movie posters.

Heading back towards Manhattan, the heavily industrialised **Long Island City** is forging a reputation as an artists' enclave. In its early days, the area of Long Island City known as Hunters' Point was linked by ferry to Manhattan, encouraging business development here. Some of the old warehouses and factories, now disused, have been redeveloped into artists' studios.

A showpiece of artistic Long Island City is the river-front **Isamu Noguchi Garden Museum**▶▶, 32–37 Vernon Boulevard. This is devoted to the work of the accomplished and acclaimed sculptor. The son of a Japanese poet who emigrated to California, Noguchi's unconventional ideas were derided by his first instructor, but his imagination and creativity is clear enough throughout the 12 indoor galleries which chart his long career (Noguchi died in 1988, aged 84), and in the gardens which hold still more of his enigmatic creations.

Steinway
Just east of Astoria, the town of Steinway was created by William Steinway when he moved his piano factory here – partly to escape the power of unions – from Manhattan in 1872. The factory still stands at 19th Avenue and 39th Street. Steinway himself, meanwhile, moved into a stonework Italianate villa overlooking the East River at 18–33 41st Street. The slightly spooky villa has certainly seen better days, as has the now entirely unsalubrious neighbourhood which surrounds it.

▶▶ **Rockefeller Center** *151C2*

47th–52nd streets between Fifth and Sixth avenues
Subway: 50th Street
This is the world's largest commercial and entertainment complex, through which a quarter of a million people pass each day. The project changed the face of American urban planning from the 1940s.

The Center is named after multimillionaire John D Rockefeller Jr, who was approached in 1928 by the Metropolitan Opera with a view to his developing a down-at-heel Midtown site, on land rented from Columbia University, as a new Opera House. Rockefeller agreed, but the Wall Street crash led to the shelving of the plans and left him with 11 acres of land and a very large debt.

In the country's first major pooled architectural project, Rockefeller commissioned several firms to erect 14 buildings on the site with the provisos that the structures form an aesthetically unified entity, and that the complex should be a pleasing environment for working, eating, shopping and relaxing.

As a result, the art deco buildings themselves take a secondary role to the numerous cafés, restaurants, underground walkways and shopping plazas secreted in and around them, allowing a flow of light and easy movement of people which became the blueprint for city-centre renewal initiatives throughout the US.

To reach the heart of the complex, enter from Fifth Avenue along the short Channel Gardens to the sunken Plaza▶, which holds an open-air restaurant and a wintertime ice-rink, and is presided over by Paul Manship's 1934 figure of *Prometheus*.

Rising above Prometheus' head, the 70-storey **GE Building** (much better known by its original title, the RCA

Rockefeller Center Facts
Number employed in construction 1931–40: 75,000.
Number of telephones: 100,000.
Number of elevators: 488.
Cost of buying Columbia University's leasehold in 1985: $400 million.

Gertrude Stein on the RCA Building, 1935
'The most beautiful thing I have seen'.

173

Summertime brings bright umbrellas and a holiday atmosphere to the sunken plaza amid the office buildings of the Rockefeller Center

Building) is the heart of the Rockefeller Center. Enter the lobby and note the murals by José Maria Sert – replacements for those of Diego Rivera, who refused to appease the anti-communist Rockefellers by removing a handsome likeness of Lenin.

Take the elevator to the **Rainbow Room** on the 65th floor where, for the price of a drink, you can gaze over Manhattan. Return to the lobby to collect a free map from the information desk, essential as you begin weaving deeper into the Rockefeller Center labyrinth.

Simple wanderings will reveal much of interest but one place not to be missed is **Radio City Music Hall**. The hall's 1932 gala opening was attended by the likes of Charlie Chaplin and Clark Gable and it instantly became one of the great American entertainment palaces. More recently a favoured location for film premieres, the hall's 6,000-seat interior is still an art-deco delight and can be seen on guided tours (tel: 632 4041).

Less glamorous but still in the realms of the showbiz world, the offices and studios of **NBC Television** can be viewed on hour-long guided tours (tel: 664 7174).

▶ **Roosevelt Island** 187A2

Once covered by 27 hospitals which kept the incurably sick and insane (and the simply scandalous, such as Mae West) segregated from the rest of New York society, Roosevelt Island is today regarded as one of the country's most successful attempts at integrated mixed-income housing. Would-be residents now have to wait several years to get an apartment in the area.

Besides near-total absence of crime, Roosevelt Island dwellers also enjoy car-free streets and a sight of the Midtown Manhattan skyline unsurpassed anywhere else in the city. For visitors, the peacefulness and the views (and the cable-car that crosses to the island – see the panel) are the only attractions, though the ruins of the old hospitals, shielded by fences at the island's southern end, add a distinctly eerie note.

174

Getting to Roosevelt Island
A road bridge crosses from Queens to Roosevelt Island, but to reach the island from Manhattan, use either the subway (lines B or Q) or (much the best choice) the cable-car, which makes a 3-minute jaunt over the East River from a terminal at Second Avenue and 60th Street.

The Roosevelt Island cable-car

► SoHo

113A2

Named for being SOuth of HOuston Street (and bordered also by Canal, Lafayette and Sullivan streets), SoHo is dominated by large cast-iron buildings put up in the mid-19th century to house factories – the notorious 'sweatshops'.

When dangerous sweatshop working conditions were outlawed in 1962 (the innumerable fires and fatalities that resulted from unsafe working practices earned SoHo the nickname 'Hell's Hundred Acres'), SoHo industries moved away and the district suffered a decade of neglect.

The determined efforts of conservationists saved the area and its unique buildings from demolition and, after 10 years of colonisation by up-and-coming artists who were attracted by spacious rooms lit by immense windows, SoHo entered a period of swift gentrification, its loft-style apartments finding favour with the city's rich and trendy – and with the art dealers who made the area internationally synonymous with contemporary art. With chic clothing stores and fashionable restaurants alongside scores of art galleries, SoHo is now transformed – but it is the dozens of remaining cast-iron buildings that shape its character.

Available through mail-order catalogues and assembled cheaply and quickly on site, prefabricated cast-iron structures represented a revolution in urban design in the mid-1800s. Their *ersatz* European decoration – be it of classical Rome or the French Renaissance – also aped the then fashionable look of the US's new business buildings, the classically themed 'temples of commerce'.

Among the earliest examples of the cast-iron form, the **Haughwout Building** (488–92 Broadway) dates from 1857 and still imposes its harmony on the surrounding streets, rising in four tiers of arched windows and Corinthian columns – a design said to be based on the Sansovino Library in Venice.

On Greene Street, numbers 28–30 and 72–6 show the artistry that later ironwork facades acquired, while the **Little Singer Building** (561–3 Broadway) suggests the next great architectural step: replacing cast-iron floor supports with steel – the basis of the modern skyscraper.

You need never look far for signs of creative endeavour in SoHo

Richard Haas' SoHo mural
Since 1973, at the junction of SoHo's Prince and Greene streets, the neighbourhood's bringing together of contemporary art and historic cast-iron buildings has been celebrated in a witty *trompe l'oeil* by Richard Haas, which cleverly confuses the actual features of the buildings with painted representations.

■ **You do not have to be an art dealer to find New York's 500 or more art galleries fascinating. Most of the galleries are clustered close together in SoHo – very much the international nerve centre of contemporary art – though others are well established on the Upper East Side and along 57th Street. Take the time to see the non-profit galleries, too, showcasing the work considered too risky by the commercial galleries ...■**

The Gallery Guide
The *New York Times*, the *Village Voice* and many specialist art publications carry art gallery listings, but the most comprehensive details are provided by *Gallery Guide*. A publication listing over 500 galleries and providing maps to help locate them, the *Gallery Guide* is published monthly and distributed free in galleries and a few selected bookshops. Be warned that the popularity of the *Gallery Guide* makes it almost impossible to find any later than the middle of the month.

Upper East Side galleries The epitome of Upper East Side elegance and sophistication, the Paris-founded **Wildenstein & Co** (19 East 64th Street) specialises in French impressionism but its holdings extend from contemporary paintings to antique *objets d'art*.

The diverse stocks of **Hirschl & Adler** are displayed in three separate galleries. The main location (21 East 70th Street) carries a broad selection of 18th- and 19th-century European pieces; at the same address, **Hirschl & Adler Folk** holds American folk art, from paintings to crafts, while **Hirschl & Adler Modern** (4th floor, 420 West Broadway, in Sotto) specialises in American and European names from the mid-1950s.

Focusing on modern American painters, the **Gagosian Gallery** (Madison Avenue between 76th and 77th streets) provides a museum-like space for lesser-known works by well-known names, including Jackson Pollock, Willem de Kooning, Andy Warhol and Cy Twombly.

57th Street galleries If you only visit one 57th Street gallery, make it **Pace** (32 East 57th Street). This deserves its place among the world's leading galleries for a stock that includes virtually every European and American name of major significance from the last 30 years.

Influential in the emergence of pop art and noted for the high quality of its purchases, the **Sidney Janis Gallery** (110 West 57th Street) has been a fixture on the New York art scene for four decades and continues to present established and new names in stimulating exhibitions.

Abstract expressionists turn up in many New York galleries but one of the better places to find works by the color field artists is the **André Emmerich Gallery** (41 East 57th Street).

If you become jaded by American and British art, the remedy might be **Galerie St Etienne** (24 West 57th Street), where some intriguing historical documents from the turbulent 1930s can be seen alongside some fine examples of German expressionism.

SoHo galleries Serious art watchers ignore the **Mary Boone Gallery** (417 West Broadway) at their peril. With a knack of latching on to developing trends before any other gallery had noticed them, through the 1980s Mary Boone helped launch some of the brightest new names in American art, such as David Salle and Julian Schnabel.

In the early 1960s, the **Leo Castelli Gallery** (2nd floor, 420 West Broadway) brought artists such as Andy Warhol, Roy Lichtenstein, Jasper Johns and Frank Stella to wide attention and is now among the world's leading galleries. The gallery has a graphic arts annexe, which can be found at 578 Broadway.

Minimalist and conceptual art is the stock-in-trade of the highly regarded **John Weber Gallery** (142 Greene Street), closely linked with established figures such as Sol Lewitt and regularly showcasing new artists with a similar outlook. Innovative and challenging sculpture, painting and photography from Europe and the US is regularly on show at **Metro Pictures** (150 Greene Street), where work by Cindy Sherman and Louise Laller is also often featured.

Guided tours of art galleries
If you want to be led through the city's art gallery labyrinth by an expert – and if you have the money (expect to spend $30–$50 per person) and the interest, this is an excellent way to get an insider's view of the world's most frenetic art scene – two small companies provide just such a service: Art Tours of Manhattan (tel: 677 6005) and Art Horizons International (tel: 969 9410).

177

Non-profit galleries **Artists' Space** (223 West Broadway) has an esteemed reputation as a launch pad for artists working with installations and video, and in the past has done wonders for Laurie Anderson, David Salle and Cindy Sherman. Each September, a group of unknowns is selected from the Artists' Space files for a group exhibition – worth seeing if you are around.

Since the mid-1970s, the Dia Art Foundation has provided funds for long-term installations and environmental pieces. Among these are two works by Walter de Maria: the **New York Earth Room** (141 Wooster Street) is a room filled with 14 tons of soil, and **The Broken Kilometer** (393 West Broadway) comprises a kilometre's worth of brass rods arranged in rows. Both are much more interesting than they sound – and could well be New York's most extraordinary sights.

The characterful streets of SoHo have become the place to go if you are interested in contemporary art. Over the past 20 years, numerous small galleries have opened in the area, providing launching pads for many new names in the art world

South Street Seaport and the cargo ship Peking

Stroll: Water Street
Water Street, between Wall Street and South Street Seaport, was New York's main riverside thoroughfare in the 19th century, lined by sailors' boarding houses, bars and brothels.

SOUTH STREET SEAPORT MUSEUM

SEPTEMBER 11,
MUSEUM ADMISSION

TICKET VALUE: $8.00

STEM IS MADE POSSIBLE BY A GENEROUS GI

▶   **South Street Seaport**   *104B3*
Eastern foot of Fulton Street
Subway: Fulton Street
A large collection of shops and restaurants, and a smattering of small museums, make up South Street Seaport, which transformed an abandoned area beside the East River – the place where New York's 19th-century maritime trade flourished – into a history-themed leisure complex, eagerly patronised by Financial District employees after work.

By day, however, most visitors come here to explore several ageing ships moored beside the South Street piers. The most interesting exhibit is the 1911 *Peking*, a four-masted cargo vessel which spent its glory days shifting nitrate from South America to the US and made several roundings of Cape Horn. Climb aboard and descend to a lower deck where a pictorial display recounts the ship's working life.

Back on dry land, the **Museum Gallery** has a minor exhibition of maritime photos and ships-in-bottles, and assorted certificates and documents attesting to New York's historical place as one of the world's great seaports.

▶▶   **Staten Island**   *48A1*
A ride on the famous Staten Island Ferry (see the panel opposite) is reason enough to make the crossing from the Financial District to the hilly chunk of land wedged between New Jersey and Brooklyn, but Staten Island has much more than a ferry to call its own.

Settled by Dutch and French farmers in 1661 and an important British base during the Revolutionary War, the island has evolved into leafy suburbia with a tranquil mood that makes it seem a million miles from the hurly-burly of the rest of New York City.

The ferry docks at St George, the island's least enthralling community (even the Staten Island Museum here can be by-passed without worry). Two miles west (take bus S40 from the ferry terminal), Sailors' Snug Harbor is a better first stop. Founded in the 1800s for 'decrepit and worn-out sailors', it is now better known as **Snug Harbor Cultural Center▶**. Restoration has kept a number of its imposing 19th-century buildings intact.

It is further south that Staten Island's real treasures are to be found (take bus S74). Visiting in 1991, the Dalai Lama himself described as 'accurate' the stone cottage on Lighthouse Hill intended to replicate a Tibetan mountain temple and provide an apt home for the **Jacques Marchais Center of Tibetan Art▶▶▶**, a wondrous stock of sculptured deities, ritual objects, incense burners and much more from the world's Buddhist cultures.

Now the largest private gathering of such material in the western world, the collection was inspired by the discovery in 1880 by the young Jacqueline Norman Klauber (who later renamed herself Jacques Marchais), of 12 Tibetan figurines which her great-grandfather had brought back from a trip to India and stored in the family attic. This stimulated a lifelong fascination with Buddhism and its

The Conference House
Students of international summitry visiting Staten Island might consider making a trip to the Conference House. In September 1776, the stone-built house became the venue of the only peace talks attempted between the British forces and the American revolutionaries. Believe it or not, the house served as a rat-poison factory before becoming a museum in 1926. The interior has period furniture and numerous items recording the revolutionary conflict – and the failed attempt to broker a peace.

The Staten Island Ferry terminal

sacraments, and no opportunity was missed to expand the collection.

Whether you are looking at the Buddhist Wheel of Life or a yak butter burner, informative explanatory texts make sense of the exhibits, and illuminate their complex symbolism. Visits are by appointment only, tel: 718/987 3478.

A mile south, the 100-acre **Richmondtown Historic Restoration▶▶** shows the fruits of half a century of gathering and restoring buildings dating from the 17th to the 19th centuries and equipping them with (usually) the original occupants' possessions. Local history buffs, dressed in period costume and keen to pass on their knowledge, help with tours around the old homes. These range from a sparsely furnished Dutch building which doubled as local church and schoolhouse to a general store packed with 1840s consumer durables – all providing a fascinating insight into forgotten ways of life.

Also within the complex, the Island Historical Museum presents a chronological record of Staten Island's growth, with many enjoyable exhibits from some of its early industries, which over the years have ranged from brewing to oyster harvesting.

The Staten Island Ferry
The actual vessel is entirely ordinary but the views from the Staten Island Ferry can be wonderful. The Statue of Liberty, Governor's Island, and the Verrazano-Narrows Bridge all appear as the skyscrapers of Lower Manhattan shrink into the distance and the green hills of Staten Island draw nearer. The ferry (pedestrians only) takes half an hour to make the 5-mile crossing and the amazingly cheap return trip fare is payable before departure only from the Staten Island terminal, at the end of Whitehall Street.

If you have time to spare, visit the **Alice Austen House▶**, a bayside home on Staten Island's eastern edge, dating from 1710 and filled by some of the 8,000 photographs taken by the untrained Alice over a 50-year period to 1934. In 1951, *Time* magazine discovered and published some of her work. Her talents were soon recognised far afield, yet at the time her fame was growing, Alice was spending her poverty-stricken old age toiling in a public workhouse.

Another small and equally unexpected collection is the **Garibaldi Meucci Museum▶**, where Giuseppe Garibaldi – one of the founders of unified Italy – spent two years in the 1850s in the home of American-Italian Antonio Meucci, both of them working in a local candle factory. Garibaldi's place in history is assured, but fate was unkinder to Meucci, an inventor who developed a prototype telephone but failed to patent the idea. To reach both this and the Alice Austin House, take bus S51 from the ferry terminal.

▶▶ Statue of Liberty 48C2

There is no greater symbol of the US and its promise of freedom and opportunity for all than the Statue of Liberty, which has held the flame of liberty above New York harbour since 1886. From Manhattan, a visit to the statue begins with a ferry ride from Battery Park Pier. Boats to the statue also put ashore at the excellent Ellis Island (see page 100).

At the statue, there are two options. If you have the time and energy, begin an assault on the 354 steps which lead up the crown – but be warned that the staircase is narrow and that you can only climb as fast as the person in front (the ascent can take three hours). Alternatively, take the elevator to the pedestal level, from which the views are only marginally less impressive than those from the crown. On the way down, visit the intriguing museum which records the creation of the statue and the effect it had on newly arrived immigrants when seeing it for the first time.

Statue of Liberty Facts
Height: 151ft 1in.
Weight: 450,000lbs.
Length of hand: 16ft 5in
Length of index finger: 8ft.
Length of nose: 4ft 6in.
Thickness of waist: 35ft.
Best film role: in Alfred Hitchcock's *Saboteur*.
Biggest fictional blunder: Liberty's torch is described as a sword in Franz Kafka's *America*.

Liberty Island is in fact closer to New Jersey than to New York, but its statue is universally regarded as a fundamental part of the city

■ **Originally intended to stand in Egypt, partly funded by a French lottery, and at first regarded in the US as a waste of money, the Statue of Liberty may be America's most famous landmark but the story of its construction is much less straightforward than most people realise ...■**

Liberty in Egypt? A sculptor with a taste for monuments on the grand scale, Frenchman Frédéric Auguste Bartholdi visited Egypt and presented to the Egyptian sultan his plans for a gigantic figure of a robed female peasant holding a torch, to be sited at the entrance to the Suez canal.

The sultan rejected the scheme but Bartholdi, on a trip to the US in 1871, found the perfect spot for his torch-carrying lady at the entrance to New York's harbour, 4,000 miles from her original intended location.

French friendship The idea of a gift from France to the US to mark the nations' shared belief in democracy had been around for some time, and Bartholdi's statue idea was taken on board by France's new Third Republic, busy modelling its constitution along US lines.

As a sign of friendship, both governments agreed that the work would be shared, Bartholdi producing the statue while its pedestal was made in New York. In France, a popular lottery raised 250,000 francs towards the project but in the US, the idea was greeted with apathy.

As *Liberty Enlightening the World* (as the statue is officially titled) took shape outside Bartholdi's Paris studio – being too large to fit inside – the pedestal had barely left the drawing board, and the American press was full of satirical cartoons and articles condemning its expense.

Raising the money After Congress rejected a bill allocating $100,000 to the work, and the mayor of New York vetoed a plan for the city to donate $50,000, newspaper publisher Joseph Pulitzer attacked the miserliness of the nation's rich, and appealed for contributions – no matter how small – from ordinary Americans.

Packed into 214 crates, the finished statue arrived in New York in June 1885. Two months later, Pulitzer announced that the goal of raising $100,000 had been reached.

The statue was hoisted on to its pedestal in May 1886, and officially unveiled in a special ceremony the following October. The response, as Pulitzer's newspaper recorded at the time, was 'one long cheer'.

Liberty Enlightening the World – a powerful symbol of welcome to generations of new arrivals in New York Harbour

The Stock Exchange

Stock Exchange   104B2

Broad Street near Wall Street
Subway: Wall Street

Housed in a 1903 neo-classical building, the New York Stock Exchange might be expected to form the highlight of a tour around the Financial District. Unless you have a vested interest in the ups and downs of the Dow Jones average, however, the exchange's 37,000sq.-ft litter-strewn dealing floor – populated by colour-jacketed brokers, reporters and pages – looks no more interesting from behind the glass of the public viewing gallery than it does on TV.

The exhibits on the exchange's history, and on share dealing in general, do nothing to lessen the sense of anti-climax. Nonetheless, if you want to view the spot where the crash of 1929 plunged the US into the Great Depression, it is best to pick up your ticket, free and time-stamped for the half-hourly tours, from the entrance soon after 9am.

▶ Theodore Roosevelt Birthplace   151A2

20th Street between Broadway and Park Avenue
Subway: 23rd Street

The nation's future 26th president, Theodore Roosevelt entered the world in 1858 in a Midtown Manhattan brownstone, a building subsequently demolished but precisely reconstructed on its original site in 1923 to house a museum honouring the only US president to have been a New York native.

The lower floor carries an absorbing exhibition on Roosevelt's life, from his childhood struggles with asthma and the tragedy of the deaths of his mother and his wife on the same day, to his entry into politics on a ticket of ending the corruption endemic in New York affairs and his rise to become the nation's youngest ever president in 1901, aged 43.

Upstairs, more than half the furnishings in the period rooms come from the original house of the Roosevelt family. Best capturing the personality of Roosevelt himself is the room stuffed with his hunting trophies and outdoor memorabilia.

▶ TriBeCa   IFCB1

Subway: Franklin Street

TriBeCa – the TRIangle BElow CAnal Street (bordered in the east by Broadway and continuing west to the Hudson River) – became the stamping ground of the artists who were priced out of their SoHo lofts (see page 175) as that district's property values soared throughout the 1970s.

Like SoHo, TriBeCa's old warehouses – formerly at the centre of New York's dairy and poultry trade – offer apartments with ample space and natural light, making perfect studios. Also like SoHo, however, TriBeCa is increasingly taking the fancy of upmarket residents in search of stylish Lower Manhattan living and a sound property investment.

Besides providing as good a picture of New York-style urban regeneration as you are likely to find, a walk through TriBeCa uncovers something of note at almost every turn. Art galleries, much less slick than their SoHo counterparts, occupy many of the former industrial build-

A radical exorcism at the Stock Exchange
The bulletproof glass screen which shields the trading floor of the Stock Exchange from the public gallery has been in place since 1967, the year when future yippie (a twist on the term 'hippie') Abbie Hoffman and friends tossed 300 one-dollar bills on to the trading floor. Traders went scurrying for the cash and one of Hoffman's co-activists described the incident as 'exorcising the evil spirits of the Stock Exchange'.

ings. A notable example is the **Clocktower** at 108 Leonard Street. Dozens of pricey restaurants nourish fashionable faces while, at 37–41 Harrison Street, a primly restored row of early-1800s Federal-style town houses makes a wholly incongruous appearance.

Trump Tower   151C2

Fifth Avenue at 56th Street
Subway: 60th Street or 59th Street
High-profile property tycoon Donald Trump was brave enough to put his name to this horrid glass tower – a monument to the booming economy of the early 1980s and the frenzied building that it financed. He also became one of the people actually to live in one of the 263 plush apartments that fill the tower's upper levels.

Although the façade is among the city's least inviting, step inside Trump Tower for some serious window-shopping. Serenaded by the tinkling of a five-storey waterfall, a host of designer-name boutiques have outlets here – though the pink marble surfaces and the obsessively manicured shrubbery might have you running for the exit surprisingly quickly.

Inside or out, nothing is understated at Trump Tower

The former Pan Am Building
Bauhaus architect Walter Gropius was among the team that designed the Pan Am Building on Park Avenue, adjoining Grand Central Terminal. The largest commercial office building ever constructed, it is also possibly the only one so closely resembling an aircraft wing. Following the demise of Pan Am, the Metropolitan Life Insurance company purchased the building in 1992 and set about removing its much-photographed Pan Am logo. The building itself remains as familiar a sight as ever, though, still blocking the view along Park Avenue.

Stroll: Duane Park
By day, the streets around TriBeCa's Duane Park provide fruitful territory for a stroll. Head northwards along Hudson Street, and turn off to explore Harrison and Leonard Streets.

UNITED NATIONS

The UN in session
During its September to December sitting, the General Assembly of the UN can be witnessed in session from the public gallery. Free tickets are issued from the information desk in the lobby on a first-come, first-served basis. In theory, the tickets are handed out at 10:30am and 3:30pm. In practice there are liable to be long delays and, with security concerns paramount, sometimes no tickets will be issued at all, even if you have been waiting all day.

The General Assembly in session. The immense hall can accommodate delegations from up to 179 countries, and proceedings are conducted in six official languages

▶ **United Nations** *151C3*

First Avenue between 42nd and 46th streets
Subway: Grand Central Terminal

Given the problems blamed on its huge and infamously cumbersome bureaucracy, it might be apt that the main building of the United Nations – the organisation of world states formed in San Francisco in 1945 and operating on this plot since 1947 – should be the Secretariat Building. This enormous building houses the UN's 16,000 pen-pushers and rises for 39 marble-and-glass storeys above the East River.

The UN's public entrance is through the General Assembly Building. The lobby carries temporary exhibitions on international themes, and from here a stairway leads down to the souvenir shop, post office (selling United Nations postage stamps, which are valid only on mail that is posted here), and also to a rather gloomy cafeteria.

To see any more of the UN, you will need to buy a ticket for a guided tour. Departing every 15 minutes or so from the lobby, the tours last around an hour and sweep through the various UN buildings, pausing on the way at displays on the work of the UN and at artworks donated by member states. None of these comes close to matching the emotional impact of the half-melted items culled from the ruins of Hiroshima and Nagasaki which are also on show.

Assuming no meetings are in session, the tour stops by the Security Council chamber – where the calmness imposed by the empty chairs and desks belies the fact that this is the only UN body with any teeth, able to impose economic sanctions and instigate military actions – and the General Assembly room, the very size of which suggests it can never be anything more than a debating chamber.

■ **The traffic gridlock that ensues whenever heads of state arrive to take their places at the United Nations now seems such an established part of New York life that it is easy to forget that the organisation came within a whisker of opting for Philadelphia as its permanent home. What is more, present-day budget problems are causing the UN to reassess not only its expenditure but also its continued presence in the Big Apple ...■**

The United Nations Charter was signed by representatives of 50 countries in San Francisco in April 1945, but the General Assembly convened its first meeting in London in 1946, a year during which the scramble among several cities to become the organisation's permanent base grew intense.

San Francisco, Boston and Philadelphia were in the running before New York's application to become the UN's home was instigated by the city's most famous (some would say most infamous) planning department chief, Robert Moses, who promised that a successful bid 'would make New York the center of the world'.

Philadelphia or New York? Among those on the city's campaign committee was Nelson Rockefeller, a member of the Rockefeller banking dynasty, who was carving a political career for himself with the ultimate ambition of becoming president. Rockefeller persuaded UN officials to use New York as their base when sizing up the rival bids during 1946, but by December it seemed certain that Philadelphia would be chosen and that city's authorities began preparing the future UN site.

Meanwhile, property developer William Zeckendorf had been buying up cheap land alongside New York's East River for residential use. Rockefeller made Zeckendorf an offer he could not refuse for the land, presented the site to the UN officials and won the bid – the land being paid for with an $8.5 million grant from Rockefeller's father. The complex of buildings was completed in 1963.

Mixed feelings Although not all New Yorkers could see the wisdom of diverting their taxes into easing the UN's arrival and providing incentives for its diplomats, the organisation's presence took the city's prestige through the roof and its spending injected millions of dollars into the local economy.

Currently, however, a question mark hangs over the UN's contribution to New York's coffers. Over-staffing and well-publicised expenses abuses caused streamlining to be ordered in 1992, while two of the organisation's largest agencies – the UN Children's Fund and the UN Development Program – have been tempted to leave their New York bases for rent-free accommodation elsewhere.

185

Considered by many to be New York's most boring building, the UN Secretariat towers above the East River and is home to the organisation's huge administrative machine

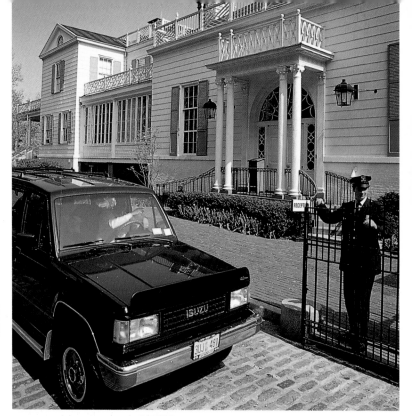

Gracie Mansion, official residence of the Mayor of New York, echoes the opulent feel of the Upper East Side

Museum Mile
The Upper East Side holds almost all of New York's finest museums on a stretch of Fifth Avenue which has become known as Museum Mile. From 79th Street going north, you will find the Metropolitan Museum of Art, the Guggenheim Museum, the Cooper-Hewitt Museum, the Jewish Museum, and the Museum of the City of New York. Just outside the officially defined mile are the Frick Collection on 70th Street, the Whitney Museum of American Art on Madison Avenue, and Museo del Barrio on 104th Street.

▶▶▶ **Upper East Side** *151D3*

Manhattan is money-mad, but nowhere is the sheer pleasure of being incalculably wealthy so clearly evident as amid the mansions, high-rent apartment blocks and ultra-chic shops of the Upper East Side, synonymous for a century with the kind of lifestyle only a bottomless bank account can buy.

A vacant space until the creation of Central Park and Manhattan's steady northward population shift made it ripe for development, the Upper East Side's first homes were modest affairs alongside new elevated train lines which ran above Park Avenue, and the streets to its east, from the 1870s.

By the 1890s, the city's wealthiest people began eyeing the two-block corridor formed by Fifth and Madison avenues. The richest of the rich erected grand mansions in styles ranging from mock-Gothic to imitation Italian Renaissance along the former, while the merely very rich moved into the fine brownstone town houses constructed along the latter.

With a few exceptions, such as the former home of Andrew Carnegie (now holding the Cooper-Hewitt Museum) and that of Henry Clay Frick (site of the Frick Collection), the Fifth Avenue mansions were demolished during the 1920s to make way for the luxury apartment blocks that stand here now, their windows giving priceless views over Central Park and their entrances guarded by white-gloved doormen.

Through the 1950s, the Madison Avenue brownstones were steadily converted to shops and offices, and it is

Walk Art and elegance

Giving a taste of the Upper East Side's elegance and taking in several interesting but often overlooked buildings, this walk also includes a couple of important art collections.

Begin on 65th Street at **Temple Emanu-El**, a 1929 synagogue with space for 2,500 people. Its design incorporates Romanesque and Byzantine features symbolising the mixing of East and West. Two blocks

UPPER EAST SIDE

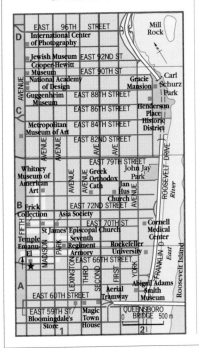

Temple Emanu-El

east and to the north, the red-brick **Seventh Regiment Armory** was built in 1880. Its drill hall is used for shows and sales, and some rooms were decorated by Louis Comfort Tiffany.

Ahead, on Park Avenue, is the **Asia Society** building (page 65), west of which stands **St James' Episcopal Church**, dating from 1884 but given its two tiers of stained-glass windows and impressive reredos during a 1924 rebuilding. Facing Fifth Avenue, the former mansion home of Henry Clay Frick holds the **Frick Collection**, mostly of European Old Masters (page 110). By contrast, four blocks north and to the east, the very best of modern American art is the speciality of the **Whitney Museum** (page 191).

here that the fashionably groomed locals mill around the art galleries, antique shops and designer clothing outlets of one of the nation's most exclusive – and expensive – commercial strips.

Strolling Madison Avenue dreamily window-shopping and eavesdropping on neighbourhood banter is the perfect way to acclimatise yourself to Upper East Side life. Further reasons to come are the so-called Museum Mile (see the panel), Gracie Mansion (see page 111) and the strongly Puerto Rican area of East Harlem, which begins to assert itself above 96th Street (see page 126).

■ 'He adored New York City. He idolised it out of all proportion'. These lines from the opening of Woody Allen's *Manhattan* could easily be applied to the director himself, whose films have regularly celebrated New York and its inhabitants – and done so more convincingly than perhaps any other film-maker ...■

Woody Allen versus Mia Farrow

In the summer of 1992, New York was gripped by the acrimony between Allen and his long-time companion Mia Farrow, following her allegations of child abuse and the revelation that Allen had had an affair with Soon-Yi, Farrow's 21-year-old adopted daughter by a previous marriage. In June 1993, Allen was found not guilty of abusing Dylan, the couple's 7-year-old adopted daughter, but was banned from seeing her for six months.

In 1942, the six-year-old Allen Konigsberg rode the subway from Brooklyn with his father and emerged on to 42nd Street. He would later recall that he was 'in love with Manhattan from the earliest memory'.

Home to New York By the mid-1950s, Konigsberg had become Woody Allen and was working as a TV gag-writer in Los Angeles when (legend has it) he proposed by phone to his Brooklyn sweetheart because he needed someone to go with to see *Casablanca* at the weekend.

Meanwhile, Lenny Bruce and Mort Sahl had reshaped US stand-up comedy and paved the way for the stage-shy Allen to progress swiftly from playing tiny Greenwich Village nightspots to becoming a major figure on the national comedy circuit.

A television appearance by Allen led to his (by then ex-) wife mounting an unsuccessful $1-million lawsuit for defamation of character, but Allen's anti-wife jokes did not prevent him from remarrying, this time to an Upper East Sider through whom he claimed to have assumed 'citizenship of Manhattan'.

The films Allen's first film to give New York a starring role was *Annie Hall* (1977). It marked a break from his earlier pastiche movies: in it Allen cast himself as a stand-up comic devoted to New York but hopelessly ill at ease in Los Angeles.

Two years later, from its George Gershwin soundtrack to its outstanding monochrome photography, *Manhattan* was as much an ode to New York as it was a tale of the 'emotional alienation of the Manhattan intelligentsia'. The key scenes unfolded in Central Park, the Whitney Museum of American Art, and the New York Aquarium.

In 1984, *Broadway Danny Rose* described the life of a New York theatrical agent through anecdotes recounted at the Carnegie Deli.

Allen's best New York film to date, however, was *Hannah and Her Sisters* (1986), exploring the complex relationships of a group of middle-class Manhattan intellectuals. City scenes are cleverly used to underscore their dilemmas.

WOODY ALLEN'S *MANHATTAN*

▶▶ The Upper West Side 151D1

Between the rampant modernism of the Lincoln Center and the turn-of-the-century campus of Columbia University, the largely residential Upper West Side is one of the few parts of Manhattan that have not greatly changed their appearance over the last hundred years.

Still standing in a neat cluster around 72nd Street are some of the city's first luxury apartment blocks. The Dakota, the earliest of them all, is described on page 96. Another one worth a glance is the Kenilworth Apartments, at the corner of Central Park West and 75th Street. The limestone twirls decorating its façade bring fresh meaning to the term 'wedding-cake architecture'. Elsewhere, gracefully ageing town houses cover large sections of the area and, close to the Hudson River, several streets hold picturesque Queen Anne-style homes.

While its buildings remain, recent decades have seen marked changes in the Upper West Side's social make-up. The park-facing apartments along Central Park West have always been occupied by the well-to-do, but much of what became the Lincoln Center was a slum during the 1950s, and not by accident was it chosen as the site of the 1960 film *West Side Story*.

The Nicolas Roerich Museum

Born in Russia in 1874, Nicolas Roerich's life was devoted to art, archaeology and philosophy. In 1929 his 'Peace through Culture' banner, intended to indicate and safeguard cultural monuments and institutions during times of war, earned him a Nobel Peace Prize nomination.

The Nicolas Roerich Museum (319 West 107th Street) remembers this remarkable character with a few of his books and possessions and many of his enigmatic paintings, often depicting a lone figure striving to find enlightenment amid Himalayan landscapes.

189

The Lincoln Center's arrival was followed by an influx of academics and media folk – many of them fleeing the rising rents of Greenwich Village. They have made the Upper West Side a liberal and cultured enclave boasting bookshops, cafés and some fashionable bars. Other new arrivals are high-earning professionals with young children, taking advantage of one of the few Manhattan neighbourhoods spared 24-hour hustle and bustle.

Social life apart, the American Museum of Natural History is one of the Upper West Side's main draws for today's visitors. From it you are well placed for further exploration on foot. Aim at some point also to investigate the curious Nicolas Roerich Museum, on the northern edge of the Upper West Side (see the panel).

Central Park West from the bridge on the Lake. The Dakota and other prestigious apartment blocks arrayed along here have much-prized views over the park

US CUSTOM HOUSE

▶ **US Custom House**　　　　*104A2*
Broadway at Bowling Green
Subway: Bowling Green

On the site of Fort Amsterdam, Manhattan's first permanent European settlement, the 1907 former US Custom House is an eloquent beaux-arts statement designed by the previously unknown Cass Gilbert.

The Custom House cost a staggering $7 million, but at the time of its construction, customs revenue was the biggest contributor to the US Treasury's coffers. New York's customs – with the city established as a major seaport – were the most lucrative of all.

Heavily endowed inside and out with symbols of maritime trade, the building's entrance is fronted by Corinthian columns topped by the head of the Roman god of commerce and holds a frieze etched with dolphins, anchors, masts, and other nautical emblems.

Raised on pedestals on the Custom House's steps, four limestone sculptures by Daniel Chester French (best known for his statue of Abraham Lincoln in Washington DC) represent the four great trading continents: Asia contemplating her navel, Europe looking to the past, Africa an unknown quantity – and America seemingly lively enough to leap from her seat and sprint across Bowling Green.

The building's interior is capped by an impressive rotunda and decorated by a series of 16 frescoes by Reginald Marsh, commissioned by the Works Progress Administration, a federal government office which created work for American artists and writers during the Depression. It shows the travels of American explorers and – much more interestingly – an ocean liner docking in New York, with Greta Garbo among the disembarking passengers.

The US Custom Service moved to the World Trade Center in 1973 and the building was closed. One section, ironically in a building packed with markers to the glories of commerce, reopened as the city's bankruptcy court.

Since 1994, the US Custom House has been the home of the National Museum of the American Indian, described on page 164.

Though no longer used by US Customs, the lavishly built Custom House at Bowling Green stands as testimony to the prosperity that maritime trade once brought to New York

▶▶ **Whitney Museum of American Art**   *187B1*

Madison Avenue at 75th Street
Subway: 68th Street

In one form or another, the Whitney Museum has ignored fashion, upset critics, baffled the general public and been single-minded in its devotion to supporting emerging American artists for eight decades. It now finds itself in possession of some of the most important names – and works – of 20th-century art.

Wealthy would-be sculptor Gertrude Vanderbilt Whitney began supporting young artists in the 1910s, purchasing and displaying their output at her Greenwich Village studio. During the 1920s, she presided over the Whitney Studio Club, a celebrated art forum which displayed the output of Edward Hopper, Stuart Davis and John Sloan.

These and other Whitney-backed artists emerged as major creative forces in contemporary American art, though they did not do much to impress the Metropolitan Museum of Art, who rejected Whitney's offer of her personal collection in 1929. The snub encouraged Whitney to found her own museum, which moved to its present home – a severe rectangular block of granite-clad reinforced concrete designed by Marcel Breuer – in 1966.

Now as much as ever, the Whitney pitches its energies towards chronicling current developments and supporting new American artists. First held in 1932 (and continuing in odd-numbered years), the Whitney Biennial continues to be a controversial, invitational exhibition of the country's latest trends – often meeting the mixed response that greeted Gertrude Whitney's earliest buys.

Throughout the year, temporary exhibitions are drawn from the extensive permanent stock, often to highlight the work of a single artist. For most visitors, however, the Highlights of the Whitney Gallery is the big draw: a chronological run-through of the gems among the museum's holdings: Claes Oldenburg, Mark Rothko, Jasper Johns, Georgia O'Keeffe, Roy Lichtenstein, Andy Warhol, Willem de Kooning, Jackson Pollock and Edward Hopper are just a few of many notables sure to be represented.

Most of the big names of 20th-century American art are represented at the Whitney Museum

The Whitney branch museums
In 1973, the Whitney opened its first branch museum – staging free exhibitions on special themes – in the Financial District. By the late 1980s it had four such branches elsewhere in Manhattan (and another one in Connecticut). Sadly, the effects of the recession have left just one branch museum remaining in the city: at the Philip Morris Building, 120 Park Avenue.

WOOLWORTH BUILDING

F W Woolworth
American rags-to-riches stories are seldom more spectacular than that of Frank Winfield Woolworth, whose retail career began as a humble clerk during the mid-1800s – an era when customers had to approach staff to ask about merchandise and, as likely as not, haggle over a price. In 1879, the first Woolworth five-and-dime store broke new ground in allowing customers to pick up and examine the stock, which was priced at either 5¢ or 10¢. By the time the Woolworth Building was commissioned, Woolworth presided over 2,000 stores and was able to uphold their no-credit credo by paying for the building in cash – a total of $13.5 million.

Stroll: World Trade Center
After visiting the World Trade Center, take a stroll towards the Hudson River, calling into the palm-tree-decorated atrium of the World Financial Center and then continuing to the riverside Esplanade of Battery Park City.

▶▶ **Woolworth Building** 104C2

Broadway between Barclay Street and Park Place
Subway: Park Place

Nowadays dwarfed – but not outshone – by the nearby towers of the World Trade Center, the Woolworth Building became the world's tallest building on its completion in 1913, when its 800ft-high tower, with Gothic pinnacles, canopies and gargoyles, became an instant city landmark.

Commissioned by F W Woolworth as a headquarters for his ultra-lucrative chain of 2,000 five-and-dime stores, the building was designed by Cass Gilbert (also responsible for the US Custom House, see page 190) and officially opened by President Woodrow Wilson. He flicked a switch in the White House to bathe the building – nicknamed 'the Cathedral of Commerce' by a commentator of the time – in the glow of 80,000 light bulbs.

The exterior may be impressive, but the lobby is the real treat. Step inside to admire the blue, green and gold mosaics on the vaulted ceiling, wonder at the grand marble staircase, and look for the sculptured caricatures of Woolworth (counting his change) and Gilbert (holding a model of the building), alongside others.

Still owned by the Woolworth company, who gave it a much-needed overhaul during the 1980s, the building remained the world's tallest structure until 1929.

Symbol of a world-famous empire: the Woolworth Building

► **World Trade Center** 104C1

Church Street between Liberty and Vesey streets
Subway: World Trade Center

Reaching more than a quarter-mile above Lower Manhattan, the twin towers of Minoru Yamasaki's World Trade Center became the world's tallest building in 1973. (They were subsequently surpassed by the Sears Tower in Chicago.) However, they are easily the least appealing of New York's better-known skyscrapers, their unadorned, stainless-steel bodies expressing monotony on a massive scale and serving to make the bland TV mast, atop the southernmost tower, look positively thrilling.

A curious fact
From the southern tower's rooftop observation level, the northerly tower of the World Trade Center is actually further away from the other tower than it is at ground level – an effect caused by the curvature of the earth.

193

The roof of the World – 1,350ft up, on the 110th floor

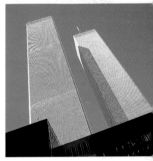

Yet over a million visitors come here each year – not for the architecture but for the views from the observation deck (tickets from the concourse level of the southernmost tower). An unexpected bonus is the elevator that speeds to the 107th floor in 58 seconds flat: you may not feel the lift move, but you will feel the air pressure change.

The enclosed observation deck gives a panoramic view across and far beyond Manhattan, though because the World Trade Center is situated at the island's southerly tip, the sight of Manhattan itself is less complete and less impressive than that from the Empire State Building. An escalator winds up further still to the vertiginous open rooftop level (closed in bad weather).

The towers are but two of the seven buildings that make up the World Trade Center, set around a 5-acre plaza that is the site of free open-air concerts in summer and holds sculptures – by Fritz Koenig, James Rosati and Masayuki Nagare – unsuccessfully intended to humanise the scale of the complex.

A better place to escape the feelings of architecture-gone-out-of-control is on the subterranean level, where an assortment of shops and restaurants serves the practical needs of the 50,000 people who work in the World Trade Center towers – employees of the many companies who rent the center's 10 million sq ft of office space.

Six people died and more than 1,000 were injured when a bomb, believed to have been planted by Muslim Fundamentalists in an underground car park, exploded in February 1993.

Adult

World Trade
Center
Observation
Deck

Excursions

When to go
Wherever you go within easy reach of New York City, you should go there between April and September. Not only will this avoid potentially chilly temperatures; it will also enable you to enjoy the dozens of local festivals which take place throughout the summer, and to visit the local museums, many of which are closed all winter.

Their affluent forebears may have had summer residences the length and breadth of the state, but many New Yorkers today go weak at the knees at the thought of leaving the familiar confines of the great metropolis and venturing beyond the commuter belt that girdles the city.

Those who take the plunge, however, are rarely less than pleasantly surprised. Within an hour's drive of Manhattan's seething streets lies a countryside thick with placid villages and abundant in blissfully rural vistas, some of which have barely changed since the times of Dutch settlement.

The Hudson Valley North of the city, the Hudson River flows through the 140-mile-long Hudson Valley (see pages 200–5). Once the major transit route into New York from New England, the river was of great strategic importance during the Revolutionary War and several forts were founded along its course, one of which evolved into the famous US Military Academy at West Point.

Though the battle sites remain, the valley no longer echoes to the sound of musket fire: its verdant hillsides and farmlands, studded with vineyards and orchards, are the embodiment of pastoral tranquillity. These are the scenes that inspired the US's first home-grown art movement, the Hudson River School; many examples of the artists' work can be seen in the region's museums.

Riverside living in the tranquil surroundings of the Hudson Valley. It is hard to believe the frenetic streets of New York City are barely 30 miles away

194

Clear skies, cool temperatures and fall colours make autumn a good time for touring the Catskills

The Catskill Mountains Halfway up the Hudson Valley, the Catskill Mountains loom to the west (see pages 196–9). The Catskills' highest peak reaches barely 4,000 feet, and rather than providing scope for rock-climbers, the so-called mountains – their sides coated by pine forests and cut by tumbling streams – provide a postcard-perfect natural setting for the dozens of tiny communities enclosed in their folds.

Photogenic views are two a penny on the lanes that wind around the hills and the Catskills' largest village, Woodstock, has a reputation for arts, crafts and culture stretching back to the early part of the century. With streets lined by clapboard homes and dozens of galleries and craft shops displaying and selling locally produced works, Woodstock is a lovely place to succumb to the Catskills' rural pace, and its sidewalk cafés are prime vantage points for people-watching.

Long Island With the Atlantic Ocean lying on one side and Long Island Sound on the other, the appropriately named Long Island (see pages 206–11) runs for 125 miles east from New York City, becoming progressively less populated as it does so.

Farming and seafaring are the traditional staples of Long Island life, but New Yorkers began frequenting the south shore's fine beaches a century ago: a group of pretty seaside villages called the Hamptons became a summer retreat for the wealthy, and to this day they remain a holiday haunt for the fashionable set.

There are more excellent sands and less social exclusiveness along the protected dune-covered sand spit of Fire Island, though many of Long Island's more intriguing stops are on the north shore, where old whaling centres and immaculately preserved farming villages nestle among mansion homes built for families such as the Roosevelts and the Vanderbilts.

Car hire and public transport
In the following pages, the excursions are described on the assumption that you are touring by car. Note, though, that you will save money by hiring a car outside New York City. All the main towns of the Hudson Valley and Long Island are well served by public transport and have offices of the major car-hire firms, so it makes sense to hire once you have arrived. A healthy alternative is to combine public transport with exploration by bicycle. Bike-hire outlets are plentiful in most towns during the summer. To discover the best of the Catskill Mountains, however, you will certainly need a car.

EXCURSIONS

Drive Catskill Mountains

The truly breathtaking scenery is found on the drive's eastward leg, on Route 23A, as it climbs from Prattsville to Hunter – famous for its winter skiing and summer festivals. An alternative route from Prattsville would take you to East Durham, worth a detour for its two museums.

Making two crossings of the ear-popping Catskill highlands and passing some of the region's most interesting villages on the way, this drive begins and ends at Kingston and Saugerties respectively.

Beyond Kingston, the drive soon reaches Woodstock and continues through several smaller settlements as it presses westwards.

The final stretch of the drive descends sharply into the Hudson Valley towards the serene village of Saugerties. A lovely, seldom crowded place, with quaint antique shops and preserved homes, Saugerties is also within easy reach of Slabsides, the log cabin of venerated local naturalist John Burroughs.

The points of interest you will pass along the route are covered in detail on pages 197–9.

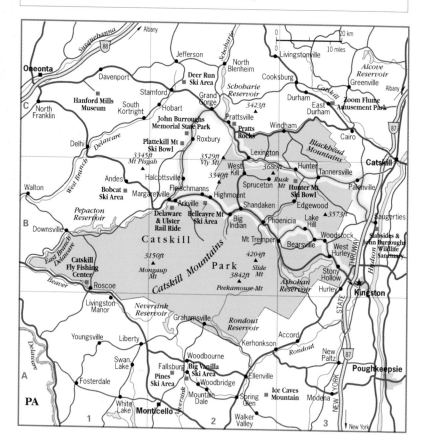

▶▶ Catskill Mountains

Kingston and Hurley While forest-covered hills and tiny villages secreted along winding lanes are what the Catskills are really all about, the region's largest town, **Kingston▶▶**, should not be overlooked. Kingston began as a Dutch trading post in 1616. By the mid-1700s it had evolved into a significant commercial base, and during the Revolutionary War it became the first capital of New York state.

At 312 Fair Street, the **Senate House State Historic Site▶** has been restored to its 1777 style to mark Kingston's two months as the seat of statehood; the senate swiftly moved south as the British approached from the north. An adjoining building displays a selection of paintings by locally born Hudson River artist John Vanderlyn and a few by his peers.

The Senate House is one of several 17th- and 18th-century Dutch-built stone houses that occupy the Stockade District, within fortifications erected in 1658 to protect the town from Native American attack. The same area holds the **Urban Culture Park Visitor Center▶▶**, outlining Kingston's history, and stands within easy reach of the **Old Dutch Church▶**. Though built in 1852, the church was founded in 1659 and its cemetery bears Dutch tombs from that time.

Kingston's second historical area is the river-front **Rondout** district, where the indoor and outdoor exhibits of **Hudson River Maritime Museum** chronicle the town's heyday as a boat-building and river trade centre.

Like Kingston, **Hurley▶**, a few miles west, enjoyed a brief spell as the state capital during 1777 and retains more than its share of Dutch-built stone houses. Ten such dwellings stand along Main Street, whose occupants open their doors for public inspection on the second Saturday in July. Should you be passing through on any other summer day, the restored 18th-century **Hurley Patentee Manor** is the place to make for.

New Paltz
New Paltz, south of Kingston on Route 32, was settled in 1677 by a refugee community of French Huguenots. They were no slouches at home building, and six of their houses remain in excellent condition along the appropriately named Huguenot Street. From the 1692 Deyo House, the local historical society leads tours of the homes, furnished in period style and giving an inkling of the trials and tribulations of local 17th-century life.

On Route 42 near Shandaken

EXCURSIONS

Woodstock The best-known and busiest of the Catskill villages, Woodstock►►► (8 miles west of Kingston on Highway 212) gave its name to the legendary rock festival of 1969, even though the actual gathering took place 60 miles away. Nonetheless, if the festival had taken place here, it would have been well in keeping with the village's long-established Bohemian character.

Hunter and its festivals
New Yorkers know Hunter (north of Woodstock on Route 214) best as a ski resort, but when the snow leaves the slopes of Hunter Mountain the area kicks into its summer season with a series of festivals remarkable for their diversity. Early July finds an Italian festival, closely followed by a German Alps festival and the first part of a country music festival. August sees the National Polka Festival, a Celtic festival, the second part of the country music festival and a Golden Oldies festival. Rounding off the season is the Mountain Eagle Native American Indian Festival, in early September.

In the early 1900s, an Englishman inspired by the Utopian ideals of John Ruskin and William Morris founded the **Byrdcliffe Arts Colony** on a 30-acre site in the hills around Woodstock (look for the signposted road off Highway 212). Artists and artisans arriving to live and work in the studios helped create a rich programme of cultural events in the village, a tradition which continues into the present day.

West from Woodstock Continuing deeper into the Catskill hills, the roads weave between peaks and pass tiny villages such as **Phoenicia** and **Shandaken**, where white-water rafting and a rich sprinkling of gourmet-class French restaurants are the main sources of local income. Both appeal to well-heeled weekending New Yorkers, who regard this area as their own piece of heaven.

On the western side of the Catskills, **Arkville** offers a touch more diversity with the **Delaware & Ulster Rail Ride►**, a 12-mile segment of a historic railway that makes a touristy but extremely photogenic jaunt to Halcottsville and back, several times a day.

Roxbury and Prattsville North of Arkville, **Roxbury** acquired the **Jay Gould Memorial Reform Church** in 1892. This imposing structure of limestone and oak was erected by the children of the unloved robber baron Gould, who was born here in 1836.

A more worthwhile call is to the **John Burroughs Memorial State Park▶**, 2 miles west. Here the Catskills' foremost naturalist was born in 1837 and was buried in 1921. Burroughs accompanied the likes of Theodore Roosevelt, Thomas Edison and Henry Ford on camping trips into the Catskills, and introduced the wonders of its nature to many more in his informative writings.

Named after local tannery-owner Zadock Pratt, **Prattsville▶▶** claims to be the first planned community in the US, and backs up this assertion with some excellently maintained 1830s houses. One of them, the home of Pratt himself, now stores the local history collections of the commendable **Zadock Pratt Museum▶**.

In **East Durham** on the Catskills' northern edge, an entertaining collection of farm tools, fossils, native American artefacts, military paraphernalia, and household furnishings makes up the **Durham Center Museum▶**, inside a former schoolhouse built in 1825. The Catskills' most bizarre souvenirs are also to be found in East Durham: ornaments made from real butterflies, produced at the **Butterfly Art Museum▶**. Founded by a lepidoptera-crazed German immigrant who arrived here in 1932, the museum has an extensive collection of mounted butterflies, and a less exotic-looking batch of preserved beetles. In complete contrast, the watery rides of the **Zoom Flume Amusement Park▶** close by on Shady Glen Road, are the perfect way to keep cool on a hot day.

Not far from **Saugerties**, back in the Hudson Valley (off route 9W near West Park) is Slabsides and the peaceful woodlands of the **John Burroughs Wildlife Park▶**.

Left, right and below: Aspects of Woodstock, the classic Catskills village

Pratt Rocks
Just outside Prattsville on Route 23, the Pratt Rocks carry engravings depicting Pratt and his horse. They were commissioned by Zadock Pratt during the 1860s, to enable an itinerant stone-cutter to earn the money to pay for lodgings.

EXCURSIONS

Drive **Hudson Valley**

Ever-changing views of the Hudson River and its tree-studded valley will guarantee lasting memories of this drive.

See map opposite.

Take two or even three days to make the most of the route, visiting some of the valley's many unique communities and historic homes – some of which have been a feature of the Hudson Valley region since its earliest European settlement. The drive ends at Albany, New York's state capital and one of the few Hudson Valley towns where modern buildings are as much in evidence as those from times long past.

The points of interest you will pass along the route are covered in detail on pages 200–5.

Philipsburg Manor and Mill

▶▶ **Hudson Valley**

Yonkers to Tarrytown Although it is entirely unrepresentative of the pastoral scenes further north, industrial **Yonkers** should be your first stop out of New York City on Interstate Highway 87. The evocative Hudson River School landscapes gracing Yonkers' **Hudson River**

Sunnyside, home of author Washington Irving, is one of several preserved buildings near Tarrytown

Museum▶ will whet your appetite for what lies ahead.

Near by, a taste of Hudson Valley history is provided by the stone-built **Philipse Manor▶**, where Frederick Philipse III – grandson of a Dutch settler who made a fortune through shipping and slavery – led a life of ease until he was imprisoned during the Revolutionary War for supporting the British. The final insult to Philipse could well be the rows of US presidential portraits which now hang above his former furnishings in the manor's museum.

Further north on Route 9, just south of Tarrytown, a neo-Gothic castle, complete with towers, spires and battlements, stands beside the river, screened by woodlands. Known as **Lyndhurst▶▶▶**, the exuberant structure is among the finest examples of American Gothic architecture and is the work of the genre's leading practitioner, Alexander Jackson Davis.

Built in 1838, Lyndhurst was purchased by the despised robber baron Jay Gould in 1880. To his credit, Gould maintained the building well and his descendants lived here until 1961. A feast for the eye, the building sits in 64 acres of sumptuously landscaped grounds and its interior is filled by a grand collection of Victoriana.

As Lyndhurst was nearing completion, author Washington Irving moved into a far less ostentatious dwelling a mile away at **Sunnyside▶▶** adding Dutch gables and a Romanesque tower to a 17th-century farmers' cottage. Guided tours explore the 17 rooms where the creator of *Rip Van Winkle* and *The Legend of Sleepy Hollow* spent the later years of his life. Besides becoming the US's first internationally known fiction writer, Irving was also a useful plumber: the taps fixed to his bathtub and the hot water tank in his kitchen were major innovations.

A short detour on Route 9 north of Tarrytown takes in the **Philipsburg Manor▶▶**, where you can see a reconstruction of the 17th-century mill at the heart of the Philipse family's empire. With livestock scurrying across the yard and the gristmill and granary in operation, the tours led by guides in 1750s attire are informative and fun.

The naming of Tarrytown
According to author
Washington Irving, local
Dutch wives were respon-
sible for the naming of
Tarrytown. It was 'due to
the inveterate propensity
of their husbands to linger
about the village tavern on
market day'. Less romanti-
cally inclined sources suggest the name was a
corruption of the Dutch
word for wheat, *Tarwe*.

*The campus of the
US Military Academy
at West Point.
Visitors here can
stroll in the footsteps
of many famous
Americans*

Little more than a pitchfork's throw from the manor, the
Old Dutch Church▶ was built at the direction of
Frederick Philipse I in 1697. Except for services, it is rarely
possible to enter the church. The cemetery is intriguing,
however: alongside the tombs of numerous Dutch set-
tlers are those of Andrew Carnegie and Washington
Irving. The headless hero of Irving's *Legend of Sleepy
Hollow* arose from his eternal slumbers here.

Tarrytown to West Point On the Hudson's west bank,
Route 9W passes close to the village of **Nyack▶**, birthplace of the great American realist artist Edward Hopper
in 1882. The artist spent much of his life here, at what is
now the **Hopper House Arts Center** (82 North
Broadway). Naturally, Hopper's finest canvases are hung
in prestigious museums elsewhere, but devotees will
find a few of his local landscapes here, plus a large number of souvenir prints and books.

Further north off Route 9W is the **Stony Point
Battlefield State Historic Site▶**, the remains of a British
fort attacked and captured in a dare-devil midnight raid by
General 'Mad' Anthony Wayne in 1779. A small visitor
centre describes the battle and its significance: Wayne's
derring-do greatly increased the prestige of the American
forces and earned him a Congressional gold medal.

Beyond Stony Point, Route 9W climbs into the **Hudson
Highlands**: an area of rare beauty, where the river narrows and the increasingly sheer tree-clad valley walls are
studded with exposed rock.

Route 218 wends a scenic route above the river, passing through the **United States Military Academy** at
West Point▶. Since 1802, West Point has sought to instil
discipline, moral fibre and leadership qualities into its

cadets. Numerous presidents, generals and astronauts have graduated here; even among the drop-outs there have been some famous names, such as 19th-century author Edgar Allan Poe and 1960s LSD guru Timothy Leary.

Ports of call here include the **West Point Museum**, room after room of mementoes – guns, flags, uniforms, medals and more – from every conflict which has ever involved the US; the remains of the Revolutionary-era **Fort Putnam**, perched 450ft above the Hudson; and the **Drill Ground** (known as the 'Plain'), where some of West Point's 4,000 cadets may sometimes be seen marching with geometric precision.

West Point to Poughkeepsie At Newburgh, the next major settlement, George Washington occupied a stone dwelling, built by Dutch settler Jonathan Hasbrouck, at 84 Liberty Street during the 16 months between the British surrender and the signing of the peace accord in Paris. Preserved as **Washington's Headquarters/Jonathan Hasbrouck House►**, the house is one of several 18th- and 19th-century homes that make a short stroll around the town worthwhile.

A better picture of the stresses of the Revolutionary period is provided by the **New Windsor Cantonment State Historic Site►►**, southwest of Newburgh near Vails Gate. Here, 10,000 of Washington's troops were accommodated in log cabins at the end of the war; only a speech by Washington himself quelled a mutiny in their ranks. During the summer months, local history buffs re-create bygone scenes here, some of them making loud bangs with replica Revolutionary-era weaponry.

North of Newburgh lie the foothill villages of the Catskill Mountains. In complete contrast, on the east bank of the Hudson, **Poughkeepsie**, founded by Native Americans, struggles to keep a grip on its past as shopping malls and new housing developments swiftly turn it into quintessential American suburbia. One venerable institution from Poughkeepsie's past which remains is **Vassar College►**, founded in 1881 as the nation's only all-women's college and the first campus to feature a museum and art gallery. Here you will find some very minor works by Rembrandt and Whistler sharing wall space with noteworthy Hudson River School landscapes.

Nothing out of place: the Plain, West Point's parade ground

A 2-mile detour south from Poughkeepsie on Route 9 leads to **Locust Grove►►**. The house was bought in 1847 by inventor Samuel Morse, who enlisted the aid of Alexander Jackson Davis to transform it into a Tuscan-style villa. The handsome building remains in fine fettle, and a pile of Morse's telegraph equipment shares the interior with a diverting cache of Victorian furnishings.

Poughkeepsie to Albany Morse may be remembered by the code that bears his name, but he could not match the achievements of a latter-day local, Franklin D Roosevelt. Destined to become the nation's longest-serving president, Roosevelt was born in a clapboard house beside the Hudson in 1882, near the hamlet of Hyde Park, on Route 9 north of Poughkeepsie.

Roosevelt converted the house into a 35-room Georgian-style mansion in 1916 and used it to treat royalty and heads of state to Hudson Valley views. It is now preserved as the **Franklin D Roosevelt National Historic Site►►**, and all and sundry are welcome to step inside and admire the Roosevelt taste in interior design.

In the grounds, the **Franklin D Roosevelt Library and Museum►** stores the presidential archive and has an exhibition on Roosevelt's life and achievements. A shuttle bus continues to the **Eleanor Roosevelt National Historic Site►**, the house used by Roosevelt's wife Eleanor as a summer resort, and as a permanent home during her widowhood.

Compared to the Roosevelts' home, the **Vanderbilt Mansion National Historic Site►►**, 2 miles further north, recalls a very shallow life. Frederick W Vanderbilt, grandson of millionaire Cornelius Vanderbilt, spent much of his life reducing the family fortune, lavishing $2 million of it on this three-storey beaux-arts mansion. Inside, the Persian rugs, Flemish tapestries, and other money-no-object features are on public display because Vanderbilt's niece could not find a buyer for the house in 1940, even at the knockdown price of $250,000 – so she donated it to the nation.

The most imaginative home in the Hudson Valley is no multi-million-dollar mansion but **Olana►►**, on Route 9G southwest of Hudson. An inspired mix of Moorish and Middle Eastern building styles, Olana arose in the 1870s as the home of a leading Hudson River School artist, Frederick Church. Decorated with Islamic and Byzantine motifs, Olana's arched doors and windows frame gorgeous views – Church himself landscaped its hilltop site. The interior is packed with rugs, ornaments and treasures from all points east.

On the final stretch towards Albany, make an eastward detour to Old Chatham, a base of the religious community known as the Shakers from 1787. Living by a code of celibacy, temperance and sharing, the Shakers' simple and superbly crafted furnishings changed the face of American applied arts. Examples are now displayed in many of the nation's museums, but the **Shaker Museum►►** at Old Chatham is undoubtedly the most comprehensive collection: eight buildings with numerous examples of Shaker achievements in carpentry, metalwork and weaving. Other exhibits detail the history of the community and its beliefs.

204

Albany's eggshell
What looks like a gigantic upturned eggshell in the centre of Albany is in fact the home of ESIPA, or Empire State Institute for the Performing Arts. Inside, the eggshell has seating for 900 and a regular programme of varied musical and theatrical events.

Marking the northern end of the Hudson Valley, Albany►► boomed during the 18th century as a trade and transport centre, becoming New York's state capital in 1797. A thorough restoration programme has kept many of Albany's 19th-century buildings in good order but what dominates the town centre is the 1960s white marble modernism of **Empire State Plaza**, whose quarter-mile pedestrian walkway is decorated by free-form sculpture. Take the elevator to the observation gallery on the 42nd floor of the plaza's tallest building, the **Corning Tower►**, for views that reach far across the valley.

At ground level, the plaza runs out beneath the pink granite exterior of the 1898 **New York State Capitol►►►**, raised at a cost of $24 million and gaining French, Italian and Romanesque features as tastes – and architects – changed during its 30 years of construction. No detail is any less ornate than it could be; a fact pointed out with relish on the hourly guided tours, which wind their way up the elegant marble staircase to the restored legislative chambers.

Across the plaza, the **New York State Museum►►►** uses copious exhibits and walk-through dioramas to pull together the region's history, shedding light on subjects as diverse as the geology of the Adirondacks and Manhattan's skyscraper architecture.

Though presented with less flair, there is more from the past on show at the **Albany Institute of History and Art►►** at 125 Washington Avenue. Much of it dates to the time of Dutch settlement – a feast of furniture, crockery and aristocratic portraiture, alongside a commendable selection of Hudson River School paintings.

The state government of New York has its offices in Albany's Empire State Plaza

The Schuyler Mansion
If travelling through the valley has not exhausted your appetite for period homes, the pick of Albany's stately residences is the 1762 Schuyler Mansion at 32 Catherine Street. It was built for the well-connected Philip Schuyler, a successful businessman who served with distinction as an officer during the Revolutionary War.

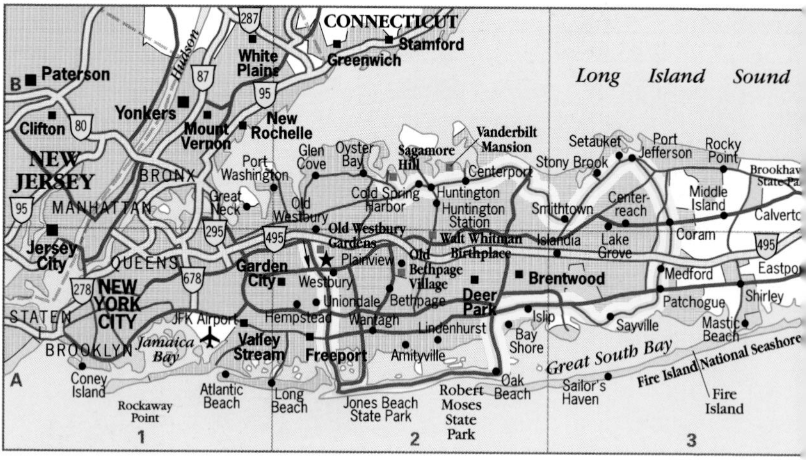

EXCURSIONS

Map with labels:

CONNECTICUT · Stamford · Greenwich · White Plains · Paterson · Yonkers · Clifton · Mount Vernon · New Rochelle · NEW JERSEY · MANHATTAN · BRONX · Port Washington · Glen Cove · Oyster Bay · Sagamore Hill · Vanderbilt Mansion · Setauket · Port Jefferson · Rocky Point · Stony Brook · Centerport · Great Neck · Old Westbury · Cold Spring Harbor · Huntington · Huntington Station · Smithtown · Center-reach · Middle Island · Calverton · Brookhaven State Park · Jersey City · Old Westbury Gardens · Walt Whitman Birthplace · Islandia · Lake Grove · Coram · QUEENS · Garden City · Plainview · Old Bethpage · Brentwood · Medford · Eastport · Westbury · Bethpage · Deer Park · Patchogue · Shirley · STATEN ISLAND · NEW YORK CITY · JFK Airport · Hempstead · Uniondale · Wantagh · Lindenhurst · Islip · Bay Shore · Sayville · Mastic Beach · BROOKLYN · Jamaica Bay · Valley Stream · Freeport · Amityville · Great South Bay · Fire Island National Seashore · Coney Island · Rockaway Point · Atlantic Beach · Long Beach · Jones Beach State Park · Robert Moses State Park · Oak Beach · Sailor's Haven · Fire Island · Long Island Sound

Drive **Long Island**

This drive takes in some of Long Island's beaches, historic homes and atmospheric fishing ports.

From the beautifully landscaped Old Westbury Gardens, the drive continues to popular Jones Beach before passing the south-shore communities of Sayville and Patchogue. The route then passes tiny farming hamlets before reaching the picturesque villages of Setauket and Stony Brook on the north shore.

The Vanderbilt mansion can be reached down a side road off the main route, or you can continue direct to Walt Whitman's birthplace and the one-time whaling settlement of Cold Spring Harbor. The final stop is at Sagamore Hill, the stately home of Theodore Roosevelt.

The points of interest you will pass along the route, as well as other highlights of a more extended visit to Long Island, are covered in detail on pages 207–11.

The beaches on Long Island's south shore are extensive enough to absorb any number of holidaying New Yorkers

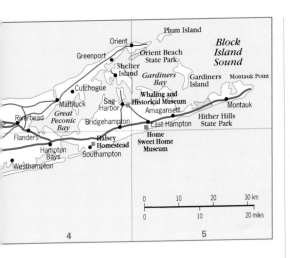

▶ Long Island

Old Westbury and Old Bethpage Much of western Long Island is now seamless suburbia criss-crossed by freeways but a century ago it was still charged with rural possibilities. John S Phipps, the son of Andrew Carnegie's business partner, chose a plot near Old Westbury as the site for a rambling country estate. Phipps' red-brick Westbury House was completed in 1903. Today, the 100-acre grounds, known as **Old Westbury Gardens▶▶**, are the main attraction for the green-fingered visitors who beat a path to the wrought-iron gates. Landscaped and planted to perfection, the gardens have thousands of mature trees, and an aromatic rose garden in their midst.

Long Island provides not only an escape from New York City but also, in **Old Bethpage Village▶▶**, an escape from the 20th century. Crushed-oystershell lanes lead into this re-creation of an early 1800s farming village, typical of those that dotted Long Island long before the days

Amityville
A house on a hill in Amityville, in deepest Long Island suburbia, caused its occupants to flee in terror during the early 1970s. After the subsequent book and film, both called *The Amityville Horror*, describing (and apparently greatly exaggerating) the events, were released, locals found themselves spending a lot of their time directing sightseers to the scene of the grisly goings-on. Not surprisingly, the house has proved difficult to sell over the years and still casts a strange spell over this otherwise rather ordinary community.

The William Floyd Estate
Close to Mastic Beach, where the road to eastern Fire Island meets the mainland, the William Floyd Estate is what is left of the plantation owned by General William Floyd, a co-signatory to the Declaration of Independence. The simple house Floyd built in 1724 remains at the centre of the 600-acre estate, greatly added to by successive generations of his descendants. The last of them lived here until 1975, while many of the others lie buried within the grounds in the family cemetery. The house's 25 rooms unfurl a fascinating tale of changing family fortunes.

of interstate freeways and creeping suburbia. As the village's tailor, blacksmith, quilters and store-owners go about their daily tasks, explaining them to visitors, it is hard not to be impressed by the thoroughness of it all.

Jones Beach and Fire Island Most New Yorkers hitting Long Island, however, are thinking not of old farming ways but about bronzing themselves on the south shore. On any summer weekend, **Jones Beach** is a picture of New York at play. For space and solitude make the short trip east to **Fire Island State Park▶**, which has the added appeal of a 19th-century lighthouse now employed as a visitor centre.

The 1,000-acre state park consumes the western extremity of **Fire Island▶▶**, longest of the sand spits that flank the southern shore of Long Island. Though never more than half a mile wide, Fire Island runs for 32 miles and, other than the road links near both ends, can be reached only by ferries from various points on the mainland.

All of Fire Island is public land although several sections are dominated by private holiday resorts, each with its distinctive social make-up. Day-trippers are not always welcomed with open arms at the more exclusive places. One welcoming day-trip spot, which can be reached by ferry from Sayville, is **Sailor's Haven▶▶**. The fine beach, the nature trails weaving around the dunes, and the hardy vegetation forming the **Sunken Forest▶**, should not be missed. A visitor centre provides absorbing background material on Fire Island's subtle ecology.

The north shore of Long Island has great appeal for New Yorkers seeking a place in the country

The Hamptons East of Fire Island, the settlements collectively known as the Hamptons sat placidly at the centre of windmill-studded farmland until the late 19th century, when wealthy New Yorkers began discovering their vacation potential and transformed them into classy seaside resorts. The Hamptons are still a getaway for the rich but retain great charm. They also have fine beaches, chic boutiques and pricey restaurants.

Southampton▶ is one of Long Island's oldest towns, and the 1648 **Halsey Homestead▶** claims to be the oldest timber-framed house in the entire state. The best-looking of the Hamptons is **East Hampton▶▶▶**, its narrow streets bordered by neatly trimmed hedgerows and picket-fenced cottages. Locally born actor and dramatist John Howard Payne liked the place so much that he composed the most sentimental of songs, 'Home Sweet Home', here; a fact duly acknowledged by the preservation of his house as

the **Home Sweet Home Museum▶**, mostly filled by 18th-century ceramics.

There is more to see in four buildings of impressive vintage maintained by the East Hampton Historical Society along Main Street. The most engrossing is the 1784 **Clinton Academy▶**, once a revered seat of learning and now carrying exhibitions on varied facets of local life.

Sag Harbor Should the 20-mile drive to the eastern extremity of Long Island fail to appeal (see panel), head

Cross the Robert Moses Causeway to reach the south shore

northwest from East Hampton to **Sag Harbor▶▶**. Though few people would believe it on first sight, this sleepy waterside community was once a busy port second only to New York City in its importance. Until 1871 it boasted the world's fourth largest whaling fleet.

Perhaps even less believably, you need to pass through a whale's jawbone framing the doorway of a former Masonic Temple to enter the town's **Whaling and Historical Museum▶▶**, where the evidence of past glories is abundant: piles of scrimshaw and nautical knick-knacks stacked to the ceiling, and a more modest assortment of household paraphernalia.

The 1789 **Custom House▶** is another survivor of Sag Harbor's seafaring heyday, as is the **Whaler's Church▶**, built in 1841 in a curious Greek-Egyptian style. As if to mark the decline of Sag Harbor's sea trade, the church's steeple – long a navigational aid to shipping – was blown down by a hurricane in 1938.

Shelter Island A quick ferry ride (pedestrians and vehicles) north from Sag Harbor, **Shelter Island** is not only a short cut to Long Island's north fork (a second ferry crosses to Greenport) but also a place of the utmost tranquillity, where narrow, weaving lanes are flanked by Victorian cottages. A picture-postcard expression of life in the middle of nowhere, Shelter Island has nonetheless enjoyed a robust past. It was a haunt of 18th-century pirates and, during prohibition, a landing point for bootleggers.

Long Island's eastern tip
If you drive east from East Hampton to Montauk, you will kick yourself for not continuing a further 5 miles to Montauk Point, the last stop before the Irish coast. A lighthouse, built on the instruction of George Washington in 1797, sits at the easternmost point. The reward for braving vertigo and dizziness to climb its 138 steps are views of Rhode Island and the Connecticut coast.

Sagamore Hill

Riverhead
One reason to visit Riverhead, a town located off the main routes between the Hamptons and the north shore, might be the Suffolk County Museum, whose exhibits range from local Native American cultures to whaling. Another reason could be the produce of the Palmer Winery (make a reservation first, tel: 516 722 WINE). If you are here in mid-August, Riverhead's Polish Street Fair and Festival should not be missed.

The north shore An exploration of Long Island's north shore should begin at **Sagamore Hill**▶▶▶, a highly desirable three-storey residence set in 80 green acres just east of Oyster Bay. The house was completed in 1884 as the summer home of Theodore Roosevelt.

Two floors of the main house hold roomfuls of Victorian furnishings and an extraordinary number of Roosevelt's hunting trophies, not least the array of moose- and deer-heads, whose dark eyes stare down at visitors. The spacious but cosy wood-panelled rooms provided the setting for Roosevelt's peace-brokering between warring Russia and Japan in 1905, for which he was awarded the Nobel Peace Prize. Further exhibits, and a short film detailing Roosevelt's life, can be viewed in the adjoining Old Orchard Home Museum, which was added by Roosevelt's son in 1938.

Continuing east on Route 25A, the **Whaling Museum** at **Cold Spring Harbor**▶ remembers the nine-ship whaling fleet based here during the mid-1880s. The exhibits include one of the few extant complete whaling vessels, and numerous smaller pieces – examples of scrimshaw, harpoons, and the grisly tools used to separate blubber from bone.

When the Cold Spring Harbor whaling fleet was still sailing the high seas, Walt Whitman – born in 1819, 2 miles away in Huntington – was busy overturning the rules of traditional verse to create *Leaves of Grass*, the work that sealed his place among America's literary greats. The two-storey shingled dwelling built in 1816 by Whitman's father is now the **Walt Whitman Birthplace State Historic Site**▶▶. One room has been reassembled as it was during Whitman's boyhood, and exhibits on the upper floor recount his adventure-filled life.

North of Centerport, the Spanish-style **Vanderbilt Mansion**▶ belonged to William K Vanderbilt II, great-grandson of Cornelius Vanderbilt. He combined his taste for opulent living with an interest in natural history, acquiring the 17,000 specimens of stuffed and mounted creatures that make a strange addition to the antiques and original furnishings on display in this shrine to luxury living. The adjacent Vanderbilt Planetarium has views of the heavens which fail to match those across Long Island Sound from the mansion's elegantly landscaped gardens.

Stony Brook and Setauket An almost too perfectly preserved village, Stony Brook▶▶ was saved from neglect by wealthy philanthropist Ward Melville during the 1930s. Melville also financed the **Museums at Stony Brook▶▶▶**, a complex which focuses on 19th-century Long Island life. Pride of place goes to the collection of vintage carriages, revealing the horse-drawn contraptions to be far more interesting than you might expect, and the paintings by William Sidney Mount, a Stony Brook resident who emerged as one of the country's most original and daring artists during the mid-1800s.

Close to Stony Brook, the similarly pretty village of Setauket▶ was a hotbed of espionage during the revolutionary years of the late 1700s, and the birthplace of what is believed to have been the nation's first spy cell. One technique employed to outwit the occupying British troops was the conveying of messages using a local housewife's clothes-line. The combination of clothing on the line corresponded to a pre-arranged code and did most damage – as far as the British were concerned – when used to alert George Washington to the approach of the French Expeditionary Force in 1780.

The Vanderbilt family spent part of their fortune on an elaborate rural retreat near Centerport

A trip to Connecticut?
Should the combination of Long Island's sea air and nautical museums give you the urge to take to the waves, you can seize the opportunity at Port Jefferson, 3 miles east of Setauket. From here, a ferry (taking both cars and pedestrians) makes the 20-mile crossing of Long Island Sound to Bridgeport in Connecticut, several times daily.

Accommodation

Hotels: the facts
The New York Convention
and Visitors' Bureau (2
Columbus Circle, New
York, NY10019; tel: 397
8222) publishes a free
guide to hotels listing their
addresses, phone numbers
and prices, and indicating
their location on a map.
More opinionated descrip-
tions of New York hotels
can be found on pages
262–9.

*You will need to
have a taste for opu-
lent living, and
ample funds, to
enjoy a stay at the
large and plush
Helmsley Palace on
Madison Avenue*

Be it a side-street sleaze-pit with naked light-bulbs or a
world-class lodging with *en suite* jacuzzi and antique furnishings, the one thing all New York hotels share is inflated prices: you will easily spend twice as much in this city
as you would for similar hotel accommodation elsewhere
in the US.

Budget hotels Any hotel room priced under about $75 is
unlikely to offer anything more than the basic necessities:
a roof over your head and a mattress under your back,
with the bathroom likely to be a shared one at the end of
a corridor and equipped with erratic plumbing.

Shabby though they may be, hotels at the rock-bottom
end of the market are usually safe, though some near
Times Square are an exception and should be approached
with caution.

Basic comforts For $75–$150, you can expect a room to
which you will be pleased to return, with colour TV (television addicts should ensure their hotel has cable channels) and a bathroom and telephone to call your own.

As you dig deeper into your budget and spend
$150–$200, rooms become larger and more elegantly furnished. The TV carries more channels, a good range of
complimentary soaps and shampoos should be found in
the bathroom, and sometimes a complimentary newspaper will be delivered to your door each morning.

Spoiling yourself To really start tasting the New York
good life means kissing goodbye to at least $200 a night.
Do this, and you will be able to stretch out on a cosy giant-
sized bed in a matching-sized room, with a fully equipped
bathroom larger than some New York apartments.
Further spending will be encouraged by 24-hour room service. You will, however, be spared from the irksome task
of turning down your own sheets: a maid will arrive to do
this, leaving a complimentary chocolate on your pillow.

Hidden extras For all but the most affluent visitor, the basic rates quoted by hotels (and given above) are frightening enough. Believe it or not, there is also a string of taxes to be added: sales tax (8.25 per cent), New York City hotel tax (5 per cent) and a $2 occupancy tax per room per night.

Therefore, what might seem an $80 bargain will actually cost $92.60, and stretching your budget to its limits for a $250 treat will land you with a bill close to $285.

Not only do quoted rates not include tax; they do not usually include breakfast either. Some hotels have restaurants, but breakfasting at a nearby coffee shop is always cheaper and more fun – and is a quintessentially New York way to start the day.

Special deals Slightly better news on the financial front is that hotel prices are lower at weekends, when many establishments seek to attract suburb-dwellers with cut-rate weekend deals. Such packages can bring savings of up to 40 per cent on regular prices and are chiefly advertised in New York area newspapers. It is always worth enquiring whether a package is available during your stay.

A few hotels also give discounts for long stays – two weeks or more – which can bring considerable savings.

Seasonal factors New York never runs short of visitors, but the peak tourist seasons match the clemency of the weather. The prime months are April, May and June. During autumn, many hotels are filled by some of the 1.8 million delegates who attend the city's business conventions each year, and the run-up to Christmas is spectacularly busy.

Even if you are arriving in the blistering heat of summer or the freezing temperatures of January, do not turn up in New York without pre-arranging accommodation, at least for your first night, and do so well in advance.

Accommodation for women Women travelling alone in New York are liable to experience problems that will not affect their male counterparts. The area near Times Square (where many hotels are situated) is especially unwelcoming for lone females. Another possible source of harassment is the staff of some up-market hotels who may suspect that an unaccompanied female is a prostitute. The good news is that several hotels provide safe accommodation exclusively for women (see pages 262–9 for some examples).

The Upper East Side is a fittingly exclusive setting for the art deco tower of the Carlyle. Every facility is provided in this truly grand hotel

Credit cards

Most hotels will accept credit cards as payment, but it is always worth checking when you first contact the establishment. Similarly, all major cards are widely accepted, although a few hotels may make a surcharge for payment with American Express.

The Raines Hotel Law

In an effort to cut down the level of alcohol consumption among the city's down-and-outs, the Raines Hotel Law of 1896 made it illegal to sell liquor in New York on a Sunday, except in hotels to accompany meals. To circumvent this law, every seedy bar with a few spare rooms declared itself a hotel and offered inedible sandwiches to its oblivion-seeking customers. The law was soon repealed.

Reservations and payment To secure a room in advance, you will be asked to place a deposit. The simplest way of doing this is by quoting your credit-card number by phone (or by fax). If you reserve a room without a deposit during a busy period and arrive after 6, you may find the room has been allocated to another guest.

Payment for your full stay (or at least a large part of it) is expected on arrival by credit card, travellers' cheque or cash (though carrying large wads of currency is not advisable in New York – see pages 54–5).

Areas of the city Manhattan is quick and simple to travel around, so you can be selective about where you stay. By far the densest concentration of hotels is in the section of Midtown Manhattan bordered by 44th and 57th streets. Some of the grandest and priciest accommodation in the city can be found here, in a knot around Grand Central Terminal, though the cheaper Midtown hotels (mostly gathered between Sixth and Eighth avenues near Times Square) can be very unappealing and you will get better value for money elsewhere.

In the southern reaches of Midtown Manhattan, where noise and traffic levels are more bearable, residential areas such as Chelsea and the Gramercy Park district hold several characterful hotels with attractive rates.

If you can afford them, a handful of classy hotels with sky-high rates sit in the moneyed environs of the Upper East Side. On the other side of Central Park, the limited number of hotels on the Upper West Side are better value, especially if you like a large room.

In Lower Manhattan, several high-rise affairs in the Financial District are squarely aimed at the international expense-account business traveller. More affordable and more interesting lodgings are to be found among the hotels dotted (albeit very thinly) through Chinatown, SoHo and Greenwich Village.

Bed and breakfast Bed-and-breakfast accommodation is an increasingly popular alternative to staying in a hotel, but prices are not significantly lower: such is the demand for accommodation of every kind in the city that real bargains are hard to come by.

New York B&Bs fall into two categories. 'Hosted' means that guests occupy a spare room or two in the apartment of a New Yorker who will provide at least a modest breakfast. Hosted B&Bs can be a source of useful insider information on the city but there is always the risk that you might find yourself at odds with the host. With 'unhosted' accommodation, guests get the run of a New York apartment whose owner is out of town.

B&B prices naturally vary according to facilities and neighbourhood. Many B&Bs are in outlying locations, so bear this in mind when booking. Hosted bed and breakfast is generally cheaper ($60–$150) than its unhosted equivalent ($80–$200). Rooms should be booked well in advance for the widest choice, although you can book the day before if necessary. Among a growing number of bed-and-breakfast agencies are City Lights (PO Box 20355, Cherokee Station, New York, NY 10028; tel: 737 7049) and Urban Ventures (PO Box 426, Planetarium Station, New York, NY 10024; tel: 594 5650).

Student halls of residence Further inexpensive accommodation is available outside term-time in the halls of residence of New York University. There is a minimum stay of three weeks, the cost per week being around $70. This type of accommodation is extremely limited, and is quickly snapped up. If you are interested, consult the New York telephone books and contact the housing office listed under the university entry.

215

Cheap and cheerful If hotels and B&Bs are beyond your budget but you are still determined to see the Big Apple, the city has three YMCAs which, for slightly less than the cost of the cheapest hotel room, offer single, double and family rooms plus a range of facilities to men, women and family groups. The West Side YMCA occupies an elegant historic building at 5 West 63rd Street (tel: 787 4400).

You do not have to be a youth or an American to stay at the American Youth Hostel Association's smart and well-equipped New York hostel (891 Amsterdam Avenue; tel: 932 2300), although you do have to be a member of the International Youth Hostel Federation. Prices depend on whether you opt for a dormitory bed or a private room, but either way are substantially lower than hotels or B&Bs. It is wise to make reservations in advance.

Home comforts, attractive bedrooms and excellent value for money make the Wyndham popular with New York regulars, so book well in advance

Food and drink

City that never sleeps it may be, but New York is also a city that never stops eating. Wherever you look – in the street, in parks, in cars – somebody, somewhere is always nibbling something.

This gastronomic obsession is easily explained: be it a burger, a blintz, catfish, dim sum, or goulash, no city on earth has such an abundance or such a variety of food available around the clock and at prices most people can afford.

Meals on the move When New Yorkers talk about 'grabbing a bite' they really mean it, breaking stride just long enough to select from a street-stand a snack which they then devour while pacing onward.

Most street-stands – the busier the street, the more stands it will have – dispense hot-dogs, knishes (a doughy pastry filled with meat or potatoes), bags of roasted chestnuts, pretzels and bagels, for around a dollar a time.

You are never far from the next snack in Manhattan

In the Financial District, the recession-torn 1990s have made expense-account lunches few and far between and many economising wheeler-dealers are to be seen not at smart restaurant tables, but eating their midday meal from rows of ethnic street-stands lining the main thoroughfares. Here steaming piles of meat or seafood and noodles are sold for a few dollars.

The deli: a New York institution Street-stands apart, what New York has more of than any other American city is delis. Found on almost every street and inside many supermarkets, delis provide takeaway breakfasts – rare is the New Yorker who can survive without an early morning coffee and a doughnut – for armies of office workers. The deli becomes even more popular at lunchtime, again for takeaways.

The larger delis have an extensive help-yourself table holding trayfuls of pasta, meats, seafood, vegetables and fruit, from which customers fill plastic containers and pay according to the weight of their food. A very healthy deli meal can be assembled for $4 or less. Eat it sitting on the nearest bench.

Tipping
In any eating place which has waiter or waitress service, you are expected to leave a tip. Restaurant and coffee-shop staff depend on tips for a large part of their income, which is why the majority will eagerly attend to your needs. The precise amount that you leave should be judged according to the standard of service, but a tip of around 15 per cent of the bill is considered average. One way to estimate a tip is to double the amount of sales tax (which is 8.25 per cent) shown on your bill.

Delis also serve a mind-boggling variety of sandwiches and rolls. Cornbeef or pastrami on rye (selecting a bread type is a critical affair; see the panel) are enduringly popular selections but you might try a 'hero' – a stack of meat, cheese or vegetables assembled to your direction inside a French bread roll, or a 'gyro', which is spit-roasted beef or pork stuffed inside a pitta bread envelope.

Bagels – soft, ring-shaped pieces of bread – are served with many weird and wonderful toppings but it is hard to beat the traditional New York way of eating them: smeared with cream cheese.

Every New Yorker has a favourite deli. Once you have found yours, start exploring the other deli delights such as soups, home-baked cakes, and blintzes – similar to crêpes with cheese or fruit fillings.

Coffee-shop breakfasts If, unlike the typical New Yorker, you are not in a rush in the morning, linger over breakfast in a coffee shop or diner. Such establishments are as prevalent as delis and street-stands, and draw an equally devoted clientele.

Sit at a table or at the coffee shop's counter and make your selection from a menu likely to include sausages, bacon, lox (smoked salmon), scrambled eggs, omelettes with a host of mix-and-match fillings, and fried eggs available in a variety of styles – choose whether you want the yolk hard or soft, and the egg fried on one side or both (see the panel).

Coffee-shop breakfasts are usually served with hash-browns (also called home-fries), which are small chunks of fried potato, and a choice of toast, a muffin or a bagel.

Strange as it may seem to Europeans, waffles also feature on New York breakfast menus and locals think nothing of starting the day by consuming one – or even a pile of pancakes – doused in syrup. Strawberries and ice-cream are other popular waffle toppings.

> **Decisions, decisions**
> In New York, as in the rest of the US, it is not enough merely to choose the meal you want, you must also precisely define the constituent parts.
>
> In the case of bread and toast, the choice usually includes white, wholewheat, rye (in dark and light varieties), and sometimes sour bread.
>
> Fried eggs come in several styles: 'sunny side up' means fried on just one side; 'over easy', is flipped over just long enough to solidify the surface of the yolk; and 'over hard', is cooked on both sides and for long enough to make the yolk firm.
>
> If you order cheese, you are faced with more choices: American, cheddar, Swiss, feta or mozzarella are the common ones.

217

A New York legend – the original Jewish deli

A coffee-shop breakfast will cost around $5. For a dollar or two more you will find something less dependent on the frying pan in a more health-conscious eatery, chosen simply by scanning the selections listed on the menu outside. Here the options might include oatmeal with raisins and hazelnuts, or fruit slices with freshly squeezed orange juice.

Lunchtime fare Coffee shops are also good places for lunch, although they vary in quality. Occasionally you will still be able to order breakfast at lunchtime (usually starting at 11 and finishing around 2), but the mouthwatering range of sandwiches is likely to be more tempting.

American sandwiches are actually entire meals. 'Open sandwiches' have a meal arranged on top of a few slices of bread, a 'triple-decker' sandwich assembles the food (various combinations of ham, beef, turkey, cheese, chopped liver and more) into finger-friendly portions by wedging it between slices of bread or toast and driving a small wooden stick through the lot.

Among New York's sandwich specialities are the 'Reuben' (corned beef with Swiss cheese and sauerkraut on rye bread), and the 'Monte Cristo' (French toast with turkey and ham topped by melted Swiss cheese). Coffee shops also serve salad platters that could feed an army and offer variations on the plain and simple hamburger such as bacon-and-cheese burgers, chili-cheese burgers, and pizzaburgers.

Lunch in a coffee shop is unlikely to cost more than $8 or so per head, but with so many people opting to eat in the streets, you will find that taking the trouble to venture inside a restaurant (posher than coffee shops, with curtains around their windows) for lunch can be worth while.

So eager are they for customers that many restaurants, whatever their culinary leaning, offer excellent-value lunch buffets for under $8, which not only means good eating at a great price but also makes lunchtime a golden opportunity to begin your investigation of the city's innumerable ethnic cuisines. Seldom will you have the chance to sample so wide a choice of restaurant fare at such affordable prices.

Italian restaurants Throughout the city, Italian restaurants can be relied upon for excellent food at very fair prices but it is to Little Italy that most New Yorkers travel if they are seeking something special. What is special about Little Italy, however, is much less the food – though there are exceptions among the tiny area's predominantly Sicilian and Neapolitan eateries – than the immensely enjoyable atmosphere.

Little Italy's prices are also higher than they deserve to be. If money is no object and you are dressed to impress, head instead for the gourmet Italian restaurants recently opened on the Upper East Side.

Chinese food Within a toothpick's throw of Little Italy, the restaurants of Chinatown are unmatched for value. Because their trade is largely drawn from New York's vast Chinese community, Chinatown's eateries can stay in profit without compromising their quality to suit western tastes.

Brunch
Now a firmly established Sunday institution, brunch is a mix of late breakfast and early lunch, usually lasting from noon to 2pm. The average brunch costs $5–$15, depending on the social esteem of the restaurant serving it and the combination of food and alcohol included in the price. The latest brunch offers are widely advertised in New York newspapers and the event has become sufficiently popular for a few restaurants to offer it on Saturdays too.

Affordable food to suit most tastes

Don't leave New York without having dim sum in Chinatown. Usually served until mid-afternoon, dim sum comprises steamed dumplings and baked buns filled with meat, seafood, and/or rice and noodles, which are chosen from trolleys pushed between the dining tables (don't bother grappling with the language difficulties; just point at what looks good – even though it might be chicken feet). When you cannot eat another thing, let the waiter or waitress know and the bill will be assessed by the number of empty plates on your table.

Anyone who thinks they know their way around a Chinese menu will relish returning to Chinatown at night, when the dinner options span Cantonese, Hunan and Szechuan specialities as well as a few more obscure regional cuisines.

Japanese food New Yorkers first got excited by Japanese sushi and sashimi during the late 1970s when a rash of new restaurants appeared. These were intended to serve the city's fast-growing Japanese population but found themselves besieged by locals entranced by the exotic combination of raw fish and tatami mats.

The city is still an excellent place for sushi and sashimi (ask any New Yorker for their suggestions) although the latest craze among devotees of Japanese food are the *okonomiyaki* restaurants, where large crêpes containing your choice of meat, seafood, vegetables or noodles are prepared on a hot slab in full view.

Meal times

To avoid crowds, or to avoid having a restaurant to yourself, be aware of the city's popular dining times. Most coffee shops open for breakfast around 6 and are at their busiest around 8. By 10, the pace has slowed as most New Yorkers are already planning their lunch. Some people eat their midday meal as early as 11:30 but around 1 is more common. By 2:30 or 3, the lunch crowds will be a distant memory as coffee shops prepare for the dinner rush, which begins around 5 and lasts until 7.

In restaurants, lunch hours tend to be similar to those of coffee shops but the peak restaurant dinner period is between 7 and 10:30, although some noted after-theatre dining spots do most of their business between 11 and midnight

Head for 6th Street in the East Village for a dazzling array of Indian restaurants

Cross-bred cuisines
New York's ethnic cuisines are quick to mix with one another. To become a gastronomic explorer at the frontiers of culinary adventure (which is sometimes a long way from culinary excellence), seek out the city's Chinese pizzerias, Kosher-Italian delis and Indian-Mexican fast-food outlets, among dozens of bizarre cross-breeds.

Korean and Indian Korean is the other Asian cuisine firmly established in New York, even though few out-of-towners ever stumble on the Korean business district. Here, within a few blocks of the Empire State Building, off Fifth Avenue in the West 30s, a number of Korean restaurants maintain a round-the-clock service.

With its emphasis on barbecued beef and pork, Korean eating might be less gastronomically adventurous than Chinese or Japanese but anyone with a liking for spicy meat should get stuck into Korean *jeyuk gui*, strips of barbecued pork smothered with a very hot sauce.

Indian food has been popular in New York for decades. The section of 6th Street between First and Second avenues in the East Village is packed with Indian restaurants, and another group is to be found in Midtown Manhattan, around Lexington Avenue between 27th and 30th streets.

Spanish and Greek New Yorkers often combine dining out with a trip to the theatre, but not if they are planning to tackle one of the gargantuan helpings of paella (which might well take most of the evening to devour) served at the convivial Spanish restaurants dotted throughout the city, with several notable examples in Greenwich Village and Chelsea.

Outside the strongly Greek-populated Astoria area of Queens, Greek food is surprisingly hard to find or disappointing, although simple Greek dishes such as spinach pie and moussaka often appear in coffee shops, many of which are managed by Greeks. The dessert choice might well include Greek pastries.

South and Central American food A lively evening is assured in any of the city's increasingly well-regarded Brazilian restaurants, which between them represent most of the country's regional cuisines.

Brazilian cooking often makes use of pigs' tails and feet but should a craving for a whole barbecued pig suddenly strike, several of the Puerto Rican restaurants along 116th Street in East Harlem will be able to oblige – barbecued pig being the island's national dish.

Less daunting Puerto Rican specialities are also served, but East Harlem can be intimidating after dark and it is sensible to restrict your food forays into the area to lunchtime.

Eastern Europe In the Yorkville district, in the 70s and 80s streets of the Upper East Side, several Hungarian, German and Czech-Slovak restaurants are reminders of the Eastern European communities that settled here before departing for the suburbs. Look no further for rich, heavy soups, stuffed cabbage, and very large portions of goulash.

Similarly solid but tasty fare turns up in the Ukrainian eateries of the East Village and in the Polish cafés that survive on the Lower East Side. In Brighton Beach's Russian restaurants, meanwhile, be ready for a Cyrillic menu – or choose from a groaning buffet table and be prepared to dodge the vodka-sozzled dancers as you are doing so.

> **Eating with children**
> The upper-crust restaurants of the Upper East Side might be an exception, but otherwise many other New York restaurants welcome children. Young diners will often be handed toys or colouring books as soon as they sit down, and those who are old enough to read may find they have their own section of the menu, where child-sized portions and perennial children's favourites such as burgers, fries, onion rings and ice-cream feature strongly.

Recipes from the regions With the foods of the world readily to hand, the regional cuisines of US battle hard to be noticed in New York. Nonetheless Cajun, Tex-Mex and Southwestern cooking all have their devotees. Fried catfish, grilled swordfish, jambalaya, gumbo soup, and even stuffed armadillo are among their offerings.

Being hungry in Harlem is a perfect excuse to discover soul food. Order a plateful of fried chicken or beef ribs coated in gravy, and don't skimp on the side dishes, such as black-eyed peas, corn bread and grits.

New York may be hard to beat for ethnic cooking, but the great all-American snack still has plenty of devoted fans

FOOD AND DRINK

Vegetarian food Street-stands, delis and coffee shops are by no means no-go areas for vegetarians, who will (provided they eat fish) also find plenty of dishes to tempt them among the regular menus of most of New York's restaurants.

Those with stricter diets, such as vegans, are provided for by a number of usually excellent specialist eateries, where very inventive and tasty dishes are concocted. Some specialise in meat-free ethnic cuisine – vegetarian Vietnamese food is one example.

Steak houses One kind of establishment into which vegetarians *will* fear to tread is New York's steak-houses. Carnivores, however, will soon be salivating in these citadels of meat-eating, where large, thick and juicy hunks of prime beef are served with a baked potato and a side salad.

The crème de la crème At the top end of the dining spectrum, New York's finest restaurants not only employ some of the world's best chefs, they also engage the top waiters (some of whom are famously surly), leading interior designers, and have a *maître d'* liable to put the fear of God into staff and diners alike.

To experience New York eating at this rarefied level requires much more than mere appetite and a strong bank balance. You will also need to make a reservation (preferably a few days in advance) and be ready to tip the *maître d'* handsomely. Unless you are an extremely famous face (and sometimes even then), you will be shown the door (or, at best, a table completely out of view of the other diners) if you are not dressed to the nines.

Once you are at the table, menu in hand, you will discover that gourmet American food is rooted in classic French cookery but is also greatly influenced – depending on the interests of the chef and the season – by aspects

Smoking in restaurants
Any smoker who can survive without the weed for the duration of a restaurant visit would be well advised to do so. Most New Yorkers are very aware of health issues and their fear of passive smoking has helped make tobacco addicts the scourge of the city. In January 1995, smoking was made illegal in restaurants seating 35 or more people, except at separate bar areas or in rooms with independent ventilation.

A revered New York institution: the steak house

of global and regional US cuisines. The results, which might be garlic-scented jumbo shrimp or calf's brains in black butter sauce, will be certain to send food buffs into raptures.

Drinks Be it coffee, Coke, carrot juice or a cocktail, New Yorkers drink as eagerly as they eat. In a coffee shop or restaurant, a glass of iced water will be rushed to your table the instant you sit down and refilled constantly throughout your meal.

Coffee and tea Unlike water, coffee has to be paid for (usually 50¢ or 75¢), but arrives in front of you – unless you are perverse enough to want to drink something else – almost as speedily. In most places your mug will be regularly topped up by free refills.

Coffee is always freshly brewed and available in 'regular' and 'de-caff' (decaffeinated) forms. Cappuccino and espresso coffee, costing $2–$3 per cup, are also popular, especially on the sidewalk tables of Italian cafés. All types of coffee may be ordered to take away from delis and street-stands, at prices graded according to the size of the cup.

Some New Yorkers have developed a taste for iced coffee, although far more have a liking for iced tea. Both are great drinks for cooling you down after a hot day on the city streets.

Most coffee shops and delis will serve hot tea if asked, but it is generally best avoided (unless you like it weak and made with lukewarm water) if it is not featured on a menu. Where it is a house speciality, tea will be offered in a variety of Chinese, Indian and herbal blends. Serious tea-drinkers should make themselves known at the city's handful of tea rooms (see the panel).

Soft drinks 'Sodas' such as Coke, Pepsi, Seven-Up, and dozens of others, are sold virtually everywhere in an array of regular, sugar-free and decaffeinated forms, for anything upwards of 75¢ a can.

Sample the day's catch in the unique surroundings of Grand Central Terminal's Oyster Bar. A quick turnover helps ensure everything is always fresh

Tea rooms
There are few more welcoming sanctuaries from the mayhem of Manhattan's streets than the city's elegant tea rooms (usually in deluxe hotels and recognised by their rather pretentious French names) between 2 and 5pm on a weekday afternoon. At this time, for a price ranging from $15 to $20, you can partake of tea – the list of blends usually spans Chinese, Indian and Russian – and nibble selectively from a silver tray laden with chicken, ham and smoked salmon sandwiches, chocolate cakes, delicate pastries, and scones topped with Devonshire cream.

FOOD AND DRINK

Relaxing outside the Victory Café on the Upper East Side

224

Happy hours

In order to attract custom in the early evening, many New York bars have 'happy hours', which are advertised with signs outside the bar and ads in the city's newspapers. Most happy hours last for more than an hour – 5pm to 7pm is a typical duration. They commonly involve special offers such as two drinks for the price of one, draught beer for $1 a glass, or margaritas for $2.50 a time. During happy hours, some bars also provide free snacks.

Sodas are fast declining in popularity among more health-conscious New Yorkers who, after a work-out at the gym or a 5-mile jog, refresh themselves instead with the nutritious fruit juices sold in the city's growing number of specialist juice bars. As well as fresh orange, grapefruit and carrot juice, some juice bars offer power-packed juices blended from parsley, ginger, spinach and root vegetables; expect to spend $1–$4 for a glassful.

Bars and beers New York can suddenly look very different when you have a glass of alcohol in your hand, not because of blurred vision brought on by over-indulgence but because you are bound to be among socialising New Yorkers.

Bars, which stay open from around midday to the early hours (legally they must stop serving at 4am), range from the chummy neighbourhood variety to those patronised almost exclusively by a particular social set – be it stockbrokers, art dealers or punk rockers. For more insights into the diversity of New York bars, see pages 114–15.

Most bars, especially larger ones and those with outdoor tables, have waiter or waitress service, though usually you can go to the bar and order drinks directly from the bartender – as you can if you sit at the bar.

Particularly in less crowded establishments, opting to sit at the bar means there is every chance that you will not need to pay until you indicate to the bartender that you are ready to leave, at which point you will be presented with a bill. In all bars, the bartender will expect you to leave a tip when buying a round of drinks or when leaving.

Mass-market American beers such as Budweiser, Miller and Rolling Rock are sold on draught and in bottles in virtually every bar. Many establishments also carry a commendable selection of bottled European lagers (occasionally found on tap) and Mexican beers. Both of these are more expensive but far higher in quality (and strength) than their US counterparts. Adventurous beer-drinkers should also investigate the output of the US's many micro-breweries: Anchor Steam Beer, brewed in California, is not the best of the bunch but is the most commonly found.

Wines and spirits Alongside the beer, New York bars also stock a selection of wines from Europe and the US. The posher the bar, the more extensive (and expensive) its wine stocks will be. Some gourmet restaurants produce wine lists on regularly updated computer print-outs.

Behind every bar will be a very well-stocked rack of spirits, usually including a selection of malt whiskies, Russian vodkas and various types of bourbon. Spirits are served in measures far more generous than in Europe but be warned that unless you ask for your drink to be served 'straight', it will come in a glassful of ice ('on the rocks').

Cocktails Besides being masters of inconsequential small-talk and capable of performing complicated mental arithmetic under the most stressful conditions, most bar-tenders can also turn their hand to mixing a mean cocktail. If you fancy an exotic tipple, ask what the bar speciality cocktails are. Some bars have their own varieties, and even if they do not the bartender will be able to suggest several dozen types featuring your favourite ingredients.

Any bar describing itself as a cocktail lounge – particularly in parts of Midtown Manhattan and in the Upper East Side – is likely to be a watering hole for the wealthy. For eavesdropping on high-society gossip and poodle-grooming tips, cocktail lounges are unrivalled, but to spend an evening inside one you will need to be very smartly dressed and not afraid to spend $10 or more on a single drink – and on no account should you topple drunkenly from your stool.

Buying beer in shops
Beer-drinkers with anti-social feelings – or anyone who wants to sample American brews in private – will find an interesting selection of domestic and imported beers in most supermarkets, delis and grocery stores. Prices are much lower than in bars: a six-pack (cans or bottles) of American beer costs around $3, imported brews are usually $5–$7 per six-pack. Note that beer is the only form of alcohol sold in the shops mentioned above; wine or spirits for home consumption can only be bought in liquor stores. On Sundays, no alcohol of any kind can be bought before noon. The minimum age to buy and consume alcohol legally is 21 – and you may well be asked to show proof of your age.

225

Views across to South Street Seaport and Lower Manhattan complement the food and wine at Brooklyn's River Café

Shopping

The Winter Antiques Fair
One way to keep warm in
New York during January
is to pay a visit to the
Winter Antiques Fair, held
at the Seventh Regiment
Armory (see page 187).
With all of New York's
antique-dealers and
antique-lovers gathered
under one roof, you might
not be able to afford anything, but eavesdropping
on the chit-chat can be
fascinating. There are
plenty of fine antiques to
admire, too.

From the ultra-exclusive antique shops of the Upper East
Side to the discount clothing stores that proliferate in
Lower Manhattan, New York is not only the most exciting
place in the world to buy things, but also the easiest and
sometimes even the cheapest. Not surprisingly, New
Yorkers really do shop until they drop.

Antiques The New York millionaires who plundered the
treasures of Europe and the Far East to furnish their mansions contributed to the city's emergence as the centre of
the international antiques trade. For serious buyers, there
is no better place to locate that elusive Japanese water-
colour or Swiss music box needed to complete a multi-
million-dollar collection. There is plenty to drool over in the
up-market antique shops of the Upper East Side. The
more affordable stuff, meanwhile, can be found in SoHo.

Among the city's top-range antiques stores, **A La Vieille
Russie** (Fifth Avenue at 59th Street) highlights the
achievements of Tsarist Russian craftsman with Fabergé
enamelware, jewel-encrusted icons, snuff-boxes, clocks
and assorted silverware – none of which would disgrace
the finest palace.

Ivory and silver pieces from 18th- and 19th-century
Japan are among the Far Eastern treasures that can be
found at **Art Asia** (Madison Avenue between 81st and
82nd streets), while well-heeled connoisseurs of art deco
will find plenty to please amid the pricey rarities at

*Once notoriously seedy, and the scene of many
demonstrations, Union Square now teems with shoppers choosing fresh produce at the popular Farmers'
Market, which is held several times a week*

Delorenzo (Madison Avenue between 75th and 76th streets).

Decorative arts items of the 20th century are the stock-in-trade of **Minna Rosenblatt** (Madison Avenue at 69th Street). The most eye-catching examples tend to be the art deco and art nouveau ornaments. Meanwhile, **America Hurrah Antiques** (Madison Avenue at 66th Street) elevates the untutored skills of early US settlers – displayed in everything from weather-vanes to decoy ducks – to the status of fine art and prices it accordingly.

Antiquated melodies accompany browsing at **Rita Ford Music Boxes** (65th Street between Madison and Fifth avenues), a colossal stash of music boxes and miniature hand-made carousels, which the staff are easily persuaded to demonstrate.

If you lack the nerve to pose as a genuine customer in the more exclusive antique shops, aim instead for the friendlier environs of the **Manhattan Art & Antiques Center** (Second Avenue between 55th and 56th streets). At the **Laura Fisher Gallery**, one of the centre's 104 separate shops, you will learn more about American quilts than you thought there was to know.

In warehouse-like shops, the mood in SoHo antique outlets is much less stuffy than the Upper East Side and the prices are far lower. Among the inventory of **Back Page Antiques** (Greene Street between Prince and W Houston streets) you will find Wurlitzer jukeboxes, vintage pool tables and vending machines.

Big Apple detritus forms the eclectic stock of **Urban Archeology** (285 Lafayette Street). This is just the place to pick up a bizarre bathroom fitting or a vintage barber-shop chair. Similar ephemera fills **Lost City Arts** (275 Lafayette Street), among it neon-lit Coke signs and dilapidated peep-show machines.

Books Bookshops are many in New York. They range from nationwide chains such as **B Dalton Bookseller** (main branch on Fifth Avenue at 52nd Street) and **Doubleday** (main branch on Fifth Avenue at 57th Street), each with formidable stocks of general fiction and non-fiction titles, to independently run outlets with more specialised fare. The main branch of **Barnes and Noble** (Fifth Avenue and 18th Street) is said to contain over 3 million volumes, making it the largest bookshop in the world. Look out, too, for the thousand and one small shops devoted to a particular genre.

Bookworms will find much to please amid the diverse stocks of **Cooper Square Books** (21 Astor Place), **Gotham Book Mart** (47th Street near Sixth Avenue) and **Coliseum Books** (Broadway between 57th and 58th streets). The city's most comfortable place to browse, however, is the oaken interior of **Rizzoli** (57th Street between Fifth and Sixth avenues).

Among the genre bookstores, crime-fiction fans are guaranteed to find their favourite authors represented in the **Mysterious Bookshop** (56th Street between Sixth and Seventh avenues) and **Murder Ink** (Broadway between 92nd and 93rd streets).

A change of identity? Anything is possible in the shops of Greenwich Village

Unusual shops
New York has an unusual shop at every turn. Among the curiosities you might stumble across are: New York Firefighter's Friend (Lafayette Street between Prince and Spring streets), selling fire-fighting paraphernalia from model fire engines to helmets and hose-nozzles; Maxilla and Mandible (82nd Street at Columbus Avenue), packed with skeletons and individual bones from humans, animals and insects; Little Rickie (First Avenue at Third Street), where an extraordinary assortment of tasteless merchandise includes Elvis Presley clocks and lamps; and Tender Buttons (62nd Street between Third and Lexington avenues), with nothing but buttons – tens of thousands of them.

SHOPPING

Museum shops
Many of New York's museums have excellent shops attached. The Museum of Modern Art (pages 158–60) and the Guggenheim Museum (pages 122–4), in particular, are excellent places to find art books, unusual badges, T-shirts, and other souvenirs marking their major exhibitions. A branch of the Guggenheim Museum in SoHo (575 Broadway) also has a good range of art-related merchandise, and the Cooper-Hewitt Museum (page 95) has tomes covering all aspects of the decorative arts.

Forbidden Planet (Broadway at 12th Street) has immense stocks of science-fiction and fantasy books and comics from the 1930s to the present, plus science-fiction paraphernalia of most imaginable kinds, from Darth Vader outfits to battery-powered robots. **The Science Fiction Shop** (163 Bleecker Street) is also devoted to the literature of the fantastic.

Although many bookshops have a special section for New York books, only at **New York Bound** (50 Rockefeller Plaza) will you find a shop entirely devoted to new, old, rare or just plain weird volumes about the Big Apple.

The Biography Bookshop (400 Bleecker Street), stocks plenty of what its title suggests, plus autobiographies, books of letters, journals and travelogues from names spanning the very famous to the surprisingly obscure.

Art books are best sought in museum gift shops (see the panel) although the SoHo branch of **Rizzoli** (West Broadway between Prince and Houston streets) carries a strong complement of fine art tomes. Near by, **A Photographer's Place** (133 Mercer Street), stocks new and used books on photographic techniques and photographers.

It may not be the oldest bookstore in the city, but the **Oscar Wilde Memorial Bookstore** (15 Christopher Street) is claimed to be the world's first gay bookshop: it opened in 1969 and stocks books and magazines of interest to gay men. **Different Light Books** (548 Hudson Street) covers much the same subject matter but also has a lesbian section.

CDs and records CDs and, to a lesser extent now, records are sold in the US at much lower prices than in Europe. Music-loving European visitors who want to save a fortune can do so amid the eclectic and vast stocks of **Tower Records** (Broadway at 4th Street).

Clothing The latest in leather, rubber and plastic street fashions can be seen being worn around the East Village but New Yorkers on the whole are conservative dressers, despite the fact that every name in international high fashion has at least one outlet in the city. Dozens of discount stores sell tried and tested American casual clothing for a song.

Clothes-conscious folk who do not need to worry about their credit limits – or about being patronised by snooty staff – do their shopping amid the designer-name outlets of Midtown Manhattan and the Upper East Side, areas cluttered with the shops of world-famous haute couture names such as **Giorgio Armani** (Madison Avenue at 68th Street), **Gucci** (two stores on Fifth Avenue at 54th Street – numbers 685 and 689), **Hermès** (57th Street, between Madison and Fifth avenues) and **Yves St Laurent** (Madison Avenue at 71st Street).

One pedigree designer you should visit for the setting alone, however, is **Polo/Ralph Lauren** (Madison Avenue at 72nd Street). The company occupies a French-Renaissance-style Upper East Side mansion which perfectly complements its range of discreetly elegant outfits.

Adventurously, Giorgio Armani also has a Lower Manhattan store, **Emporio Armani** (Fifth Avenue at 16th Street). This is pitched at the younger designer-dresser, though you will need much more than pocket money to afford anything inside.

The person of average income in search of quality clothing should aim instead for the scores of discount outlets, where designer togs are unceremoniously off-loaded for as little as half their regular prices. A rummage through the racks of **NBO** (Broadway at 67th Street), **Syms** (45 Park Place, near City Hall), or the menswear-only **BFO** (Fifth Avenue at 21st Street) is likely to reap sartorial dividends. Another potential source of bargains is **Gabay's** (First Avenue between 13th and 14th streets), which carries seconds from Manhattan department stores.

Lower-priced (but not cheap) designer stores include **Banana Republic** (205 Bleecker Street), specialising in chic clothes and accessories for the style-conscious traveller. **Betsey Johnson** (130 Thompson Street, one of three Manhattan branches) adopts New York street fashion into loud and colourful garments.

Lower Manhattan is a good area for bargain clothing shops and stalls such as this one on West Broadway

Sales and special offers.
Rarely do New York shops keep their sales and special offers secret. Usually the details are advertised all over the city's newspapers. The Sunday edition of the *New York Times* is just one likely place to find the latest price-busting offers. In addition, the numerous free tourist magazines found in hotel lobbies are packed with discount vouchers, typically knocking $10 off a purchase at a particular store.

SHOPPING

A note for bargain-hunters Photographic and electrical goods can bring real bargains for European visitors to New York. It is vital, however, to know exactly what you want before entering a store and to resist the seductive patter of the salesperson. This is especially true of electrical goods, most of which are not convertible from American to European voltages – even if the sales pitch suggests otherwise.

The largest photographic discount store is 47th St Photo (main branch on 47th Street between Fifth and Sixth avenues; others listed in Yellow Pages). It also carries a large range of videos, computers and all manner of electrical gadgets.

Mainstream American-made clothing, particularly Levi jeans, represents exceptionally good value for the European visitor; prices are lowest in the scores of discount stores on and around the SoHo section of Broadway: the biggest is **Canal Jean** (between Broome and Spring streets), with a massive stock of jeans, T-shirts, jackets, sunglasses, beachwear, loud ties and all kinds of practical travelling accessories at extremely tempting prices.

Army/Navy (328 Bleecker Street, one of three Manhattan branches) is another dependable provider of items such as jeans, plaid shirts, T-shirts and well-priced leather jackets.

Department stores Immortalised in film, fiction and folklore, Manhattan's department stores are the stuff of legend. Generations of New Yorkers have grown up unable to imagine life without these totems to 20th-century consumerism and while they are superficially similar, each one has a character and *cachet* very much its own, and its own band of loyal supporters.

Among them, **Macy's** (34th Street and Sixth Avenue) is famously described as the world's largest department store. The claim seems justified as you wind up its ten floors and find half a million items for sale. There is even a section for buying pets, and a branch of the Museum of Modern Art's gift shop. Large it may be but, despite revamping its image during the 1970s, Macy's is far from being the world's most exciting department store, having built its reputation by supplying middle-income family purchasers with middle-of-the-road tastes.

By contrast, **Bloomingdale's** (Third Avenue at 59th Street) is consummate high-style New York consumerism. A glamorous cross between a trendy disco and a Middle Eastern bazaar, Bloomies (as it is widely called) has low ceilings and crowded aisles which contribute to feelings of claustrophobia. Despite this, shopping here, or even just visiting, is always something of an adventure, not least because of the special promotions that regularly transform the whole store.

Bloomingdale's was the first department store to feature now established designers such as Yves St Laurent, Calvin Klein and Ralph Lauren, and supports many newer ones.

Elsewhere, there are cosmetics (perfumes are sprayed by eager salespeople at unsuspecting passersby), the latest in electrical gadgetry, a well-stocked bookshop, and a food level which devotes a whole section to caviar.

Bloomingdale's is expensive but it is a thrift store compared to **Bergdorf Goodman** (Fifth Avenue between 57th and 58th streets). This is where the ladies of the Upper East Side shop beneath crystal chandeliers for clothes, jewellery, perfumes and other luxury items. Their

Everything under one (huge) roof: Macy's occupies an entire block of 34th Street

Personal shopping
If the prospect of many hours of roaming the city's department stores in search of what you want fills you with dread, each store has a team of personal shoppers who will make your purchases for you. All you have to do is pay for them – and for the personal shopper.
Telephone for details: Bergdorf Goodman (tel: 753 5300); Bloomingdale's (tel: 705 3135); Macy's (tel: 560 4181); Saks Fifth Avenue (tel: 940 4200).

latest husbands, meanwhile, sift through the $100-a-piece tie racks of **Bergdorf Goodman Men**, directly across Fifth Avenue.

The antidote to glitz and ostentatious wealth is **Saks Fifth Avenue** (Fifth Avenue between 49th and 50th streets), which simply offers tasteful, quality merchandise – clothing, linens, cosmetics – in an orderly setting with efficient service.

Jewellery Dozens of jewellers occupy Manhattan's 'diamond district', filling a block of 47th Street immediately west of Fifth Avenue. More famous outlets include **Tiffany & Co** (Fifth Avenue between 56th and 57th streets), with three floors of highly desirable pieces, and the more conservative **Cartier** (Fifth Avenue at 52nd Street), worth a call not least for the landmark building which it occupies. Lower Manhattan is the place to find adventurous contemporary jewellery: leading the field is **Artwear** (Broadway between Prince and Houston streets).

Shoes Shoe shops are two-a-penny in New York and if you cannot find what you want, be it hand-made Italian loafers or street-smart trainers, you are simply not trying. Aside from numerous up-market outlets on the Upper East Side, and the extensive stocks of most department stores, many Lower Manhattan discount stores offer good deals in footwear. Manhattan also has two 'shoe districts', where you will see rows of shoe shops – on West 8th Street and on 34th Street between Fifth and Sixth avenues.

If you simply must have the best that money can buy between you and the Manhattan sidewalks, go to **Susan Bennis/Warren Edwards** (Park Avenue and 56th Street) where the handmade, limited-edition footwear for men and women comes in all manner of styles.

Nightlife

New York nightlife is never boring. Be it the $100-a-seat Metropolitan Opera or an avant-garde East Village nightclub, the city's after-hours entertainment is more plentiful and more diverse (and often of a higher standard) than you will find almost anywhere else in the world. To enjoy it, all you need is energy and, in most cases, plenty of money.

Most New York-based publications carry extensive nightlife listings. The most thorough are the *Village Voice* and the Friday and Sunday editions of the *New York Times*. For new films and plays, the *New Yorker* is also an excellent source of opinionated information.

Theatre From the *Ziegfeld Follies* to *The Phantom of the Opera*, the theatre has been an integral part of New York nightlife for years. The section of Broadway nearest sleazy Times Square has long been established as the flag-carrier of commercial American theatre.

Big-time New York theatre has hit a rough patch, however. Incredibly high production costs have resulted in high seat prices (as much as $65) and only financially low-

risk plays seem to be contemplated. The result is an endless stream of lavish musicals, comedies, and unadventurous lightweight drama, usually with a big name or two. The hit shows continue to be packed every night, but overall Broadway theatres have been hit by declining attendances and have had more flops than ever before.

Nonetheless, even if you expect the show to be disappointing, one reason for splashing out on a night inside one of the 34 official Broadway theatres is to enjoy the sumptuous auditorium and imbibe a little of the history and folklore which every Broadway theatre has in abundance.

Among them, the **Belasco** (111 West 44th Street) was built by the legendary director David Belasco in 1907 and equipped with a host of then futuristic technical devices for his spectacular productions. The **Martin Beck** (302 West 45th Street) was the country's first Byzantine-style theatre when it opened in 1924, and saw the first showing of *The Iceman Cometh* by Eugene O'Neill. The **Music Box** (239 West 45th Street) was designed by Irving Berlin to house his Music Box Revue in 1921, while the **Walter Kerr** (219 West 48th Street) has undergone an expensive restyling in order to re-create the style and grandeur of the 1920s.

Smaller than their Broadway counterparts, Off-Broadway theatres (seating 100–499) are a little more

Theatre tickets
For most Broadway and Off-Broadway productions, New York theatregoers usually order tickets by phone (Tele-Charge, HIT-TIX, Ticketmaster) or buy tickets through a ticket agent (listed in Yellow Pages and local newspapers) rather than going to the theatre box office.

Half-price day-of-performance tickets are sold from Manhattan's two branches of TKTS (on 47th Street between Broadway and Seventh Avenue, and in the south tower of the World Trade Center; tel: 768 1818) between 3 and 8 for evening shows, and from 10 until 2 for Wednesday matinee shows.

Another way to cut costs is with a 'two-fers' – a coupon entitling the holder to two tickets for the price of one. These are commonly used to boost audience numbers at otherwise poorly attended shows and are handed out at ticket queues and found in hotel lobbies.

The Public Theater's Quixtix outlet sells half-price day-of-performance tickets and also issues free tickets for rehearsals – a perfect alternative for drama enthusiasts who also happen to be flat broke.

adventurous and between them offer a choice of musicals, comedies, revivals, classics and new works that few cities can equal. Top playwrights and leading professional actors are no strangers to Off-Broadway productions, and many of the more successful make the transition to Broadway.

Most of the leading Off-Broadway theatres are located in and around Greenwich Village and they include the **Circle in the Square Downtown** (159 Bleecker Street; tel: 254 6330); the **Circle Repertory Company** (99 Seventh Avenue; tel: 924 7100); **Orpheum** (Second Avenue at 8th Street; tel: 477 2477) and the **Provincetown Playhouse** (133 MacDougal Street; tel: 477 5048).

The dozens of tiny Off-Off-Broadway theatres (seating under 100) are often housed in places like converted churches or disused schoolrooms. It is here that daring and experimental plays are performed by unknown but often very talented actors. Seldom will you pay more than $15 for a seat.

Off-Off-Broadway venues also stage performance art and alternative cabaret. Among the longer-lasting are **The Kitchen** (19th Street between Tenth and Eleventh avenues; tel: 255 5793); the **Performing Garage** (Wooster Street between Grand and Broome streets; tel: 966 3651); and **PS122** (First Avenue at 9th Street; tel. 477 2588).

Another venerable New York dramatic institution is the **Joseph Papp Public Theater** (425 Lafayette Street; tel: 598 7150). Here you will discover provocative new plays and controversial adaptations of the classics in six separate theatres.

Theatre information
Besides the extensive listings in the *New Yorker*, *New York Times* and *Village Voice*, round-the-clock recorded information on what is playing where, and on ticket availability, can be found by calling the NYC/ON STAGE hotline (tel: 768 1818) and The Broadway Line (tel: 563 2929).

Shakespeare in the Park
The Public Theater's former director, Joseph Papp, instigated the popular 'Shakespeare in the Park' series, bringing two of the bard's plays to Central Park's open-air Delacorte Theater (near the 81st Street entrance on the Upper West Side) between June and August. Tickets are free but limited to two per person. A very long queue begins forming around noon, the tickets being distributed at 6.

233

Big names and bright lights in the theatre district

The golden age of neon may be long since gone, but the gaudy excitement of Times Square remains legendary

Cinema New York has always had a special relationship with the cinema, playing a part in countless films over a period of more than 60 years (see pages 14–15 and 188). The city is also a great place to watch films. Not only do most high-budget Hollywood features get their first screenings here in state-of-the-art cinema complexes, but dozens of smaller film houses specialise in new independent films and rarely seen foreign movies. Nostalgia buffs are in for a treat, too, with oldies – from world cinema classics to kitsch 1940s musicals – regularly on offer.

Multi-screen complexes show the latest releases all over the city; most art house and revival cinemas are located in Lower Manhattan. They include the six-screen **Angelika Film Center** (Houston Street at Mercer Street; tel: 995 2000); the **Anthology Film Archives** (Second Avenue at 2nd Street; tel: 505 5181); **Bleecker Movie House** (144 Bleecker Street; tel: 807 9205); **Cinema Village** (12th Street between Fifth and Sixth avenues; tel: 924 3363); **Film Forum** (Houston Street at Varick Street; tel: 727 8110); the **Public Theater** (425 Lafayette Street; tel: 598 7150); **Theatre 80** (80 St Mark's Place between First and Second avenues; tel: 254 7400); and the **Walter Reade Theater** (70 Lincoln Center Plaza; tel: 875 5600).

Many of the city's museums have projection facilities and often mount film series linked to a particular exhibition. The **Museum of Modern Art** and the **Metropolitan Museum of Art** also have extensive film archives of their own, and the **Museum of TV and Radio** (see page 161) is another potential source of delight for film-lovers.

The New York Film Festival
Each September, specially selected new American and foreign-made films are screened at the New York Film Festival, held at the Alice Tully Hall at Lincoln Center. The festival is organised by the Film Society of Lincoln Center, and tickets tend to be in short supply (tel: 875 5610).

Classical music New York reverberates to the sound of classical music all the year round, From free open-air recitals to concerts featuring the biggest in big names, the serious music lover will find plenty to cheer about.

Lincoln Center's Avery Fisher Hall is the home of the **New York Philharmonic**, whose season runs from mid-September to May (for tickets, tel: 721 6500). During July, the orchestra undertakes a free concert series in the parks of each of the city's five boroughs.

The Mostly Mozart Festival
For six weeks each July and August, New Yorkers shake off their summer slumbers with the enormously popular Mostly Mozart Festival, held at Lincoln Center's Avery Fisher Hall. Featuring many star performers and conductors, the festival is also the only chance many people get to afford front row seats: for the festival, all seats are charged at a single (low) price.

The **New York Chamber Orchestra** (tel: 996 1100) is based at the 92nd Y (92nd Street at Lexington Avenue). The oak-walled **Kaufmann Concert Hall** is strong on both acoustics and atmosphere, and is a popular venue with visiting soloists and other chamber groups.

At the Lincoln Center, the **Alice Tully Hall** (tel: 875 5050) is another important place for chamber music, and all around the city a plethora of other (usually small and inexpensive) venues regularly give all forms of classical music an airing. The historic **Carnegie Hall** (Seventh Avenue and 57th Street; tel: 247 7800) has a steady diet of chamber music and solo recitals; the compact **Merkin Concert Hall** (67th Street between Broadway and Amsterdam Avenue; tel: 362 8719) specialises in more unusual fare, such as ethnic music; and a broad-ranging programme is offered at the **Town Hall** (43rd Street between Sixth Avenue and Broadway; tel: 840 2824).

Music fans of meagre means should scan the newspapers' listing section for free concerts, held at the Financial District's **St Paul's Chapel** and the Upper West Side's **Riverside Church**, and at the city's numerous schools of music – the major one being the **Juilliard School of Music** at the Lincoln Center.

Ballet and dance New York is a happy hunting ground for dance fans. Some of the world's most respected companies and most accomplished directors are based in the city.

New York's leading ballet company is the world-renowned **New York City Ballet**, based at the Lincoln Center's **New York State Theater** (tel: 870 5570). Their performance seasons run from November to February and from April to June, with a special Christmas airing of the *Nutcracker*. Tickets vary widely in price and often sell out in advance. Returns are sold on the day of performance.

Many of the world's finest dancers perform at the Met

Half-price tickets
Half-price day-of-performance tickets for many classical music, dance and opera events (though seldom for the Metropolitan Opera) are sold from a ticket booth (tel: 382 2323) at Bryant Park, Sixth Avenue at 42nd Street. Credit cards are not accepted.

Based at the Lincoln Center's **Metropolitan Opera House**, the **American Ballet Theatre** (tel: 362 6000) regularly garners rave reviews for its interpretations of classical and contemporary pieces. The season runs from April to June. When the ABT is on tour, top international guest companies, such as the Bolshoi or the Paris Opera, are likely to be found taking their place. Ticket prices vary greatly, and you should bear in mind that the cheaper seats are very high and very far from the stage, not necessarily making them the best bargain in the theatre.

Another important but much more intimate dance venue, **City Center** (55th Street between Sixth and Seventh avenues; tel: 239 6200), hosts a trio of innovative companies: the **Alvin Ailey American Dance Theater**; the **Dance Theater of Harlem**; and the **Merce Cunningham Dance Company**.

A further small but interesting venue is the **Bessie Schonberg Theater** (19th Street between Seventh and Eighth avenues; tel: 924 0077), where the **Dance Theater Workshop** pioneers experimental dance.

The promising talent of many future dance stars can be seen in the student shows of the prestigious **American School of Ballet** (tel: 874 7515) at the Lincoln Center's **Juilliard School of Music**.

Such is the quality of its productions that dance-loving Manhattanites make a rare crossing of the East River to attend shows at the **Brooklyn Academy of Music** (tel: 718/636 4100). Established as a major centre of modern dance, it hosts the spectacular Next Wave festival each autumn.

'The Gate' is just one of Greenwich Village's many popular nightspots

Opera During its late September to mid-April season at the Lincoln Center's vast **Metropolitan Opera House**, the **Metropolitan Opera** company's performances (tel: 362 6000) are as much social as musical occasions, with the city's great and good attending in all their finery. The company is criticised as unimaginative but seldom turns in anything other than exceptionally polished performances. Tickets are highly priced and can be hard to get without booking a long time in advance.

Also based at the Lincoln Center is the increasingly innovative **New York City Opera** (tel: 870 9259), usually performing at the **New York State Theater**.

Among a sprinkling of smaller opera companies, with lower prices and cosier settings, are the **Amato Opera Company** (319 Bowery; tel: 228 8200) and the **Bel Canto Opera Company** (31st Street and Madison Avenue; fax: 535 5231), who tackle the standards with vigour. Also worth catching is the **Opera Orchestra of New York**, who perform at the atmospheric Carnegie Hall (57th Street at Seventh Avenue; tel: 799 1982).

From June to August, **New York Grand Opera** (tel: 360 2777) mounts free shows at Central Park's Summer Stage.

The Poets' Slam
Listening to unknown poets reciting their latest verse can be an unexciting way to pass an evening, but at the Nuyorican Poets' Café (3rd Street between avenues B and C; tel: 505 8183), the Friday night 'Poets' Slam' finds a bunch of rowdy poets locked in combat, each one hoping to impress the audience, and a panel of invited judges, with their work. A winner is chosen at the end of this lively and bizarre – but very New York – event.

237

Music is a way of life for many New Yorkers. The city offers plenty of scope for talented performers

Comedy clubs New York's comedy clubs have given a leg-up to the careers of Eddie Murphy, David Letterman, Robin Williams and innumerable others over the years. Don't expect Las Vegas-style gags and routines – New York comedy clubs can be boisterous places and the crowds can be cruel if they take a dislike to a particular performer.

Most clubs have two shows nightly. Reservations are wise on Fridays and Saturdays. Expect to pay more (if you can get tickets) for an established name, but 'open mike' nights (when amateurs take a turn, usually on Mondays) are almost always free. The most extensive comedy club listings are carried by the *Village Voice*.

With a range of up-and-coming talent, and the occasional big name, the most reliable clubs are **Caroline's Comedy Club** (Broadway between 49th and 50th streets); the **Comic Strip Inc** (Second Avenue between 81st and 82nd streets; tel: 861 9386); **Dangerfield's** (First Avenue between 61st and 62nd streets; tel: 593 1650); and **Stand Up NY** (78th Street and Broadway; tel: 595 0850).

NIGHTLIFE

Nightclubbing at the Palladium

Showing ID
However old you are, there is every chance you will be asked to show ID when entering a New York night-club. If you are under 21 – the legal minimum age to buy alcohol – you may be turned away. Clubs that attract many under-21 cus-tomers often issue club-goers old enough to buy alcohol with special wrist-bands (or some similar non-transferable form of ID) which must be shown when using the bar.

Nightclubs New York nightclubs are in a permanent state of flux. The last 15 years have seen the rise and fall of the jet-set chic Studio 54, the arty Mudd Club, which helped rejuvenate SoHo, and a batch of punky East Village clubs which reshaped many New Yorkers' notions of what a night out could be.

The city's nightclub scene in general is now thriving again, after a period when it could have been said to lack sparkle. One recent development is that the action has tended to move Downtown, but there are still scores of places of different kinds where you can dress up (or dress down), pose, preen, or just dance – well into the small hours.

For non-regulars, the biggest potential hazard at any club is the doorman, who will decide whether you are a suitable person (judged by your clothes and general man-ner) to be admitted. The arrogance of doormen is leg-endary, but if you are turned away, simply try somewhere else.

No nightclub worth its salt gets into gear before 1 or 2 in the morning (most are open until 4). Arrive before mid-night and you will probably have the place to yourself. One advantage of arriving early, however, may be a reduced admission charge. Drinks in nightclubs are more expensive than in bars, sometimes extortionately so.

Many clubs have different entertainment, and therefore an entirely different crowd, on particular nights of the week: always phone ahead to check.

New York nightclubs open, close and change address with incredible rapidity; the following suggestions are intended as a representative cross-section of what is available.

One of the longer-established up-market clubs, the polo-stick-and-croquet-mallet-decorated **Au Bar** (58th Street between Madison and Park avenues; tel: 308 9455) attracts a designer-dressed and rather staid crowd, dancing primly to fairly bland disco music.

Occasionally visited by rock-and-roll celebrities, the **China Club** (Broadway at 75th Street; tel: 877 1156) is an enjoyable mainstream rock-and-roll disco. Likewise, **Webster Hall** (11th Street between Third and Fourth avenues; tel: 353 1600) is unadventurous musically, but is much appreciated by its regular crowd of hedonistic suburbanites.

Lively and youthful, and packed to the gills on busy nights, **Red Zone** (54th Street between Ninth and Tenth avenues; tel: 582 2222) has the top House and hip-hop DJs, and also features salsa on some nights. There are more Latin American rhythms – and mambo lessons – at **SOBs** (Varick Street at Houston Street; tel: 243 4940).

If you are not particularly style-conscious, **The Bank** (Houston Street at Essex Street; tel: 505 5033), a slick if

Radio City Music Hall is a popular rock venue

sometimes run-of-the-mill disco, makes for a reasonable night out – or try the **Palladium** (14th Street between Third and Fourth avenues; tel 473 7171), a cavernous room and dance-floor with video monitors designed by leading architect Arata Isozaki.

Opening in the mid-1980s, the subdued ambience of **Nell's** (14th Street between Seventh and Eighth avenues; tel: 675 1567) was intended as an antidote to flashing lights and pulsating music; this Victorian-style living room has faded from fashion but is still worth a visit.

Rock music Rock music's big names always include New York on their international touring schedules. If they are not popular enough to fill the 55,000-capacity Shea Stadium in Queens, they are most likely to be found in venues such as the **Beacon Theater** (Broadway at 75th Street; tel: 496 7070), **Madison Square Garden** (Seventh Avenue between 31st and 33rd streets; tel: 465 6000), or **Radio City Music Hall** (Sixth Avenue at 50th Street; tel: 247 4777).

239

Gay and lesbian nightclubs
New York has many gay and lesbian nightspots and many Lower Manhattan nightclubs are intended predominantly or exclusively for gay men or lesbians on certain nights of the week. The latest details can be found by reading the *Village Voice* and the many smaller gay- and lesbian-aimed publications found in specialist bookstores such as *Different Light Books*, 548 Hudson Street.

NIGHTLIFE

Rock music tickets
Tickets for major rock shows (usually $15–$30) and for most shows at medium-sized venues ($10–$20), can be booked by phone and paid for by credit card through Ticketmaster (tel: 307 7171).

Up-and-coming bands from the US and Europe who have outgrown the small club scene but are not yet ready for the large concert halls turn up most nights of the week in mid-sized venues such as **Academy** (43rd Street between Seventh and Eight avenues; tel: 249 8870), the **Marquee** (21st Street near Tenth Avenue; tel: 249 8870), styled on its more famous London namesake, and **Roseland** (52nd Street between Eighth Avenue and Broadway; tel: 249 8870), the legendary ballroom of the Big Band era.

Other venues worth checking out are **The Bottom Line** (4th Street near Fifth Avenue; tel: 228 6300), showcasing new signings to major labels and also booking some ageing 1960s cult names, and **Wetlands** (Hudson Street, three blocks south of Canal Street; tel: 966 4225), with 1960s psychedelic décor, organic food and books and pamphlets on ecological issues – as well as a full roster of rock, reggae and funk bands.

New York's own rock music scene is highly incestuous – some bands might be huge in a particular neighbourhood but unknown outside it. Plenty of exotically named hopefuls can be heard every night for free, or a few dollars, in dozens of tiny clubs secreted throughout the East Village and SoHo. For details, read the ads in the *Village Voice* or look for the handwritten notices pinned up in local cafés and bars.

Talking Heads and Blondie were just two of the big names who emerged from the New York punk scene of the mid-1970s, which focused on the still-surviving **CBGB** (Bowery at Bleecker Street; tel: 982 4052). Unknown bands play here every night of the week, while performance art and readings are also billed at the **CB's Gallery** next door (tel: 388 2529).

Experimentally minded musicians explore rock's avant-garde fringe at the **Knitting Factory** (Houston Street near Mulberry Street; tel: 219 3055). If you just want a loud rocking noise to accompany an evening of beer-swilling, try **Desmond's Tavern** (Park Avenue between 29th and 30th streets; tel: 684 9472).

Jazz and blues Since the 1940s, New York has been well endowed with smoky jazz clubs, usually occupying basements in Greenwich Village. Their floorboards will have been trodden by many of jazz's most illustrious figures.

Most jazz clubs have two or three nightly shows. Cover charges range from around $8 to $20 or more. Sometimes there will also be a two-drink minimum charge (around $6).

The long-established **Village Vanguard** (Seventh Avenue at 11th Street; tel: 255 4037) epitomises the dark-and-smoky Greenwich Village basement jazz club. Many

A popular jazz venue on the Upper West Side, Birdland is named after a club that was a 1940s legend

Greenwich Village jazz: a costlier night out than 50 years ago, but the atmosphere remains the same

top names play here regularly. Major jazz stars are also frequent visitors to the atmospheric **Blue Note** (3rd Street at MacDougal Street; tel: 475 8592), where cover charges can sometimes be very steep.

A couple of lower-key Greenwich Village venues are **Sweet Basil** (Seventh Avenue at Bleecker Street; tel: 242 1785) and **Bradley's** (70 University Place; tel: 228 6440), where quality piano and bass duos thrive in an intimate atmosphere.

Elsewhere around town, the pricey **Michael's Pub** (55th Street at Third Avenue; tel: 758 2272) specialises in New Orleans-style jazz. An unannounced Woody Allen will sometimes add his clarinet to the exuberant musical melee. An appreciative audience helps make **Fat Tuesday's** (Third Avenue between 17th and 18th streets; tel: 533 7902) a likely place to catch emerging talents, and the **Knickerbocker Bar and Grill** (9th Street and University Place; tel: 228 8490) offers some star line-ups. Far from the smoky haunts of Greenwich Village, **Birdland** on Broadway at 105th Street (tel: 749 2228), is cast in the mould of a 1940s supper club. It offers three nightly jazz sets as well as a Sunday jazz brunch.

Blues and R&B, meanwhile, seldom come rawer or raunchier than the nightly acts at the **Dan Lynch Blues Bar** (Second Avenue at 14th Street; tel: 677 0911), where admission is free except on Fridays and Saturdays.

Folk Greenwich Village was the epicentre of the early 1960s folk revival. The days of hootenannys are long gone, but legendary folk venues like the **Bitter End** (147 Bleecker Street; tel: 673 7030) and the **Speakeasy** (corner of MacDougal and Bleecker streets; tel: 598 9670), still remain and feature folk acts on most nights.

Country music
Listening to country music seems somewhat incongruous in ultra-urban New York, but the large and brassy Lone Star Roadhouse (52nd Street between Broadway and Eighth Avenue; tel: 245 2950) features a mixture of new wave and traditional country sounds. Smaller country venues are O'Lunney's (44th Street near Fifth Avenue; tel: 840 6688) and the Rodeo Bar (Third Avenue at 27th Street; tel: 683 6500).

New York for children

242

For children in the Outer Boroughs

Brooklyn's Children's Museum (145 Brooklyn Avenue) is an architecturally innovative affair, with exhibits to encourage understanding of the basics of science and nature. Older children might prefer a romp through the vintage subway carriages displayed at the New York Transit Museum (see page 76).

A ride on the Staten Island Ferry is enjoyable in its own right and, once ashore, the Richmondtown Historic Restoration (page 179) has traditionally attired guides bringing local history to life in a colourful and informative way.

Elsewhere, the Bronx Zoo (pages 70–1) has a children's section; in Queen's, the New York Hall of Science (page 171) has a mass of entertaining hands-on exhibits.

A number of Manhattan museums have sections intended for children but only the **Children's Museum of Manhattan** (in the Tisch Building, 83rd Street between Broadway and Amsterdam Avenue) is purpose-designed: a wonderful play-as-you-learn facility using computerised interactive exhibits and displays. The Children's Museum's four floors of informative fun include the Brainatarium, exploring the functions of the human brain, and the Time Warner Center for Media, where little hands can film, edit and star in their own videos. Outside, the Urban Tree House explores the environmental conflicts between city life and the natural world.

At the **Children's Museum of the Arts** (72–8 Spring Street, tel: 941 9198) young people from 18 months to 10 years can enjoy a whole series of creative play areas based around the visual and performing arts.

Still with an educational role, the **American Museum of Natural History** (see pages 63–4), with its dinosaur skeletons, giant model whale and scores of stuffed creatures, is another place where the squeals of infant joy are regularly heard.

For city views, if you have children in tow, the **World Trade Center**, with its speedy elevator ride, wins out over the **Empire State Building**, although the latter's Guinness World of Records Exhibition steals many a young heart. A boat trip (see page 67) might then be combined with a clamber around the historic ships of **South Street Seaport** (see page 178).

In Central Park, the main **Central Park Zoo** is located behind the Arsenal at 64th Street and Fifth Avenue (tel: 408 0271). For sheer entertainment value, the sea-lion

Alice and friends in Central Park

243

feeding times at 11:30, 2 and 4 are hard to beat. Also in the park, story-telling takes place on Saturdays at the Hans Christian Andersen statue by Conservatory Water (tel: 794 6564 for details).

When it is time for treats, go to the **Enchanted Forest** (85 Mercer Street), where expensive stuffed animals inhabit a make-believe medieval forest, or **FAO Schwarz** (Fifth Avenue between 58th and 59th streets), packed from floor to ceiling with the kind of toys most children can only dream about.

Above: Getting to grips with the game in Central Park

Above left: The Bronx Zoo, described on pages 70–1

Left: Rollerblading – the latest Central Park craze

New York for free

Free in the Outer Boroughs
The Brooklyn Historical Society is free every day. Throughout the summer, the Brooklyn Arts Council (for details, tel: 718/625 0080) hosts free musical events at several locations, including Brighton Beach. The Bronx's Hall of Fame for Great Americans (page 71) is always free, as is the Bronx Zoo (pages 70–1) from Tuesday to Thursday, although a voluntary donation is expected. In Queens, the New York Hall of Science (page 171) does not make an admission charge but suggests a donation. Staten Island's Garibaldi Meucci Museum (page 180) has free admission, and there is no charge for the July concert series at Snug Harbor (tel: 718/448 2500).

Window-shopping, Manhattan-style: a live window display at Macy's department store

Millionaires may have made Manhattan what it is but even paupers can have fun in the Big Apple. Many of New York's finest things – architecture, pulsating streetlife, distinctive neighbourhoods, fantastic department stores – can be seen and enjoyed without spending a cent. Study the suggestions below for even more ways to enjoy New York without opening your wallet.

Free in Manhattan Several of the city's major museums described in the A to Z section of this book offer free admission on selected weekday evenings: the **Cooper-Hewitt Museum** (Tuesdays 5–9); the **Guggenheim Museum** (Tuesdays 5–8); the **Museum of Modern Art** (Thursdays 5–9; a voluntary donation is expected); and the **Whitney Museum of American Art** (Thursdays 6–8).

Among the smaller institutions with temporary shows, the **National Academy of Design** allows free entry to its exhibitions on Tuesday evenings (5–8), as does the **International Center of Photography**.

Museums and galleries to which admission is always free are the **American Numismatic Society** (page 65); the **American Bible Society** (page 61); the **Forbes Magazine Galleries** (page 107); the **Hispanic Society of America** (page 126); the **Museum of American Folk Art** (page 155; there is a suggested donation of $2); the **Museum of American Illustration** (page 62); the **Nicolas Roerich Museum** (page 189); and the **Police Academy Museum** (page 152).

Visiting **Federal Hall** (page 102) and the **General Grant Memorial** (page 110) costs nothing, and both the **Lincoln Center** (page 134) and the **Stock Exchange** (page 182) offer free guided tours. When tickets are available, you can listen for free to delegates' speeches at the **UN General Assembly** (page 184).

Free musical and theatrical entertainment can be found during the summer in **Central Park** (tel: 360 2777), at the **Rockefeller Center** (tel: 698 8901), on the plazas of the **Lincoln Center** (tel: 875 5400) and the **World Trade Center** (tel: 435 4170), and at **South Street Seaport** (tel: 669 9400).

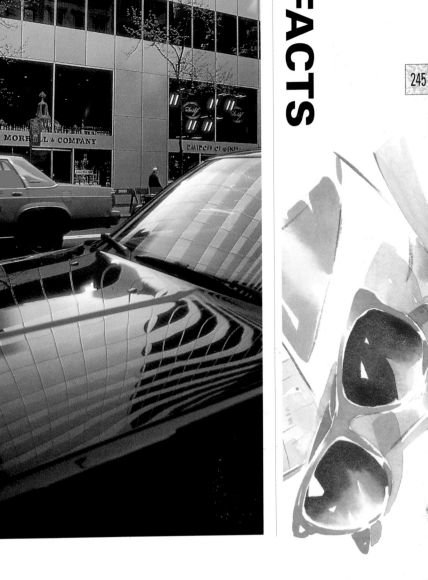

TRAVEL FACTS

Arriving

Entry formalities British citizens require a full 10-year passport to visit the US but, like the citizens of most European countries, do not need a visa if their intended stay in the US is less than 90 days and they have a return ticket. It is necessary, however, to fill out the green visa-waiver form issued on the plane.

Before landing, passengers will also be given US customs and immigration forms to complete. These forms require fairly simple information about the duration of your stay and the address where you will be spending your first night and should present no difficulties if you are visiting the US on holiday.

Should you be planning to live and/or work in the US, however, you need to obtain permission to do this – and the relevant paperwork – from a US embassy before arranging your flight.

If your holiday is long (more than three weeks, for example) you are likely to be asked to show evidence of sufficient funds to support yourself during your stay. A wallet full of credit cards and a thick wad of travellers' cheques will soon put the minds of suspicious immigration officials (who might think you are planning to work illegally in the US) at ease.

If you are travelling with a major airline, it is possible that an immigration check (a computer check of the pas-

Use only licensed cabs from the official airport taxi ranks

sengers' names against those of known miscreants) will be carried out when you check in at the airport. A sticker will then be attached to your passport to speed your passage through immigration control when you land.

Otherwise, anticipate a wait of at least an hour to be processed by immigration. Once you reach the desk, hand to the officer your passport and the immigration form that you filled in on the plane, and have your return ticket ready for inspection.

Assuming there are no problems, your passport will be stamped with the date and part of the immigration form will be fixed to your passport showing the date by which you must leave the country (usually three months ahead); this is removed only when you leave the US.

By air International flights into New York land either at John F Kennedy Airport (in Queens, about 15 miles east of Manhattan) or Newark (in New Jersey, about 15 miles west of Manhattan). Both these airports also receive domestic flights, as does the city's third airport, La Guardia (also in Queens, 8 miles east of Manhattan).

Wherever you land, travel into Manhattan should be fairly straightforward if somewhat time-consuming: once clear of immigration and customs, allow at least an hour and a half to travel between the airport and the city. Each airport has a Ground Transportation Desk where you can check routes, timings and fares into the city.

Besides the public transport services detailed below, taxis operate from each of the three airports and should be taken from the clearly sign-posted official taxi ranks, which will be pointed out by uniformed airport staff. Any taxi driver who approaches you in person is likely to be unlicensed, and therefore uninsured, and may overcharge (or possibly even rob) you.

Taxi fares from the airports into Manhattan are high: expect to spend around $40–$50 (road and bridge tolls are extra) from JFK or Newark, $20–$30 from La Guardia. Bear in

Helicopters provide a speedy but costly way to sightsee or reach the airport. Most travellers prefer to use the bus

mind, too, that traffic can be dense around each airport and can add further to taxi charges.

From JFK Free shuttle buses run to the nearest subway station, at Howards Beach, which leaves a 60-minute ride into Manhattan. Other buses link the airport to other subway lines, intended for New Yorkers who want to get home without changing lines. (Before using the subway, see **Public transport** on pages 256–8.)

Nervous tourists arriving at JFK for the first time and carrying luggage should ignore the subway and instead use the Carey Express Airport Coach service (tel: 800/284 0909), which departs for six stops in Midtown Manhattan every 20 minutes between 6am and midnight. One-way tickets can be bought, for much less than half the cost of a taxi, from the uniformed attendants outside the airport terminals.

Another option – slightly more expensive but potentially quicker – is to use a shared minibus. Gray Line Air Shuttle (tel: 800/451 0455) operate minibuses from JFK to any address in Manhattan between 7am and 11pm.

If money is no object, you can zip between the airport and Manhattan by helicopter. The helicopter service takes 10 minutes to reach the 34th Street Heliport (tel: 800/645 3494).

From Newark The New Jersey Transit Bus (tel: 762 5100) runs to Manhattan's Port Authority Bus Terminal (42nd Street and Eighth Avenue) around the clock. The journey takes about 30 to 45 minutes. Alternatively, the Olympia Trails Airport Express (tel: 964 6233) travels from Newark to three locations in Midtown and Lower Manhattan between 6.15am and midnight, departing every 20 minutes.

As from JFK, Gray Line Air Shuttle (tel: 800/451 0455) operate shared minibuses from Newark airport to any address in Manhattan.

From La Guardia Local buses run to the rest of Queens, but to reach Manhattan the choice is between the Carey Express Airport Coach (tel: 800/451 0909), which departs for six Midtown Manhattan stops every 20 minutes between 6am and midnight, and a shared Gray Line Air Shuttle minibus (tel: 800/451 0455) to any address in Manhattan, available between 7am and 11pm.

By sea New York's great days as a seaport may be long gone but the QE2 keeps the tradition, and the sheer luxury, of transatlantic ocean-liner travel very much alive. After the ocean crossing, you will glide into New York beneath the Statue of Liberty and put ashore at Midtown Manhattan's gleaming Passenger Ship Terminal, which is situated on Twelfth Avenue between 50th and 52nd streets.

By bus Long-distance buses into New York complete their journeys at the country's largest and busiest bus station: Port Authority Bus Terminal (tel: 564 8484) at the junction of 42nd Street and Eighth Avenue.

By rail Most local commuter trains pull into Grand Central Terminal, at 42nd Street and Park Avenue, while long-distance trains pull into New York's other station, the Pennsylvania Railroad Station (known as 'Penn Station'), at 31st Street and Eighth Avenue. For information on US train travel, tel: 800/872 7245.

Car breakdown

In the unlikely event of your rental car breaking down, phone the breakdown number which should be prominently displayed on or near the dashboard (if it is not, simply phone the car rental firm you hired from). With luck, the rental company representative will shortly arrive with another car in which you can continue your journey.

Should you be unfortunate enough to break down far from a phone, stay with your vehicle and wait for a Highway Patrol to come by. If any other passing motorist stops to offer help, there is every chance that the approach will be genuine – but treat the offer with caution. Usually, the best help such a person can provide is driving on to a public telephone and making a call on your behalf.

The view that confirms you have really arrived in the Big Apple

Car rental

With traffic lights on almost every block and a lack of affordable parking, as well as being infamous for its gridlock, Manhattan – and New York City generally – is a dire place in which to drive. For excursions outside the city, however, a rental car is a near-essential accessory.

Many package holiday deals to the US from Europe will include car rental at a temptingly low cost. All the major international car-rental companies have desks at New York's airports (and offices in the city), where you can collect a pre-booked car or hire one on the spot. Without a rental car as part of your holiday package, you will save time and money if you travel out of the city by public transport and then rent a car in a smaller town.

The address of the nearest major car-rental outlet can be found by calling the following toll-free numbers: Avis (tel: 800/331 1212); Budget (tel: 800/527 0700); Hertz (tel: 800/654 3131); National (tel: 800/227 7368); Thrifty (tel: 800/367 2277). Many more rental firms are listed in the Yellow Pages, though the big international companies are often safest.

Wherever you rent a car, check the small print very carefully, particularly with regard to Collision Damage Waiver (CDW), a compulsory form of insurance that can add considerably to costs. Check also whether or not the vehicle has to be returned with a full tank of fuel.

Without booking ahead, any non-US citizen under the age of 25 and/or without a credit card may have problems renting a car in New York.

Climate

New York City attracts visitors all the year round. Those who avoid the hot, sticky months of July and August (when many New Yorkers flee the city) and the snowfalls and sub-zero temperatures which are common between December and February, get the best deal in terms of climate.

The city generally emerges from its winter freeze by mid-March. By April, the numerous outdoor events that make New York so appealing are getting into full swing, making springtime a good period to be around. After the

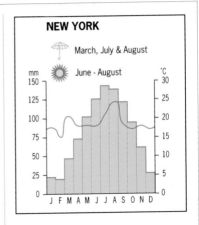

NEW YORK

March, July & August

June - August

ferocious summer heat, when air-conditioning machines are run at full-pelt and New Yorkers tend to become irritable, the autumn finds the humidity disappearing although temperatures remain appealingly mild, usually well into October.

For advice on when to travel outside New York City, where summers are much more pleasant, see the panel on page 194.

Crime

New York is among the world's most notorious cities for crime against the person. Careful advance planning, staying alert on the street and in the subway, and reading the Survival guide on pages 54–5 of this book, however, will all help to reduce what is already a statistically very slender chance of your being robbed or attacked.

Theft of money and valuables from your hotel room is easy to avoid simply by handing them over to the staff for safe keeping. The chances of street robbery can be reduced by not carrying easily snatched handbags and not having your wallet sticking out of your back pocket.

Lost or stolen travellers' cheques are relatively easy to replace (read the instructions when you buy the cheques and make a note of the relevant details). Replacing a stolen passport can be much harder and begins with a visit or telephone call to your country's nearest consular office (see **Embassies and consulates** on pages 252–3).

Customs regulations

Duty-free allowances for non-US citizens entering the country include one US quart (just under a litre) of alcoholic spirits or wine (no one under 21 may bring alcohol into the US), 200 cigarettes or 50 cigars, and up to $100-worth of gifts. Among things you may not bring into the US are meat, fruit, plants, chocolate liqueurs and lottery tickets.

Be warned that bottles of pills and other forms of medication are likely to excite the interest of US customs officers if they discover such things during a search of your luggage. Unless you have a doctor's certificate, even drugs which are available over the counter in the UK may be confiscated if they are prescription-only in the US.

Travellers with disabilities

In New York, as in the US generally, facilities for travellers with disabilities are not only impressive, but are also improving all the time. By law, public buildings have to be at least partially wheelchair-accessible and all must provide toilets for people with disabilities (the design of which sometimes differs from those found in Europe). Almost all New York buses have rear-door lifts for wheelchair-users and most are also able to 'kneel' to make access easier from the kerb.

US trains and airlines are obliged to provide services for people with

Elevated subway in Williamsburg

disabilities if requested, and Amtrak (the US train service) has earned a reputation for doing this well. Though less comfortable than the trains, Greyhound buses are more frequent and allow a companion to travel free provided you have a doctor's certificate stating that this is necessary.

Some major car-rental companies can arrange vehicles with hand controls provided they receive advance notice.

For more information about New York's services for people with disabilities, contact the Mayor's Office for People with Disabilities, tel: 788 2830.

Domestic travel

Should you be combining your trip to New York with travel further afield in the US, you will find that the country's domestic transport services are (considering the distances involved) usually far cheaper than their European counterparts. Foreign visitors are often entitled to discounted passes which can reduce costs still further.

By air Not only the fastest way to get between cities, air travel in the US can also be a bargain. Seemingly no end of cut-price domestic air fares are advertised by US travel agents and airlines as they seek to fill seats on flights outside peak periods. Look in any newspaper or travel agent's window for the latest bargains.

Non-US citizens can also choose from a bewildering variety of 'Visit USA' air passes which, for a fixed price, entitle the holder to unlimited flights within a particular time span (such as 30 or 60 days) or to a certain number of flights with no time restriction. Most transatlantic airlines offer these passes; the full details can be checked at your local travel agent.

By bus Long-distance bus services in the US are run by Greyhound and, by a few dollars, are the country's cheapest form of long-distance travel. All departures from New York are from the Port Authority Terminal (see **Arriving**, page 248).

Although Greyhound buses are comparatively comfortable – with air conditioning, reclining seats, toilets

on board, and stops every few hours for refreshments and leg-stretching – journeys can be very long (five hours from New York to Boston, for example) and monotonous. The buses nearly always take the fast but tedious Interstate Highways rather than more scenic country or coastal roads.

Costs over several very long journeys can be reduced with an Ameripass ticket, which offers unlimited Greyhound travel over a fixed period – from 4 to 30 days. Ameripass tickets can only be bought outside the US. Details can be obtained from your local travel agent.

By car If you are travelling beyond New York or embarking on any of the excursions described on pages 194-211, the cheapest and most convenient way to do so is by car. In the US, petrol costs a fraction of its European price and car-rental rates (outside New York City) are very reasonable. For further details, see Car rental (page 249).

Driving in the US is legal with a valid licence of most European countries or with an International Driver's Licence. For an idea of what you might encounter once behind the wheel, see Driving tips (page 252).

By train Before the advent of cheap domestic air travel, rail was the swiftest and most stylish way to travel around the US and New York's Grand Central Terminal was truly the gateway to the continent. These days, the trains – equipped with sleeping berths, dining cars, and comfortable carriages – are as plush as ever, but prices are often no lower than the cheapest air fare on the same route. For non-US citizens touring the country (or part of it) by train, a variety of regional and country-wide rail passes can save money over regular fares provided they are used to their fullest extent.

Visitors from Europe should note that the US rail network is far from comprehensive and, in many instances, services between major cities are not particularly frequent.

All departures from New York are from Grand Central Terminal or Penn Station (see Arriving, page 248).

CONVERSION CHARTS

FROM	TO	MULTIPLY BY
Inches	Centimetres	2.54
Centimetres	Inches	0.3937
Feet	Metres	0.3048
Metres	Feet	3.2810
Yards	Metres	0.9144
Metres	Yards	1.0940
Miles	Kilometres	1.6090
Kilometres	Miles	0.6214
Acres	Hectares	0.4047
Hectares	Acres	2.4710
US Gallons	Litres	3.7854
Litres	US Gallons	0.2642
Ounces	Grams	28.35
Grams	Ounces	0.0353
Pounds	Grams	453.6
Grams	Pounds	0.0022
Pounds	Kilograms	0.4536
Kilograms	Pounds	2.205
US Tons	Tonnes	0.9072
Tonnes	US Tons	1.1023

MEN'S SUITS

UK	36	38	40	42	44	46	48
Rest of Europe	46	48	50	52	54	56	58
US	36	38	40	42	44	46	48

DRESS SIZES

UK	8	10	12	14	16	18
France	36	38	40	42	44	46
Italy	38	40	42	44	46	48
Rest of Europe	34	36	38	40	42	44
US	6	8	10	12	14	16

MEN'S SHIRTS

UK	14	14.5	15	15.5	16	16.5	17
Rest of Europe	36	37	38	39/40	41	42	43
US	14	14.5	15	15.5	16	16.5	17

MEN'S SHOES

UK	7	7.5	8.5	9.5	10.5	11
Rest of Europe	41	42	43	44	45	46
US	8	8.5	9.5	10.5	11.5	12

WOMEN'S SHOES

UK	4.5	5	5.5	6	6.5	7
Rest of Europe	38	38	39	39	40	41
US	6	6.5	7	7.5	8	8.5

Driving tips

Driving in New York City is not recommended (not least because New Yorkers drive like maniacs and parking can sometimes cost $10 an hour), nor is it necessary. Venture beyond the city to the Catskill Mountains, the remoter parts of the Hudson Valley, Long Island or New Jersey – or further afield – and wheels of your own become essential (see pages 194–211).

On US roads, signposted distances are always given in miles (although elsewhere distances may be expressed in terms of the time it takes to drive somewhere). Traffic travels on the right-hand side, and overtaking is permitted on both the inside and outside lanes of Interstate Highways.

A speed limit of 55mph or 65mph is in force on Interstates (in some places there may also be a minimum limit) In built-up areas lower speed limits are indicated. An extremely dim view is taken of drinking and driving for which hefty fines and prison sentences are frequently imposed. Parking infringements also attract stiff fines, so read the signs carefully. Never park within 10 feet of a fire hydrant.

The Interstates and US Highways are part of the federally run road network. State Highways and State Roads tend to be smaller and are financed by the state government. Occasionally you may find yourself travelling on County Roads – typically winding lanes through isolated rural areas.

Except for some minor routes, the roads are of a high standard with petrol ('gas') stations easy to find in all but the most secluded or inhospitable regions. Virtually all cars use unleaded petrol, sold by the US gallon (3.8 litres).

Be warned that tolls are charged for some Manhattan bridges, and for some stretches of road in the Outer Boroughs.

If you are a member of a motoring organisation at home, check its links with its US counterparts, several of which provide a range of free services to suitably affiliated foreign drivers.

It is illegal to overtake a stationary school bus

Electricity

The US electrical supply is 110 volts (60 cycles) and appliances use two-pin plugs. European appliances are designed for 220 volts (50 cycles) and can only be used with an adapter, which can be bought before leaving (though first make sure it is suitable for the US) or in the US.

Many electrical goods such as computers, videos and CD players are sold in New York at prices much lower than in Europe and the rest of the US. If you are tempted, be sure to check (preferably with the manufacturer rather than the eager-to-please sales assistant) whether or not the item is compatible with European electricity supplies.

Embassies and consulates

Most countries have their US embassy in Washington DC. The following are consular offices in New York: **Australia**, 636 Fifth Avenue (tel: 408 8400); **Canada**, 1251 Sixth Avenue (tel: 596 1700); **Denmark**, 825 Third Avenue (tel: 223 4545); **France**, 934 Fifth Avenue (tel: 606 3600); **Germany**, 460 Park Avenue (tel: 308 8700); **Ireland**, 515 Madison Avenue (tel: 319 2555); **Italy**, 690 Park Avenue (tel: 737 9100);

Netherlands, 1 Rockefeller Plaza (tel: 246 1429); New Zealand, 630 Fifth Avenue (tel: 832 4038); Norway, 825 Third Avenue (tel: 421 7333); Portugal, 630 Fifth Avenue (tel: 246 4580); Sweden, Dag Hammarskjöld Plaza (tel: 751 5900); United Kingdom, 845 Third Avenue (tel: 745 9200).

Emergency telephone numbers

For ambulance, police or fire, dial 911 (no money required) and ask for the relevant service.

Other emergency numbers include Crime Victim's Hotline (tel: 577 7777), New York Gay and Lesbian Anti-violence Unit (tel: 807 0197), Rape Helpline (tel: 267 7273).

Health and health insurance

It is essential, though not compulsory, to have insurance when you travel anywhere in the US. Besides the obvious benefits of compensation for stolen articles and disrupted travel, taking out travel insurance will guard against an astronomical bill if you are unfortunate enough to need medical treatment while in the US.

Comprehensive insurance cover for

City streetlife takes many forms in the Big Apple

a stay in New York should include medical insurance of at least $1 million. If you book a package tour to New York, incidentally, you are likely to find that the optional insurance cover offered will be more expensive and/or less comprehensive than that available from a specialist insurance company. For a reduced rate, some insurance companies offer cover for the US which includes only medical bills.

If you need to see a doctor or dentist, find one by looking under 'Physicians and Surgeons' or 'Dentists' in the *Yellow Pages*, or phone one of the doctor and dentist referral services, tel: 876 5432.

New York hospitals with 24-hour casualty departments include St Luke's Roosevelt (59th Street at Ninth Avenue) and St Vincent's (Seventh Avenue and 11th Street).

Language

New Yorkers not only talk fast, they also talk American English, a language only superficially resembling English English. Besides well-known variations such as 'elevator' instead of lift, 'sidewalk' instead of pavement, and 'being through' instead of having finished, Americans also commonly use 'sir' and 'madam'

(usually abbreviated to 'Ma'm') as a polite way of addressing strangers, and will say 'excuse me' rather than 'pardon' if they mishear or do not understand somebody.

Most New Yorkers, of course, have learned their English in New York, so 'excuse me' will become a very familiar and frustrating phrase to English-speakers who do not make at least a token attempt at conversing in American English, regardless of how weird it may make them feel.

Lost property

Lost at JFK Airport, tel: 718/656 4120.
Lost at La Guardia Airport, contact the relevant airline.
Lost at Newark Airport, tel: 201/961 2230.
Lost in a taxi, tel: 840 4734.
Lost on a bus or the subway, tel: 718/330 3000.

Media

New York has hundreds of TV and radio channels, and newspapers and magazines. Free publications aimed at visitors litter every hotel lobby, the best single source of what's-on information being the new *Critic's Choice*. Also excellent is the weekly *Village Voice*. For a full run-down on the city's media, see pages 132–3.

Street advertising is an art form New York could call its own

Money matters

Before arriving in the US, convert your spending money to US dollar travellers' cheques, which can be used as cash (simply sign and hand over the cheque, then wait for your change) in New York and all over the country in hotels, restaurants and the larger shops. Most hotel cashiers will happily exchange guests' US dollar travellers' cheques for cash.

Trying to change foreign currency – or foreign-currency travellers' cheques – in the US is much more of an ordeal, although New York (rarely among US cities) does boast several banks with foreign-exchange desks, and a small number of exchange bureaux. Money can also be changed on arrival at JFK and Newark airports.

Companies that offer currency exchange include American Express (tel: 640 2000) and Thomas Cook (tel: 757 6915). Both have several branches throughout the city and phoning the number above will elicit the address of the nearest one to you.

US dollar travellers' cheques can be changed for cash in a bank, but you will have to show ID and may be charged a commission fee. Ask first.

Regular New York banking hours are Monday to Friday from 9 to 3 or 3:30 (6 on Thursday at some branches).

Credit cards are a common form of payment and all the major cards are widely accepted. Europeans who know their credit card PIN number can also get cash through American cash-dispensing machines (known as ATMs) which display the appropriate credit-card symbol.

The US currency you will be handling most frequently are the identically sized and coloured notes: $20, $10, $5 and $1; and the variously sized coins: 25¢ (a 'quarter'), 10¢ (a 'dime'), 5¢ (a 'nickel') and 1¢ (a 'penny').

National holidays
Banks and all public offices will be closed on all the following holidays, though shops may be open on some of them: New Year's Day (1 January), Martin Luther King's Birthday (third Monday in January), Lincoln's Birthday (12 February), Washington's Birthday (third Monday in February), Memorial Day (third Monday in May), Independence Day (4 July), Labor Day (first Monday in September), Columbus Day (second Monday in October), Veterans' Day (11 November), Thanksgiving Day (fourth Thursday in November), Christmas Day (25 December). In addition, Good Friday is a half-day holiday and Easter Monday is a full-day holiday. In some cases, the actual dates vary if the holiday falls on a weekend.

Opening hours
New York shop opening hours vary greatly. Many big shops will open on weekdays and Saturdays from 9 to 5 or 6, but smaller or more specialist stores may open as late as 11 or noon and close at 9 or 10.

Museum opening times also vary. Many are open from 10 or 11 to 6 on weekdays and Saturdays (though several are closed on Monday). Some also open on Sundays, and several keep late hours on Tuesdays.

Bank opening hours are Monday to Friday from 9 to 3 or 3:30 (6 on Thursday at some branches).

St Paul's Chapel on Fulton Street was built in 1766

Pharmacies
Pharmacies are plentiful in New York. Visitors from Europe will find many familiar medicines under unfamiliar names. Some drugs that are available over the counter in Europe are available in the US only with a prescription.

If you are using medication regularly, the safest course is to bring a supply with you (but see the relevant section of **Customs regulations** on page 250). Should you be intending to buy prescription drugs while in New York, bring a note from your own doctor. (To find a doctor in New York, see **Health** on page 253.)

Places of worship
New York's places of worship are many and varied. Some of the principal ones are described in the A to Z section of this book, and on pages 120–1. Your hotel reception will be able to advise of those in your neighbourhood, and the telephone book carries a comprehensive list.

Police

Popularly known as 'New York's Finest', the city's police are helpful and efficient in almost every situation. Besides patrolling in cars, officers are regularly seen on the street and the police are well represented in crowd situations.

If you are unfortunate enough to be the victim of theft, you will need to call at a police station to have your insurance claim authorised. Every New York neighbourhood has a police station. To find the one nearest you, dial 374 5000. If you need the police in an emergency, dial **911**.

Post offices New York's main post office, at Eighth Avenue and 34th Street, stays open around the clock, every day of the week. Elsewhere in the city, larger post offices are open on Monday to Friday from 8 to 6 and on Saturdays from 8 to 1. The many smaller post offices keep shorter hours. Post-boxes are blue.

As well as from a post office, stamps can be bought (at inflated prices) through vending machines found in some shops and in many hotel lobbies.

Public transport

Spending most of your time in Manhattan will leave you much less reliant on public transport than you might expect. Not only are distances small, but much of Manhattan is best seen on foot. If you are exhausted, in a rush, planning to visit the Outer Boroughs or simply commuting between nightclubs, however, you will need to make use of the city's buses, subway or taxis.

City buses Substantially slower than subway trains, New York buses at least allow passengers to view the city as they travel through it. Many people find them less intimidating than the underground transit system. The bus network is comprehensive (free maps are available from the tourist information office listed on page 260) and the majority of routes run north-south, with free transfers provided to change on to east-west 'crosstown' buses.

Bus stops are close to street corners – marked by a blue sign and a yellow-painted section of kerb – and most have a route map and frequency schedule for the buses that use that stop. The route is displayed on the front of each bus. Most buses stop every two or three blocks; those marked 'limited' (which only run at rush-hour) make fewer stops, usually only at major junctions.

As with the subway, there is a flat fare (currently $1.25) for all journeys. This can be paid in coins (exact change only; no dollar bills) or with a subway token (see below), either of which should be dropped into the box beside the driver.

If you need a transfer, ask the driver as you pay and he or she will hand you a transfer slip. Transfers can be used only for continuing travel, not as return tickets. They are valid for one hour from the time punched on them, and can only be used on the bus routes printed on the back of the transfer slip.

Especially during rush-hours, New York buses can become solidly packed. If you are wedged in a

Stamps can be bought from vending machines

crowded bus and think your stop may be coming up soon, start making your way towards the exit doors (which are in the middle of the bus – though you can also get off at the front door where you entered) in plenty of time; otherwise there is every chance you will not reach the doors before they shut and the bus moves on.

The subway The much-maligned New York subway system is a swift, inexpensive and largely efficient way to get about the city. The system is also in the throes of an expensive clean-up campaign, intended to replace the notoriously smelly and graffiti-strewn carriages with sleek and spotless air-conditioned models.

Even though security measures have also been stepped up, the subway system still has more than its share of crime, and riding it should be done with caution – see pages 54–5.

A tangle of lines denoted by numbers and letters, the subway system map (available free from subway station token booths and from the tourist information office listed on page 260) initially seems hopelessly confusing. In fact, the system is relatively easy to use provided you remember that 'Uptown' trains go north (towards the Upper West and East sides and Harlem) and 'Downtown' trains travel south (towards Lower Manhattan). Any train labelled 'Brooklyn Bound' is indeed bound for Brooklyn but will stop in Lower Manhattan on the way.

What can be more confusing is the choice between 'Express' and 'Local' trains. While local trains stop at all stations on a particular line, express trains stop only at selected stations. Board an express train by mistake and you could find yourself some distance from where you want to be, and possibly in a dangerous neighbourhood. If this happens then take the next train back as soon as possible.

Provided you know which line and which direction you want before entering the station, follow the relevant signs to the platform. If you do not know, enquire at the ticket booth or ask a uniformed transit police officer. On the platform, approaching trains are usually announced over loudspeakers (though such announcements can often be inaudible). Each train has the relevant letter or number and its destination shown along its side, in a colour that corresponds to the colours on the subway map.

During the day, trains arrive every 10–15 minutes (more during rush-hours). Between midnight and 5am (the service operates around the clock) the usual wait is around 20 minutes.

To enter the subway system, you will need to drop a subway token (currently costing $1.25) into a slot and pass through a turnstile. Subway tokens can be bought from the token booths found at every station (their opening hours are shown above the station entrance) and also from a few major museums. These tokens are due to be replaced by electronic swipe cards. Contact the New York Convention and Visitors Bureau (see page 260) for further details.

Take care on the subway

TRAVEL FACTS

Taxis New York taxis are expensive, and liable to be stuck in traffic for agonisingly long periods of time. If you cannot resist the thrill of riding in a yellow cab, however, simply hail the next empty one to pass by.

Once inside, tell the driver your destination. Do not be surprised if he (or she) does not know how to get there – in New York, taxi-driving is a traditional occupation of the newly arrived immigrant. The driver may also have problems understanding English.

Once under way, it is a good idea to follow your route on a map. This helps if the driver gets lost, and also prevents any 'scenic detours' intended to increase the fare.

Use only the official 'medallion' cabs. These are yellow with 'NYC Taxi' stencilled on the side and with a light and a medallion on the roof. Any other vehicle touting for passengers will be unlicensed (known colloquially as a 'gypsy cab') and should be ignored. It will probably be uninsured and you may be overcharged.

Official taxi charges currently begin at $1.50 and gain 25¢ for each 1/5 mile travelled and 25¢ for each minute of waiting time; a 20 per cent tip is the norm.

Student and youth travel

Coming from Europe, students in full-time education and anyone under 26 may qualify for discounted transatlantic flights offered by travel agents that specialise in youth and student travel. Students carrying International Student Identity Cards (ISICs) will also find themselves entitled to reduced admission to many New York museums and other attractions.

While not exclusively for young and student travellers, the city's YMCAs and youth hostels (see page 215) offer budget-priced accommodation and a chance to socialise with other young New York visitors from around the world.

On the down side, travellers under 21 should remember that US law forbids them to buy alcohol; they may also be denied admission to some New York nightclubs. Under-25s may also encounter problems hiring a car in some parts of the US.

Telephones

Americans are inclined to pick up the telephone for routine enquiries much more frequently than their counterparts in Europe. One reason for this is that US telephones – even public ones – nearly always work. Many businesses have toll-free numbers (prefixed 800) allowing the public to phone them free of charge, and the common 'touch-tone' phones – each push-button number issuing a different electronic tone as you press it – enables extensions to be accessed with a single call (any necessary instructions are provided by a computer-generated voice).

Public telephones are easy to find: in the street, in hotel lobbies, in train and bus stations, in bars and restaurants, and in most public buildings.

The telephone has slots for quarters, dimes and nickels, which should be inserted before dialling. By European standards, phone calls are cheap. A local call costs 20¢ for three minutes (with a 25¢ minimum). The definition of 'local', however, often only covers an area of a few square miles; calls further afield – from Manhattan to Staten Island, for example – can be costly.

Almost without exception, hotel room telephones have charges much higher than those of public telephones. Sometimes hotels even charge for dialling toll-free numbers.

Emergency calls (dial 911) and calls to the operator (dial 0) or the international operator (dial 1 800 874 4000) are free.

Throughout this book, toll-free numbers are given where available. The area code for Manhattan (212) is omitted on the assumption that you are calling from another Manhattan number. If you are not, you will need to add 212 to the Manhattan numbers (except toll-free ones) given in the text. Before dialling an area code or an 800 number, you must first dial '1'.

Time
New York uses Eastern Standard Time, 5 hours behind the UK, 6 hours behind the rest of western Europe, and 13–15 hours behind Australia. These differences are liable to vary by an hour for a few weeks in March/April and October/November, when US Daylight Saving Time begins and ends.

Tipping
Nothing causes as many problems or as much potential embarrassment for European visitors to the US as tipping. In the US, tipping is a long-established fact of life and many people in jobs that involve serving the general public rely on tips to make up

From a restaurant meal to a shoe-shine...don't forget that tipping is expected in the US

a large proportion of their relatively low wages.

How much you tip is entirely up to you, but the general rule in a restaurant or coffee shop is to leave the person who served you 15–20 per cent of the total bill. (An easy way to calculate the approximate amount is to double the sales tax figure – which is 8.25 per cent – shown at the bottom of the bill.) The money should be left on the table, or in a box beside the cashier. Do not leave a tip at any food outlet where you serve yourself or where the food is sold to be taken away.

After a taxi ride, it is customary to tip the driver around 15–20 per cent of the fare. The amount need not be exact, however, and most people (if the amount works out within reason) allow the driver to keep the change as they pay for the fare.

Tipping hotel porters is also the done thing, especially if they are red in the face and short of breath after carrying your bulging suitcases up several flights of stairs. Again, the amount you tip is entirely discretionary, but reckon on 50¢–$1 per bag. If a porter simply helps move your luggage from the lobby into a taxi outside the hotel, a total of $1–$2 should usually be sufficient.

In some hotels, envelopes bearing the maid's name are left in guests' rooms. These are intended to hold tips for the maid, though you need not feel obliged to leave anything, particularly if your stay is only lasting a few nights.

Toilets

Public toilets on the New York streets are usually grim, filthy affairs, and are often frequented by unsavoury types. Fortunately, every public building is obliged to provide public toilets (look for the signs saying 'Rest Rooms' or 'Bathrooms'). These are almost always in immaculate condition, as are the toilets in hotel lobbies, restaurants and most bars.

Tourist information

The multilingual staff of the New York Convention & Visitors' Bureau, 2 Columbus Circle, at the junction of 59th Street and Broadway, can answer visitor queries and provide free bus and subway maps. The office (open on weekdays from 9 to 6 and at weekends from 10 to 6; tel: 800 NYC VISIT or 397 8222) also has racks of free leaflets and brochures detailing New York hotels, restaurants and tourist attractions.

Women travellers

Many women in New York hold powerful, high-profile jobs but, as in any other city, females on their own – be they residents or visitors – may attract unwelcome attention. This is likely to be more annoying than threatening, and can usually be dealt with simply by ignoring it or, if you have been in the city long enough, by delivering some of the choice insults you will have heard New Yorkers throw at each other.

A woman travelling alone is by no means uncommon in New York. The Directory gives details of selected women-only accommodation (see pages 262–8), but obviously common sense dictates that women on their own should avoid cheap hotels in seedy areas which are unsafe at night.

Otherwise, women travellers face many of the same problems as their male counterparts – see the survival tips on pages 54–5. If you need help and are in trouble, see the **Emergency telephone numbers** listed on page 253.

Beneath Brooklyn Bridge

HOTELS AND RESTAURANTS

HOTELS AND RESTAURANTS

The following recommended hotels and restaurants have been divided into three price categories:

- **budget** (£)
- **moderate** (££)
- **expensive** (£££)

Prices do not include taxes; refer to Hidden extras on page 213. Note also that telephone numbers prefixed 800 are free outside the 212 code area when dialled within the US (dial '1' first); local toll numbers follow the toll-free number, the code for Manhattan being 212.

ACCOMMODATION

CHINATOWN

Holiday Inn Downtown (££) 138 Lafayette Street, at corner of Howard Street (tel: 800/HOLIDAY; 966 8898). The only hotel in Chinatown, with very small rooms offering two telephones, in-room movies and individual climate control. Eat in the excellent Pacifica restaurant, or head for the many cheaper alternatives in the busy streets around.

FINANCIAL DISTRICT

Manhattan Seaport Suites (££) 129 Front Street (tel: 800/77SUITE; 742 0003). Sited at the foot of Wall Street and within walking distance of South Street Seaport, rooms here range from tidily furnished studios to one- or two-bedroom suites equipped with microwave ovens, fridges and well-stocked bars.

Millenium (£££) 55 Church Street (tel: 800/835 2220; 693 2001). A black-glass tower rising 55 storeys opposite the World Trade Center, the Millenium was designed for the Downtown business exec, with room rates to match. In return, you get an impressive array of services including a sky-lit swimming pool and choice of two restaurants – the Taliesin and the less formal Grille, both offering 24-hour full-menu room service. Ask for an upper-floor room as the view is unforgettable.

New York Marriott Financial Center (£££) 85 West Street (tel: 800/242 8685; 385 4900). A traditional hotel catering mainly for business people, the Marriott Financial Center exudes the confidence of knowing exactly what it is trying to do, and doing it well. Service is speedy and professional, and public rooms have plenty of soul. The Liberty Lounge serves snacks and cocktails, or you can dine in JW's restaurant. Rooms are small, with the compensation of generously sized bathrooms and spectacular views. Weekend rates are very low, and make this a good base for exploring southern Manhattan.

New York Vista (£££) 3 World Trade Center (tel: 800/HILTONS; 938 9100). Another state-of-the-art shrine to the needs of the high-flying corporate business traveller, the Vista provides a fitness center and indoor swimming pool to hone the muscles before clinching those crucial Wall Street deals. Tourists benefit from weekend deals which include guided tours of nearby neighbourhoods and a free shuttle bus to Midtown Manhattan.

GREENWICH VILLAGE

Washington Square Hotel (£) 103 Waverly Place (tel: 800/222 0418; 777 9515). There is no better placed or better priced Greenwich Village base, this hotel being situated just opposite a corner of Washington Square Park. The rooms tend to be small but are clean and pleasantly furnished, and the staff are helpful. In a previous life as the Hotel Earle, this was the first New York home of Bob Dylan and was where a homesick John Phillips of the Mamas and the Papas penned the hit song 'California Dreamin'.

LITTLE ITALY AND SOHO

Off-SoHo Suites (££) 11 Rivington Street (tel: 800 OFF SOHO; 979 9808). These mini-apartment-style suites are good value if you want to be within walking distance of SoHo, Little Italy and the Lower East Side. Rates are inexpensive because the suites are tiny, and the area, just the wrong side of the Bowery, can be chancy. For budget accommodation, though, this is well worth considering. Each suite has cable TV and VCR, and there is a laundry and fitness room on the premises. Make use of the hotel's 24-hour discount cab service.

MIDTOWN MANHATTAN

Aberdeen (£) 32nd Street between Fifth Avenue and Broadway (tel: 800/551 2303; 736 1600). Now part of the Chatwal chain of reasonably priced hotels, the Aberdeen offers unelaborate but functional rooms in the heart of the compact Korean business district, almost in the shadow of the Empire State Building.

Algonquin (££) 44th Street between Fifth and Sixth avenues (tel: 800/548 0345; 840 6800). It took a Japanese company to restore this literary landmark (home of the Round Table, presided over by Dorothy Parker and friends from 1919) to its former glories. Above the sumptuous lobby and bar areas, however, the Algonquin's rooms are only adequate, and there are plenty of better value alternatives in the area.

Allerton House (£) 57th Street at Lexington Avenue (tel: 753 8841). A women-only and largely residential hotel with tiny but clean, tidy and very low-priced rooms. Private bathrooms are a few dollars extra.

Ameritania (£) Broadway at 54th Street (tel: 800/922 0330; 247 5000). A glitzy, inexpensive hotel on the great white way, next to the old Ed Sullivan theatre and six blocks from Central Park. Everything is brand new, from the black marble bathrooms to the neon-lit lobby with waterfall. There is also an Italian restaurant and a busy pizza parlour and coffee shop on the premises. The low prices are a major attraction – be sure to book early.

Beekman Tower (£££) 3 Mitchell Place at First Avenue and 49th Street (tel: 800/MESUITE; 689 5200). The 1928 Gothic-style Beekman Tower rises above the East River and holds an all-suite hotel providing sensibly priced accommodation especially attractive for long-term stays – which explains its popularity with officials from the nearby United Nations. All the suites have kitchenettes with microwave ovens and coffee-makers, and there is also a fully equipped fitness centre.

Beverly (££) 50th Street between Lexington and Second avenues (tel: 800/223 0945; 753 2700). Some much-needed renovations are smartening up The Beverly, whose spacious, one-bedroom suites, equipped with kitchenettes, are very good value. Also on the premises is a 24-hour pharmacy.

Box Tree (£££) 49th Street at Second Avenue (tel: 758 8320). The perfect place for an indulgent weekend, The Box Tree fills two (soon to be three) adjoining brownstones in the Turtle Bay area of Midtown. *Trompes-l'oeil* decorate the walls, and a Gaudiesque main staircase leads from the restaurant to a series of tiny private dining rooms, most on Versailles-like themes, upstairs. The 13 bedrooms are decorated in different styles – take your pick from Chinese, Egyptian or Japanese – and although bathrooms are tiny, you are again paying for style rather than space.

Carlton Arms (£) 25th Street at Third Avenue (tel: 679 0680). Each wacky, threadbare room is designed and decorated by a different (unknown) artist, and what the Carlton Arms lacks in cleanliness and creature comforts (which is quite a lot) it just about makes up for through its sheer eccentricity. If this sounds like it's for you, book well in advance for a room with

a bathroom. Many struggling artists make this their New York home, so expect bizarre fellow guests and exceptionally low prices. If you pay for six nights, you get a seventh for free.

Chatwal Inn (££) 45th Street at Sixth Avenue (tel: 800/CHA-TWEL; 921 7600). Behind its drab façade the Chatwal Inn offers simple but nicely furnished rooms with cable TV and round-the-clock room service. The location is handy, and a free breakfast of coffee and pastries is served in the lobby.

Chelsea Hotel (££) 23rd Street between Seventh and Eighth avenues (tel: 243 3700). Arthur Miller reputedly relocated here from the Plaza Hotel because he was fed up with having to put on a tie to go down to the front desk to collect his mail. The Chelsea still attracts refugees from more formal establishments, with its laid-back but solicitous service and the atmosphere of a run-down but arty apartment building. For the full story of the writers and artists who have stayed in this landmark New York hotel, see the feature on page 85.

Comfort Inn Murray Hill (££) 35th Street between Fifth and Sixth avenues (tel: 800/221 2222; 947 0200). This branch of the nationwide chain predictably has

higher rates than its far-flung counterparts but nonetheless represents good value for New York City, with tidy, comfortable rooms.

Doral Inn (£££) Lexington Avenue at 49th Street (tel: 755 1200). A deservedly popular hotel in an excellent location, the Doral's public rooms are decorated in a stylish 1990s version of Grecian architecture, and the staff are helpful and friendly. If tramping the New York streets has left you with any energy, you can use the inn's private squash courts – or simply relax in the fitness centre's sauna.

Drake Swissôtel (£££) Park Avenue at 56th Street (tel: 800/DRAKENY; 421 0900). The lobby's wood and brass fittings (and the bowls of complimentary Swiss chocolates) set a comfortable, low-key mood which continues into the comfortable, airy rooms.

Edison (££) 47th Street at Eighth Avenue (tel: 800/637 7070; 840 5000). A partial refurbishment has made some of the Edison's rooms bright, airy and welcoming affairs, while others remain rather shabby and depressing. The good rooms come at a fair price although the hotel's sheer size (1,000 rooms) and its theatre-district site means it is very much a tourist hotel, with little atmosphere.

HOTELS AND RESTAURANTS

Elysée (££) 54th Street between Madison and Park avenues (tel: 753 1066). Recent refurbishment has sadly obliterated the highly individual 'Lucy goes to Hollywood' older rooms, but the new management has kept some of the original furnishings and incorporated them into the brand-new, Regency-inspired rooms. Most of the doubles are small – opt for a suite if you want to spread out. VCRs are standard features, as are marble bathtubs and in-room safes. Next in line for redecoration is the Monkey Bar, which will re-open some time in the future for drinks, meals and light entertainment.

Essex House Hotel Nikko (£££) Central Park South between Sixth and Seventh avenues (tel: 800/654 5687; 247 0300). From the etched brass and black marble features of the art deco lobby to the amply proportioned and tastefully furnished rooms, the Essex House is stylish throughout and enjoys an enviable position facing Central Park. To get the best views, however, splash out on one of the luxurious suites.

Four Seasons (£££) 57th Street between Park and Madison avenues (tel: 800/332 3442; 758 5700). The Four Seasons is not only the tallest hotel in New York – designed by the celebrated I M Pei, it rises 52 stories high – but it is also the most opulent. On average, each room costs a million dollars to deck out in stylish contemporary art-deco form and acquire amenities such as bathtubs that fill within 60 seconds and are large enough to wash an elephant.

Gorham New York (££) 55th Street between Sixth and Seventh avenues (tel: 800/735 0710; 245 1800). An excellent location to enjoy the best features of Midtown Manhattan. The staff are noted for their courtesy and friendliness, and the more costly of the very comfortable rooms feature jacuzzis, kitchenettes with microwave ovens, and the latest in temperature-controlled baths.

Gramercy Park (££) 21st Street and Lexington Avenue (tel: 800/221 4083; 475 4320). Facing Gramercy Park (keys to this private park are available to hotel guests from the porter), this gracefully ageing hotel may have tardy elevators and few recent furnishings, but it does have character in large amounts, offers discounts at weekends and for long stays, and is usefully placed on the borders of Midtown and Lower Manhattan.

Helmsley Middletowne (££) 48th Street between Lexington and Third avenues (tel: 800/843 2157; 755 3000). Owned by the controversial hotelier Leona Helmsley (but not to be confused with the Helmsley Palace – see below), the Middletowne occupies a 17-storey former residential town house not far from the United Nations complex. The property has a mellow, homely ambience and the pleasant rooms include kitchenettes and fridges. Some rooms open on to terraces.

Herald Square (£) 31st Street near Fifth Avenue (tel: 800/727 1888; 279 4017). Occupying the 1893 *Life* magazine building, with mementoes of the publication easy to spot, the rooms here are small and spartan but with clean, tiled bathrooms. Most have colour TV and phones, but you probably wouldn't want to spend too much time in the room. The main attractions are the cheap prices, offset by the noisy and relatively uninteresting location.

Inn on 57th Street (££) 440 West 57th Street (tel: 800/231 0405; 581 8100). Unexciting but dependable branch of a nationwide chain, within easy reach of the Midtown Manhattan sights but occupying a lacklustre location.

Iroquois (£) 44th Street between Fifth and Sixth avenues (tel: 800/332 7220; 840 3080). A much-needed refurbishment greatly improved this always dependable but once very shabby hotel. The pricier rooms are equipped with kitchenettes; almost all are nowadays tastefully decorated in relaxing pastel shades. People who have stayed here recently say that the service sometimes leaves a lot to be desired.

Journey's End (££) 40th Street between Fifth and Madison avenues (tel: 800/668 4200; 447 1500). Unfussy but crisply decorated rooms with all the usual amenities in a good location at a very fair price.

Lexington (££) Lexington Avenue at 48th Street (tel: 800/448 4471; 755 4400). Beyond the marble-floored lobby with its rosewood pillars and beautiful flower arrangements are two types of accommodation – the dated older rooms and the newly decorated (and more expensive) Tower rooms. Although both types are small, there is plenty of space in which to spread out elsewhere. A coffee shop, a northern Italian restaurant, a highly acclaimed Chinese restaurant, and the western-style nightclub, Denim and Diamonds, are on the premises. The Winter Citysaver rates are by far the best value.

Macklowe (£££) 44th Street between Sixth Avenue and Broadway (tel: 800/MACK-LOWE; 768 4400). Though situated in the heart of the Times Square theatre district, the Macklowe is geared more toward business travellers than tourists. But if the price is affordable, there are few better-appointed or more up-to-date options in the vicinity.

Mansfield (£) 44th Street between Fifth and Sixth avenues (tel: 800/255 5767; 944 6050). A place with few pretensions but offering very affordable rooms in a prime Midtown Manhattan location (the more famous Algonquin Hotel is just across the street). The turn-of-the-century building was designed by noted New York architect Stanford White.

Marriott East Side (£££) Lexington Avenue at 49th Street (tel: 800/242 8684; 755 4000). Erected as an apartment house slightly more recently than the medieval-style gargoyles on the façade might suggest, the 34-storey Marriott East Side has successfully moulded spacious 1920s New York residential rooms into comfortable hotel accommodation. Each room contains useful extras such as an iron and a filter-coffee machine, though if you prefer not to do all this for yourself, the service is helpful and there is a club-like bar downstairs.

Martha Washington (£) 30th Street between Park and Madison avenues (tel: 689 0023). Women-only accommodation in a semi-residential area. The rooms are gloomy and range from small to comparatively spacious; pay extra for a private bathroom and TV. Bookable by the night or at very tempting weekly rates; additional discounts for longer stays (one month maximum).

Michelangelo (£££) 51st Street at Seventh Avenue (tel: 800/237 0990; 765 1900). Genuine 18th- and 19th-century European art and a wealth of marble and crystal help the Michelangelo to rank among New York's most luxurious hotels. The large rooms come in art deco, Empire or country French styles with seemingly every possible amenity, including TV in the bathroom. There is even a free unpacking service if you have too much luggage to tackle alone. The atmosphere is a bit hushed, but this de luxe, self-styled palazzo is one of the fanciest places to stay around Broadway.

Milford Plaza (££) 45th Street at Eighth Avenue (tel: 800/221 2690; 869 3600). Not the most characterful or luxurious of hotels (in fact reminiscent of an airport lounge), the Milford Plaza has its share of cramped rooms, but a prime location on Times Square makes it a hit with money-conscious tourists and business travellers alike. The immediate area can be dangerous at night, but hotel security is good.

Morgans (£££) Madison Avenue between 37th and 38th streets (tel: 686 0300). The brainchild of the former owners of the extremely chic Studio 54 nightclub, Morgans has a minimalist design and a colour scheme based on black, grey and white. The bathrooms feature unique stainless steel basins and fittings, and every room has a video player. The clientele is predominantly young and fashionable – and not short of a dollar or two.

Parker Meridien (£££) 56th Street between Sixth and Seventh avenues (tel: 800/543 4300; 245 5000). From the glitzy interior architecture to the pricey French nouvelle cuisine served in its restaurant, everything about Parker Meridien symbolises conspicuous wealth. The ideal guest must be rich, beautiful, and inclined to pose for hours at the rooftop swimming pool.

Penn Plaza (£) 34th Street between Seventh and Eighth avenues (tel:800/633 1911; 947 5050). Small, functional rooms are adequate for a night's rest if you don't mind the slightly sleazy location, opposite Penn Station. Each room has cable TV and a private bathroom, with the low prices being the main attraction.

Pickwick Arms (£) 51st Street between Second and Third avenues (tel: 800/PIC-KWIK; 355 0300). A sumptuous lobby, a cocktail lounge and a roof garden go some way towards compensating for the small rooms. This is a well-priced option for the area, just a few minutes' walk from the heart of Midtown Manhattan.

Plaza (£££) Fifth Avenue at Central Park South (tel: 800/759 3000; 759 3000). New York's leading hotel since it opened in 1907, the Plaza's past guests have included Teddy Roosevelt, F Scott and Zelda Fitzgerald, the Beatles, and Solomon Guggenheim, who lived in one of the Plaza's suites and decorated its walls with the art which later became the core of the Guggenheim Museum's collection. Property tycoon Donald Trump snapped up the Plaza for $400 million in 1988 and put his then wife Ivana in control of a $100-million facelift. Still the epitome of posh, the Plaza has every facility you can think of. Some of the infamously tiny viewless rooms have been converted into suites; the pricier accommodation has unbelievable panoramas of Fifth Avenue or Central Park.

Portland Square Hotel (£) 47th Street between Sixth and Seventh avenues (tel: 800/388 8988; 382 0600). An unknown James Cagney was just one among many struggling actors who used this long-established budget-priced hotel in the heart of the Broadway theatre district. The rooms have a few more frills than the Portland's sister hotel, Herald Square: there are places to sit in the lobby, lockers, and a drinks- and ice-machine. Parts of the immediate area can be intimidating after dark.

Remington (£) 46th Street between Broadway and Sixth Avenue (tel: 221 2600). Clean, no-frills accommodation in the theatre district. The cheapest rooms lack private bathrooms, but all are fair value for their low price. Very close to Times Square, which is not a place for aimless night-time strolling.

Roger Smith (££) Lexington Avenue at 47th Street (tel: 800/445 0277; 755 1400). Tucked just north of Grand Central Terminal, the Roger Smith offers attractively

265

furnished rooms and the intimate, personal atmosphere most Midtown Manhattan hotels can only strive for.

Roger Williams (£) 31st Street between Madison and Park avenues (tel: 800/637 9773; 684 7500). Located in a quiet semi-residential area of Midtown, the Roger Williams is one of the friendlier budget hotels. Every room has a kitchenette and cable TV, and there is a good choice of suite accommodation for families. The furnishings may have seen better days, but the hotel is good value.

Roosevelt (££) Madison Avenue at 45th Street (tel: 800/223 1870; 661 9600). Once a pre-eminent New York hotel catering to the thousands of train travellers who poured into the city at nearby Grand Central Terminal, the Roosevelt has matured into a slightly down-at-heel though dependable hotel. Renovations are now in progress – one of the first areas to be spruced up was the beautiful, vast, neo-classical lobby. Many of the rooms have been upgraded too; with the very reasonable room rate this is one of Midtown's better deals.

Royalton (£££) 44th Street between Fifth and Sixth avenues (tel: 800/635 9013; 869 4400). Another ultra-trendy hotel from the team that created Morgans (see

page 265), the Royalton is designed with a cool artistry throughout and finds favour with the young and good looking.

St Moritz on the Park (££) Central Park South at Sixth Avenue (tel: 800/221 4774; 755 5800). You will pay the usual high rates for a park view, but in general this is one of the less exclusive and more affordable hotels facing Central Park. The St Moritz draws a mixture of guests, ranging from airline crew to people on intensive Fifth Avenue shopping sprees, and there is usually a busy crowd milling around the lobby, the bar and Rumpelmayer's ice-cream parlour. Rooms are small, but fine for a stay of a couple of days.

Salisbury (££) 57th Street between Sixth and Seventh avenues (tel: 800/223 0680; 246 1300). A welcoming, professionally run, small hotel across the road from the Russian Tea Room and convenient for shopping. Décor is frumpy, but rooms are spotless and comfortable, the most recently renovated ones offering brand new microwave and fridge. If you want even more space, opt for one of the apartment-sized suites.

San Carlos Hotel (££) 50th Street between Lexington and Third avenues (tel: 800/722 2012; 755 1800). Little sets it apart from other Midtown Manhattan hotels,

but the San Carlos offers good quality rooms with ample cupboard space and adequately equipped kitchenettes.

Sherry Netherland (£££) Fifth Avenue at 59th Street (tel: 355 2800). One of the grand French chateau-style buildings put up along Fifth Avenue across from Central Park during the 1920s, the Sherry Netherland offers soaring park views and impeccable service. Rooms are spacious and individually decorated, with VCRs and microwaves, and plenty of personal touches. The sky-high rates are worth it if you have a huge range of hard-to-satisfy demands. Room service is by the acclaimed restaurant, Harry Cipriani, located at ground level.

Tudor (£££) 42nd Street between First and Second avenues (tel: 800/879 8836; 986 8800). A stylish hotel located in a planned Tudor-style residential section of Midtown Manhattan, a few minutes' walk from the Chrysler Building, Grand Central Terminal and the UN. Rooms are spacious, furnished in deep, rich colours, and offer trouser press, mini-bar, cable TV and safe. The corporate discounts and dual-line phones with data ports favour the business traveller, but there is plenty for others, from the balustraded Regency Lounge and Carvery to the sauna and fitness centre.

United Nations Plaza (£££) First Avenue at 44th Street (tel: 800/233 1234; 758 1234). The rooms in this modern, architectural-award-winning structure do not begin until the 28th floor, the lower levels being UN office space. Chrome, marble and mirrors are prevalent throughout, and every room has a stunning view. The sports facilities are excellent. You will find many a UN delegate using the indoor tennis courts, swimming pool and sauna.

Vanderbilt-YMCA (£) 47th Street between Second and Third avenues (tel: 755 9600). Make an early book-

ing to stay at the most popular and best-located of New York's YMCAs. Open to men and women, it has newly renovated small single and double rooms at very low prices plus extra facilities such as a brand new restaurant, left-luggage lockers, a swimming pool, a gym and a self-service launderette.

Waldorf-Astoria (£££) Park Avenue between 49th and 50th streets (tel: 800/HILTONS; 355 3000). After the Plaza, the Waldorf-Astoria is New York's most famous hotel. It was the birthplace of the charity ball and the prime rendezvous for New York high society from the 1930s – although it has taken a $150-million restoration to bring back the grandeur of times gone by. A sense of opulence strikes as soon as you enter the art-deco lobby, and all the rooms are stylishly appointed with marble bathrooms. Only in the top-price suites, however, will you encounter a level of luxury to match the hotel's rich history.

Warwick (£££) 65 West 54th Street (tel: 800/223 4099; 247 2700). Built by William Randolph Hearst in 1927, the recently renovated Warwick is popular with business travellers. It has over 400 rooms (all with TV and telephone), plus a restaurant and fitness facilities, and it is convenient for all the main Midtown sights.

Wellington (££) Seventh Avenue at 55th Street (tel: 800/652 1212; 247 3900). Except perhaps for the lobby, there is nothing fancy about the sizeable Wellington, where the rooms are clean and simple and very reasonably priced for their prized central location.

Wolcott (£) 31st Street at Fifth Avenue (tel: 268 2900). For a remarkably low rate, the Wolcott offers smallish but smartly furnished, comfortable rooms complete with private bathrooms and cable TV, and some interesting photos of New York on the walls. The mirror-lined, baroque-style lobby is an unexpected bonus in this impressive budget hotel.

Wyndham (££) 58th Street between Fifth and Sixth avenues (tel: 800/257 1111; 753 3500). The Wyndham feels more like an apartment building than a hotel, and is especially popular with Broadway performers who could easily afford to stay elsewhere. Such good-sized rooms in this area and price bracket are very unusual; all are individually and tastefully decorated. The low prices mean early booking is essential.

UPPER EAST SIDE

Barbizon (££) 63rd Street at Lexington Avenue (tel: 800/753 0360; 838 5700). By the standards of the high-priced Upper East Side, the Barbizon is remarkably good value for its smallish but cosy rooms and the dozen terraced suites (some with good views of the New York skyline) that occupy the red-brick building's Gothic tower. Until 1981, the Barbizon was a women's residential hotel and its roll-call of famous former guests includes Grace Kelly, Candice Bergen and Liza Minelli.

Carlyle (£££) 76th Street at Madison Avenue (tel: 744 1600). For years, the understated elegance of the Carlyle has provided a home away from home for high-ranking international dignitaries and those so accustomed to being fabulously wealthy that they have no need to flaunt their affluence. Crystal chandeliers hang above the public spaces, and the guest rooms are decorated with antiques, tapestries and fresh flowers. Most also have fax machines. Sink into the marble bath-tub and you will also find that you have a phone at your elbow.

Lowell (£££) 63rd Street between Park and Madison avenues (tel: 838 1400). A small, luxurious hotel, the Lowell occupies an art deco building in the landmark district of the Upper East Side. Chinese porcelain, 18th- and 19th-century prints and wood-burning fireplaces decorate the rooms; service is personal (staff greet you by name within minutes of checking in). There is a fitness room for the use of all guests, but if you like your work-outs to be private then go for the Gym Suite, said to be inspired by one-time guest Madonna.

Mark (£££) 77th Street at Madison Avenue (tel: 800/843 6275; 744 4300). In-room jacuzzis, video players (select the film you want to watch from a well-stocked library) and reliable and courteous staff help the Mark attract a fashionable, jet-setting clientele.

Mayfair Hotel Baglioni (£££) Park Avenue at 65th Street (tel: 800/223 0542; 288 0800). With its turn-of-the-century-style public rooms, white-gloved elevator attendants, and plenty of thoughtful extras, the Mayfair Hotel Baglioni is one of the city's consistently top places to stay. The spacious rooms are decked out in chintz and fresh flowers; many of the world's great and good arrive for repeat stays. An added attraction is Le Cirque, one of New York's finest restaurants, next door.

Pierre (£££) Fifth Avenue at 61st Street (tel: 800/332 3442; 940 8101). There is absolutely nothing surreal about the mural-lined corridors or the enormous, well-furnished rooms of the Pierre, even though this was Salvador Dali's favourite New York hotel. Packed with antiques and lined by lush carpets, the hotel's aristocratic ambience is heightened by the afternoon tea served daily beneath the rotunda.

Plaza Athénée (£££) 64th Street between Park and Madison avenues (tel: 734 9100). With Louis XIV-style furniture filling every corner and marble and crystal fittings wherever you look, the Plaza Athénée is intended to evoke the grandeur of a European royal palace. Even though some find it pretentious, plenty of wealthy guests bask happily in the pre-revolutionary Versailles atmosphere, and standards of service are high.

Regency (£££) Park Avenue between 60th and 61st streets (tel: 800/23 LOEWS; 759 4100). The lobby may be stuffed with French antiques, but the Regency, while extremely stylish, is a lot less snooty than many of its Upper East Side rivals. Be they financial wheeler-dealers or rock stars on the rise, the clientele appreciate the tastefully furnished, airy rooms and the efficient, attentive staff.

Stanhope (£££) Fifth Avenue at 81st Street (tel: 800/828 1123; 288 5800). With high-quality reproduction Louis XIV furniture filling the lobby and antique porcelain sitting beside state-of-the-art electronic gadgets in every guest room, the Stanhope is an interesting blend of old and new but has a rather hushed and hallowed atmosphere.

Surrey (£££) 76th Street at Madison Avenue (tel: 800/ME-SUITE; 288 3700). A small, quiet and welcoming hotel, where all the rooms include kitchenettes – though it is hard to imagine the tidily bank-rolled guests opting for self-made snacks when room service operates around the clock and an acclaimed French restaurant is located on the premises.

Wales (££) Madison Avenue at 92nd Street (tel: 876 6000). One of New York's longest-serving hotels, the Wales has been in business since 1900, and the attractive rates reflect its location on the northern edge of the neighbourhood – though public transport links to Midtown and Lower Manhattan are swift. The price of the nicely but not opulently furnished rooms

includes afternoon tea and a light breakfast.

Westbury (£££) Madison Avenue at 69th Street (tel: 800/321 1569; 535 2000). American elegance takes on an English appearance at the Westbury, where genuine Chippendale furniture decorates the lobby and a generous number of top-class reproductions fill the guest rooms. Splash out for a deluxe room and you can stretch out on a four-poster bed. Extras include a well-equipped gymnasium for guests' use.

UPPER WEST SIDE

Beacon (££) Broadway at 75th Street (tel: 800/572 4969; 787 1100). A bustling, professionally run small hotel, ten blocks north of the Lincoln Center and within easy reach of most Upper West Side attractions. The large rooms all come with cable TV and kitchenette, and Zabar's, the city's best gourmet deli, is just across the road. A very good deal, especially the newly renovated rooms.

Broadway American (£) Broadway at 77th Street (tel: 362 1100). Mid-sized hotel with competitive rates. All rooms come with colour TV and fridges. A few dollars can be saved by opting for a shared rather than an *en-suite* bathroom.

Esplanade (£) West End Avenue at 74th Street (tel: 874 5000). Filling a large, red-brick building in a residential part of the Upper West Side, the Esplanade is an attractively priced, mainly suite-oriented hotel. All rooms are well proportioned; those facing west get views of the sunset across the Hudson River. Be aware, however, that the area, while perfectly safe during daylight, should be regarded as off-limits at night

Excelsior (£) 81st Street between Central Park West and Columbus Avenue (tel: 800/368 4575; 362 9200). Standard but entirely acceptable rooms with spotless, old-fashioned bathrooms make this a good stand by,

in a residential section of the Upper West Side. Central Park, the American Museum of Natural History and the Columbus Avenue bars and restaurants are all within easy walking distance.

Malibu Studios (£) Broadway between 102nd and 103rd streets (tel: 800/647 2227; 222 2954). Bordering a district which can be intimidating at night, though close to Columbia University and the Cathedral Church of St John the Divine, the Malibu offers student-residence-style accommodation at very low rates. Rooms are unelaborate but homely, and spending a few extra dollars brings a colour TV, kitchen facilities and private bathroom.

Mayflower on the Park (££) Central Park West at 61st Street (tel: 800/223 4164; 265 0060). On the border with Midtown Manhattan, and with some rooms overlooking Central Park, the Mayflower offers tidily appointed rooms a stone's throw from the Lincoln Center. Stars of stage and screen sometimes number among the guests.

Milburn (£) 76th Street near Broadway (tel: 800/833 9622; 362 1006). One of the Upper West Side's best budget choices, the Milburn offers not only a quiet, graceful lobby and rooms with brand-new kitchenettes (with microwaves), but also prompt, friendly service. The spacious suites make ideal family accommodation (children under 12 stay with their parents free); there is a self-service laundry on the premises.

New York International Youth Hostel (£) Amsterdam Avenue at 103rd Street (tel: 932 2300). The largest youth hostel in the US occupies an architectural landmark – dating from 1883, the building was designed by the man responsible for the base of the Statue of Liberty. Very clean and welcoming, with small dormitory rooms and a host of additional services for the budget traveller.

Olcott (£) 72nd Street between Central Park West and Columbus Avenue (tel: 877 4200). Worn furnishings and offhand service may put some off, but others – including theatrical and musical performers – stay here for the inexpensive weekly rates. Shorter stays are subject to availability; early booking is essential (no credit cards).

Radisson Empire (££) Broadway at 63rd Street (tel: 800/221 6509; 265 7400). A luxury chain hotel, recently refurbished to the tune of $30 million, offering small, well-furnished rooms all with CD and tape deck as well as colour TV and VCR. The grand, high-ceilinged lobby displays a beautiful collection of model stage sets – appropriate for a hotel just a few steps from the Lincoln Center.

Riverside Tower (£) Riverside Drive at 80th Street (tel: 800/877 5200; 877 5200). Located in an unexciting residential section of the Upper West Side, the Riverside Tower's spartan and somewhat dreary rooms have phones, colour TVs and superb views over the Hudson River. There are no other facilities – use this as a low-cost place to sleep.

West Side YMCA (£) 63rd Street near Central Park West (tel: 787 4400). Book well ahead for these simple but usefully situated and reasonably priced rooms, which are available as singles or doubles in a large, echoey building close to the Lincoln Center. The price includes use of a well-equipped gym and a large swimming pool, safe-deposit boxes, coin-op launderette and 24-hour security.

RESTAURANTS

THE BRONX

Dominick's (££) 2335 Arthur Avenue (tel: 718/733 2807). The southern Italian cuisine is far from exceptional, but dining at Dominick's is strong on atmosphere, not least because the place is usually crowded with noisy diners and the menu is not written, but recited by the harassed waiters.

Mario's (££) 2342 Arthur Avenue (tel: 718/584 1188). Often as busy as Dominick's (above), but with a slightly better standard of food, much of it Neapolitan.

BROOKLYN

Aunt Sonia's (££) Eighth Avenue at 12th Street (tel: 718/965 9526). Handy for the Brooklyn Museum, though the menu is unpredictable and depends entirely on the daily whims of the chef. Seldom do the culinary creations disappoint, however.

Gage and Tollner (££) corner of Fulton and Jay streets, Downtown Brooklyn (tel: 718/875 5181). Excellent fresh seafood dishes – many of them southern US specialities – served in a noted 19th-century interior, complete with gas lamps.

Lichee Hut (£) 162 Montague Street, Brooklyn Heights (tel: 718/522 5565). A variety of Hunan and Szechuan dishes plus an excellent selection of vegetarian meals; especially good value at lunchtime.

Montague Street Saloon (£) 122 Montague Street, Brooklyn Heights (tel: 718/522 6770). Low-cost American staples; a nicely placed option if you are exploring Brooklyn Heights.

Mrs Stahl's Delicious Knishes (£) 1001 Brighton Beach Avenue (tel: 718/648 0210). Delivers exactly what its name suggests: expertly made knishes available in a host of fillings. Buy several.

New Prospect Café (£) 393 Flatbush Avenue (tel: 718/638 2148). Lively locals' eating spot, within easy reach of the Brooklyn Museum.

Odessa (££) 1113 Brighton Beach Avenue (tel: 718/332 3223). Come with several friends. One price buys a bottle of vodka and all you can eat from the Russian/Georgian buffet table. Be ready to dance, too.

Primorski (££) 282 Brighton Beach Avenue (tel: 718/891 3111). Borscht and assorted Georgian specialities at remarkably low prices during the day; at night, the three-course dinners are accompanied by rowdy live entertainment.

River Café (£££) 1 Water Street (tel: 718/522 5200). Set beneath the Brooklyn Bridge with breathtaking views of the Manhattan skyline, the River Café also boasts some adventurous and successful modern American cuisine.

Santa Fe Grill (££) 60 Seventh Avenue, corner of Lincoln Place (tel: 718/636 0279). Large portions of spicy Cajun and Tex-Mex food served from lunchtime, but the place really gets into gear during the evenings, when it is used for drinking as much as for eating.

Teresa's (£) 80 Montague Street, Brooklyn Heights (tel: 718/797 3996). Very filling, very well-priced Polish food.

CHINATOWN

Bo Ky (£) 80 Bayard Street (tel: 406 2292). Nothing fussy about the decor but nourishing bowls of steaming noodle soup with seafood or duck are served at rock-bottom prices.

First Taste (££) 53 Bayard Street (tel: 962 1818). Serves an eclectic mix of Hong Kong favourites and, as the name suggests, makes a good spot to begin exploring the intracacies of this regional cuisine.

Golden Unicorn (££) 18 East Broadway (tel: 941 0911). A favourite for large family banquets or big parties. Large selection of dishes, from savoury appetisers through dim sum to duck, fresh fish and bean curd.

Hong Fat (£) 63 Mott Street (tel: 962 9588). A locals' favourite for steaming noodles and meat dishes, served in a boisterous but friendly eat-and-run setting.

House of Vegetarian (£) 68 Mott Street (tel: 226 6572). If the meat- and fish-intensive fare of most Chinatown eateries leaves you unimpressed, this totally vegetarian cubby hole does wondrous things re-creating regular Chinese dishes but using nothing that ever walked, crawled or swam.

HSF (££) 46 Bowery (tel: 374 1319). A fair bet for lunchtime dim sum, especially for first-time western visitors who will not feel as left out of the culinary fun here as they might in some Chinatown eateries, not least for the picture chart showing some of the options.

Hunan House (££) 45 Mott Street (tel: 962 0010). One of the first places to make spicy Hunan fare available in predominantly Cantonese Chinatown, and still carrying a good range of tasty, fiery dishes.

King Fung (££) 20 Elizabeth Street (tel: 964 5256). Good choice of well-prepared Cantonese food in a setting that is a cut above most neighbourhood eateries; also lunchtime dim sum.

Mandarin Court (£) 61 Mott Street, near Canal Street (tel: 608 3838). Wonderfully chaotic dim sum parlour, busiest on Sundays when the communal tables are packed. Once you are seated, be ready for a lot of shouting and pointing to get what you want from the passing trolleys.

Mon Bo (£) 65 Mott Street (tel: 964 6480). Cantonese cooking at its plain and simple best. The noodle soups are delicious – but then so is almost everything else.

Mweng Thai (££) 23 Pell Street (tel: 406 4259). A variety of tantalising Thai dishes. Anyone who wants to keep the roof on their mouth should take care when venturing among the spicier items.

Nice Restaurant (£) 35 Broadway (tel: 406 9510). A big and always busy venue for quality Cantonese dishes at very low prices. Come for

the lunchtime dim sum to see the place at its liveliest.

Nom Wah Tea Parlour (£) 13 Doyers Street (tel: 962 6047). Long-established and immensely popular for the wonderful selection of dim sum served throughout the day. Plenty of gastronomically thrilling and exotically filled dumplings and pastries fill the passing trays, although regulars claim standards have dropped.

Noodle Town (£) 28 Bowery (tel: 349 0923). Providing plenty of what its name suggests in many more varieties than you ever imagined possible.

Peking Duck House (££) 22 Mott Street (tel: 227 1810). Here, at what former New York City mayor Ed Koch regarded as 'the best Chinese restaurant in the world', you will find a range of crispy pork and beef dishes. If you are feeling flush and hungry, opt for the full Peking Duck dinner, which cuts no corners and costs around $30.

Phoenix Garden (££) 46 Bowery Arcade (tel: 233 6017). Slightly dearer than many Chinatown restaurants but worth paying the extra for sophisticated Cantonese food which makes few concessions to Western eating habits; salt-and-pepper shrimp is one speciality.

Saigon House (£–££) 89–91 Bayard Street (tel: 732 8988). Small and unpretentious venue for enjoying highly regarded Vietnamese specialities at a bargain price.

Sun Say Gay (£) 220 Canal Street (tel: 964 7256). Hole-in-the-wall rice shop dispensing simple dishes – bits of meat, vegetables and pickles on generous piles of rice – at absurdly cheap prices.

Thailand (£) 106 Bayard Street (tel: 349 3132). Inexpensive Thai favourites, and some lesser-known dishes, filling a lengthy, mouthwatering menu.

Triple 8 Palace (££–£££) 59 Division Street (tel: 941 8886). On the top floor of a

building beneath the Manhattan Bridge, this is wildly popular with locals who show up mostly for the lunchtime dim sum, although the menu carries a large and appetising range of Hong Kong cuisine.

20 Mott Street (££) 20 Mott Street (tel: 964 0380). Spread over three floors and offering a massive and (to Westerners) largely indecipherable menu, this is one of Chinatown's most celebrated restaurants. Its reputation is definitely for the food rather than the service – often you will need to be very determined to get your order taken. Come for the lunchtime dim sum or for a memorable dinner, even though you may not be certain what you are eating.

Viet-Nam (£) 11 Doyers Street (tel: 693 0725). A completely unpretentious setting for the best and probably most authentic Vietnamese cuisine in New York.

Wong Kee (£) 113 Mott Street (tel: 226 9018). Fine selection of Cantonese dishes at irresistible prices; deservedly crowded.

EAST VILLAGE AND LOWER EAST SIDE

Acme Bar and Grill (££) 9 Great Jones Street (tel: 420 1934). Cajun cooking and lots of it – gumbo, jambalaya, and deep fried oyster are among the choices — plus a range of hot sauces to tempt the devil-may-care diner.

Angelica Kitchen (£) 12th Street between First and Second avenues (tel: 228 2909). Tasty and very inexpensive natural foods.

Around the Clock Café (££) 8 Stuvesyant Street (tel: 598 0402). Sports a cosy East Village ambience and earns a place in the hearts of nocturnal locals by being open 24 hours a day. The menu is simple pasta-to-burgers fare.

B&H Dairy (£) Second Avenue at St Mark's Place (tel: 505 8065). If you have never sampled blintzes, this is the place to start. Also a dependable outlet for vegetarian meals.

Benny's Burritos (£) Avenue A at 6th Street (tel: 254 2054). Burritos (folded tortillas) with a host of inventive fillings are dispensed here to a lively East Village crowd before or after they spend the night clubbing.

Café Orlin (£) 41 St Mark's Place (tel: 771 1447). The outside tables are excellent vantage points for watching the weird and wonderful East Village folk go about their daily business while you sip a coffee and munch a pastry.

Café Tabac (£££) Ninth Street between Second and Third avenues (tel: 674 7072). Rare is the New York celebrity who has not dined at this ultra-trendy rendezvous patronised by supermodels and rock stars; classy contemporary American cuisine but sometimes brusque service for the non-celebrity diner.

Caffè della Pace (£) Seventh Street between First and Second avenues (tel: 529 8024). Low-key spot that is worth seeking out for its stylishly presented Italian food at very reasonable prices.

Dojo (£) 24 St Mark's (tel: 674 9821). An intriguingly combined Japanese and health-food restaurant, much prized among its predominantly youthful and trendy clientele for remarkable low prices and the health-boosting potential of its offerings.

Great Jones Café (££) 54 Great Jones Street (tel: 674 9304). This is where you will find the cutting-edge East Village faces selecting their late-afternoon breakfasts from the daily specials – hearty and homely American fare – chalked on a blackboard.

Gulshan (£) Second Avenue at 6th Street (tel: 979 6572). Not the finest Indian food in the area but especially good for vegetarians and all at extremely low prices; all-you-can-eat lunchtime specials at weekends.

Haveli (££) Second Avenue between 5th and 6th streets

(tel: 982 0533). One of the few East Village Indian eateries to put as much care into the decor as into the food, and serving some fine southern Indian specialities among a predominantly north Indian menu.

Indochine (££) Lafayette Street between Astor Place and 4th Street (tel: 505 5111). Dine amid palm fronds on a tremendous mix of Vietnamese, Thai and Cambodian fare; open for dinner only.

Katz's Delicatessen (£) East Houston Street near Orchard Street (tel: 254 2246). Legendary for providing pastrami and corned beef sandwiches to fussy eaters for over a century, Katz's found additional fame in the 1989 film *When Harry Met Sally*.

Kiev (£) Second Avenue at 7th Street (tel: 674 4040). Eastern European specialities such as pirogi and generously filled blintzes are served around the clock, as are a selection of more familiar omelettes and burgers.

Mitali (££) 6th Street between First and Second avenues (tel: 533 2508). The quality Indian cuisine brings adventurous diners from all over New York; expect tables to be at a premium on Friday and Saturday evenings.

Ratner's Dairy Restaurant (£) Delancey Street between Norfolk and Suffolk streets (tel: 677 5588). Established in 1905, Ratner's is well past its prime but still pulls in old-time Lower East Siders for its mushroom barley soup, lox and many other Jewish favourites.

Rectangle's (££) Second Avenue at 10th Street (tel: 677 8410). Intriguing array of Yemeni and Israeli dishes, all of them extremely affordable.

Second Avenue Kosher Deli (££) Second Avenue at 10th Street (tel: 677 0606). Landmark family-run Jewish deli and one of the last remaining places where you can sample kasha, kugel, knishes and knaidels in

authentic forms, besides more common fare such as pastrami and chopped liver sandwiches and steaming chicken soup. Eat in the back room and you will be surrounded by memorabilia from the Lower East Side's Yiddish Theater.

Sugar Reef (££) Second Avenue between 5th and 6th streets (tel: 477 8427). Colourful and lively setting for Caribbean (mostly Dominican) cuisines – the zesty seafood dishes are particularly good – or for downing rum-based cock-tails at the bar.

Two Boots (£) Avenue A at 2nd Street (tel: 505 2276). Enterprising and successful mixing of Italian and Cajun cookery: shrimp pizza is just one example.

Ukrainian Restaurant (££) Second Avenue at 9th Street (tel: 529 5024). Be it borscht or stuffed pirogi – just two of many popular traditional dishes – you will find it hard to finish your meal, so large are the helpings.

Veselka (£) Second Avenue at 9th Street (tel: 228 9682). Earthy, filling Ukrainian and Polish fare served around the clock and in large quantities to a sur-prisingly diverse East Village crowd. If you want something comparatively light, stick to the blintzes.

Yaffa Café (£) 97 St Marks Place (tel: 674 9302). Popular, easy-going hang-out for East Village charac-ters, happily grazing on croissants or burgers inside or out in the garden.

FINANCIAL DISTRICT, SOHO AND TRIBECA

American Harvest (£££) 3 World Trade Center, in the New York Vista (tel: 938 9100). Most top-notch New York restaurants offer 'con-tinental' cuisine based on classic European dishes, but American Harvest lives up to its name by adjusting its menu seasonally to take advantage of the best meat, fish, fruit and vegeta-bles available from all

271

across the US. Usually, the formula works extremely well.

Au Mandarin (£) World Financial Center (tel: 385 0313). A well-priced selection of Chinese meals is offered on the ground floor of this bustling, architecturally innovative structure, notable for its indoor palm trees.

Big Kitchen (£) 5 World Trade Center (tel: 938 1153). Great selection of delis and ethnic food booths providing tasty, nourishing fare at low cost to grateful World Trade Center employees and visitors.

Bridge Café (££) Water Street at Dover Street (tel: 227 3344). If you have just crossed the Brooklyn Bridge on foot, reward yourself with a slap-up lunch in this cosy red-brick dining room sited just beneath the bridge itself. Along with the usual American lunch and dinner favourites, there is an appetising selection of well-prepared seafood.

Cellar in the Sky (£££) 1 World Trade Center (tel: 938 1111). Although it is on the 107th floor, nobody comes to Cellar in the Sky for the views. The attraction is a specially chosen, fixed-price, multi-course dinner served with selected wines; the details change every two weeks. The price is astronomical, smart attire is necessary, and you will need to make a reservation; the results should be worth the effort.

Delphi (£) West Broadway near Reade Street (tel: 227 6322). Wonderful portions of Greek food served at giveaway prices.

Duane Park Café (££) Duane Street between West Broadway and Hudson Street (tel: 732 5555). Fashionable dining spot with an impressive menu bearing culinary influences from Italy, Japan and California.

Ecco (££) Chambers Street between West Broadway and Church Street (tel: 227 7074). Plush interior and fine Italian food served to well-heeled financiers and art dealers.

Ellen's Café and Bake Shop (£) Broadway at Chambers Street (tel: 962 1257). Delicious selection of fresh-baked goodies, ideal for a snack or lunch in the company of lawyers from the nearby courts and beneath the photos of the former beauty-queen owner.

Fraunces Tavern (££) 54 Pearl Street (tel: 269 0144). A reconstruction of a landmark 18th-century site (see page 107), the Fraunces Tavern is an atmospheric dining place, but the food, regular American fare, is seldom above average.

Greene Street Café (££) Greene Street between Prince and Spring streets (tel: 925 2415). Set in a spacious loft decorated by stylish artworks and with soothing live jazz in the evenings, this makes for a very SoHo dining experience even before you reach the menu and its classy American-style nouvelle cuisine.

Harry's at Hanover Square (£) 1 Hanover Square (tel: 425 3412). Essential stop for seekers of the ultimate burger: Harry's hamburgers are lovingly grilled over charcoal and apple wood and come with a range of toppings from caviar to avocado.

Japonica (£) 100 University Place, between 11th and 12th streets (tel: 243 7752). Sushi and tempura bar which is a favourite for its good value – especially brunch on Saturdays and Sundays.

McDonald's (£) Broadway at Liberty Street (tel: 385 2063). McDonald's like you have never seen it before, with a doorman, flowers and a pianist soothing diners. Besides the usual burgers (carried on silver trays to marble tables) you can also order grapes, strawberries or a cappuccino.

Nosmo King (££) 54 Varick Street (tel: 966 1239). Excellent, healthy fare completely free of meat and butter and certain to thrill the tastebuds; the name is a reference to the house policy towards tobacco users. Open weekdays only.

Odeon (£££) West Broadway at Thomas Street (tel: 233 0507). American nouvelle cuisine served in an art-deco and neon-decorated setting to appreciative diners. Draws its share of semi-celebrities.

Omen (££) Thompson Street between Spring and Prince streets (tel: 925 8923). A stylish place to soothe stressed nerves, the house speciality of this relaxed Japanese restaurant is indeed Omen – a spicy soup dish with vegetables and noodles.

Pipeline (££) Ground Floor, World Financial Center, between Vesey and Liberty streets (tel: 945 2755). The exposed pipes and gantry walkways of this architecturally themed eatery may distract your attention from some interesting lunch and dinner dishes. A takeaway picnic box is also available.

Raoul's (££) Prince Street between Sullivan and Thompson streets (tel: 966 3518). A winning New York version of a French restaurant, with a tempting selection of main courses, devilish desserts, an impressive wine list, plus comfortable seating and a convivial atmosphere.

Sloppy Louie's (££) 92 South Street, at South Street Seaport (tel: 509 9694). Informal surroundings and a seafood menu that has been pleasing fish fanciers since 1930. The chowders are a speciality, but there is plenty more to choose from.

SoHo Kitchen and Bar (£) 103 Greene Street (tel: 925 1866). Good burgers, fajitas and steaks, plus a superb selection of wines. Try one of their 'flights' – different wines grouped together according to grape variety and served in sample sizes.

Tennessee Mountain (££) Spring Street at Wooster Street (tel: 431 3993). Highly calorific offerings – fried chicken, onion rings, thick burgers and bowls of chili – are eagerly consumed here (along with the flavoured margaritas) by a noisy crowd.

TriBeCa Grill (££) Greenwich Street at Franklin Street (tel: 941 3900). Co-owned by actor Robert de Niro and set in what is now a film company building, the TriBeCa Grill draws a star-spotting crowd but its real attraction is the gourmet-pleasing food, especially the carefully crafted fish dishes.

Windows on the World (£££) 1 World Trade Center (tel: 938 1111). Top-class gourmet fare served on the 107th floor. The food and views (fog permitting) are stunning.

GREENWICH VILLAGE

Acme Bar and Grill (£) 9 Great Jones Street, near Broadway (tel: 420 1934). Casual, lively Cajun joint with what seems like the world's largest hot-sauce collection ranged along the tiled walls. The frozen margaritas are a steal during the happy hour.

Anglers and Writers (£) Hudson Street at St Luke's Place (tel: 675 0810). Plays up the neighbourhood literary links and serves snacks, tea and coffee amid a jumble of antiques and rows of frequently thumbed books.

Apple Restaurant (£) 17 Waverly Place (Tel: 473 8888). Vietnamese/vegetarian cuisine.

The Bagel (£) Fourth Street at Cornelia Street (tel: 255 0106). Though it has general deli fare and offers meals throughout the day, you should come here for the Village breakfast, the house speciality of strawberries and pancakes.

Benny's Burritos (£) 113 Greenwich Avenue (tel: 633 9210). Like their branch in the East Village (see above), Benny's offers folded tortillas stuffed with as much cheese, beans, meat or vegetables as they will hold.

Black Sheep (£££) 344 West 11th Street (tel: 242 1010). French provincial cuisine is the stock-in-trade of this

long-established and long-popular restaurant, which offers a five-course fixed-price dinner or Sunday brunch.

Café Loup (££) 13th Street between University Place and Fifth Avenue (tel: 255 4746). Delightful French bistro providing classy food with a minimum of fuss in a welcoming setting at equally welcoming prices.

Caffè Dante (£) 79 MacDougal Street (tel: 982 5275). Excellent place to people-watch while munching a home-baked cake and sipping a freshly made espresso or cappuccino.

Caffè Reggio (£) 119 MacDougal Street (tel: 475 9557). Claimed to be the country's oldest coffee shop, with a dark, atmospheric interior and a selection of pleasing coffees and cakes.

Caribe (£) 117 Perry Street (tel: 255 9191). Find a table amid the plastic palm trees and blazing tropical decor to sample spicy West Indian delights such as curried goat, jerk chicken and conch fritters.

Cent' Anni (££) 50 Carmine Road (tel: 989 9494). Modest surroundings disguise what locals know to be a place of magical Florentine cuisine, where great things are done with flavourful sauces, angel-hair pasta and carefully cooked meat.

Chumley's (££) 86 Bedford Street (tel: 675 4449). A onetime speakeasy, Chumley's is a compact and atmospheric location for either a drink or a meal chosen from a menu of dependable American fare.

Cornelia Street Café (££) 29 Cornelia Street (tel: 989 9319). The reliable if unimaginative range of European-accented fare served in this three-room restaurant attracts a regular Greenwich Village clientele. There is also a space for poetry read-ings and performance art.

Corner Bistro (£) 331 West 4th Street (tel: 242 9502). Busy, no-frills stop for eat-and-go American food such

as burgers, chicken wings and fries, consumed to the strains of a jukebox.

Cottonwood Café (££) 415 Bleecker Street (tel: 924 6271). Eat-till-you-drop Texas-style fare to thrill carnivores with enormous appetites. The steak fried in breadcrumbs rarely disappoints, but there is lots more besides – and live Texan music most nights.

Cowgirl Hall of Fame (£) 519 Hudson Street (tel: 633 1133). Photos of famous cowgirls grin down from the walls and country music plays on the jukebox as plaid-shirted staff ferry substantial helpings of Tex-Mex fare – and potent margaritas – to customers.

Cucina Stagionale (£) 264 Bleecker Street (tel: 924 2707). Simple, inexpensive and very pleasing Italian food; be prepared to wait in the queue and to bring your own alcohol.

Elephant and Castle (££) 68 Greenwich Avenue (tel: 243 1400). Great selection of breakfast omelettes; other healthy fare at lunch and dinner times. The mellow setting encourages relaxed eating.

Eva's (£) 11 West 8th Street (tel: 677 3496). Enormous vegetarian platters and some meat dishes, served at unbeatable prices in a fast-food setting.

Florent (££) 69 Gansevoort Street (tel: 989 5779). In-vogue bistro specialising in, but not limited to, delectable meat dishes. Being open around the clock with a breakfast menu available from midnight results in an intriguing assortment of club-going New Yorkers arriving through the small hours.

Gotham Bar and Grill (£££) 12th Street at Fifth Avenue (tel: 620 4020). From the perfect architecture to the perfectly presented food, the Gotham Bar and Grill is impeccably stylish and very much the place to be seen. Even people who don't want to be seen still come – the food, fish especially, is a dream.

HOTELS AND RESTAURANTS

The Grange Hall (£) 50 Commerce Street (tel: 924 5246). Lovely spot deservedly popular with locals for its inexpensive Portugese food.

Hudson Corner Café (£) 570 Hudson Street (tel: 229 2727). Attractive diner serving some interesting pasta dishes, alongside more common – but good quality – American fare.

India Pavilion (££) 35 West 13th Street (tel: 243 8175). Fine Indian food consumed in pleasant surroundings. The menu is short but filled with chef's specialities and includes some promising vegetarian selections.

Jane Street Seafood Café (££) Eighth Avenue at Jane Street (tel: 243 9237). Brick walls, wood floors and casually attired staff make this a cosy and unpretentious spot to sample New England-style seafood: only the freshest catches form the daily specials, which are chalked up on the blackboard.

John's Pizzeria (£) 278 Bleecker Street (tel: 243 1680). Long popular – not least with Woody Allen – for perfect oven-baked pizzas in more than 50 varieties. Also a great place to eavesdrop on Greenwich Village gossip.

La Bohème (££) 24 Minetta Lane (tel: 473 6447). A diminutive eatery decorated in rural French style and bringing a French culinary influence to its wood-fired pizzas (try the snail topping), pastas and other succulent dishes.

Little Mushroom Café (£) 10th Street at Seventh Avenue (tel: 242 1058). Likeable locals' diner, short on elbow space but strong on value.

Louisiana (££) Broadway between Bleecker and Houston streets (tel: 460 9633). Artfully presented Cajun and Creole classics, sure to be spicy and good.

Minetta Tavern (££) Minetta Lane and MacDougal Street (tel: 475 3850). A historic Greenwich Village saloon decorated with artworks and memorabilia of local life in the 1930s, the Minetta Tavern provides a welcomingly informal place for very satisfying Italian lunches and dinners.

One If By Land, Two If By Sea (£££) 17 Barrow Street (tel: 228 0822). Occupying a converted 19th-century carriage house, this is a classy venue for a candle-lit dinner. Beef Wellington is a speciality, and the stunning desserts are home made.

Patisserie Lanciani (£) 271 West 4th Street (tel: 929 0739). Some of the best pastries in the city, and good espresso and cappuccino too. A favourite breakfast or late-night spot.

Peacock Caffè (£) 24 Greenwich Avenue (tel: 242 9395). Opera plays in the background as locals skim their newspapers over coffee, cakes and pastries.

Pink Teacup (££) 42 Grove Street (tel: 807 6755). Should a craving for black-eyed peas or collard greens suddenly strike, this long-running soul-food restaurant has both – and much more – in ample supply. The prices, however, reflect the fashionable location.

Pot Belly Stove (£) 98 Christopher Street (tel: 242 8036). Serving burgers, omelettes, sandwiches and other all-American favourites around the clock to an interestingly diverse crowd.

Ray's Original Pizza (£) Sixth Avenue at 11th Street (tel: 243 2253). Ray's Pizza outlets are all over New York but this is the first and best of the lot, serving pizza by the slice to take away or eat at one of the few tables.

Spain Restaurant (££) 13th Street between Sixth and Seventh avenues (tel: 929 9580). Under-acclaimed but long-standing neighbourhood restaurant serving very fine traditional Galician fare.

Tea and Sympathy (£) 108 Greenwich Avenue (tel: 807 8329). Comfort food for homesick Brits – as well as the traditional high tea, they also serve shepherd's pie, fish cakes and 'school dinner' puddings.

3Z Café (£) 60 University Place (tel: 777 7370). Brightly lit and crisply efficient coffee shop serving breakfasts, lunches (the sandwiches are gigantic) and dinner. The Greek cakes are also worth sampling.

Tortilla Flats (£) Washington Street at 12th Street (tel: 243 1053). There is rarely a dull moment at this shaking Tex-Mex eatery, where the emphasis is on rowdy good times as much as on consuming fiery food and alcohol in very large amounts.

University Place (£) University Place and 12th Street (475 7727). Often crowded coffee shop which provides the usual diner fare at low prices. Many come for the excellent waffles, best covered by ice-cream or strawberries.

Villa Mosconi (££) 69 MacDougal Street (tel: 673 0390). Home-made pasta and some tasty seafood dishes served beneath Italian paintings in surroundings conducive to happy eating.

White Horse Tavern (£) Hudson Street at 11th Street (tel: 243 9260). Famous as the bar where Dylan Thomas drank one too many whiskies, the White Horse Tavern also has a fair range of food. Regulars swear by the burgers.

Whole Wheat 'n Wild Berrys (££) 57 West 10th Street (tel: 677 3410). Friendly and comfortable small basement restaurant specialising in healthy, vegetarian fare chosen from the lengthy menu or the host of daily specials.

HARLEM

Copeland's (££) 145th Street between Broadway and Amsterdam Avenue (tel: 234 2356). Where the high-flyers of Harlem don their finery and dine on a creative mix of soul food and nouvelle cuisine.

Sylvia's (££) Lenox Avenue between 126th and 127th streets (tel: 996 0660). A landmark soul-food restaurant, seemingly as popular with busloads of tourists as with locals, Sylvia's serves massive helpings of southern US favourites such as spicy barbecued ribs and chicken, and follows the main courses with devilishly stodgy desserts.

LITTLE ITALY

Angelo's (£) 146 Mulberry Street (tel: 966 1277). Not the best but one of the most visited Little Italy restaurants, serving southern Italian dishes which few of its predominantly tourist customers ever find anything to complain about.

Assaggio (££) 178 Hester Street (tel: 226 2686). Not as rowdy as some Little Italy establishments, and with much that is good among its southern Italian staples.

Benito's (£) 163 and 174 Mulberry Street (tel: 226 9012 and 226 9171). Two branches of the same trattoria, each with dependable, fairly priced dishes.

Caffè Biondo (£) 141 Mulberry Street (tel: 226 9285). Popular spot for arty, dressed-in-black SoHo types to choose from a wide selection of coffees and pose by the oversized front window.

Caffè Roma (£) 385 Broome Street (tel: 226 8413). In business since the 1890s, Caffè Roma offers excellent coffee and freshly baked pastries.

Ferrara (£) 195 Grand Street (tel: 226 6150). Lacks the atmosphere of Caffè Roma (see above), but a nice place to sip a cappuccino and nibble your selection from a tempting array of baked goods while watching the world go by from one of the sidewalk tables.

Luna's (£) 12 Mulberry Street (tel: 226 8657). Small and atmospheric southern Italian eatery entered by way of the kitchen. A place to visit for its food rather than its decor.

Puglia (££) 189 Hester Street (tel: 226 8912). Be it for baked mussels or a thousand and one pasta variations, Puglia's always

draws an excited, boisterous crowd because its prices are astonishingly low, the wine is home made, and live music often accompanies the dining.

Taormina (££) 147 Mulberry Street (tel: 219 1007). A touch pricier and classier than its neighbours, Taormina serves Neapolitan dishes in a sedate setting conducive to pleasant eating.

MIDTOWN MANHATTAN

East and West Midtown

Argentine Pavillion (££) 46th Street between Fifth and Sixth avenues (tel: 921 0835). A slightly touristy restaurant, but if the ever-sizzling grill at the front window tempts you, then the traditionally prepared Argentine seafood and meat dishes will not disappoint.

Christine's (££) Lexington Avenue at 40th Street (tel: 953 1920). Serves omelettes, salads and sandwiches, but knowing regulars choose the Polish dishes – tripe,

homemade *pierogi* or *blintzes* – and leave room for the *babka* as dessert.

Delegates' Dining Room (££) United Nations, First Avenue at 46th Street (tel: 963 7626). Armed with a reservation and proper attire, the general public can rub shoulders with United Nations officials and delegates (those who eat here are unlikely to be famous faces, however) on any weekday lunchtime. Top value is the buffet.

Dosanko (£) 45th Street between Lexington and Third avenues (tel: 697 2967). Perhaps not the finest but almost certainly the cheapest Japanese food in New York is provided by the small chain of Dosanko restaurants, dispensing wonderful soups and noodle dishes with a minimum of fuss.

Four Seasons (£££) 52nd Street between Park and Lexington avenues (tel: 754 9494). At the helm of new-wave American cuisine, the Four Seasons rarely offers

anything from its changing daily menu that will fail to delight the true gourmet – or the New York power brokers who gather here for million-dollar deals over lunch. What is more, the restaurant has an entrance decorated by a large Picasso and sits inside the architecturally significant Seagram Building, designed by Mies van der Rohe and Philip Johnson.

Grand Central Oyster Bar and Restaurant (££) Lower level of Grand Central Terminal (tel: 490 6650). A lengthy seafood menu particularly strong on oysters and doing a roaring trade with office managers, eating slowly and talking fast beneath an extraordinary vaulted ceiling.

Kaplan's Deli (££) 59th Street between Park and Madison avenues (tel: 755 5959). An unexciting but reliable standby for sandwiches, soups and the usual deli fare in an otherwise pricey area.

Keens Chophouse (££) 36th Street between Fifth and Sixth avenues (tel: 947 3636). Keens has been providing no-fuss meat-and-potatoes fare since 1885; mutton chop with mint is what they do best, although there is a wide choice of other meat dishes and some hearty seafood options.

La Bonne Soupe (££) 55th Street between Fifth and Sixth avenues (tel: 586 7650). Tasty and affordable provincial French fare: an array of soups, omelettes and meat-based dishes.

Lipstick Café (££) Third Avenue at 54th Street (tel: 486 8664). Around the corner from Vong's (see below), the same celebrated chef oversees the creation of near-perfect American breakfasts and lunches at reasonable prices.

Lou G Seigel (££) 38th Street between Seventh and Eighth avenues (tel: 921 4433). Kosher deli established since 1917 and still serving chopped liver, gefilte fish, chicken soup – and much more, to local

workers and long-distance regulars.

Lutèce (£££) 50th Street between Second and Third avenues (tel: 752 2225). You will not find culinary innovation at Lutèce, but you will find classic French cooking, with an Alsatian bias, at its very best. The fixed-price lunch and dinner menus are exceptional value. Book well in advance.

Manganaro's Hero Boy (£) Ninth Avenue between 37th and 38th streets (tel: 947 7325). The claim that the 'hero' – a sandwich of immense length, made with French bread – was born here in 1940 is quite believable; you can still order your meal-sized sandwich by the foot.

New York Deli (££) 57th Street near Sixth Avenue (tel: 541 8320). The least costly and least pretentious branch of this well-known local deli chain, and offering a fair meal at a fair price.

Rainbow Room (£££) 65th floor, 30 Rockefeller Plaza (tel: 632 5000). The food may be no more than reasonable value for the money but the restored art-deco setting is a delight and comes complete with a 12-piece band providing 1940s favourites and roaming cigarette girls. You will need a reservation, smart attire, and 20-20 vision to enjoy to the full the stunning views of New York stretching out below.

Secret Harbor Bistro (££) Lexington Avenue at 37th Street (tel: 447 7400). Chic place to start the day, offering pastries, yoghurt and fresh juices, or to end it with a choice of well-prepared dishes ranging from vegetable lasagne to blackened tuna in lemon leek sauce.

Vong (£££) 200 East 54th Street (tel: 486 9592). Well known to choosy New Yorkers and the brainchild of one of the city's most talented chefs, Jean-Georges Vongerichten. You must call weeks in advance if you want to make a reservation to sample the French/Thai food.

Zarela (££) Second Avenue between 50th and 51st streets (tel: 644 6740). Without a frozen margarita in sight, Zarela's raises Mexican cuisine to lofty heights with exotic creations stressing subtlety in taste and texture.

Theater District
Broadway Diner (££) Broadway at 55th Street (tel: 765 0909). Good range of better-than-average diner staples, but you pay extra for the 1940s-style fittings.

Cabana Carioca (££) 45th Street between Sixth and Seventh avenues (tel: 581 8088). Hefty servings of Brazilian food, well-cooked meat in abundance and black beans by the bowlful. The bar serves lethal cocktails, and the diners come in party mood.

Café 44 (££) 44th Street between Eighth and Ninth avenues (tel: 581 3080). The fluffy breakfast omelettes and ample-sized sandwiches and burgers proffered for lunch are reason enough to visit Café 44, but the seafood and pasta dinners are also a hit with the pretheatre crowd.

Café 57 (££) 57th Street between Eighth and Ninth avenues (tel: 489 9767). Under the same ownership as **Café 44** (see above) and equally worth a visit.

Carnegie Delicatessen (££) Seventh Avenue at 55th Street (tel: 757 2245). Landmark showbiz eatery with a rich mix of sit-down deli fare – from enormous corned beef and pastrami sandwiches to luscious cakes. Many of the dishes are named after Broadway legends.

Dish of Salt (£££) 47th Street between Sixth and Seventh avenues (tel: 921 4242). With high prices and reservations strongly recommended, this Chinese eaterie is a far cry from the budget options of Chinatown, serving wonderful Cantonese food (dinner only on Saturday) in a stylishly decorated, split-level room.

India Pavilion (£–££) 56th Street between Broadway and Eighth Avenue (tel: 489 0035). Very fairly priced and extremely good quality Indian and Pakistani food, served in an intimate and unpretentious setting.

Jezebel (££) Ninth Avenue at 45th Street (tel: 582 1045). Earthy soul-food favourites, such as fried chicken, catfish and grits, offered at up-market prices in a setting themed as a Deep South bordello.

Joe Allen (££) 46th Street between Eighth and Ninth avenues (tel: 581 6464). Burgers, bowls of chili and other simple American food served in large portions amid Broadway show posters.

Landmark Tavern (££) Eleventh Avenue at 46th Street (tel: 757 8595). Purveying hearty lunches and dinners – fish and chips, and shepherds' pie alongside the ubiquitous burgers and sandwiches – to appreciative diners in appealing wood-panelled rooms dating from 1856.

Manhattan Chilli Company (£) Broadway at 43rd Street (tel: 730 8666). Chilli in more varieties than you ever thought possible, plus a selection of other south-western US dishes. Those who like their chilli ultra-hot should aim for the Texas Chain Gang chilli, made with fiery jalapeño peppers.

Munson Diner (£) 49th Street at Eleventh Avenue (tel: 246 0964). Being trapped in an out-of-the-way location near the Hudson River has not stopped this no-frills spot from satisfying the hunger pangs of its regulars since 1908.

Russian Tea Room (£££) 57th Street between Sixth and Seventh avenues (tel: 265 0947). Founded by homesick Russian ballet dancers in the 1920s, the Russian Tea Room is a fixture for New York showbiz high society, serving top-notch caviar, borscht and smoked salmon – plus champagne, vodka and tea from the samovar. If your face is not familiar, however, beware of banishment to 'Siberia', the upstairs dining room.

Sardi's (££) 44th Street between Broadway and Eighth Avenue (tel: 221 8440). A noted theatrical hang-out and gossip-columnists' lair, Sardi's is well past its prime, but the caricatures of Broadway stars still line its walls and the service is still as offhand as ever. Choose from an Italian menu.

Stage Deli (££) Seventh Avenue at 54th Street (tel: 245 7850). Long-time rival of the Carnegie Deli (see above), the Stage Deli provides much the same staple deli fare in equally generous portions, though the staff can often be less than gracious.

Murray Hill, Gramercy and Chelsea

America (££) 9 East 18th Street between Fifth Avenue and Broadway (tel: 505 2110). Large and warehouse-like, with a long, slick bar well placed for people-watching. The food is also good – a mixture of American, Italian and Tex-Mex.

An American Place (££) Park Avenue and 32nd Street (tel: 684 2122). Some innovative and exciting American nouvelle cuisine, inspired by the country's regional cookery.

Annapurna (££) Lexington Avenue between 27th and 28th streets (tel: 679 1284). For service and decor, this is a cut above the other Indian restaurants in the immediate vicinity but still very reasonably priced.

Burke & Burke (£) Seventh Avenue at 29th Street (tel: 564 0273). One of a city-wide chain of small and reliable, but otherwise largely undistinguished, delis.

Chelsea Place (££) Eighth Avenue between 17th and 18th streets (tel: 924 8413). Pass through an antiques shop and then through a smoky and crowded pseudo-speakeasy bar to the comparatively sedate downstairs restaurant and your reward will be some fine Northern Italian food. The best bets are among the daily specials.

Choshi (££) Irving Place between 18th and 19th streets (tel: 420 1419). Japanese food, especially sushi and sashimi, stylishly presented to stylish diners and best eaten at the side-walk tables.

Coffee Shop (££) 16th Street and Union Square West (tel: 243 7669). Eat-and-run coffee shops abound around Union Square, but this, despite its name, is actually a lively and fashionable spot for consuming American-Brazilian food and generally being seen by the right faces.

Cola's (£) Eighth Avenue between 17th and 18th streets (tel: 633 8020). The lack of a liquor licence (bring your own booze) helps to keep the prices low at this pleasant Italian diner, which attracts a trendy local crowd.

Cottage (£) Irving Place between 15th and 16th streets (tel: 505 8600). Inexpensive Hunan and Szechuan dishes. If you have no appetite when you arrive, you will have one by the time you have read through the enormous menu.

Empire Diner (£) Tenth Avenue at 22nd Street (tel: 243 2736). Retro-style decor and good, down-to-earth diner food at reasonable prices, catering around the clock to a modish clientele.

Frank's (££) 14th Street between Ninth and Tenth avenues (tel: 243 1349). Operating in the so-called 'meat-packing district' since 1912, this honest-to-goodness steak and seafood spot offers food of far higher quality than the sawdust-on-the-floor decor might suggest. Local butchers feature prominently among the lunchtime diners.

Friend of a Farmer (££) Irving Place between 18th and 19th streets (tel: 477

2188). Popular and attractive restaurant serving wholesome American country fare with finesse for breakfast, lunch or dinner.

Galaxy (£) Eighth Avenue at 16th Street (tel: 463 7460). If you have to choose between getting something to eat and visiting the Hayden Planetarium at the American Museum of Natural History, you could compromise by coming here and consuming the ordinary coffee-shop fare while gazing at the cosmos-inspired decor.

La Colombe D'Or (££) 26th Street between Third and Lexington avenues (tel: 689 0666). Excellent French provincial cuisine served in an elegant brownstone town house.

Live Bait (££) 23rd Street between Madison and Fifth avenues (tel: 353 2400). Styled as a rustic southern fishing shack, Live Bait is a busy bar and also dispenses filling southern-style sandwiches, burgers and salads.

Lola (££) 22nd Street between Fifth and Sixth avenues (tel: 675 6700). American food bearing a West Indian influence, and some genuine Caribbean and South American dishes, is prepared to an exceptional standard. A 'gospel brunch' is also served on Sundays.

Lox Around the Clock (£) Sixth Avenue at 21st Street (tel: 691 3535). With its junkyard furnishings and multiple video screens, this place is aimed at the peckish East Village nightclub crowd. It provides a decent range of coffee-shop nourishment long into the night, and around the clock at weekends.

Marchi's (£££) 31st Street between Second and Third avenues (tel: 679 2494). Long-established Italian restaurant where the diners dress in their finest clothes and celebrate birthdays, weddings, and other special occasions by tackling the five/six-course fixed menu of Italian/American fare.

Mary Anne's (£) Eighth Avenue at 16th Street (tel: 633 0877). Dependable Mexican fare, slightly costlier than elsewhere but worth a few extra dollars for the better quality and wider choice.

Newsbar Inc (£) 19th Street between Fifth and Sixth avenues (tel: 255 3996). Serves breakfast, lunch, and early dinner, but the real reason to visit this minimalist-designed café is to sip coffee, people-watch and scan the racks of international newspapers.

Park Bistro (££) Park Avenue between 28th and 29th streets (tel: 689 1360). Among the better of New York's many French bistro-style restaurants, and deservedly popular for providing lovely food in a lovely setting.

Peter's Place (£) Third Avenue between 20th and 21st streets (tel: 260 2900). You will not be hungry after eating at Peter's Place, a cosy coffee shop where the menu includes immense sandwiches, gigantic Belgian waffles, and smoked salmon on a jumbo bagel.

Pete's Tavern (££) 18th Street at Irving Place (tel: 473 7676). A bar popular with the after-work crowd and an ideal place for sidewalk dining. The food includes the usual American fare and a wide choice of pasta dishes.

Raymond's Café (££) Seventh Avenue between 15th and 16th streets (tel: 929 1778). Calf's liver in sherry sauce and squid in linguine pasta are just two of the house dishes; Raymond's also serves a good brunch on Saturdays and Sundays.

Tullio Trattoria (££) 22nd Street between Fifth and Sixth avenues (tel: 691 4188). Delightfully intimate and low-key Italian restaurant, with a matching small but uniformly good-quality menu.

Union Square Café (££) 16th Street and Union Square West (tel: 243 4020). French

and Italian cuisine and tempting grilled seafood predominate in this trendy eatery which draws many image-conscious New York media folk.

Young Fu Noodle Shop (£) Madison Avenue at 31st Street (tel: 447 5400). Popular locals' Chinese pit-stop, especially strong on spicy Szechuan dishes and offering lunch specials at rock-bottom prices.

QUEENS

Happy Dumpling (£) 135–29 40th Road, Flushing (tel: 718/445 2163). Chinese fare, and rarely bettered for stuffed dumplings or noodle dishes.

Jackson Diner (£) 74th Street between Roosevelt and 37th avenues (tel: 718/672 1232). Probably the best priced of a glut of Indian restaurants in this section of the borough. The food is far better than the decor might suggest.

Ko Hyang (£) 42–96 Main Street, Flushing (tel: 718/463 3837). Informal Korean restaurant with a wide selection of meals and snacks.

Kuala Lumpur (£) 135–31 40th Road, Flushing (tel: 718/933 8333). Tasty Malaysian fare in a fast-food setting.

Lefkos Pyrgos (£) 22–85 31st Street, Astoria (tel: 718/932 4423). The pick of Astoria's many Greek cafés, offering an array of sweet things certain to alarm your dentist.

Taverna Vraka (££) 23–15 31st Street, Astoria (tel: 718/721 3007). An institution in this Greek-dominated neighbourhood for its old-style Greek food and entertainment.

Yao Han (£) 135–21 40th Road, Flushing (tel: 718/359 2828). Chinese and Vietnamese food, and another great find for noodle-lovers.

UPPER EAST SIDE

Arcadia (£££) 62nd Street between Madison and Fifth avenues (tel: 223 2900). Few New York foodies would dispute that Arcadia is

among the finest restaurants in the city. Its selective menu is adjusted according to ingredients in season and may include anything from smoked lobster to roast quail on dandelions.

Arizona 206 (£££) 60th Street between Second and Third avenues (tel: 838 0440). The American Southwest re-created on Manhattan's Upper East Side, with desert-style decor and southwestern cuisine of exceptional quality.

Daniel (£££) 76th Street between Fifth and Madison avenues (tel: 288 0033). The French chef from Le Cirque (see below) already had such an exalted reputation among New York foodies that this, his own restaurant, was an instant success when it opened in 1993. Dinner reservations entail an eight-week wait; alternatively, hope for a lunch cancellation.

Dumpling Queen (£) 85th Street at Third Avenue (tel: 249 0362). Very cheap Chinese food, including dim sum, in no-frills dining room.

E.A.T. (£) Madison Avenue between 80th and 81st streets (tel: 772 0022). Yuppies come here after racketball, shoppers come at the weekend, and locals come all the time for the Continental/Jewish snacks and sinful desserts.

1st Wok (££) First Avenue at 74th Street (tel: 535 8598). One branch of a widely found chain delivering tasty, healthy Chinese food to your table within a few minutes of ordering.

Fu's (£££) Second Avenue between 72nd and 73rd streets (tel: 517 9670). Varied Chinese food of outstanding quality, but decor and prices which are a long way from Chinatown.

Jackson Hole Wyoming (£) Second Avenue between 83rd and 84th streets (tel: 737 8788). Burger outlets are comparatively few in the style-conscious Upper East Side, but this branch of the city-wide chain offers its

usual formidable hunks of beef-between-buns with many exciting toppings.

JG Melon (£) Third Avenue at 74th Street (tel: 650 1310). American diner fare which is a cut above the average, served at low cost in the homely environment of a wood-panelled bar.

Jo Jo (££) 160 East 64th Street, near Lexington Avenue (tel: 223 5656). Superb 'international' dining; prices are remarkably low for the quality so reservations are a must. Choose between the main dining area – usually loud and packed – and the more serene rear room.

Le Cirque (£££) 65th Street between Park and Madison avenues (tel: 794 9292). Famous faces are regularly spotted at Le Cirque's close-together tables, though if you can afford to eat at one of the city's priciest restaurants you should concentrate on the food rather than celebrity-spotting.

Mocca (££) Second Avenue between 83rd and 84th streets (tel: 734 6470). Excellent Hungarian dishes, and liveliest at weekends when gypsy fiddlers entertain the diners.

Ottomanelli's Café (£) York Avenue between 81st and 82nd streets (tel: 737 1888). One of several Upper East Side branches of this well-known New York eatery. This particular one has a tempting selection of

freshly baked goods among the usual range of salads, pastas, burgers and sandwiches.

Petaluma (££) First Avenue at 73rd Street (tel: 772 8800). Mesquite-grilled swordfish, boneless chicken in garlic and fried calamari are among the options in this inventive California-style Italian restaurant.

Pig Heaven (££) Second Avenue between 80th and 81st streets (tel: 744 4887). Has pig-themed decor as well as many intriguing pig dishes (such as shredded pigs' ears) alongside a host of stylish Chinese dishes and some moreish American desserts.

Post House (£££) 63rd Street between Park and Madison avenues (tel: 935 2888). If you have an ample budget but detest French food, this might be the answer: a classy place, but best for no-nonsense portions of seafood and steak.

Red Tulip (££) 75th Street between York and First avenues (tel: 734 4893). More Hungarian folk music and food and a more intimate mood than Mocca (see above); strong on stuffed cabbage, goulash and well-cooked meats.

Ruby's River Road Café (£) Second Avenue at 93rd Street (tel: 348 2328). A party atmosphere prevails as boisterous diners gorge on spicy southern US dishes and cool themselves with pitchers of beer.

Rusty's (££) Third Avenue at 73rd Street (tel: 861 4518). The gigantic salads and bowls of meal-in-itself soup are reason enough to come, but you might choose instead to tackle the well-filled platefuls of spicy Cajun-style cooking.

7th Regiment Mess (£) 643 Park Avenue between 66th and 67th streets (tel: 744 4107). American home-cooking is served up in an old wood-panelled restaurant inside the Seventh Regiment Armory. This place is great for children; booking is advisable.

Wilkinson's Seafood Café (£££) York Avenue between 83rd and 84th streets (tel: 535 5454). A mouthwatering variety of always-fresh seafood is on offer at Wilkinson's. Usually the choice includes lobster, red snapper, crab cakes, swordfish and salmon – all prepared to perfection and stylishly presented to well-dressed, appreciative and mostly local diners.

Zucchini (££) First Avenue between 71st and 72nd streets (tel: 249 0559). A delicious and nutritious

assortment of salads and pastas is on offer here, using vegetables and seafood.

UPPER WEST SIDE

Akaihana (£) Broadway between 76th and 77th streets (tel: 724 8666). New Yorkers are passionate about sushi, and this is one of the best places in the city to sample it without spending a fortune.

Alcala (££) Amsterdam Avenue between 75th and 76th streets (tel: 769 9600). Spanish food which can be nibbled as tapas – tempting morsels laid out in dishes on the bar – or consumed more heartily from the menu's choice of well-prepared and delicious seafood and meat dishes.

Barney Greengrass (The Sturgeon King) (££) Amsterdam Avenue between 86th and 87th streets (tel: 724 4707). The epitome of a New York Jewish deli-diner and in the ownership of the Greengrass family since 1908. The proud claims for the sturgeon are justified, and salmon is another house speciality; breakfast and lunch only.

Blue Nile (££) 77th Street at Columbus Avenue (tel: 580 3232). One of New York's few Ethiopian restaurants and an essential call for adventurous eaters. Forget about knives and forks. The food is scooped up and devoured with spongy chunks of injera bread.

Café des Artistes (£££) 67th Street at Central Park West (tel: 877 3500). The 1930s Howard Chandler Christy murals of ethereal nudes add to the joy of consuming what might well be the best food in New York. Reservations are essential for dinner and also for the restaurant's divine Sunday brunch.

Café Lalo (£) 83rd Street at Amsterdam Avenue (tel: 496 6031). Trendy spot for would-be neighbourhood writers, artists and media folk to imbibe cappuccino by the gallon and gorge themselves on a selection of irresistible cakes.

Café Luxembourg (£££) 70th Street between Amsterdam and Columbus avenues (tel: 873 7411). This is an art deco bistro aiming for a 1930s Parisian ambience. The top-rated food – a mix of French, Italian and regional US cuisines – draws fashionable faces from all over the city.

Diane's Uptown (£) Columbus Avenue between 71st and 72nd streets (tel: 799 6750). A comfortable and extremely cheap restaurant, offering dishes such as burgers, omelettes and sandwiches.

EJ's Luncheonette (£) Amsterdam Avenue between 80th and 81st streets (tel: 873 3444). Retro diner complete with chrome fittings and historic Coke advertisements. The sandwiches (the grilled Cajun chicken breast is recommended) are big enough to feed an army.

Empire Restaurant (£) Broadway at 97th Street (tel: 663 6004). Immense choice of Szechuan and Hunan fare. Dim sum is also on offer at weekend lunchtimes.

Fishin Eddie (££) 71st Street between Central Park West and Columbus Avenue (tel: 874 3474). A dinner-only seafood restaurant with a strong reputation for unusual Italian dishes such as *cioppina* – a type of fish stew – served in large portions.

Good Enough To Eat (££) Amsterdam Avenue between 83rd and 84th streets (tel: 496 0163). Grand selection of ever-popular American staples, from ham and eggs to strawberry waffles, for breakfast, lunch or dinner in cosy surroundings.

H&H (£) Broadway at 80th Street (tel: 595 8000). Round-the-clock baking means the bagels sold here are guaranteed hot and fresh. They are available with a multitude of fillings.

India Garden (££) Amsterdam Avenue between 90th and 91st streets (tel: 787 4530). Distinguished from the neighbourhood Indian restaurants by its goat dishes, available in biryani, vindaloo, saag and badami forms.

Indian Café (££) Broadway at 108th Street (tel: 749 9200). Competitively priced Indian food including especially inventive vegetarian selections, such as chick peas with spinach and tomato, and sauteed lentils with garlic and ginger. Alternatively, feast on a selection of appetisers.

Isola (££) Columbus Avenue at 84th Street (tel: 362 7400). Draws a devoted local crowd for its predominantly Sicilian and Sardinian fare, plus a mouthwatering selection of wood-fired pizzas.

Jackson Hole Wyoming (£) Columbus Avenue at 85th Street (tel: 362 5177). Multifarious burgers, usually large enough to feed two.

La Caridad (£) Broadway at 78th Street (tel: 874 2780). Intriguing and inventive Chinese-Cuban dishes served without fuss in informal surroundings.

La Traviata (£) 101 West 68th Street (tel: 721 1101). A hole-in-the-wall outlet popular with locals and dispensing tasty pizza by the slice.

Lucy's (££) Columbus Avenue between 84th and 85th streets (tel: 787 3009). Tex-Mex food is boisterously consumed in the back room as the fashionable faces of the Upper West Side prop up the bar.

Museum Café (££) Columbus Avenue at 77th Street (tel: 799 0150). Facing the American Museum of Natural History, and offering a delicious assortment of generous salads and melt-in-the-mouth pasta dishes.

Ollie's Noodle Shop (£) Broadway at 84th Street (tel: 362 3111). Noodles and dumplings are among the no-nonsense Chinese fare prepared in full view of diners. The noodle soups, in particular, are flavourful and very cheap.

Olympic Flame (£) Ninth Avenue at 58th Street (tel: 765 7965). Laid-back diner which is something of an oasis in this hectic area. Select from coffee-shop staples or simply linger over a refreshing mugful of coffee.

Piccolino (££) Amsterdam Avenue, between 81st and 82nd streets (tel: 873 8004). Fabulous place for pasta, with nearly 30 varieties to choose from.

Popover Café (£) Amsterdam Avenue between 87th and 88th streets (tel: 595 8555). Salads, soups and sandwiches, and popovers (small balls of pastry served with jam and butter) are the specialities of this quaintly decorated place.

Rancho Mexican Café (££) Amsterdam Avenue between 82nd and 83rd streets (tel: 362 1514). Potent frozen margaritas accompany the Mexican fare – you will get a free one by ordering dinner during the early evening happy hour. Hosts a riotous

Sunday brunch, too.

Sarabeth's Kitchen (££) Amsterdam Avenue between 80th and 81st streets (tel: 496 6280). A polite and refined place in which to indulge in smoked salmon sandwiches or fluffy omelettes. Also has a scintillating selection of home-baked cakes.

Shark Bar (£) 74th Street between Columbus Avenue and Broadway (tel: 496 6600). Be it Tallahassee grilled shrimp, Louisiana fried crab cakes or pan-blackened catfish, the Shark Bar has the spiciest, tastiest fare from all over the American south.

Symposium (£) 113th Street at Amsterdam Avenue (tel: 865 1011). Authentic, inexpensive Greek fare – spinach pie, moussaka and more – especially popular with students from nearby Columbia University. In summer you can dine in the garden.

Tavern on the Green (£££) 67th Street at Central Park West (tel: 873 3200). More famous as a New York landmark than as a home of fine dining, the Tavern on the Green serves erratic – but usually excellent – meals beneath the Venetian chandeliers of the Crystal Room or outside in the garden, mostly to pre-theatre diners.

Terrace (£££) 119th Street at Morningside Drive (tel: 666 9490). Dimly lit and plushly furnished with views across Upper Manhattan, the Terrace has a reputation for variable culinary quality, but overall the French-influenced fare is extremely unlikely to disappoint. Smart attire and reservations are essential.

Zabar's Café (£) Broadway at West 80th Street (tel: 787 2000). Just stools, stand-up counters and not much elbow room at this cheerful establishment, but some of the best cappuccino in town, along with excellent pastries, croissants and sandwiches.

Index

A

283

INDEX